What?! Volume 3?!
Tsutsui
yeah!

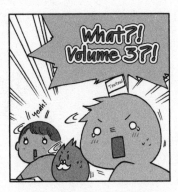

We're already on volume 3!
I'm overflowing with gratitude and appreciation to have had your support for three volumes now!
I've finally gotten used to drawing the weekly chapters, so I decided to renew my gym membership and address my extreme lack of fitness. I got carried away and swam way too much, and the next day I was so fatigued that my whole body ached and I even had a fever—but I still had to draw my chapter. Don't tell my editor!
So, whether your muscles are extremely sore or not very sore at all, I'd like to offer you this rom-com comic as a balm!

• Taishi Tsutsui •

We Never Learn

We Never Learn

Volume 3 • SHONEN JUMP Manga Edition

STORY AND ART **Taishi Tsutsui**

TRANSLATION Camellia Nieh
SHONEN JUMP SERIES LETTERING Snir Aharon
GRAPHIC NOVEL TOUCH-UP ART & LETTERING Erika Terriquez
DESIGN Shawn Carrico
SHONEN JUMP SERIES EDITOR John Bae
GRAPHIC NOVEL EDITOR David Brothers

Printed in the U.S.A.

Published by VIZ Media, LLC
P.O. Box 77010
San Francisco, CA 94107

10 9 8 7 6 5 4 3 2 1
First printing, April 2019

VIZ MEDIA
viz.com

SHONEN JUMP
shonenjump.com

ratings.viz.com
RATED T+ OLDER TEEN

PARENTAL ADVISORY
WE NEVER LEARN is rated T+ for Older Teen and is recommended for ages 16 and up. This volume contains mild language and sexual themes.

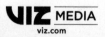

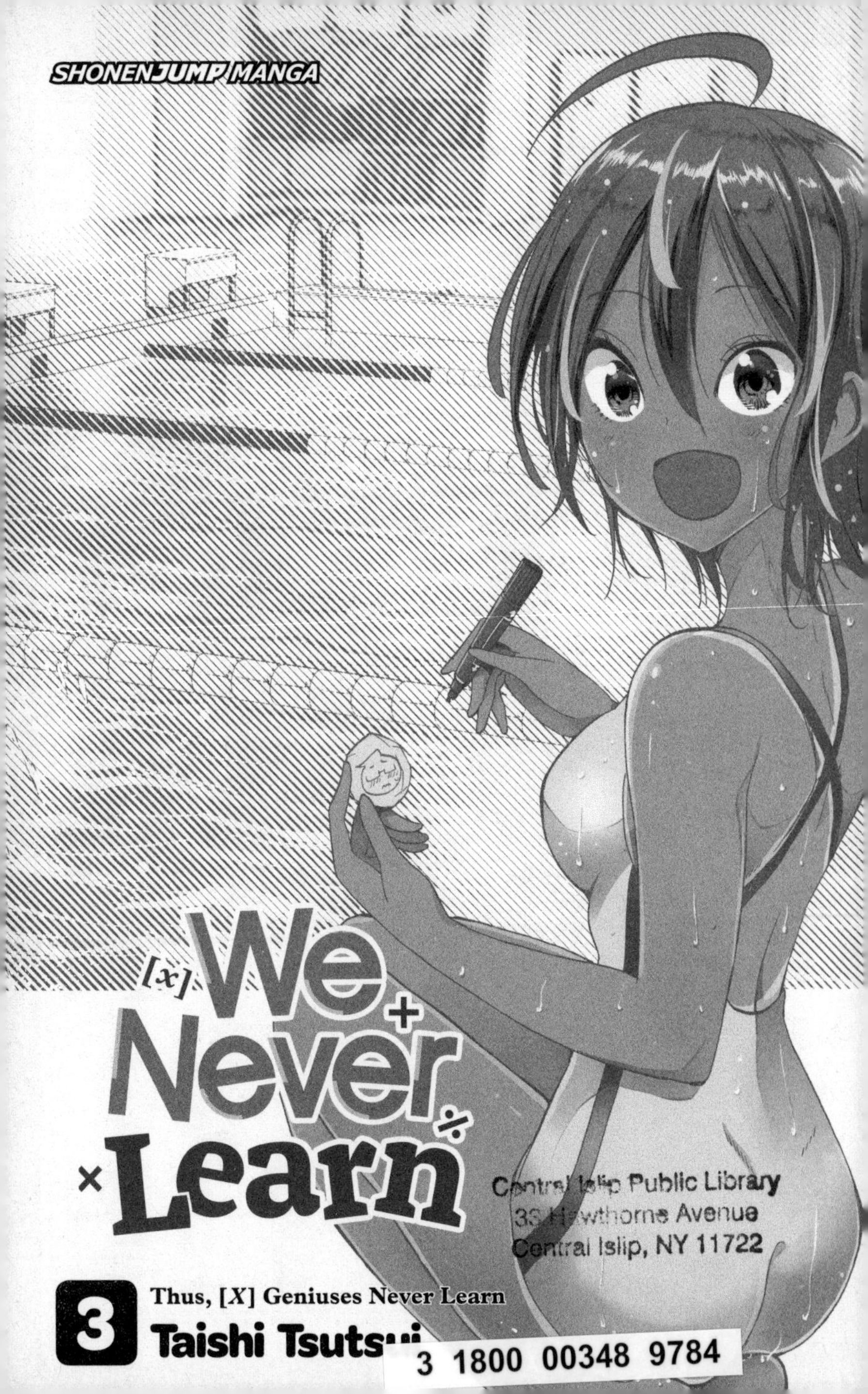

SHONEN JUMP MANGA

[x] We Never Learn

3

Thus, [X] Geniuses Never Learn

Taishi Tsutsui

We Never Learn

Nariyuki Yuiga and his family have led a humble life since his father passed away, with Yuiga doing everything he can to support his siblings. So when the principal of his school agrees to grant Nariyuki the school's special VIP recommendation for a full scholarship to college, he leaps at the opportunity. However, the principal's offer comes with one condition: Yuiga must serve as the tutor of Rizu Ogata, Fumino Furuhashi and Uruka Takemoto, the three girl geniuses who are the pride of Ichinose Academy! Unfortunately, the girls, while extremely talented in certain areas, all have subjects where their grades are absolutely rock-bottom. How will these three struggling students ever manage to pass their college entrance exams?!

On an overnight study trip, Rizu and Nariyuki accidentally kiss. Soon after, Nariyuki is summoned for a meeting with Kirisu Sensei... What other surprises will shake up their final year of high school?!

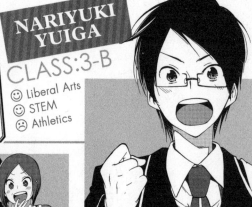

NARIYUKI YUIGA

CLASS:3-B

☺ Liberal Arts
☺ STEM
☹ Athletics

A bright student from an ordinary family. Nariyuki lacks genius in any one subject but manages to maintain stellar grades through hard work. Agrees to take on the role of tutor in return for the school's special VIP recommendation.

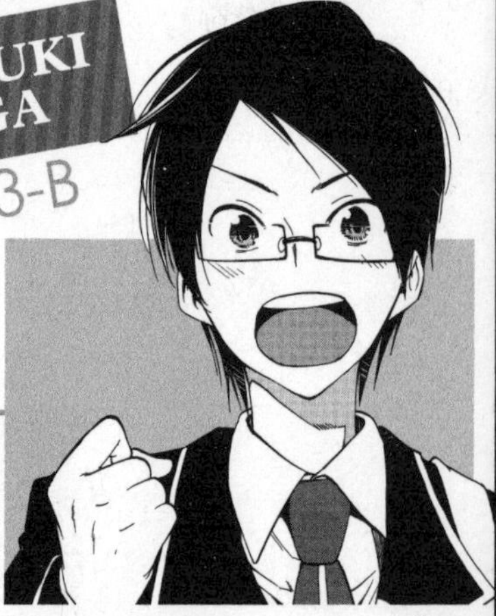

The Yuiga Family

A family of five consisting of Nariyuki, his mother and his siblings, Mizuki, Hazuki and Kazuki.

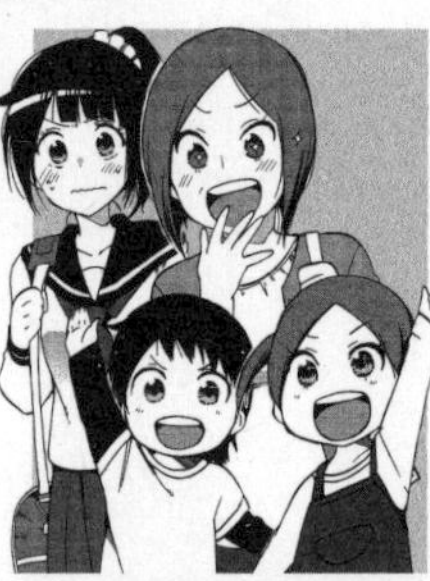

Kobayashi and Omori

Nariyuki's friends.

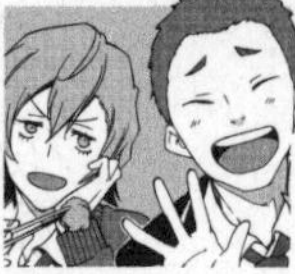

Sawako Sekijo

The head of the science club and a rival of Rizu's, but she secretly adores her.

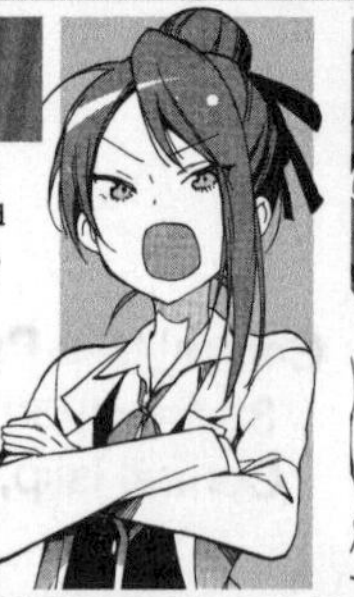

Kawase and Umihara

Uruka's friends.

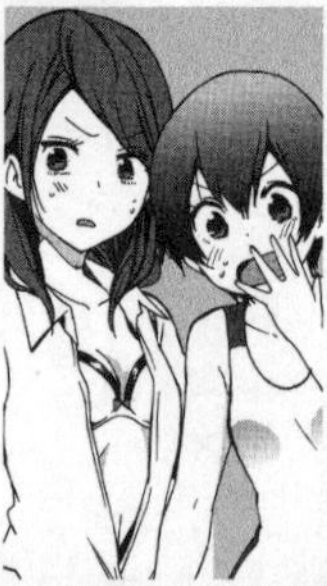

Principal

Assigns Nariyuki the role of tutor.

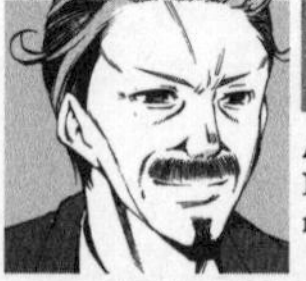

RIZU OGATA

CLASS:3-F

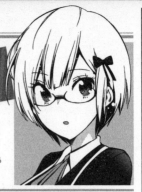

☹ Liberal Arts ☺ STEM ☹ Athletics

Known as the Thumbelina Supercomputer, Rizu is a math and science genius, but she's a dunce at literature, especially when human emotions come into play. She chooses a literary path to learn about human psychology—partially because she wants to learn how to be better at board games.

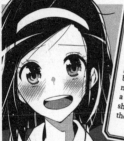

FUMINO FURUHASHI

CLASS:3-A

☺ Liberal Arts
☹ STEM
☺ Athletics

Known as the Sleeping Beauty of the Literary Forest, Fumino is a literary wiz whose mind goes completely blank when she sees numbers. She chooses a STEM path because she wants to study the stars.

URUKA TAKEMOTO

CLASS:3-D

☹ Liberal Arts ☹ STEM ☺ Athletics

Known as the Shimmering Ebony Mermaid Princess, Uruka is a swimming prodigy but terrible at academics. In order to get an athletic scholarship, she needs to meet certain academic standards. She's had a crush on Nariyuki since junior high.

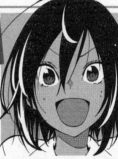

MAFUYU KIRISU

TEACHER

☺ Pedagogy
☹ Home Economics

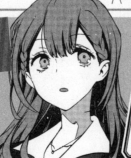

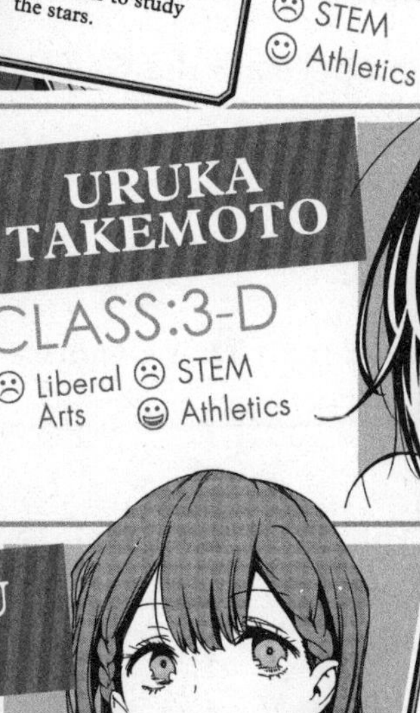

A teacher at Ichinose Academy, and Rizu and Fumino's previous tutor. She believes people should choose their path according to their talents and pressures Rizu and Fumino to change course. However, deep down, she's a caring person. She's also surprisingly slovenly for a teacher!

TITLE

We Never Learn

CONTENTS

VOLUME 3 Thus, [X] Geniuses Never Learn

NAME Taishi Tsutsui

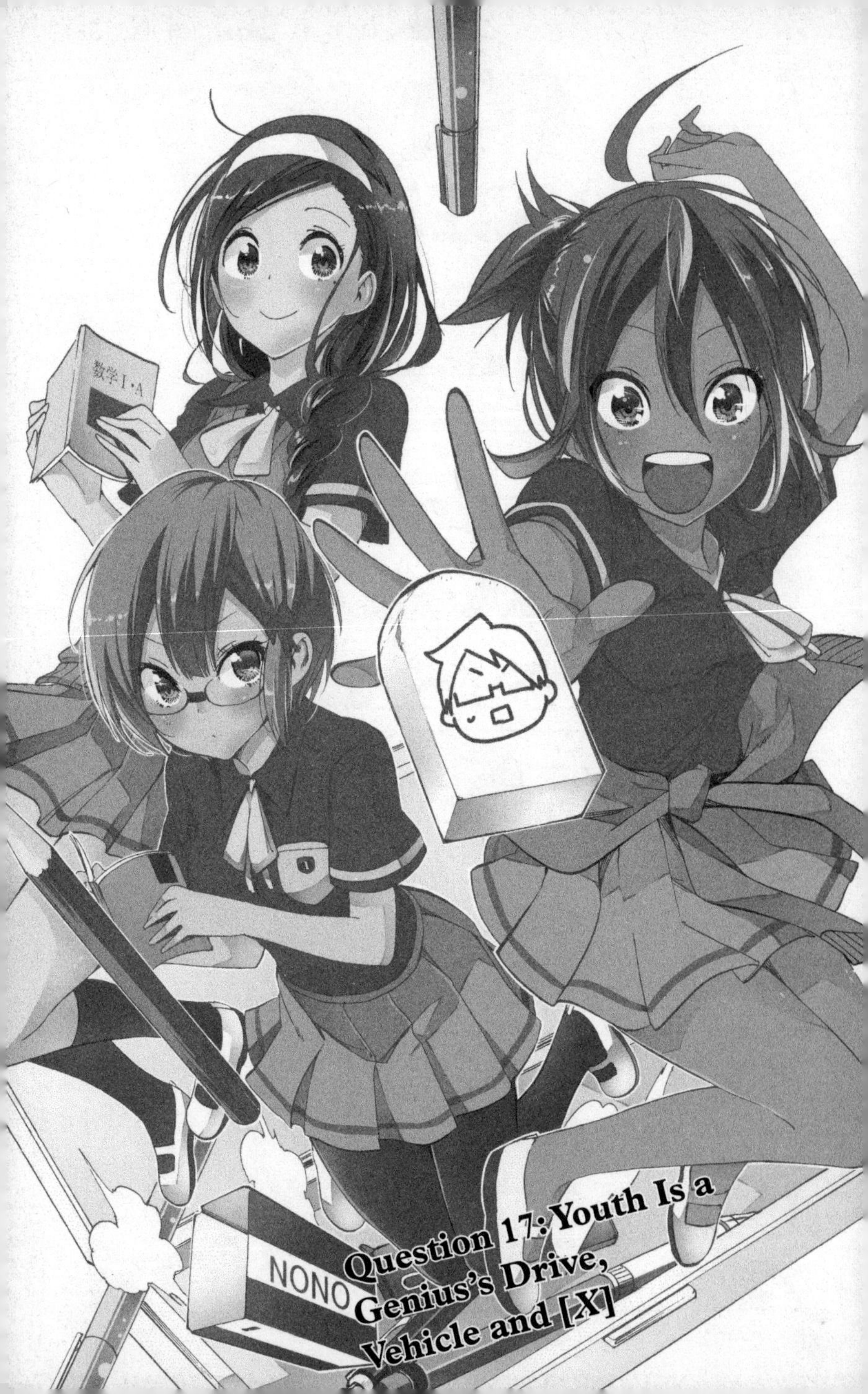
数学I・A
NONO

Question 17: Youth Is a Genius's Drive, Vehicle and [X]

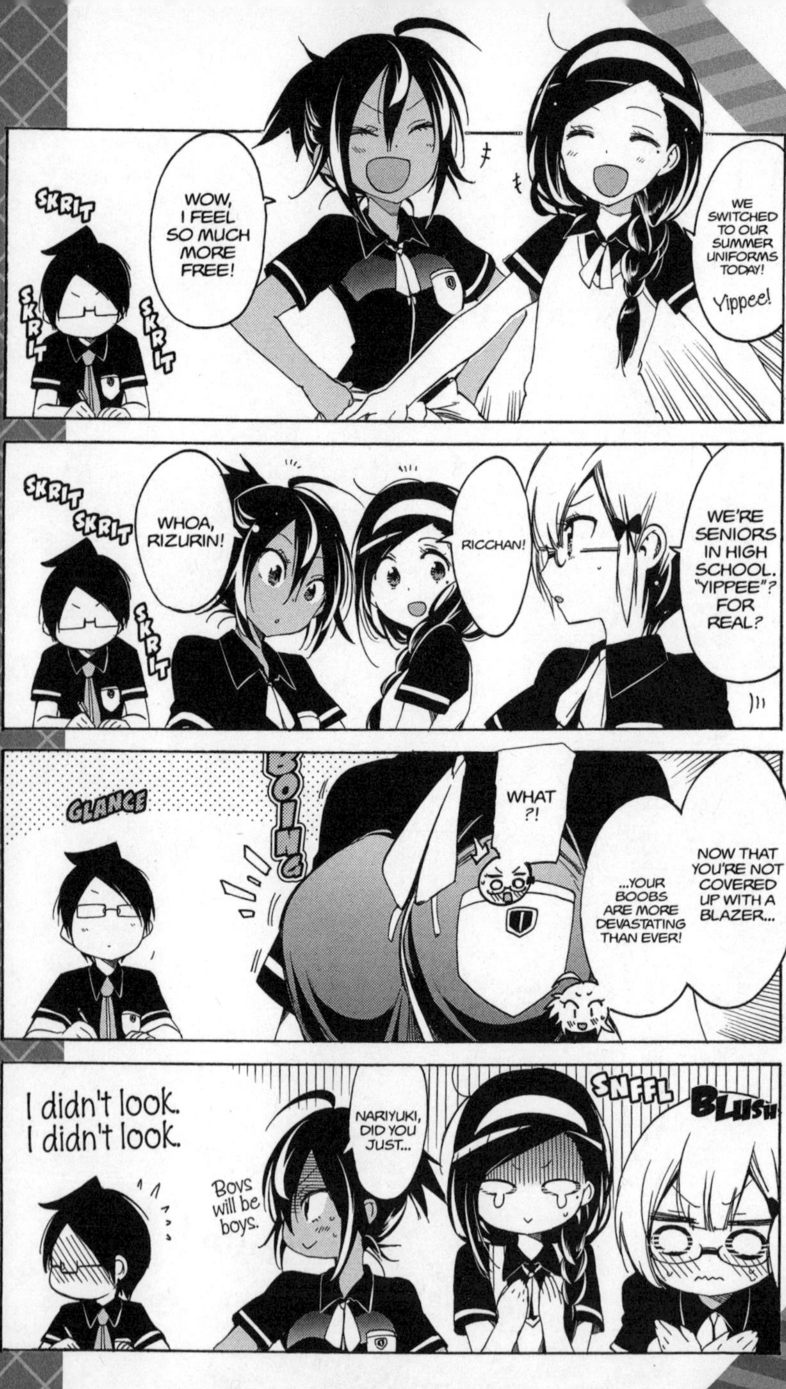
WE SWITCHED TO OUR SUMMER UNIFORMS TODAY!
Yippee!
WOW, I FEEL SO MUCH MORE FREE!
SKRIT
SKRIT
SKRIT
WE'RE SENIORS IN HIGH SCHOOL. "YIPPEE"? FOR REAL?
RICCHAN!
WHOA, RIZURIN!
SKRIT
SKRIT
SKRIT
NOW THAT YOU'RE NOT COVERED UP WITH A BLAZER...
...YOUR BOOBS ARE MORE DEVASTATING THAN EVER!
WHAT?!
BOING
GLANCE
BLUSH
SNFFL
NARIYUKI, DID YOU JUST...
Boys will be boys.
I didn't look. I didn't look.

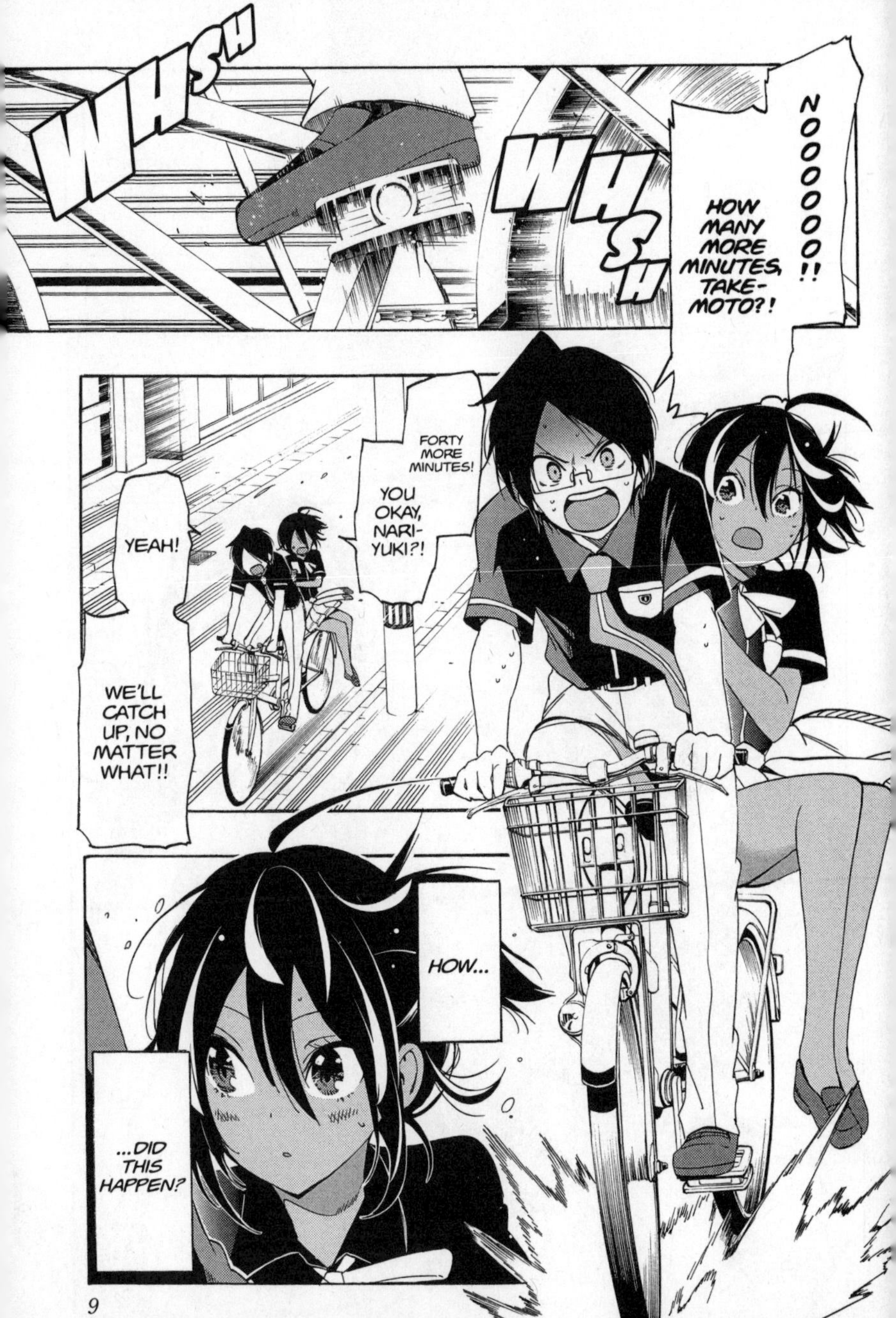
NOOOOOOO!!
HOW MANY MORE MINUTES, TAKE-MOTO?!
WHSH
WHSH
FORTY MORE MINUTES!
YOU OKAY, NARI-YUKI?!
YEAH!
WE'LL CATCH UP, NO MATTER WHAT!!
HOW...
...DID THIS HAPPEN?

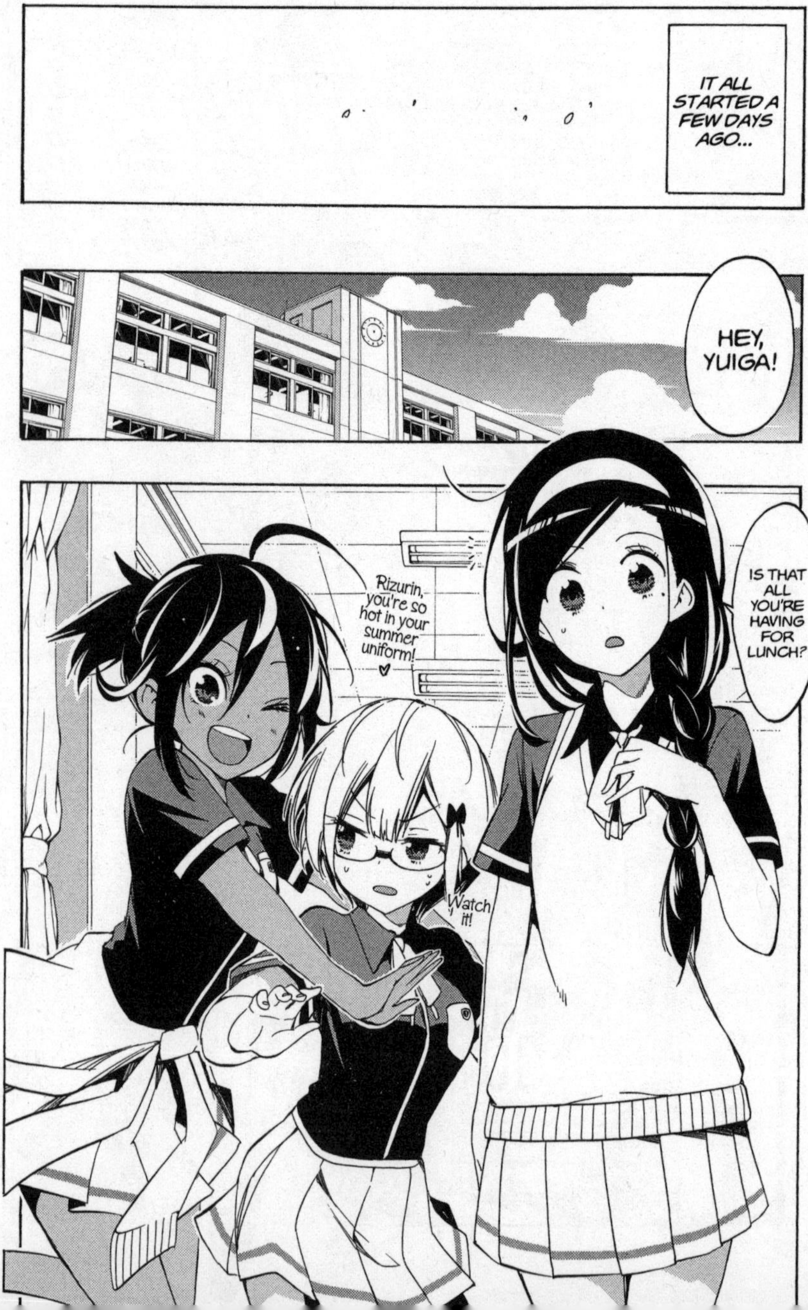
IT ALL STARTED A FEW DAYS AGO...
HEY, YUIGA!
IS THAT ALL YOU'RE HAVING FOR LUNCH?
Rizurin, you're so hot in your summer uniform! ♥
Watch it!

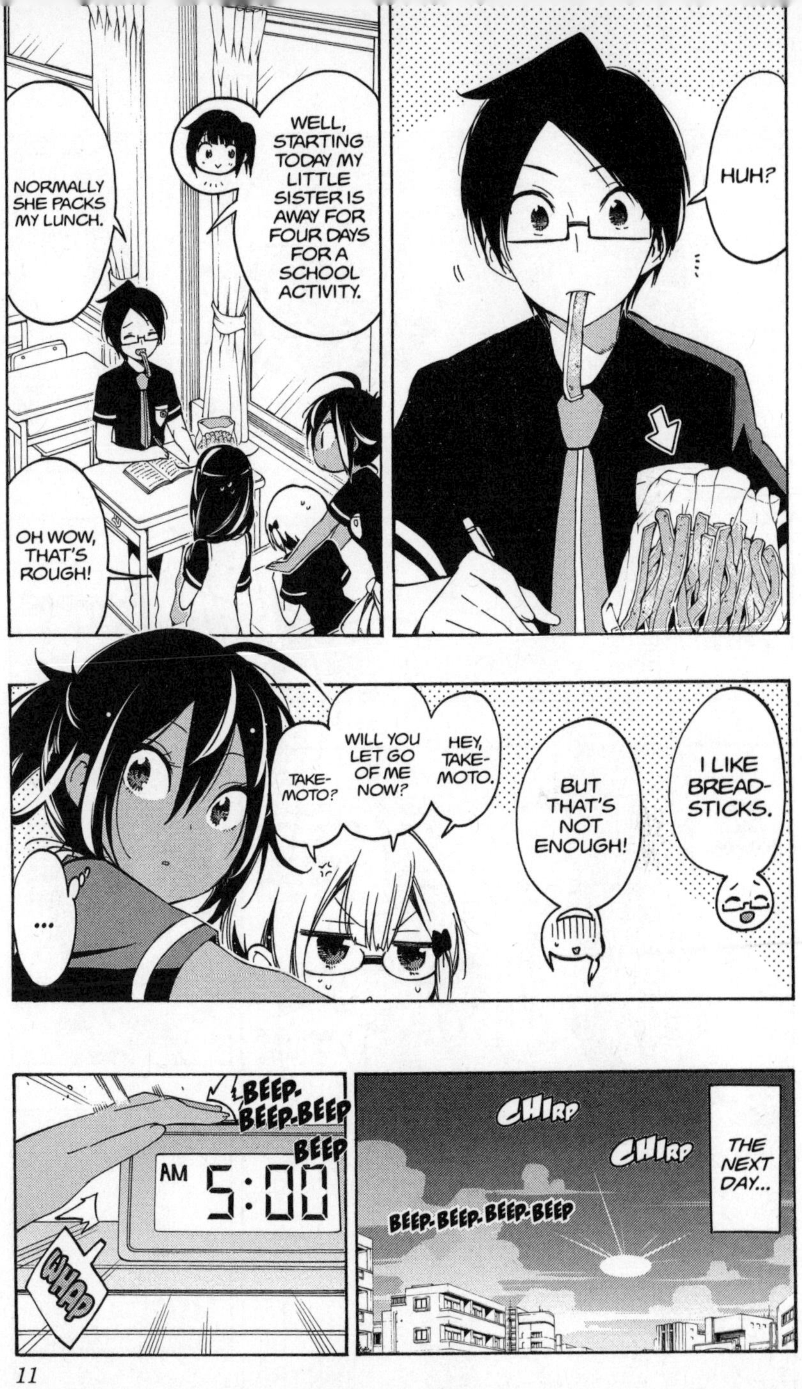
HUH?
WELL, STARTING TODAY MY LITTLE SISTER IS AWAY FOR FOUR DAYS FOR A SCHOOL ACTIVITY.
NORMALLY SHE PACKS MY LUNCH.
OH WOW, THAT'S ROUGH!
I LIKE BREAD-STICKS.
BUT THAT'S NOT ENOUGH!
HEY, TAKE-MOTO.
WILL YOU LET GO OF ME NOW?
TAKE-MOTO?
...
THE NEXT DAY...
CHIRP
CHIRP
BEEP-BEEP-BEEP-BEEP
BEEP-BEEP-BEEP
BEEP
AM 5:00
WHAP

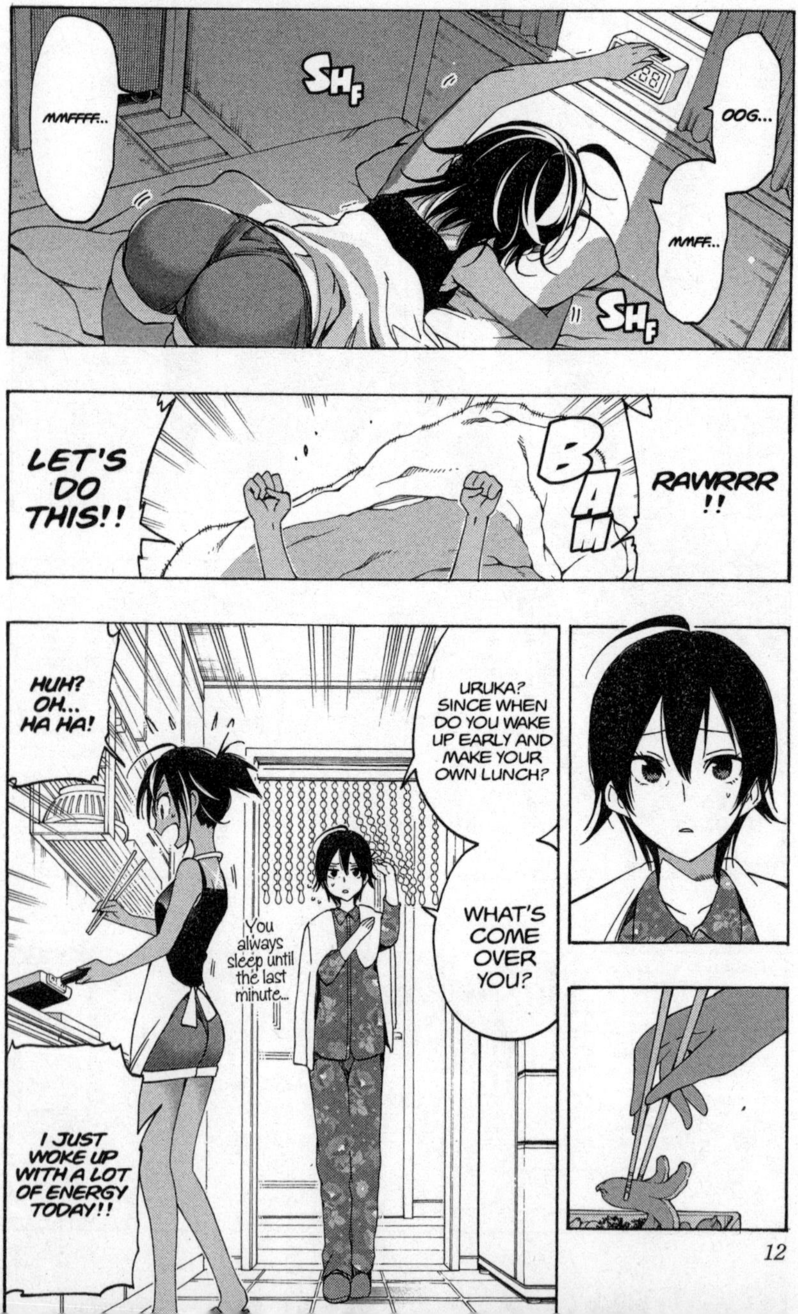
OOG...
MMFF...
SHF
SHF
MMFFFF...
RAWRRR!!
BAM
LET'S DO THIS!!
URUKA? SINCE WHEN DO YOU WAKE UP EARLY AND MAKE YOUR OWN LUNCH?
WHAT'S COME OVER YOU?
You always sleep until the last minute...
HUH? OH... HA HA!
I JUST WOKE UP WITH A LOT OF ENERGY TODAY!!

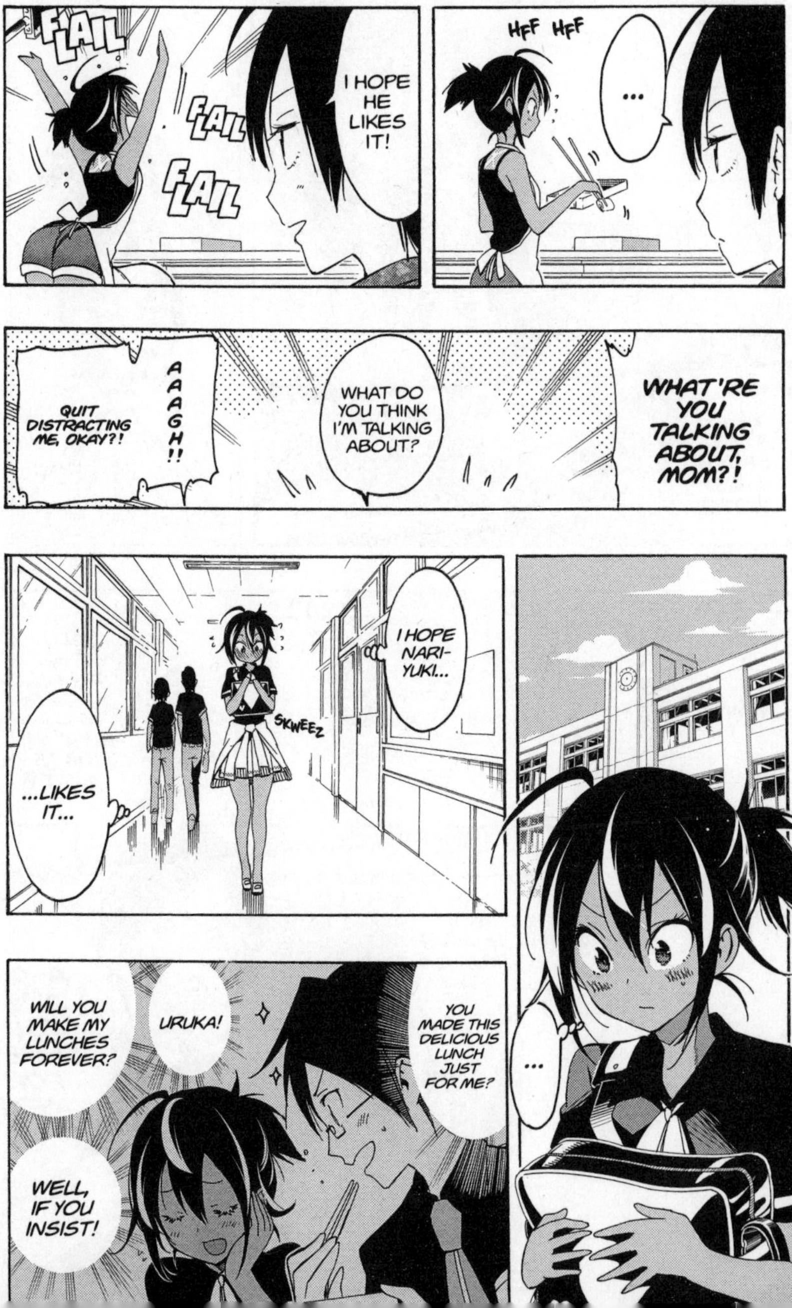
HFF HFF
...
FLAIL
I HOPE HE LIKES IT!
FLAIL
FLAIL
WHAT'RE YOU TALKING ABOUT, MOM?!
WHAT DO YOU THINK I'M TALKING ABOUT?
AAAGH!!
QUIT DISTRACTING ME, OKAY?!
...
I HOPE NARI-YUKI...
SKWEEZ
...LIKES IT...
YOU MADE THIS DELICIOUS LUNCH JUST FOR ME?
URUKA!
WILL YOU MAKE MY LUNCHES FOREVER?
WELL, IF YOU INSIST!

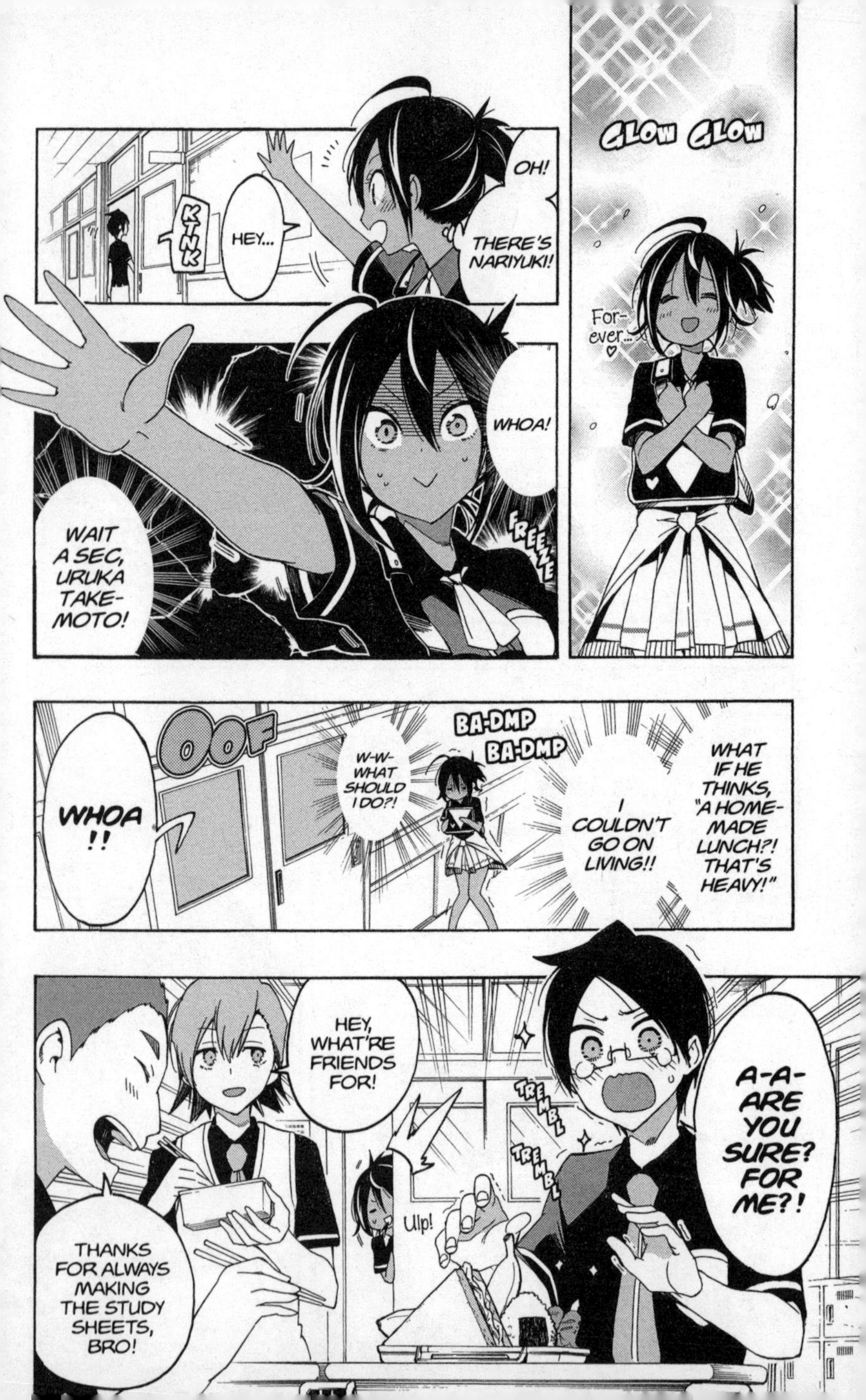
GLOW GLOW
For-ever... ♡
OH!
THERE'S NARIYUKI!
HEY...
KTNK
WHOA!
FREEZE
WAIT A SEC, URUKA TAKE-MOTO!
WHAT IF HE THINKS, "A HOME-MADE LUNCH?! THAT'S HEAVY!"
I COULDN'T GO ON LIVING!!
BA-DMP
BA-DMP
W-W-WHAT SHOULD I DO?!
OOF
WHOA!!
A-A-ARE YOU SURE? FOR ME?!
TREMBL
TREMBL
Ulp!
HEY, WHAT'RE FRIENDS FOR!
THANKS FOR ALWAYS MAKING THE STUDY SHEETS, BRO!

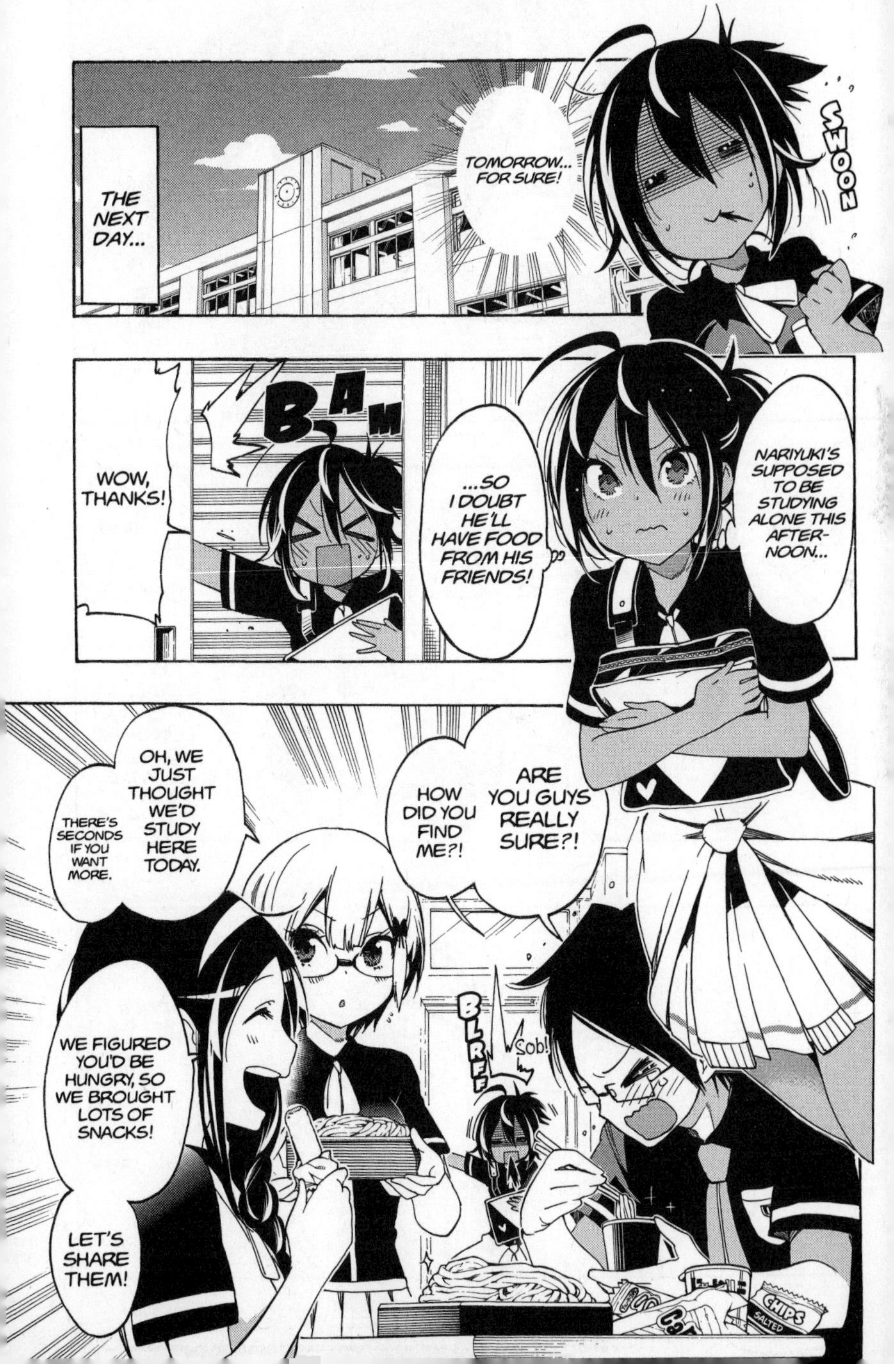
SWOON
TOMORROW... FOR SURE!
THE NEXT DAY...
NARIYUKI'S SUPPOSED TO BE STUDYING ALONE THIS AFTER-NOON...
...SO I DOUBT HE'LL HAVE FOOD FROM HIS FRIENDS!
BAM
WOW, THANKS!
ARE YOU GUYS REALLY SURE?!
HOW DID YOU FIND ME?!
OH, WE JUST THOUGHT WE'D STUDY HERE TODAY.
THERE'S SECONDS IF YOU WANT MORE.
BLRFF
Sob!
WE FIGURED YOU'D BE HUNGRY, SO WE BROUGHT LOTS OF SNACKS!
LET'S SHARE THEM!
CHIPS
SALTED

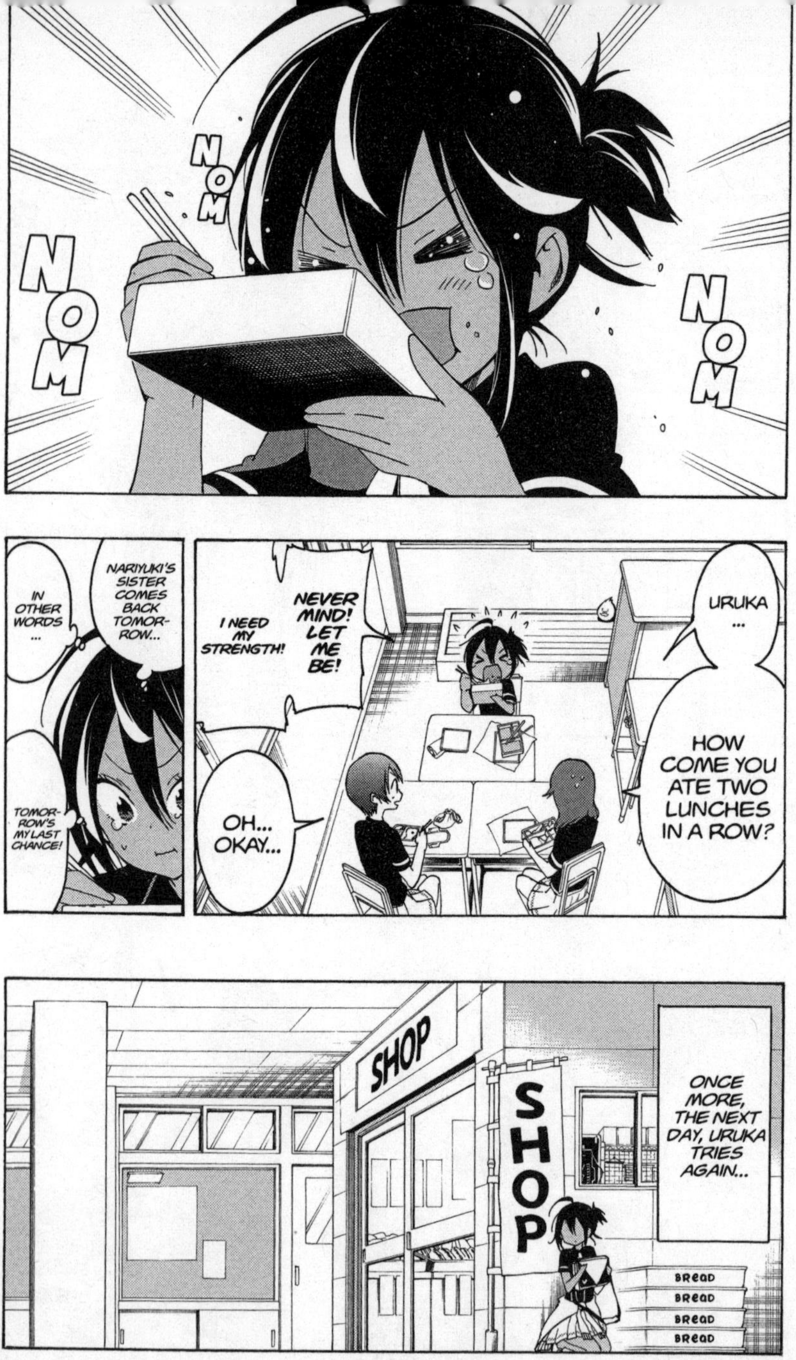
NOM NOM
NOM
NOM NOM
URUKA...
HOW COME YOU ATE TWO LUNCHES IN A ROW?
NEVER MIND! LET ME BE!
I NEED MY STRENGTH!
OH... OKAY...
NARIYUKI'S SISTER COMES BACK TOMOR-ROW...
IN OTHER WORDS...
TOMOR-ROW'S MY LAST CHANCE!
ONCE MORE, THE NEXT DAY, URUKA TRIES AGAIN...
SHOP
SHOP
BREAD
BREAD
BREAD
BREAD

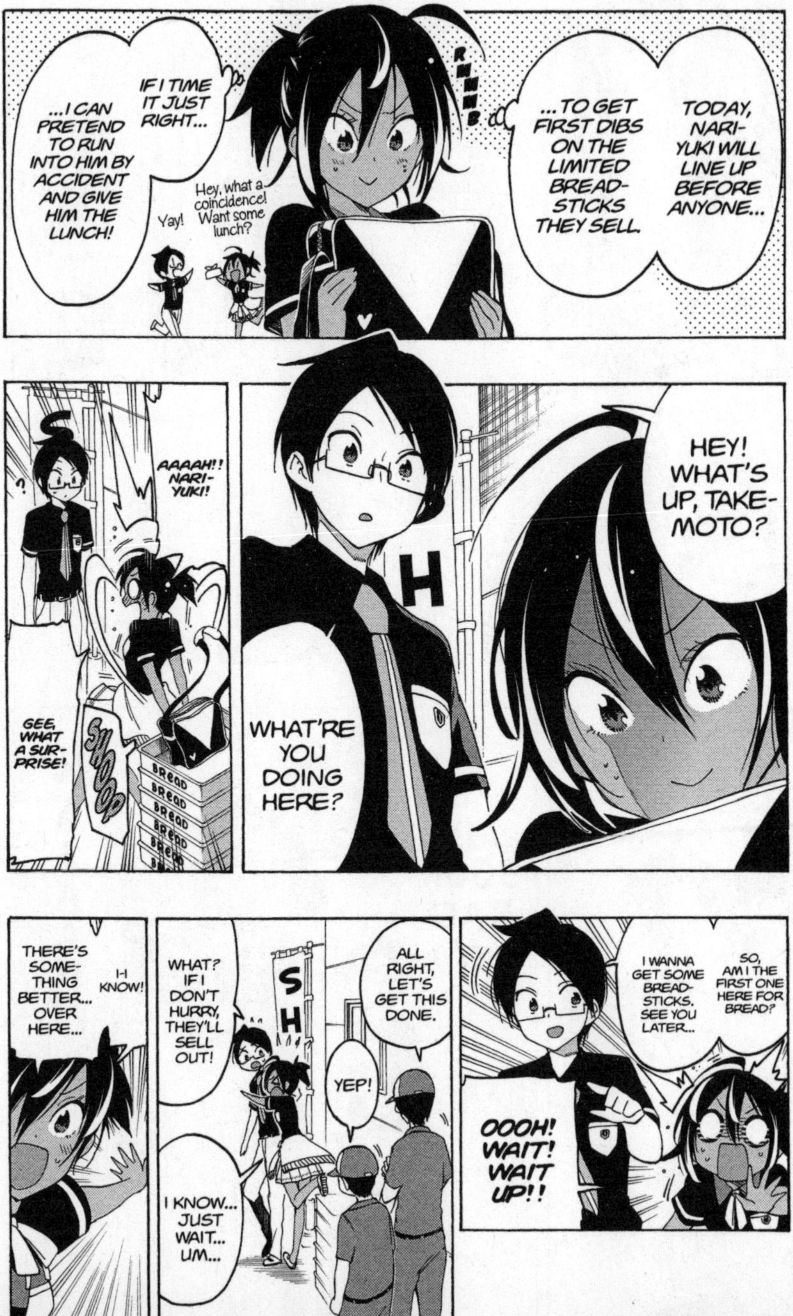
TODAY, NARI-YUKI WILL LINE UP BEFORE ANYONE...
...TO GET FIRST DIBS ON THE LIMITED BREAD-STICKS THEY SELL.
IF I TIME IT JUST RIGHT...
...I CAN PRETEND TO RUN INTO HIM BY ACCIDENT AND GIVE HIM THE LUNCH!
Hey, what a coincidence! Want some lunch?
Yay!
HEY! WHAT'S UP, TAKE-MOTO?
H
WHAT'RE YOU DOING HERE?
AAAAH!! NARI-YUKI!
GEE, WHAT A SUR-PRISE!
SHOOP
BREAD
SO, AM I THE FIRST ONE HERE FOR BREAD?
I WANNA GET SOME BREAD-STICKS. SEE YOU LATER...
OOOH! WAIT! WAIT UP!!
ALL RIGHT, LET'S GET THIS DONE.
YEP!
SH
WHAT? IF I DON'T HURRY, THEY'LL SELL OUT!
I KNOW... JUST WAIT... UM...
I-I KNOW!
THERE'S SOME-THING BETTER... OVER HERE...

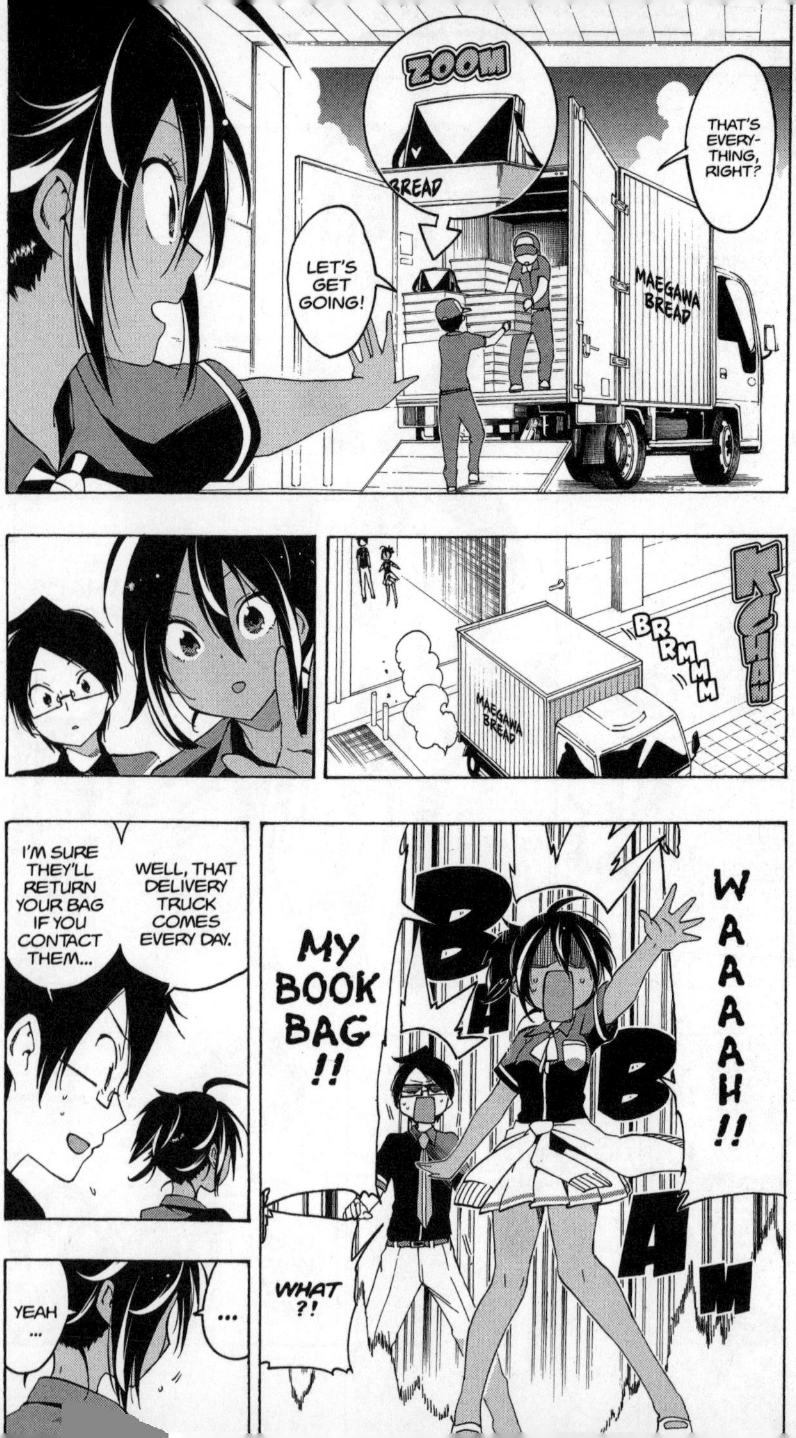

THAT'S EVERYTHING, RIGHT?
ZOOM
BREAD
LET'S GET GOING!
MAEGAWA BREAD
KCHA!
BRRMMM
MAEGAWA BREAD
WAAAAAH!!
BAM
MY BOOK BAG!!
WHAT?!
WELL, THAT DELIVERY TRUCK COMES EVERY DAY.
I'M SURE THEY'LL RETURN YOUR BAG IF YOU CONTACT THEM...
...
YEAH ...

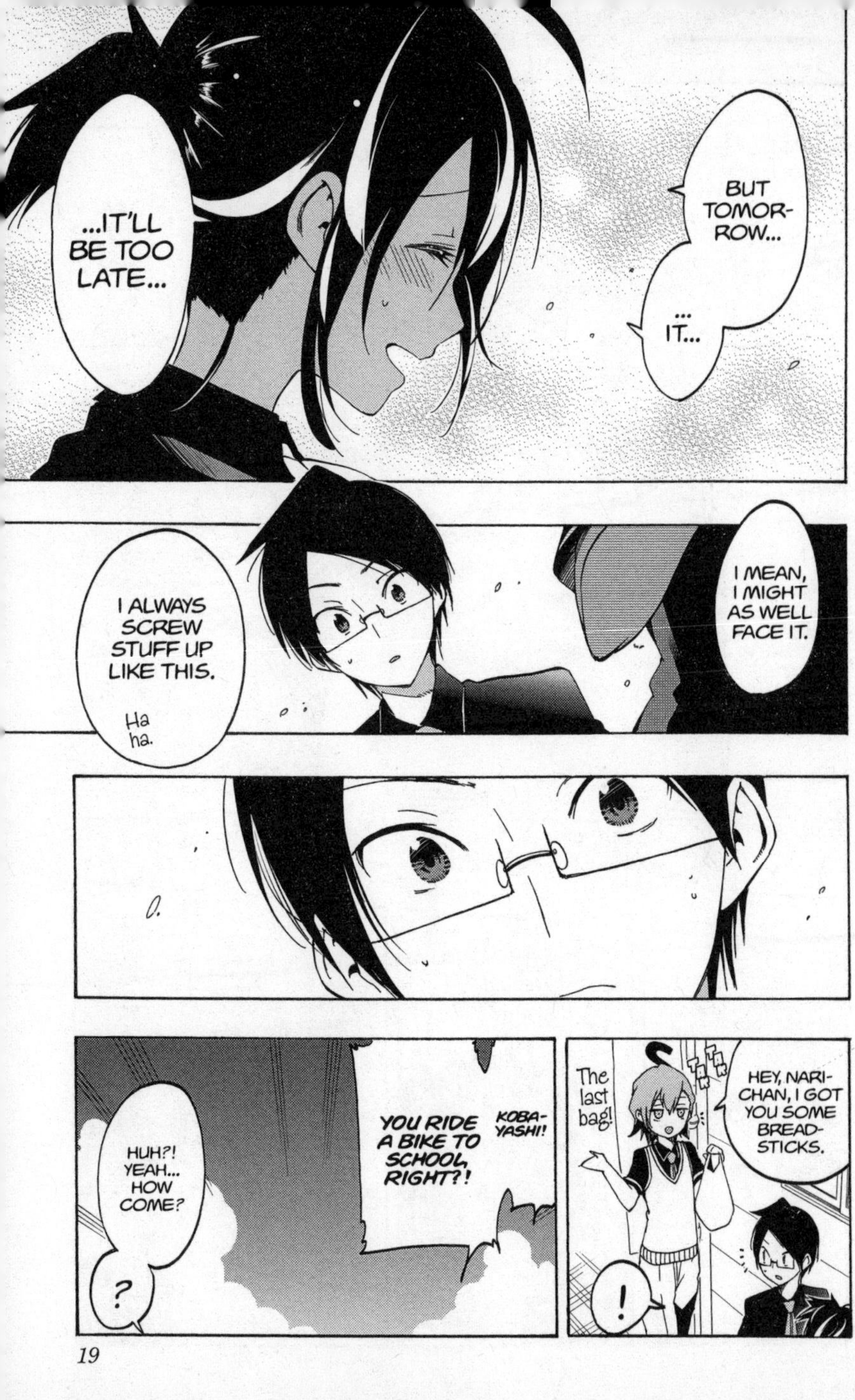
BUT TOMORROW...
... IT...
...IT'LL BE TOO LATE...
I MEAN, I MIGHT AS WELL FACE IT.
I ALWAYS SCREW STUFF UP LIKE THIS.
Ha ha.
HEY, NARI-CHAN, I GOT YOU SOME BREAD-STICKS.
TAK TAK
The last bag!
!
KOBAYASHI!
YOU RIDE A BIKE TO SCHOOL, RIGHT?!
HUH?! YEAH... HOW COME?
?

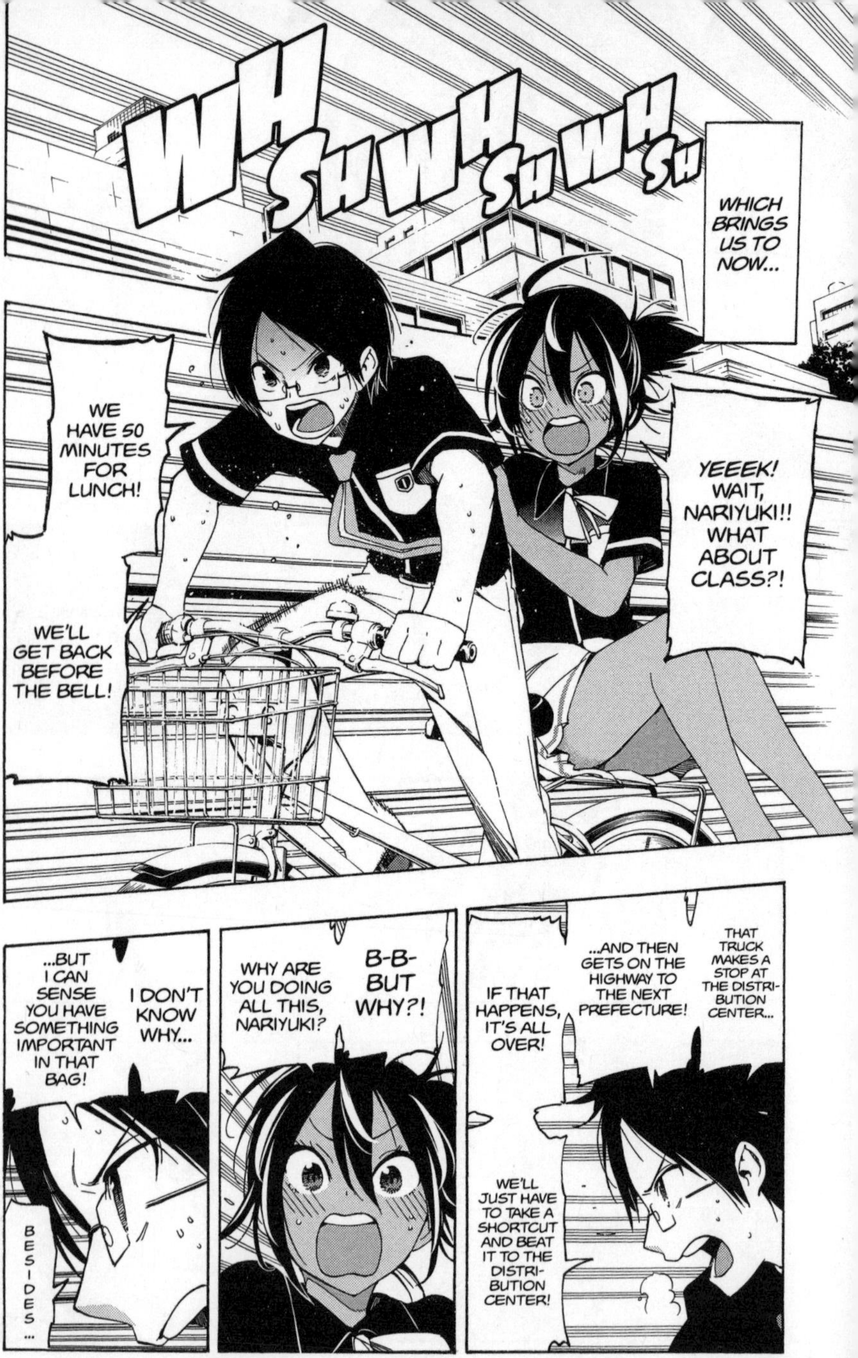
WHSHWHSHWHSH
WHICH BRINGS US TO NOW...
YEEEK! WAIT, NARIYUKI!! WHAT ABOUT CLASS?!
WE HAVE 50 MINUTES FOR LUNCH!
WE'LL GET BACK BEFORE THE BELL!
THAT TRUCK MAKES A STOP AT THE DISTRIBUTION CENTER...
...AND THEN GETS ON THE HIGHWAY TO THE NEXT PREFECTURE!
IF THAT HAPPENS, IT'S ALL OVER!
WE'LL JUST HAVE TO TAKE A SHORTCUT AND BEAT IT TO THE DISTRIBUTION CENTER!
B-B-BUT WHY?!
WHY ARE YOU DOING ALL THIS, NARIYUKI?
I DON'T KNOW WHY...
...BUT I CAN SENSE YOU HAVE SOMETHING IMPORTANT IN THAT BAG!
BESIDES...

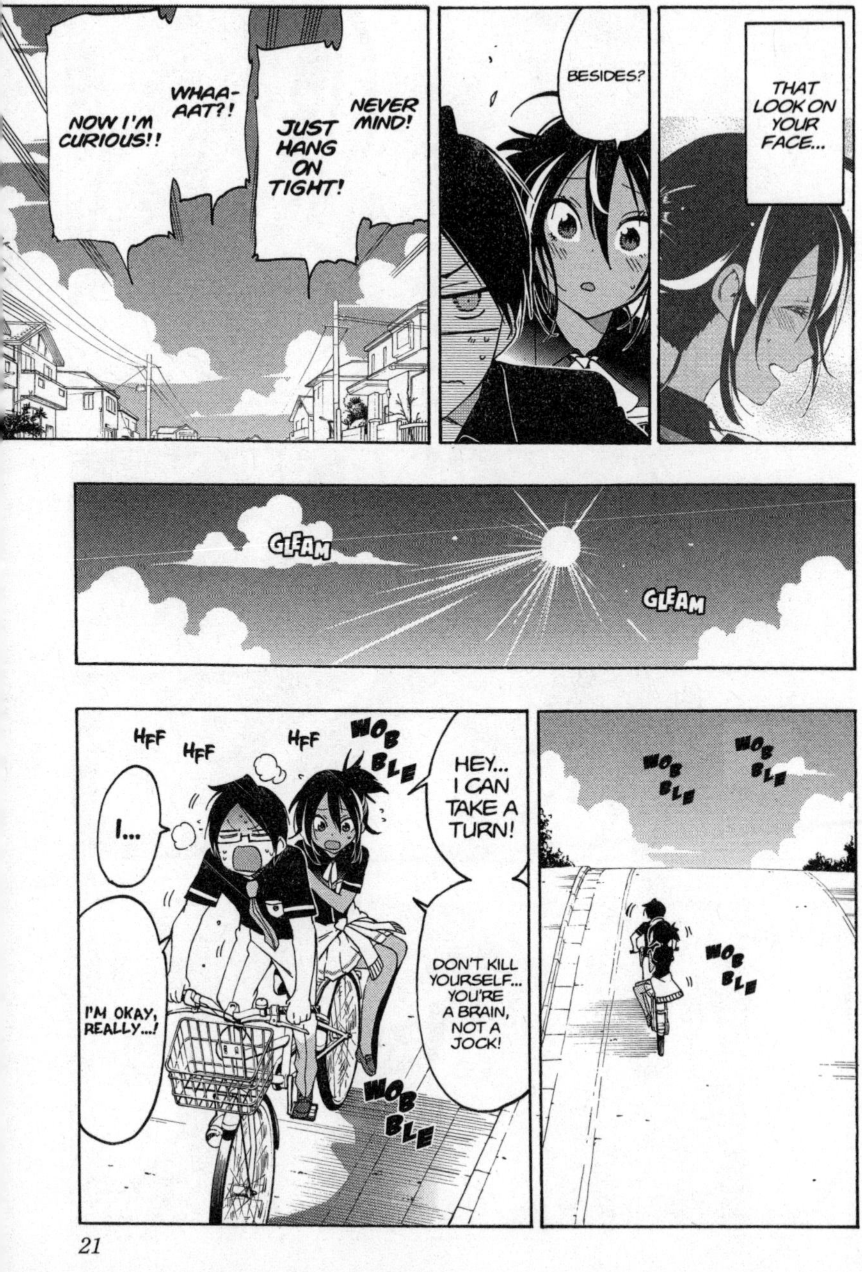
THAT LOOK ON YOUR FACE...
BESIDES?
NEVER MIND!
JUST HANG ON TIGHT!
WHAAA-AAT?!
NOW I'M CURIOUS!!
GLEAM
GLEAM
WOBBLE
WOBBLE
WOBBLE
HEY... I CAN TAKE A TURN!
WOBBLE
HFF
HFF
HFF
DON'T KILL YOURSELF... YOU'RE A BRAIN, NOT A JOCK!
I...
I'M OKAY, REALLY...!
WOBBLE

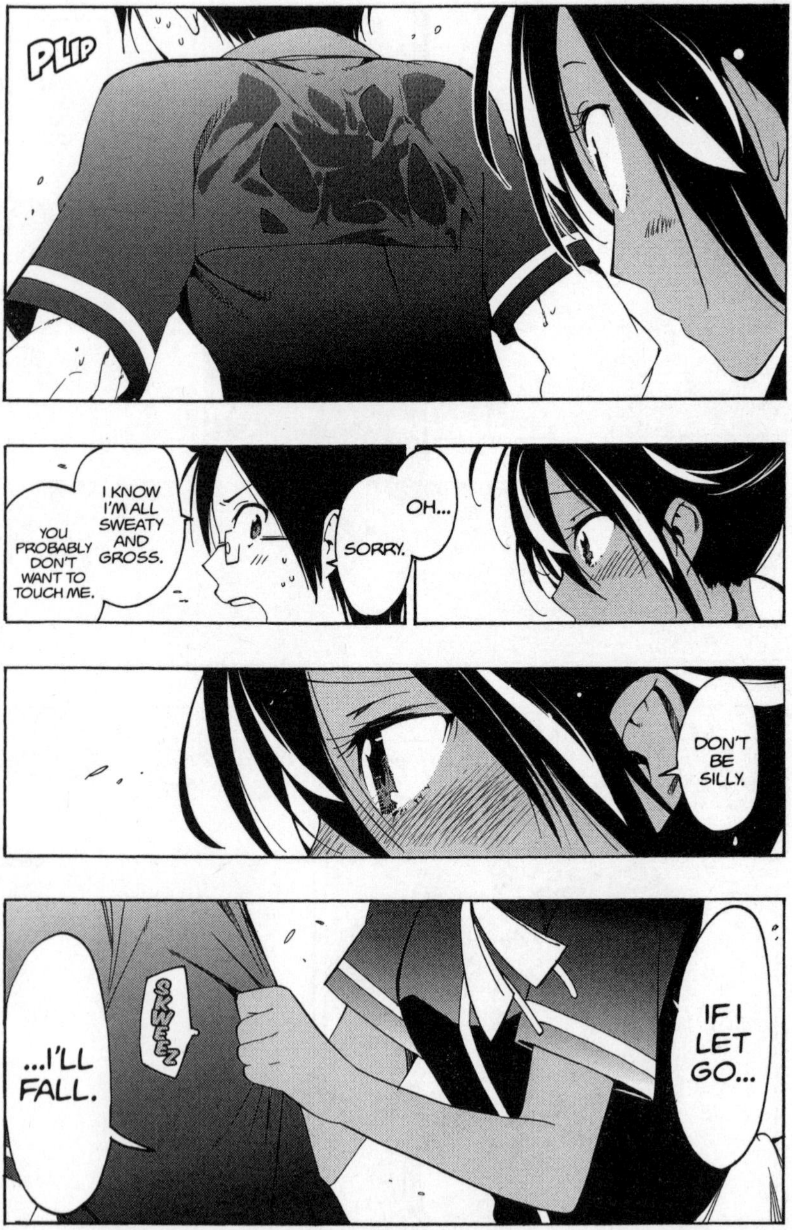
PLIP
OH... SORRY.
I KNOW I'M ALL SWEATY AND GROSS.
YOU PROBABLY DON'T WANT TO TOUCH ME.
DON'T BE SILLY.
IF I LET GO...
SKWEEZ
...I'LL FALL.

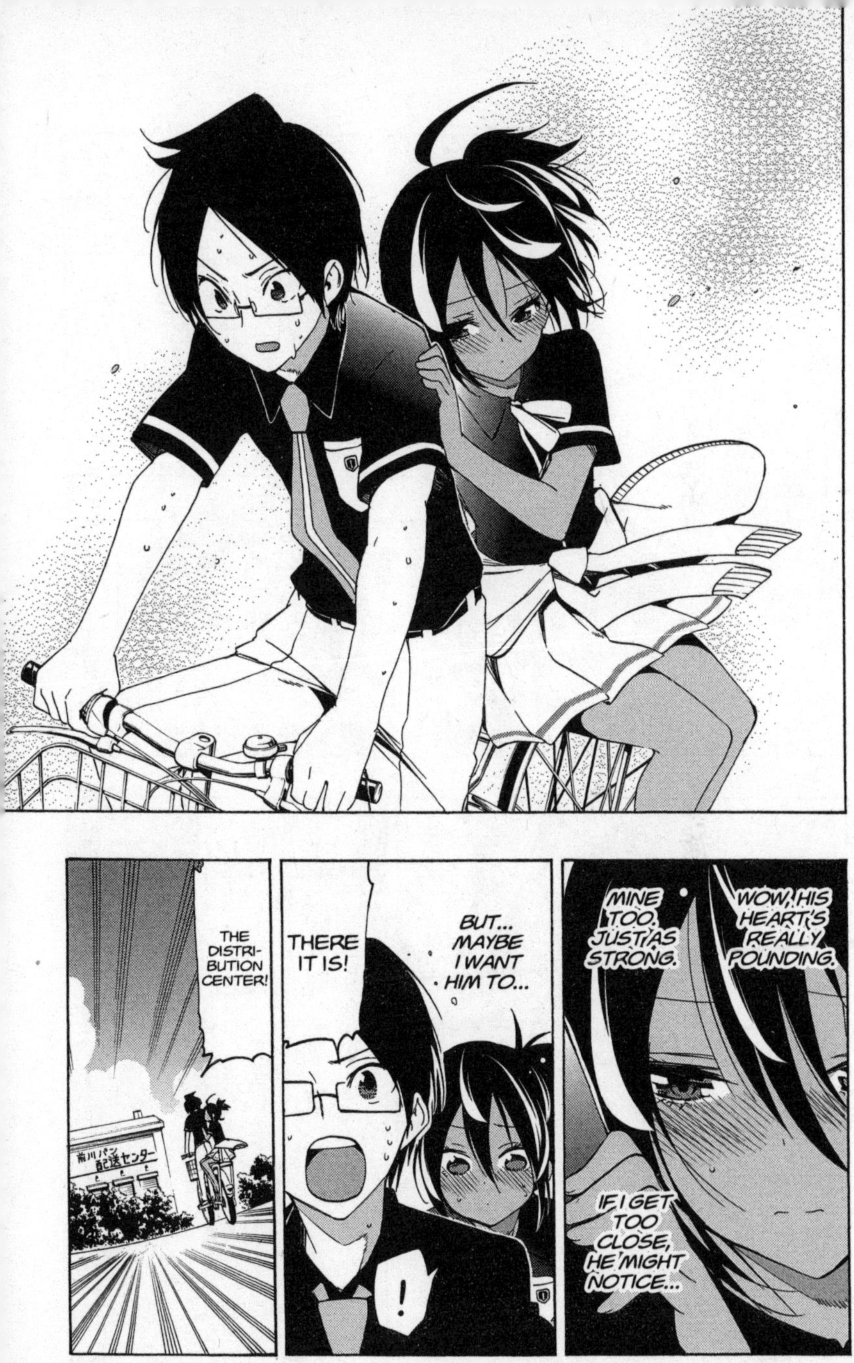
WOW, HIS HEART'S REALLY POUNDING.
MINE TOO. JUST AS STRONG.
IF I GET TOO CLOSE, HE MIGHT NOTICE...
BUT... MAYBE I WANT HIM TO...
THERE IT IS!
!
THE DISTRI-BUTION CENTER!
前川パン 配送センター

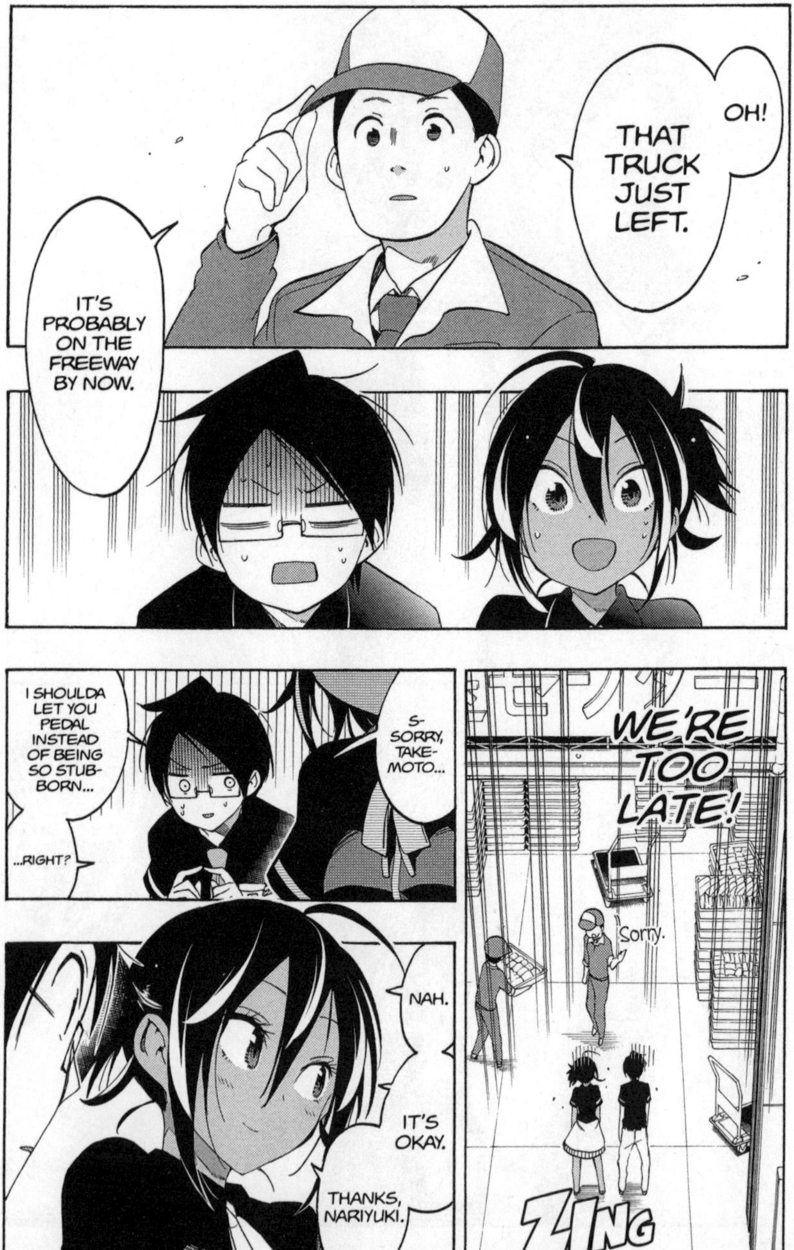
OH!
THAT TRUCK JUST LEFT.
IT'S PROBABLY ON THE FREEWAY BY NOW.
WE'RE TOO LATE!
Sorry.
ZING
S-SORRY, TAKE-MOTO...
I SHOULDA LET YOU PEDAL INSTEAD OF BEING SO STUB-BORN...
...RIGHT?
NAH.
IT'S OKAY.
THANKS, NARIYUKI.

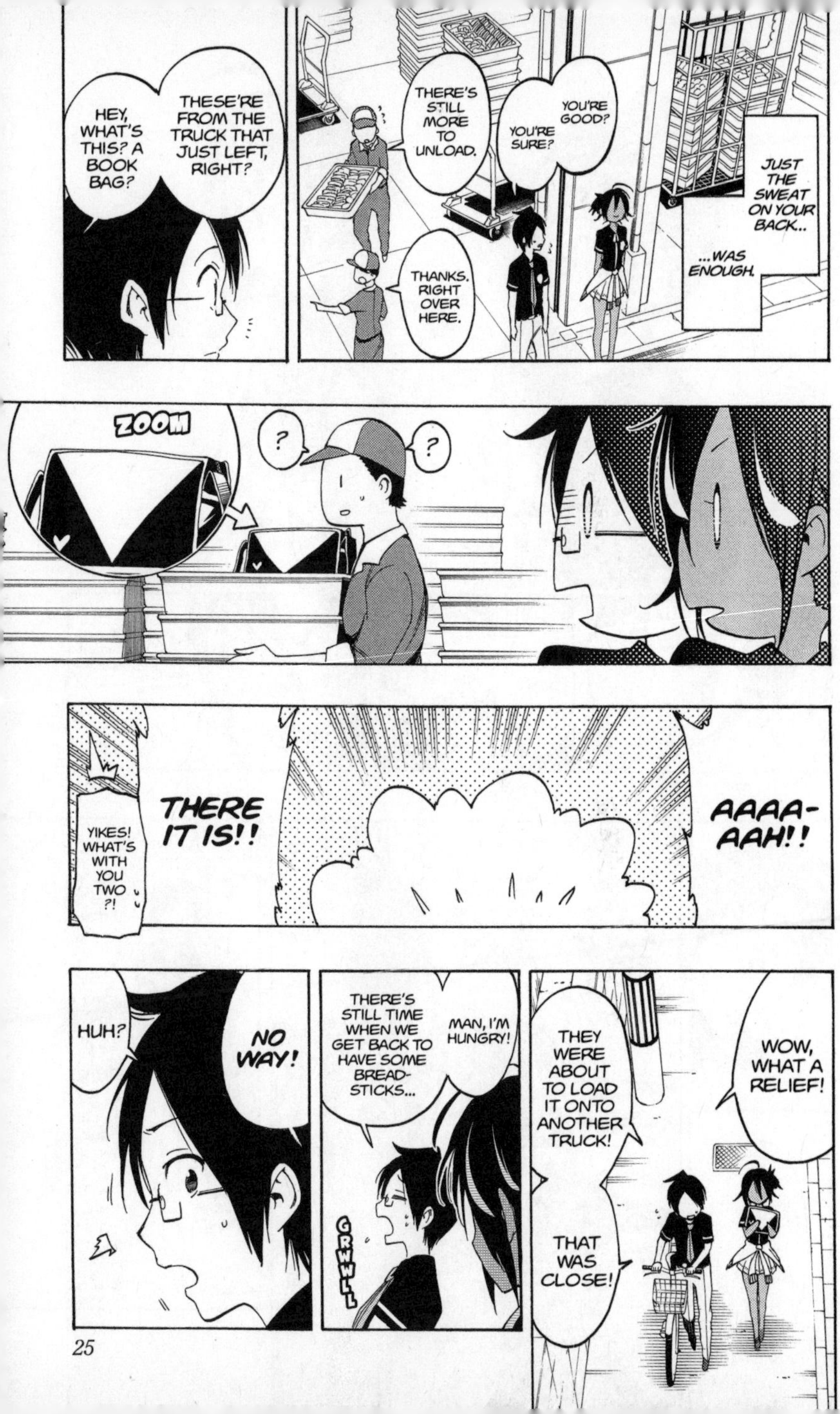
JUST THE SWEAT ON YOUR BACK...
...WAS ENOUGH.
YOU'RE GOOD?
YOU'RE SURE?
THERE'S STILL MORE TO UNLOAD.
THANKS. RIGHT OVER HERE.
THESE'RE FROM THE TRUCK THAT JUST LEFT, RIGHT?
HEY, WHAT'S THIS? A BOOK BAG?
?
?
ZOOM
AAAA-AAH!!
THERE IT IS!!
YIKES! WHAT'S WITH YOU TWO?!
WOW, WHAT A RELIEF!
THEY WERE ABOUT TO LOAD IT ONTO ANOTHER TRUCK!
THAT WAS CLOSE!
MAN, I'M HUNGRY!
THERE'S STILL TIME WHEN WE GET BACK TO HAVE SOME BREAD-STICKS...
GRWLL
NO WAY!
HUH?

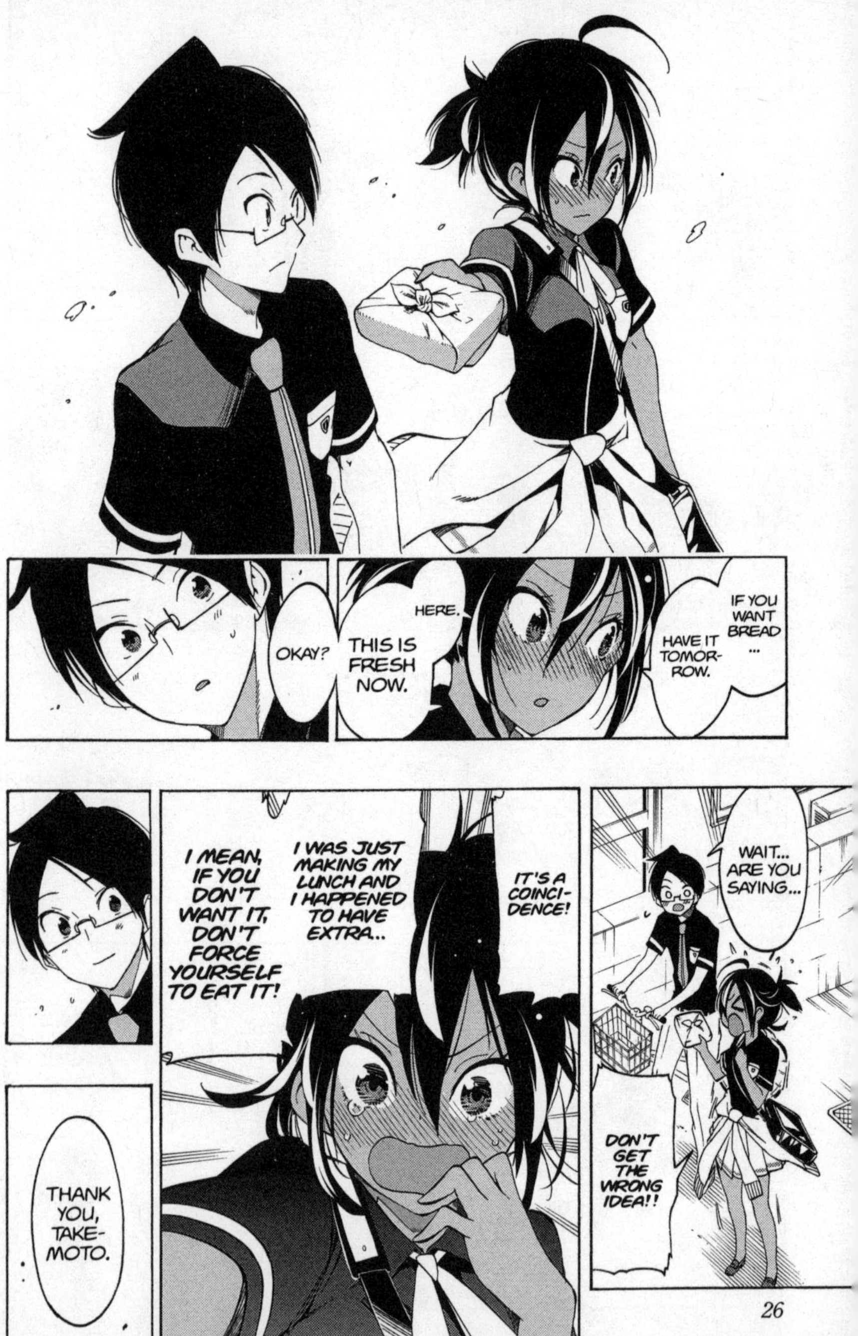
IF YOU WANT BREAD...
HAVE IT TOMORROW.
HERE.
THIS IS FRESH NOW.
OKAY?
WAIT... ARE YOU SAYING...
DON'T GET THE WRONG IDEA!!
IT'S A COINCIDENCE!
I WAS JUST MAKING MY LUNCH AND I HAPPENED TO HAVE EXTRA..
I MEAN, IF YOU DON'T WANT IT, DON'T FORCE YOURSELF TO EAT IT!
THANK YOU, TAKEMOTO.

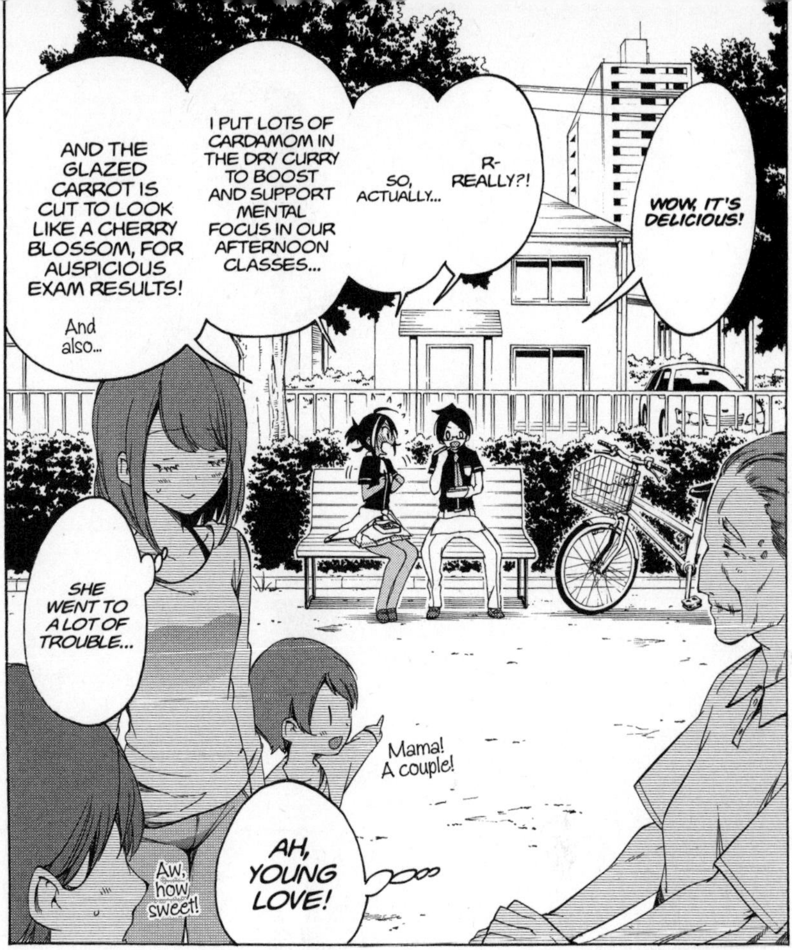
WOW, IT'S DELICIOUS!
R-REALLY?!
SO, ACTUALLY...
I PUT LOTS OF CARDAMOM IN THE DRY CURRY TO BOOST AND SUPPORT MENTAL FOCUS IN OUR AFTERNOON CLASSES...
AND THE GLAZED CARROT IS CUT TO LOOK LIKE A CHERRY BLOSSOM, FOR AUSPICIOUS EXAM RESULTS!
And also...
Mama! A couple!
AH, YOUNG LOVE!
SHE WENT TO A LOT OF TROUBLE...
Aw, how sweet!

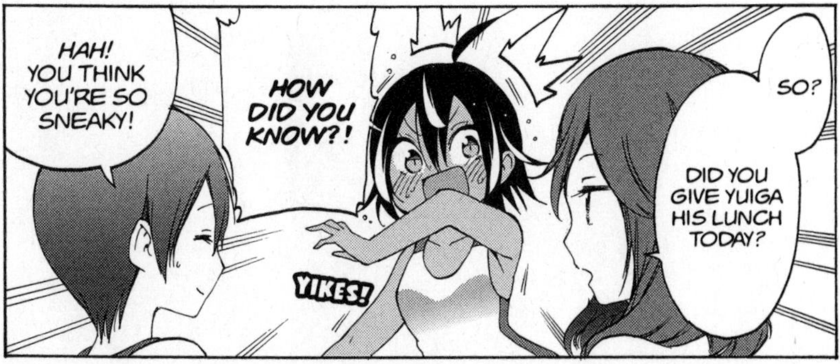
SO?
DID YOU GIVE YUIGA HIS LUNCH TODAY?
HOW DID YOU KNOW?!
YIKES!
HAH! YOU THINK YOU'RE SO SNEAKY!

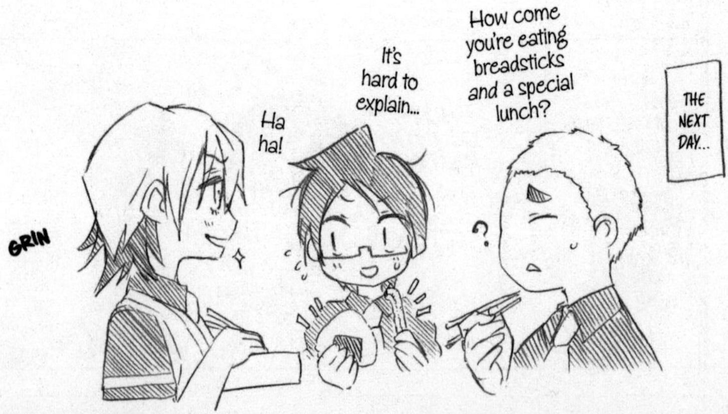
THE NEXT DAY...
How come you're eating breadsticks and a special lunch?
?
It's hard to explain...
Ha ha!
GRIN

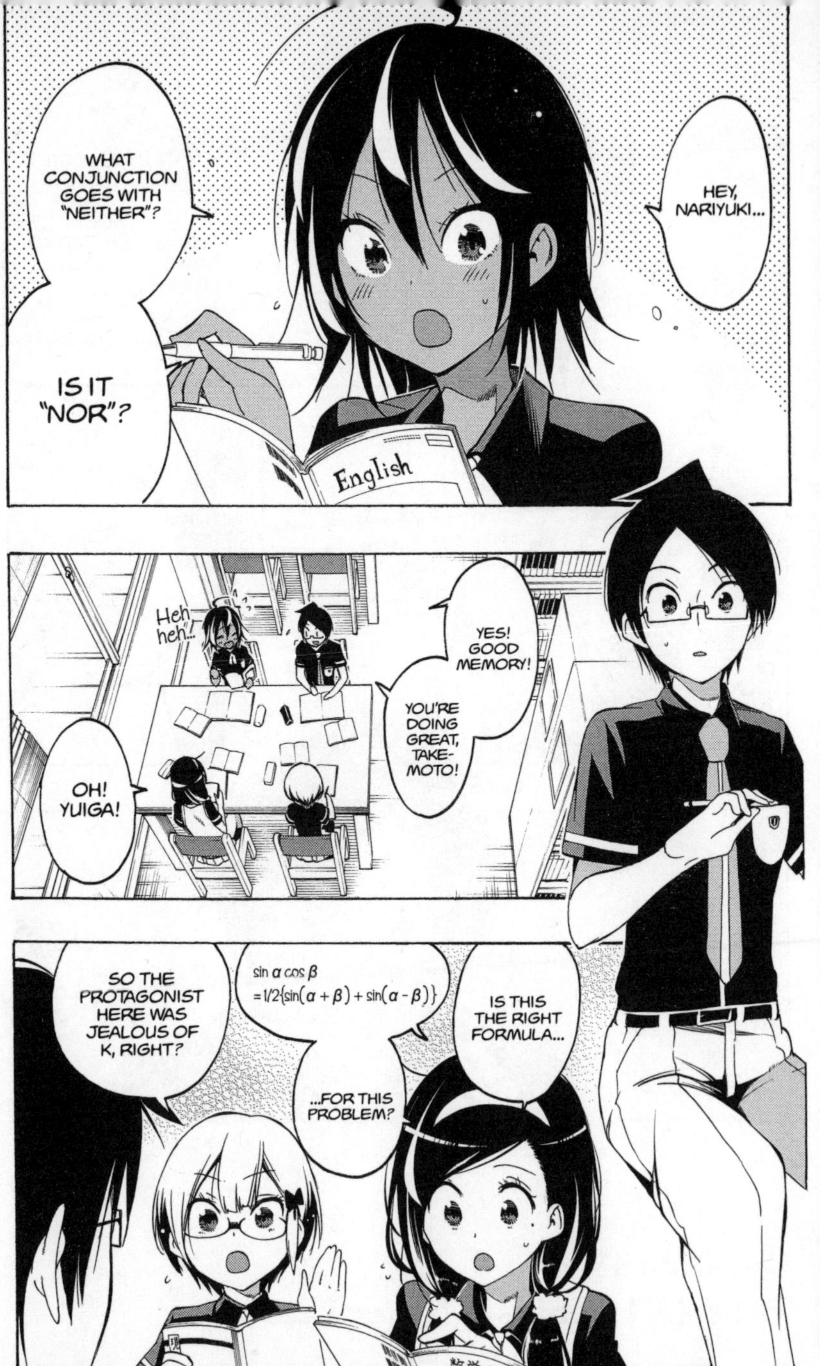
HEY, NARIYUKI...
WHAT CONJUNCTION GOES WITH "NEITHER"?
IS IT "NOR"?
English
YES! GOOD MEMORY!
YOU'RE DOING GREAT, TAKE-MOTO!
Heh heh...
OH! YUIGA!
IS THIS THE RIGHT FORMULA...
sin α cos β
= 1/2{sin(α + β) + sin(α - β)}
...FOR THIS PROBLEM?
SO THE PROTAGONIST HERE WAS JEALOUS OF K, RIGHT?

Question 18: Thus, [*X*] Geniuses Never Learn

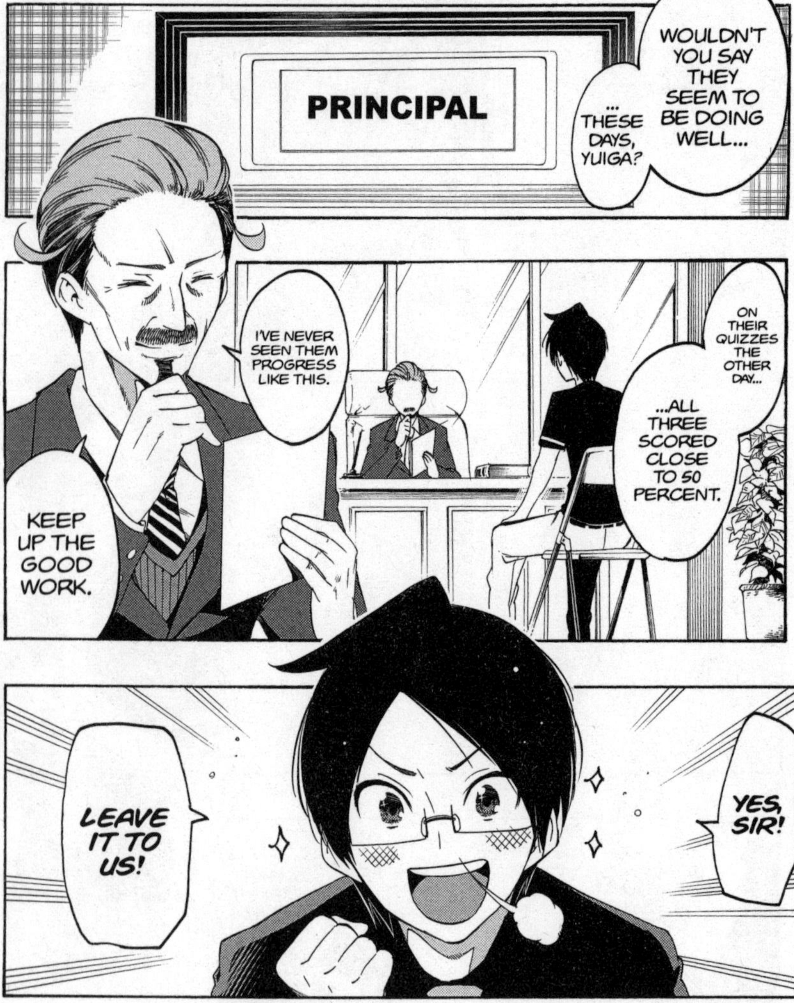
WOULDN'T YOU SAY THEY SEEM TO BE DOING WELL...
...THESE DAYS, YUIGA?
PRINCIPAL
ON THEIR QUIZZES THE OTHER DAY...
...ALL THREE SCORED CLOSE TO 50 PERCENT.
I'VE NEVER SEEN THEM PROGRESS LIKE THIS.
KEEP UP THE GOOD WORK.
YES, SIR!
LEAVE IT TO US!

Question 18:
Thus, [*X*] Geniuses Never Learn

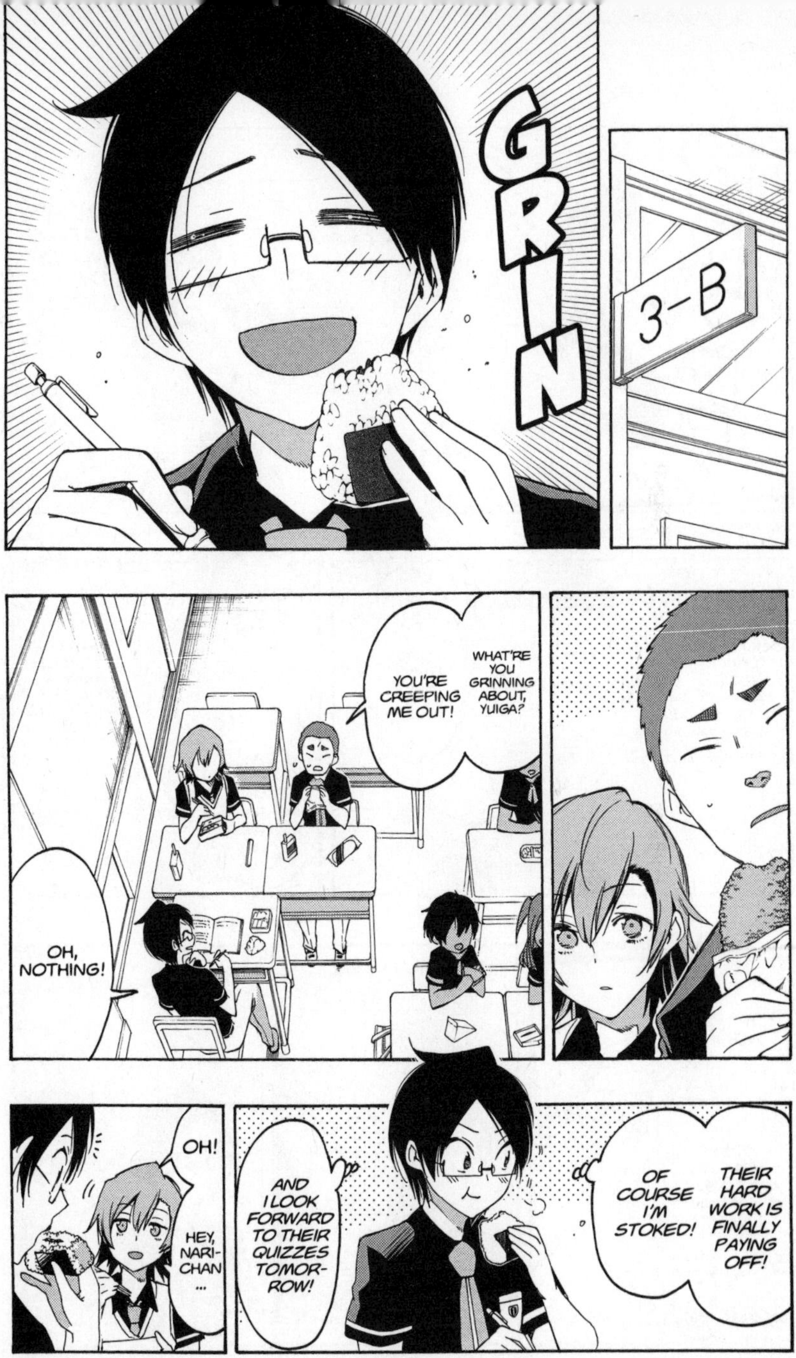
3-B
GRIN
WHAT'RE YOU GRINNING ABOUT, YUIGA?
YOU'RE CREEPING ME OUT!
OH, NOTHING!
THEIR HARD WORK IS FINALLY PAYING OFF!
OF COURSE I'M STOKED!
AND I LOOK FORWARD TO THEIR QUIZZES TOMORROW!
OH!
HEY, NARI-CHAN...

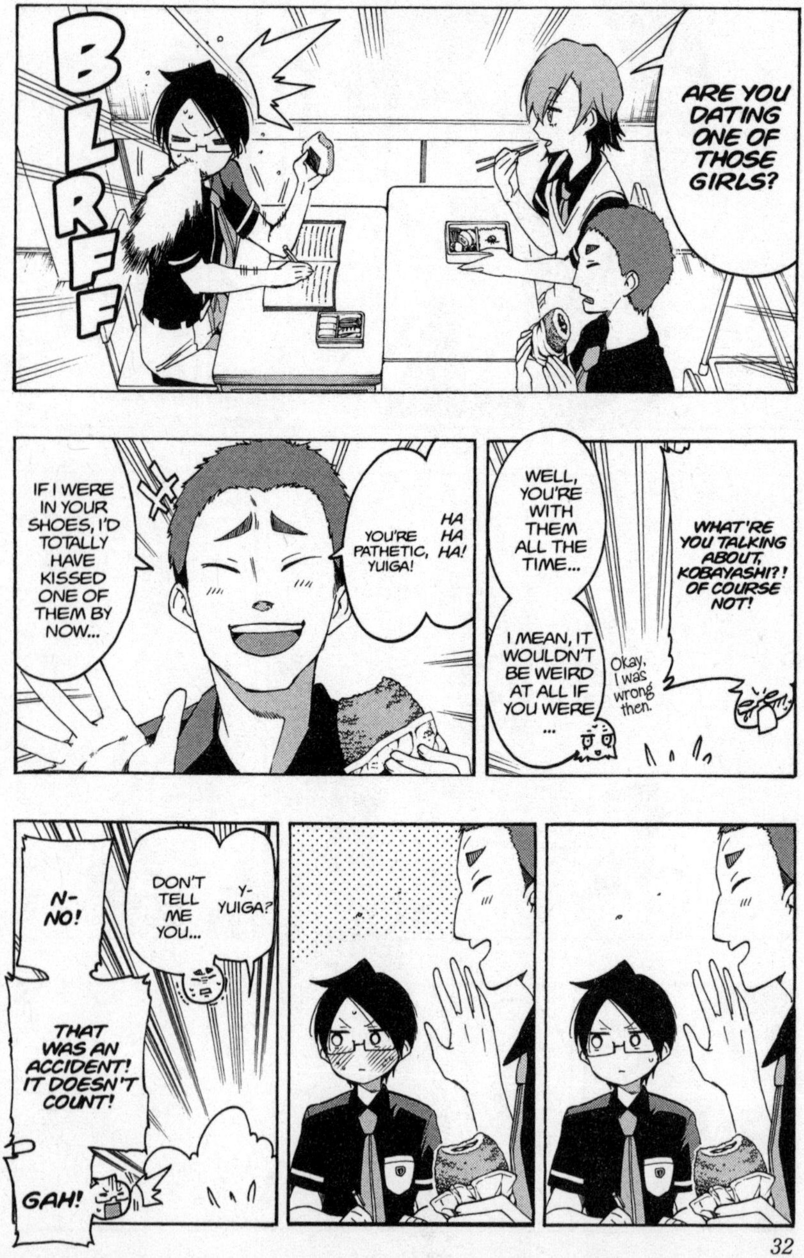
ARE YOU DATING ONE OF THOSE GIRLS?
BLRFF
WHAT'RE YOU TALKING ABOUT, KOBAYASHI?! OF COURSE NOT!
WELL, YOU'RE WITH THEM ALL THE TIME...
I MEAN, IT WOULDN'T BE WEIRD AT ALL IF YOU WERE...
Okay, I was wrong then.
HA HA HA!
YOU'RE PATHETIC, YUIGA!
IF I WERE IN YOUR SHOES, I'D TOTALLY HAVE KISSED ONE OF THEM BY NOW...
Y-YUIGA?
DON'T TELL ME YOU...
N-NO!
THAT WAS AN ACCIDENT! IT DOESN'T COUNT!
GAH!

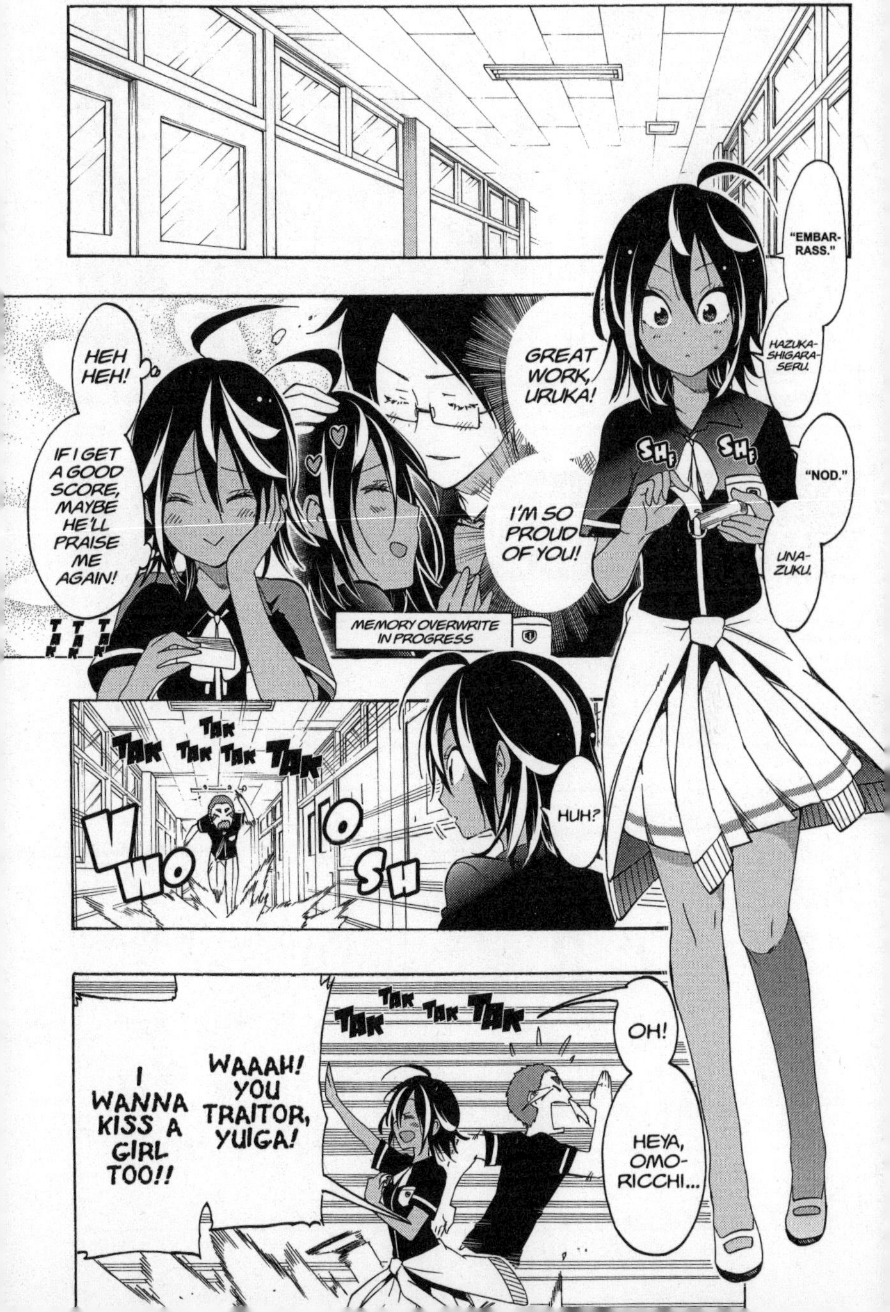

"EMBARRASS."
HAZUKA-SHIGARASERU.
"NOD."
UNA-ZUKU.
SHF SHF
GREAT WORK, URUKA!
I'M SO PROUD OF YOU!
MEMORY OVERWRITE IN PROGRESS
HEH HEH!
IF I GET A GOOD SCORE, MAYBE HE'LL PRAISE ME AGAIN!
TAK TAK TAK
HUH?
TAK TAK TAK TAK TAK
VWOOSH
OH!
HEYA, OMORICCHI...
TAK TAK TAK TAK
WAAAH! YOU TRAITOR, YUIGA!
I WANNA KISS A GIRL TOO!!

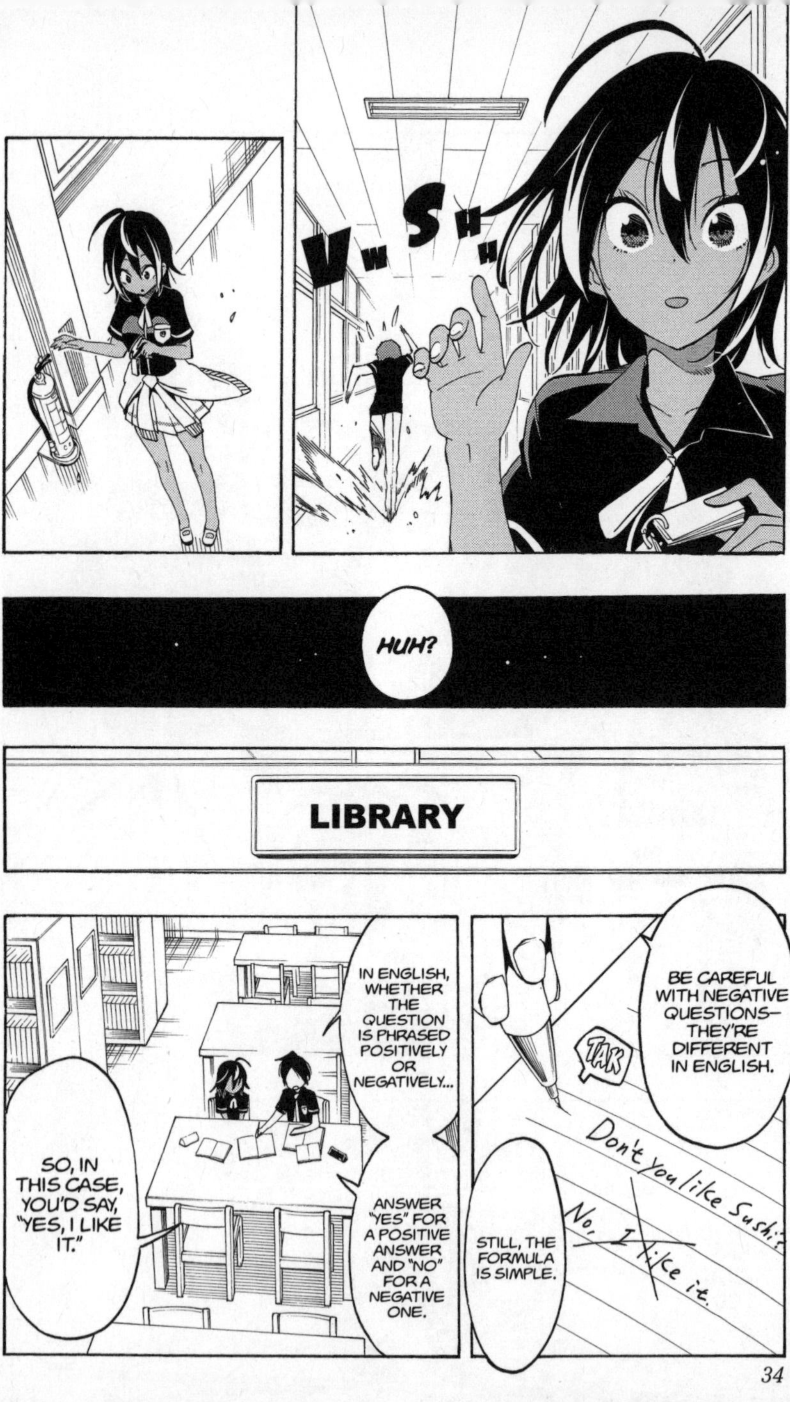

VwSHH
HUH?
LIBRARY
BE CAREFUL WITH NEGATIVE QUESTIONS—THEY'RE DIFFERENT IN ENGLISH.
TAK
Don't you like Sushi?
No, I like it.
STILL, THE FORMULA IS SIMPLE.
IN ENGLISH, WHETHER THE QUESTION IS PHRASED POSITIVELY OR NEGATIVELY...
ANSWER "YES" FOR A POSITIVE ANSWER AND "NO" FOR A NEGATIVE ONE.
SO, IN THIS CASE, YOU'D SAY, "YES, I LIKE IT."

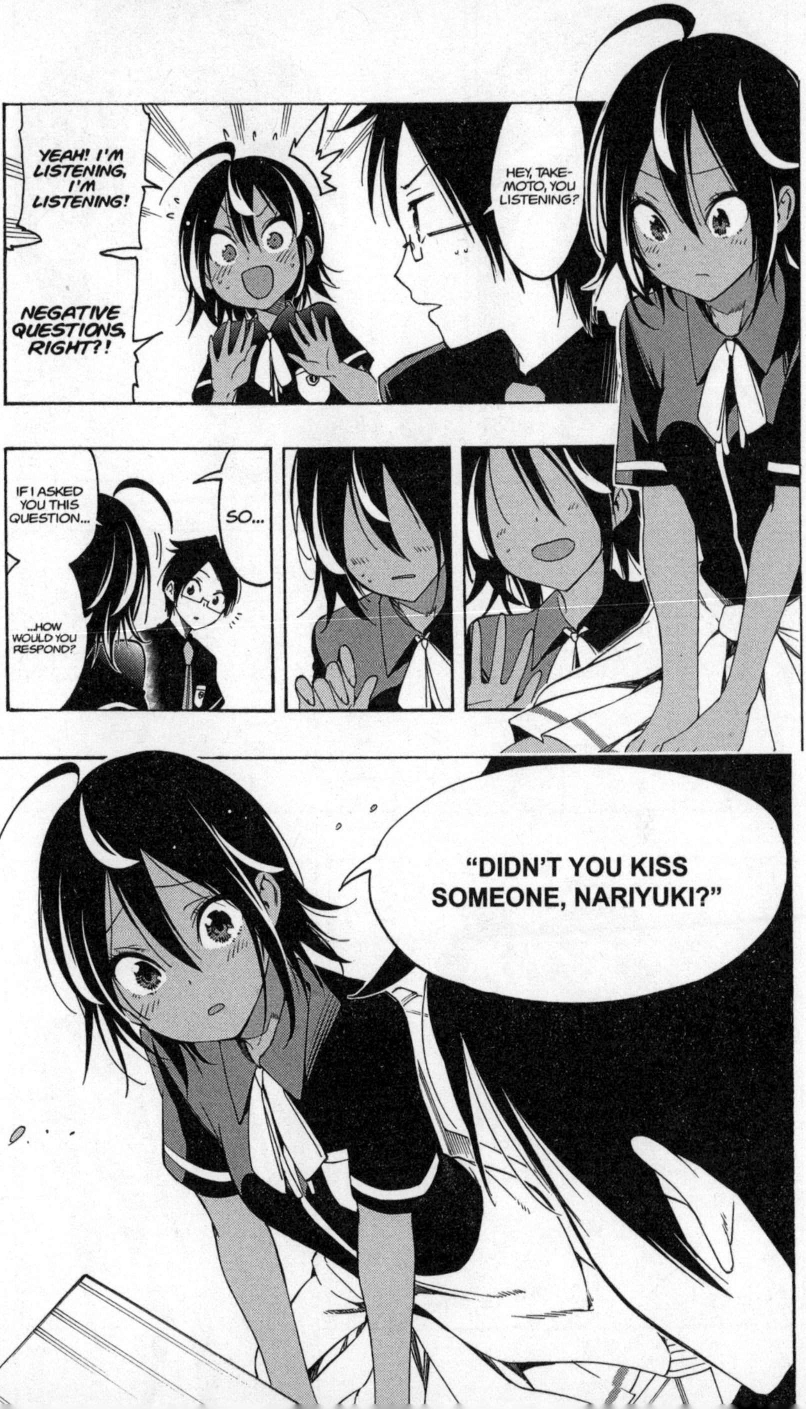
HEY, TAKE-MOTO, YOU LISTENING?
YEAH! I'M LISTENING, I'M LISTENING!
NEGATIVE QUESTIONS, RIGHT?!
SO...
IF I ASKED YOU THIS QUESTION...
...HOW WOULD YOU RESPOND?
"DIDN'T YOU KISS SOMEONE, NARIYUKI?"

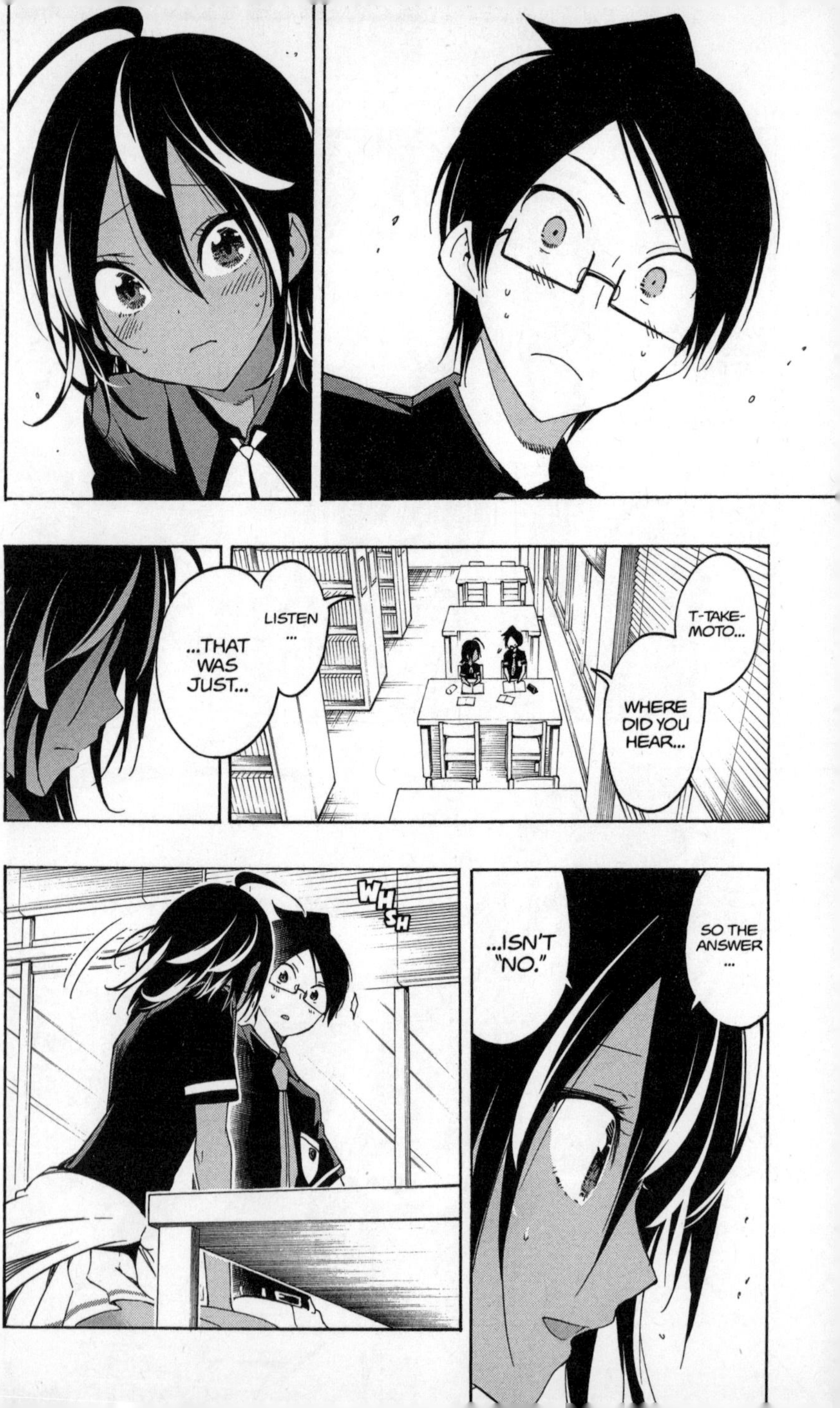
T-TAKE-MOTO...
WHERE DID YOU HEAR...
LISTEN...
...THAT WAS JUST...
SO THE ANSWER...
...ISN'T "NO."
WHSH

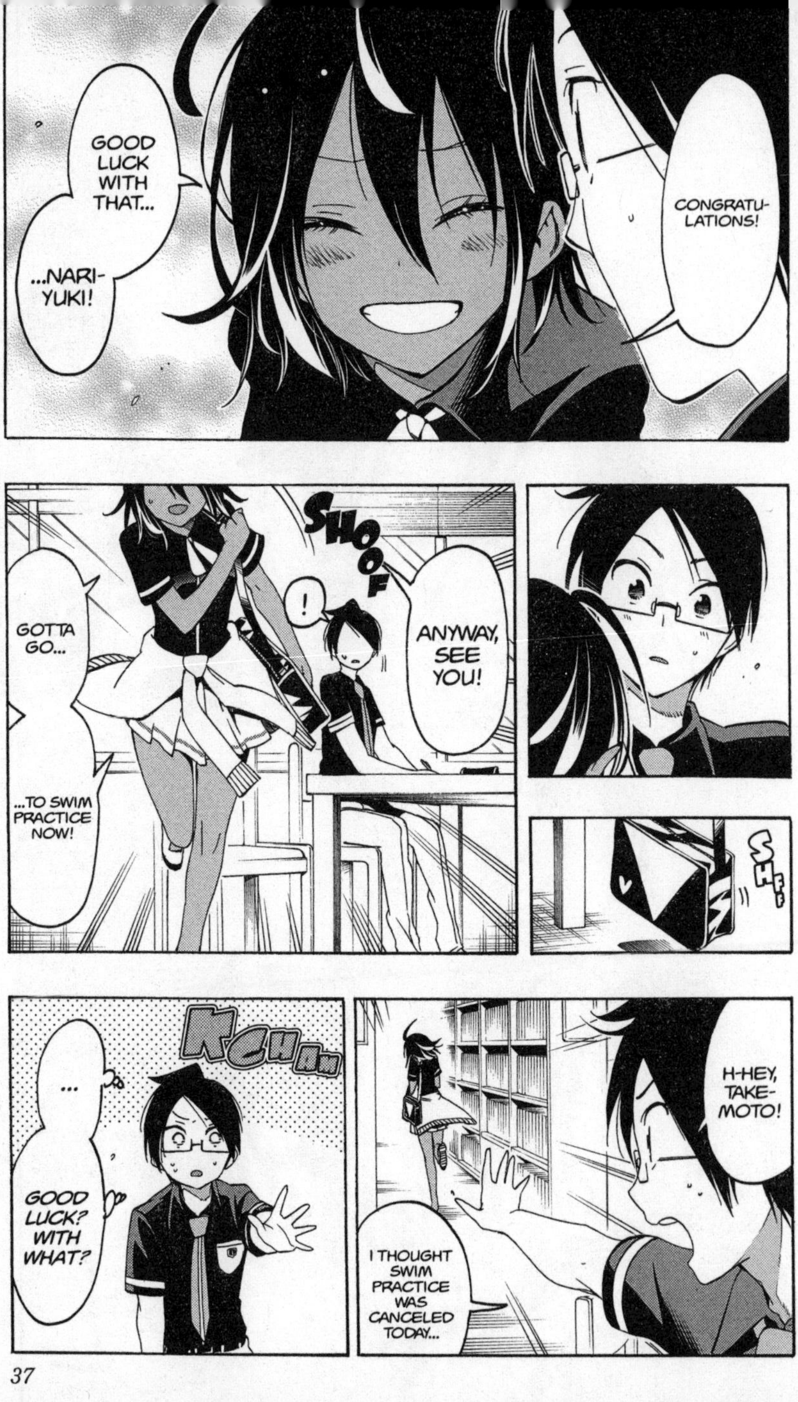
CONGRATULATIONS!
GOOD LUCK WITH THAT...
...NARI-YUKI!
SHF
SHOOF
ANYWAY, SEE YOU!
!
GOTTA GO...
...TO SWIM PRACTICE NOW!
H-HEY, TAKEMOTO!
I THOUGHT SWIM PRACTICE WAS CANCELED TODAY...
KCHAN
...
GOOD LUCK? WITH WHAT?

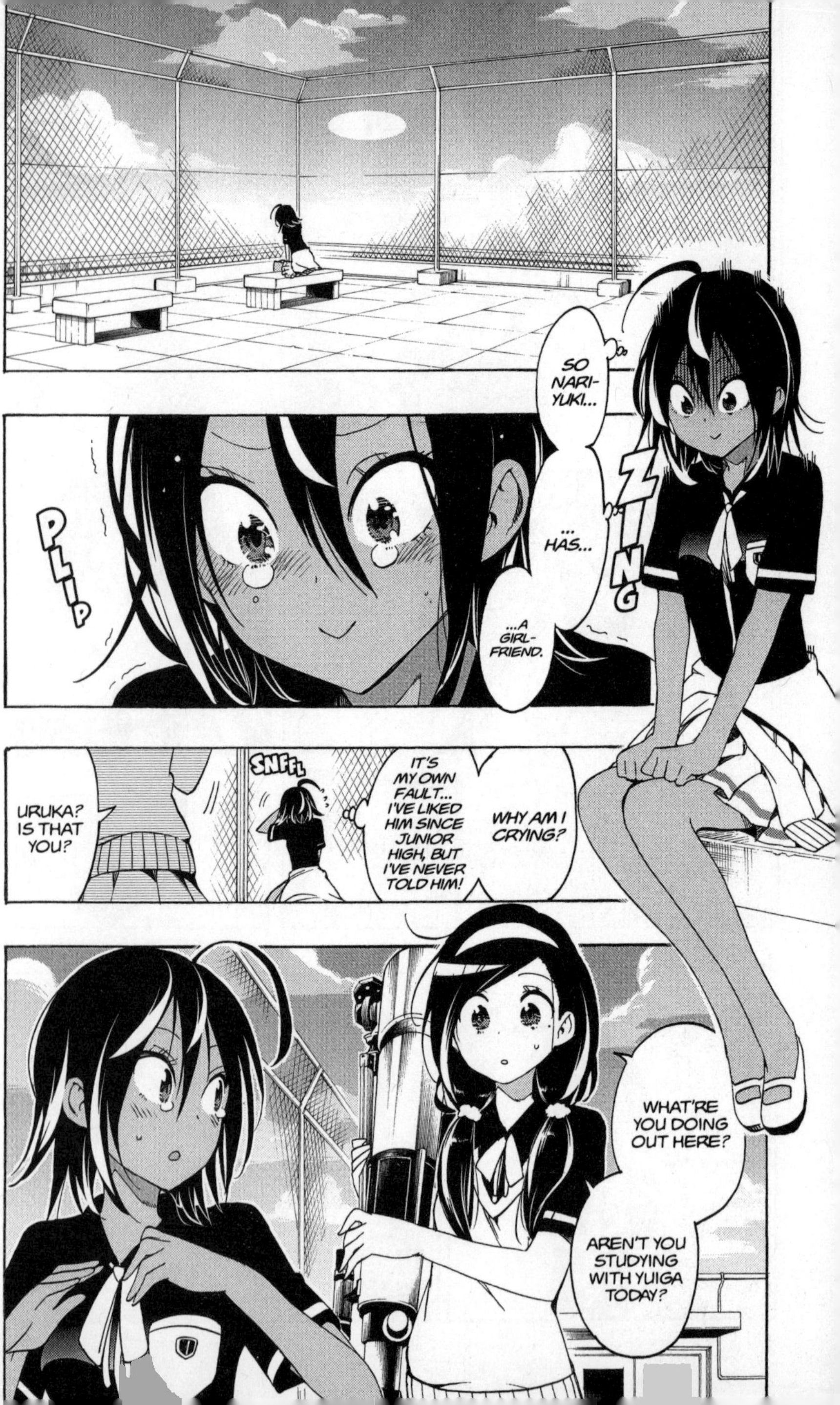
SO NARI-YUKI...
...HAS...
...A GIRL-FRIEND.
ZING
PLIP
WHY AM I CRYING?
IT'S MY OWN FAULT... I'VE LIKED HIM SINCE JUNIOR HIGH, BUT I'VE NEVER TOLD HIM!
SNFFL
URUKA? IS THAT YOU?
WHAT'RE YOU DOING OUT HERE?
AREN'T YOU STUDYING WITH YUIGA TODAY?

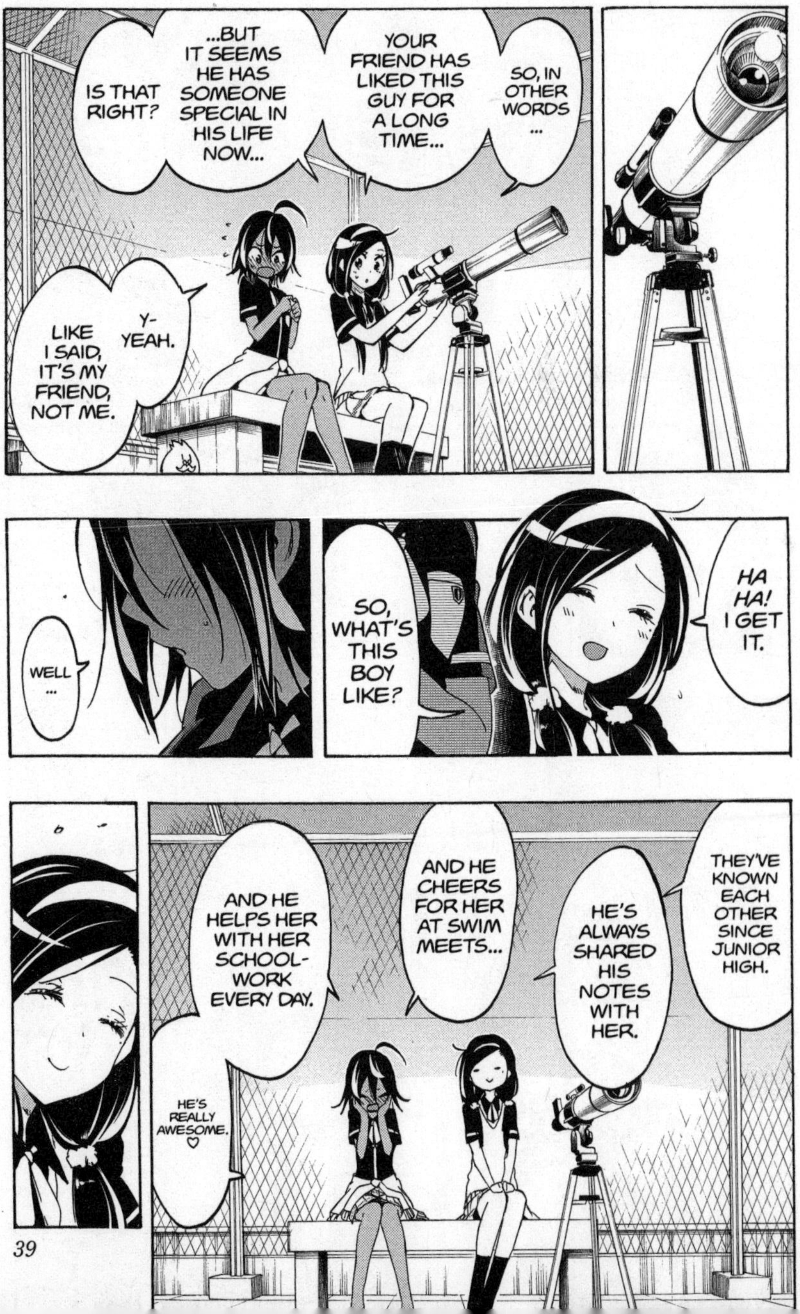
SO, IN OTHER WORDS...
YOUR FRIEND HAS LIKED THIS GUY FOR A LONG TIME...
...BUT IT SEEMS HE HAS SOMEONE SPECIAL IN HIS LIFE NOW...
IS THAT RIGHT?
Y-YEAH.
LIKE I SAID, IT'S MY FRIEND, NOT ME.
HA HA! I GET IT.
SO, WHAT'S THIS BOY LIKE?
WELL...
THEY'VE KNOWN EACH OTHER SINCE JUNIOR HIGH.
HE'S ALWAYS SHARED HIS NOTES WITH HER.
AND HE CHEERS FOR HER AT SWIM MEETS...
AND HE HELPS HER WITH HER SCHOOL-WORK EVERY DAY.
HE'S REALLY AWESOME. ♡

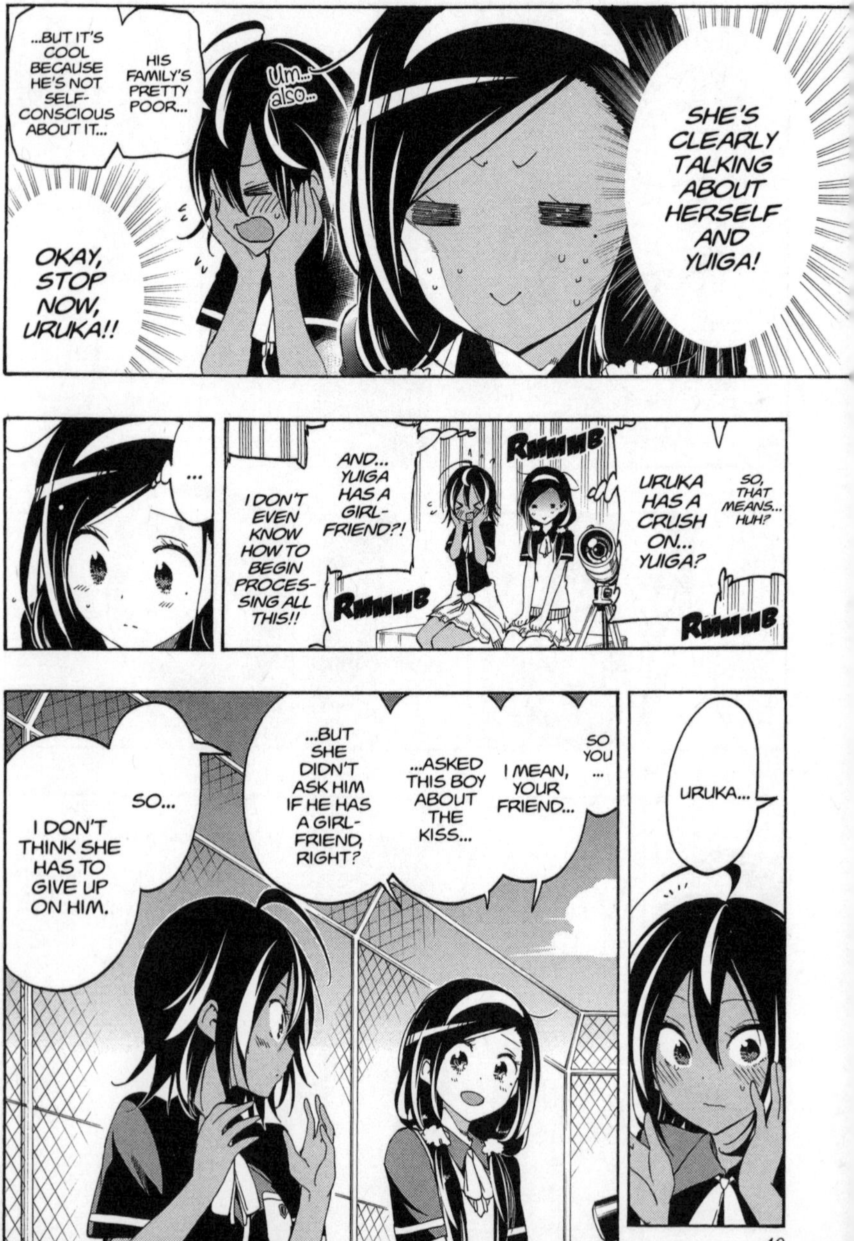
SHE'S CLEARLY TALKING ABOUT HERSELF AND YUIGA!
Um... also...
HIS FAMILY'S PRETTY POOR...
...BUT IT'S COOL BECAUSE HE'S NOT SELF-CONSCIOUS ABOUT IT...
OKAY, STOP NOW, URUKA!!
SO, THAT MEANS... HUH?
URUKA HAS A CRUSH ON... YUIGA?
RMMMB
AND... YUIGA HAS A GIRLFRIEND?!
I DON'T EVEN KNOW HOW TO BEGIN PROCESSING ALL THIS!!
RMMMB
RMMMB
...
URUKA...
SO YOU ...
I MEAN, YOUR FRIEND...
...ASKED THIS BOY ABOUT THE KISS...
...BUT SHE DIDN'T ASK HIM IF HE HAS A GIRLFRIEND, RIGHT?
SO...
I DON'T THINK SHE HAS TO GIVE UP ON HIM.

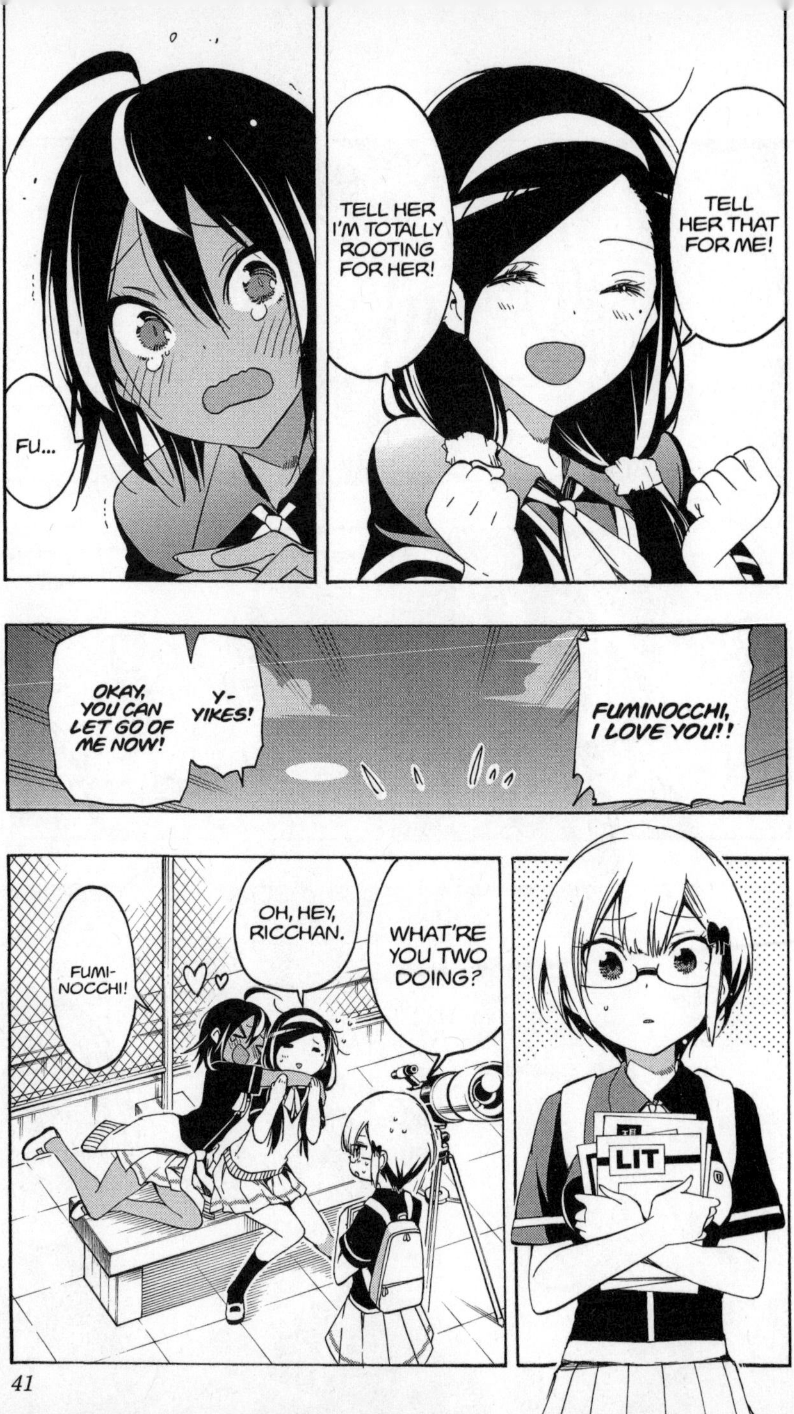
TELL HER THAT FOR ME!
TELL HER I'M TOTALLY ROOTING FOR HER!
FU...
FUMINOCCHI, I LOVE YOU!!
Y-YIKES!
OKAY, YOU CAN LET GO OF ME NOW!
LIT
WHAT'RE YOU TWO DOING?
OH, HEY, RICCHAN.
FUMI-NOCCHI!

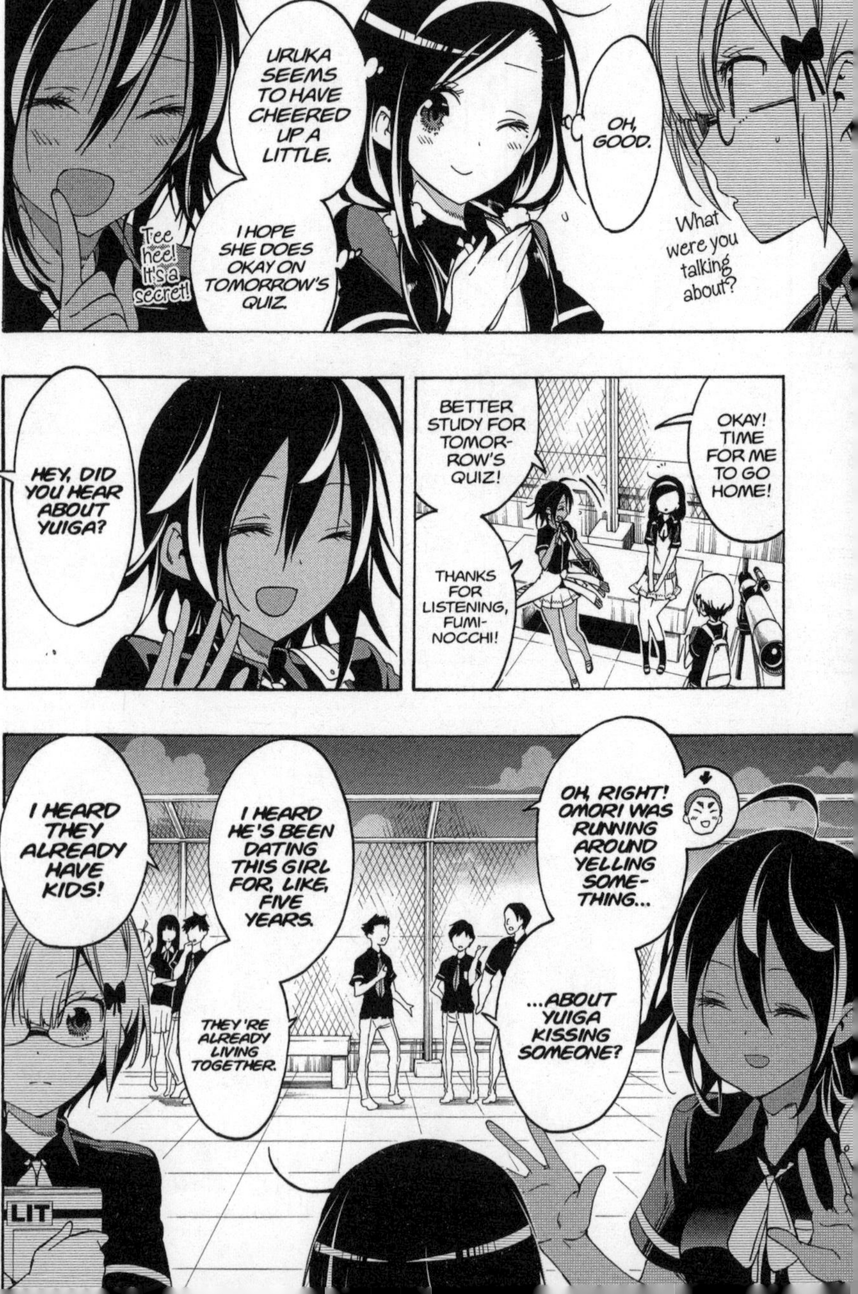
OH, GOOD.
What were you talking about?
URUKA SEEMS TO HAVE CHEERED UP A LITTLE.
I HOPE SHE DOES OKAY ON TOMORROW'S QUIZ.
Tee hee! It's a secret!
OKAY! TIME FOR ME TO GO HOME!
BETTER STUDY FOR TOMORROW'S QUIZ!
THANKS FOR LISTENING, FUMINOCCHI!
HEY, DID YOU HEAR ABOUT YUIGA?
OH, RIGHT! OMORI WAS RUNNING AROUND YELLING SOMETHING...
...ABOUT YUIGA KISSING SOMEONE?
I HEARD HE'S BEEN DATING THIS GIRL FOR, LIKE, FIVE YEARS.
THEY'RE ALREADY LIVING TOGETHER.
I HEARD THEY ALREADY HAVE KIDS!
LIT

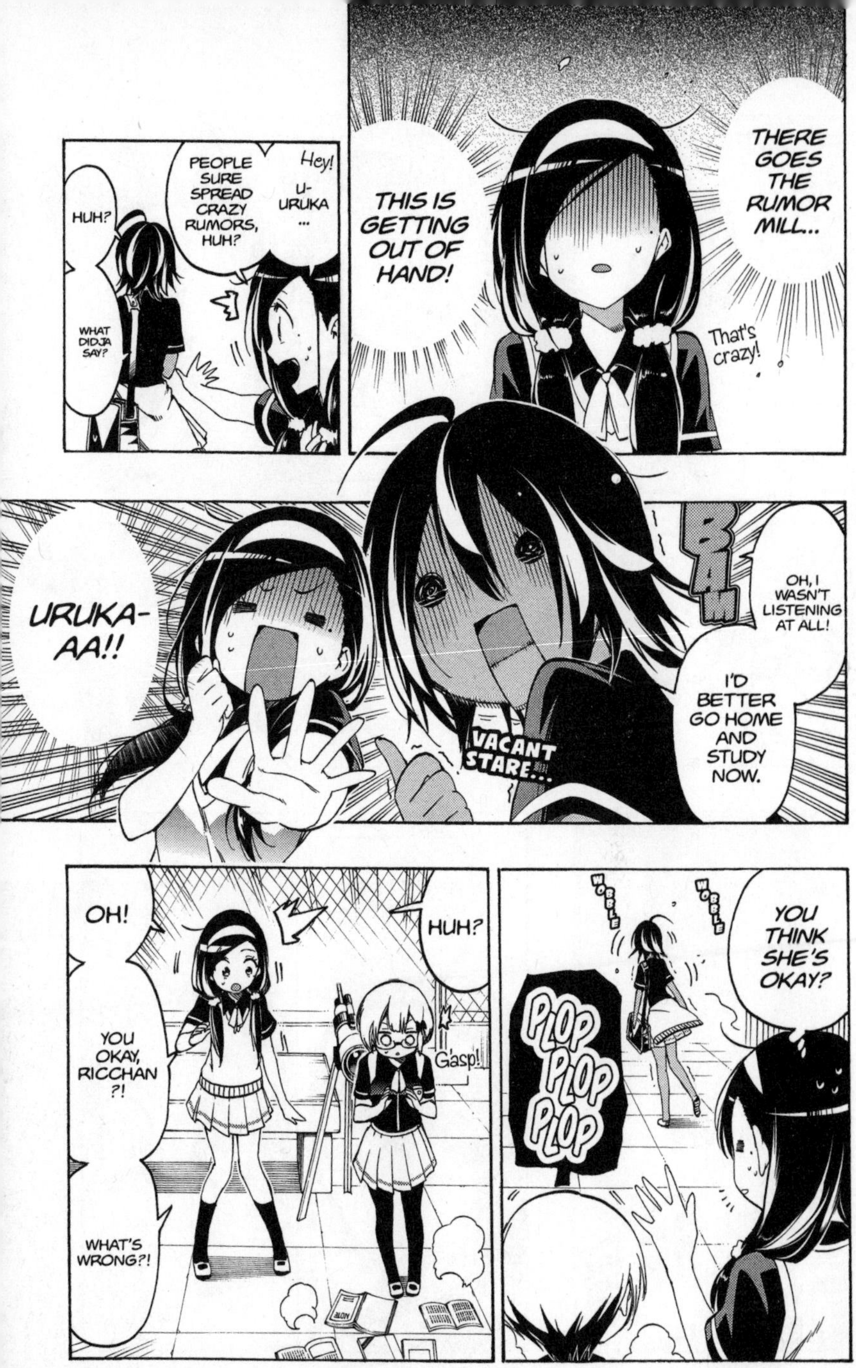
THERE GOES THE RUMOR MILL...
THIS IS GETTING OUT OF HAND!
That's crazy!
Hey!
U-URUKA...
PEOPLE SURE SPREAD CRAZY RUMORS, HUH?
HUH?
WHAT DIDJA SAY?
BAM
OH, I WASN'T LISTENING AT ALL!
I'D BETTER GO HOME AND STUDY NOW.
VACANT STARE...
URUKA-AA!!
WOBBLE
WOBBLE
YOU THINK SHE'S OKAY?
PLOP PLOP PLOP
HUH?
OH!
Gasp!
YOU OKAY, RICCHAN?!
WHAT'S WRONG?!

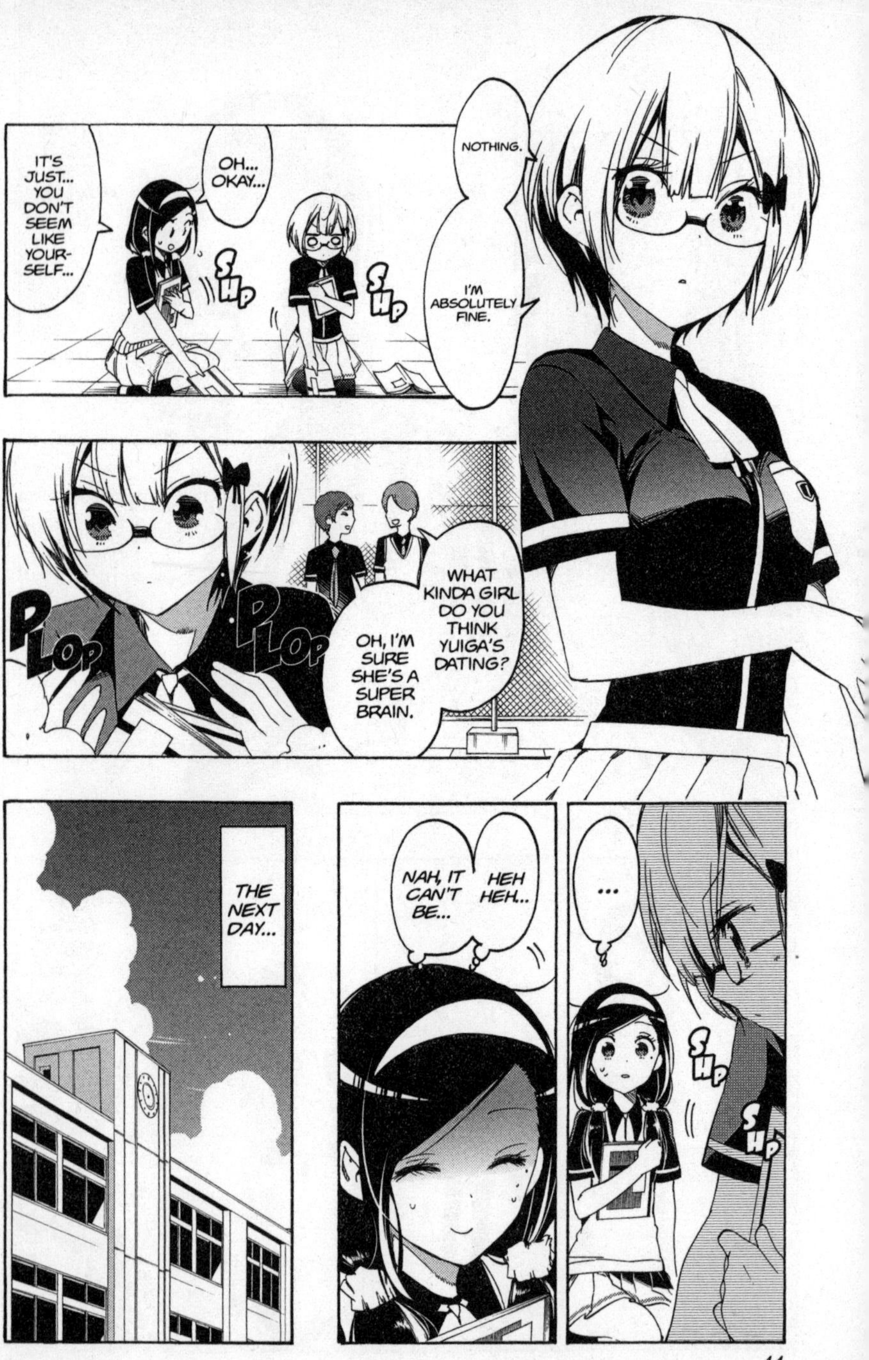
NOTHING.
I'M ABSOLUTELY FINE.
OH... OKAY...
IT'S JUST... YOU DON'T SEEM LIKE YOURSELF...
SHP
SHP
WHAT KINDA GIRL DO YOU THINK YUIGA'S DATING?
OH, I'M SURE SHE'S A SUPER BRAIN.
PLOP
PLOP
...
SHP
SHP
HEH HEH...
NAH, IT CAN'T BE...
THE NEXT DAY...

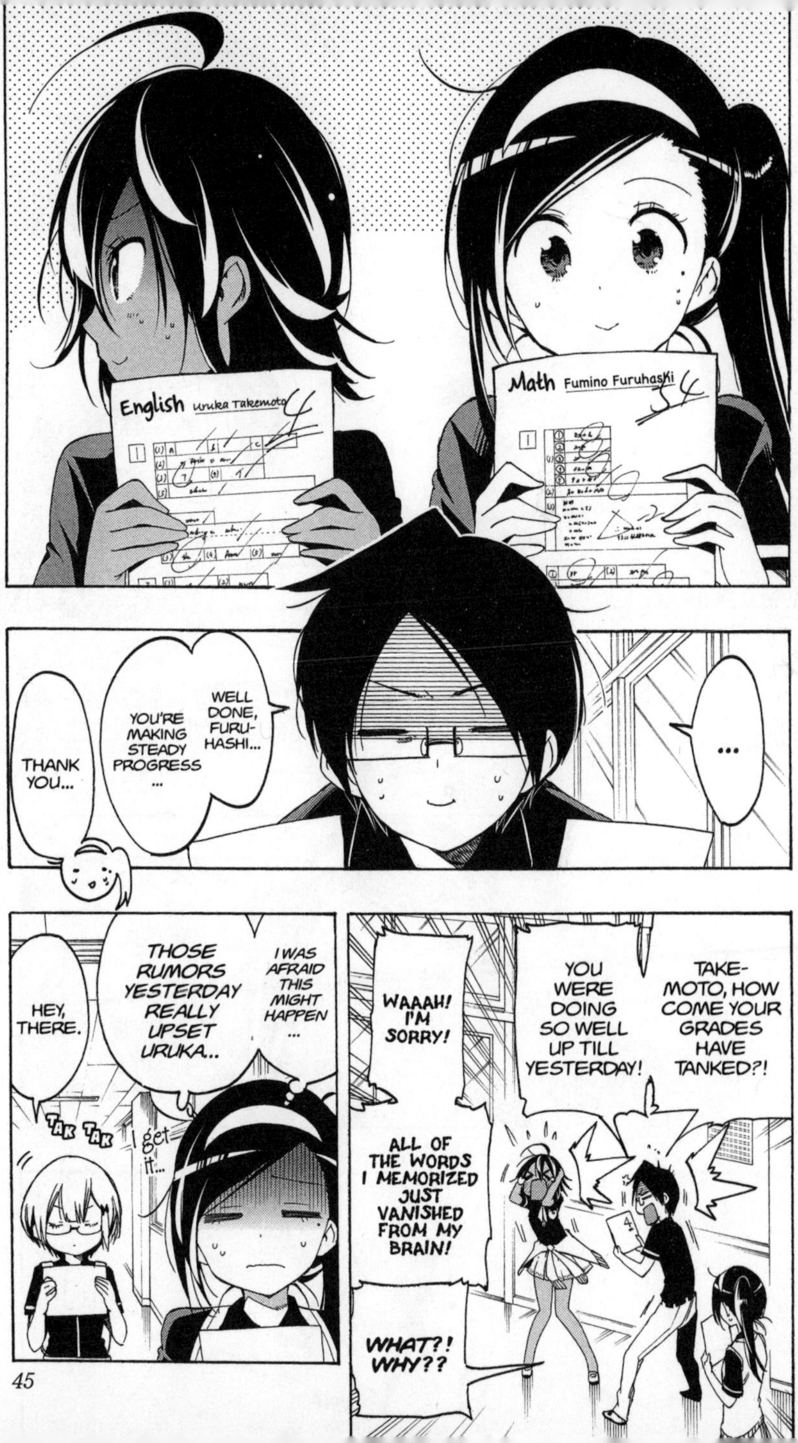
Math Fumino Furuhashi
English Uruka Takemoto
...
WELL DONE, FURUHASHI...
YOU'RE MAKING STEADY PROGRESS...
THANK YOU...
TAKEMOTO, HOW COME YOUR GRADES HAVE TANKED?!
YOU WERE DOING SO WELL UP TILL YESTERDAY!
WAAAH! I'M SORRY!
ALL OF THE WORDS I MEMORIZED JUST VANISHED FROM MY BRAIN!
WHAT?! WHY??
I WAS AFRAID THIS MIGHT HAPPEN...
THOSE RUMORS YESTERDAY REALLY UPSET URUKA...
HEY, THERE.
I get it...
TAK TAK

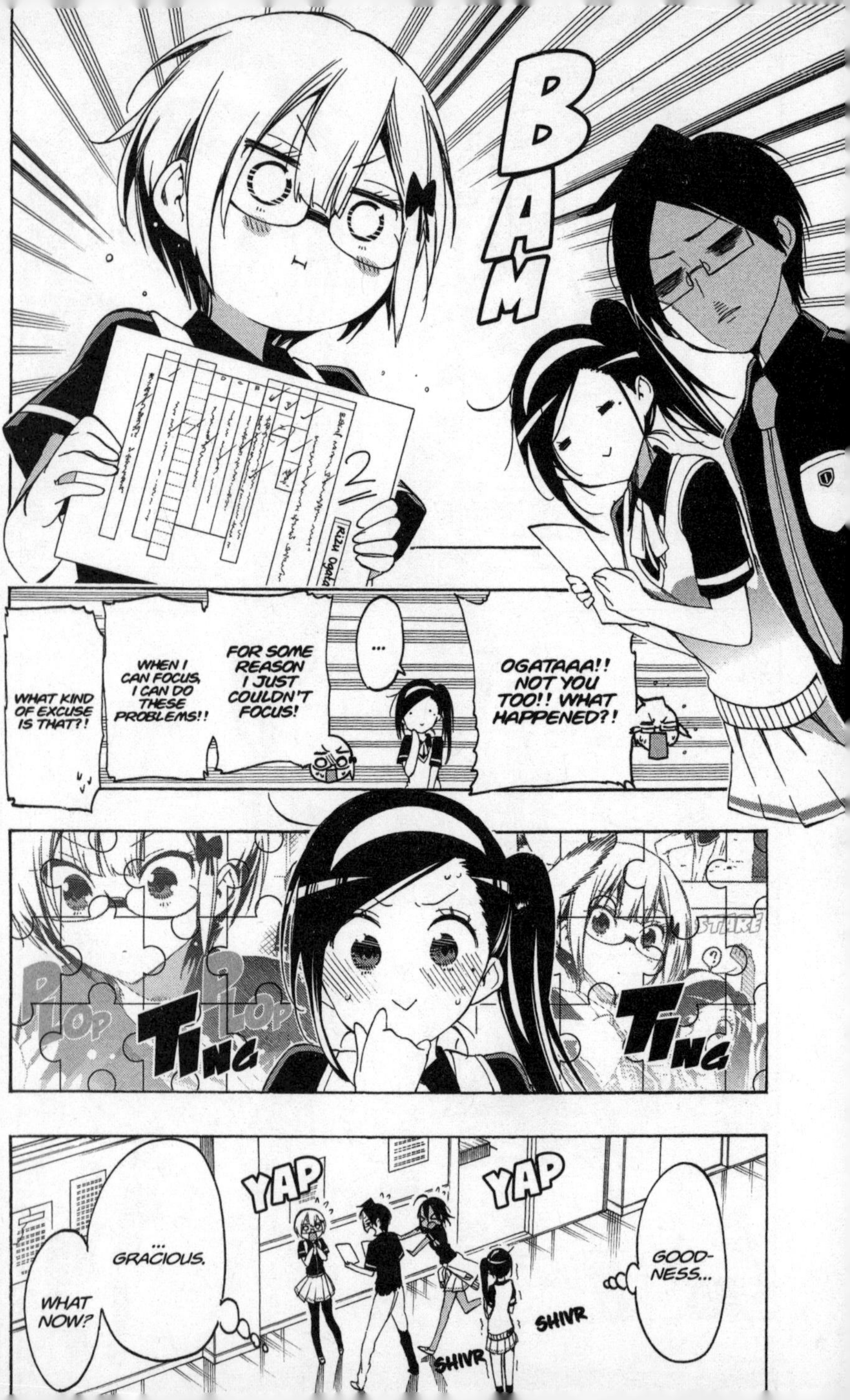
BAM
Rizu Ogata
OGATAAA!! NOT YOU TOO!! WHAT HAPPENED?!
...
FOR SOME REASON I JUST COULDN'T FOCUS!
WHEN I CAN FOCUS, I CAN DO THESE PROBLEMS!!
WHAT KIND OF EXCUSE IS THAT?!
STARE
?
TING
TING
PLOP
PLOP
YAP
YAP
GOOD-NESS...
SHIVR
SHIVR
... GRACIOUS.
WHAT NOW?

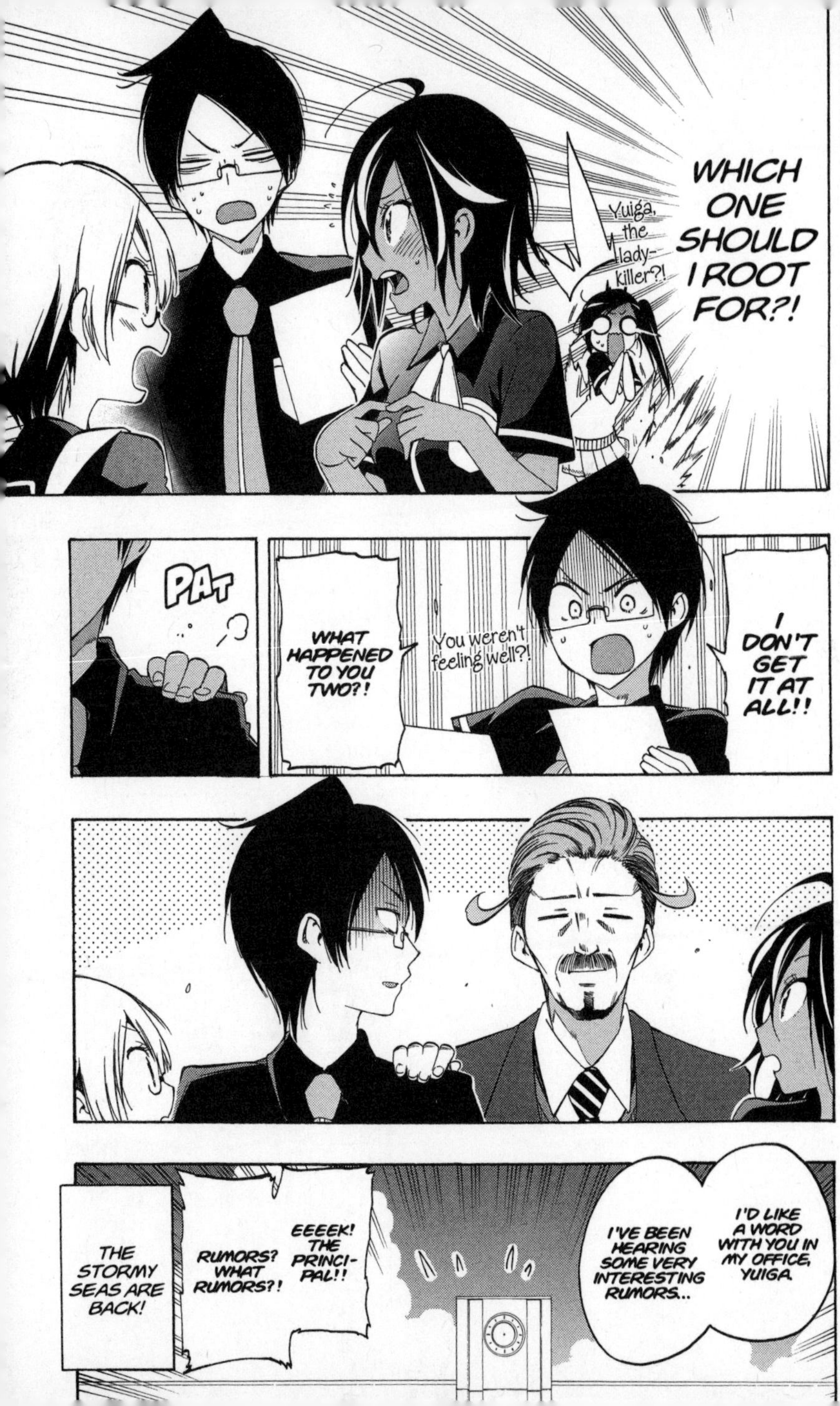
WHICH ONE SHOULD I ROOT FOR?!
Yuiga, the lady-killer?!
I DON'T GET IT AT ALL!!
You weren't feeling well?!
WHAT HAPPENED TO YOU TWO?!
PAT
I'D LIKE A WORD WITH YOU IN MY OFFICE, YUIGA.
I'VE BEEN HEARING SOME VERY INTERESTING RUMORS...
EEEEK! THE PRINCI-PAL!!
RUMORS? WHAT RUMORS?!
THE STORMY SEAS ARE BACK!

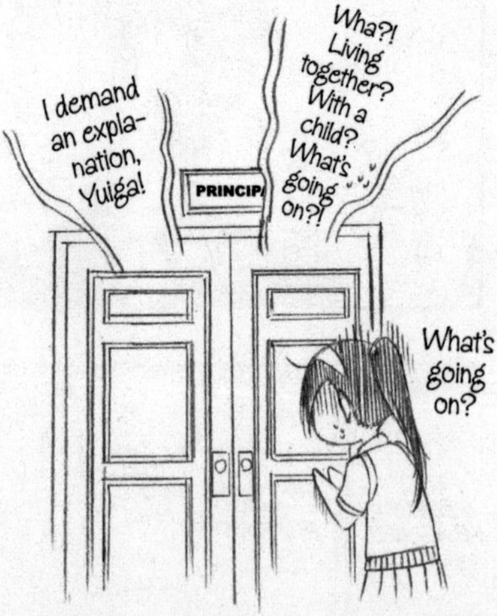
Wha?! Living together? With a child? What's going on?!
I demand an explanation, Yuiga!
PRINCIPA
What's going on?

Question 19: A Genius and [*X*] Take the Weather for Granted

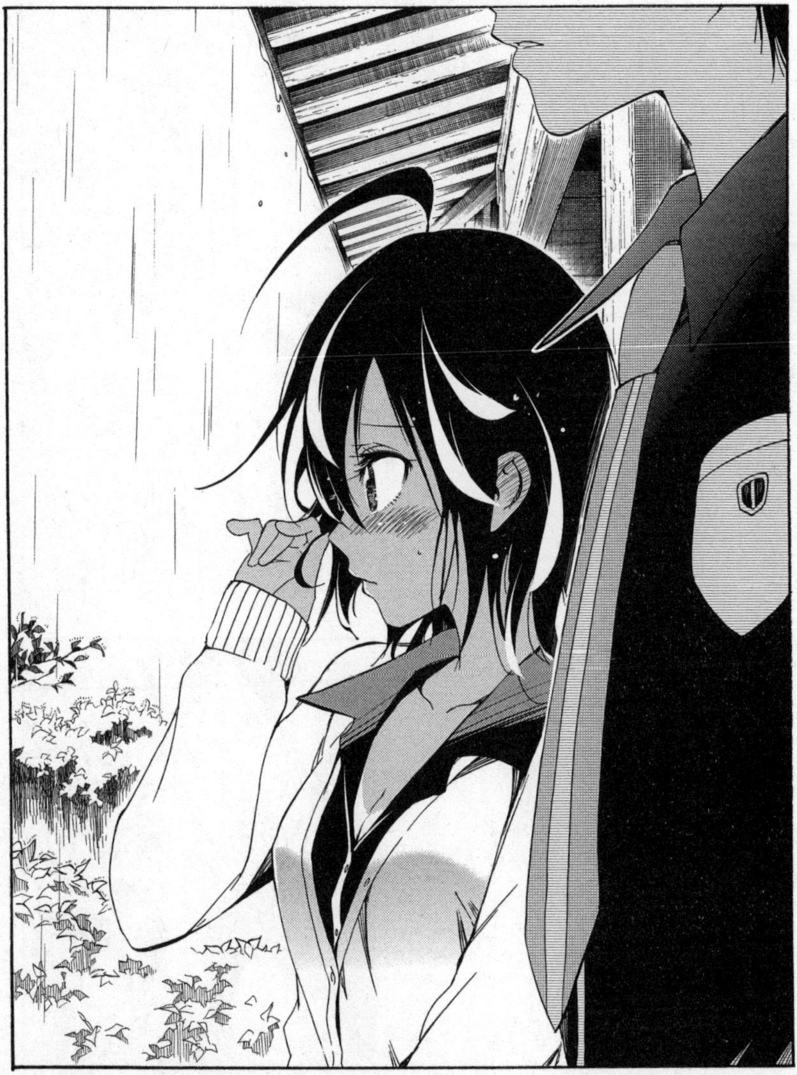

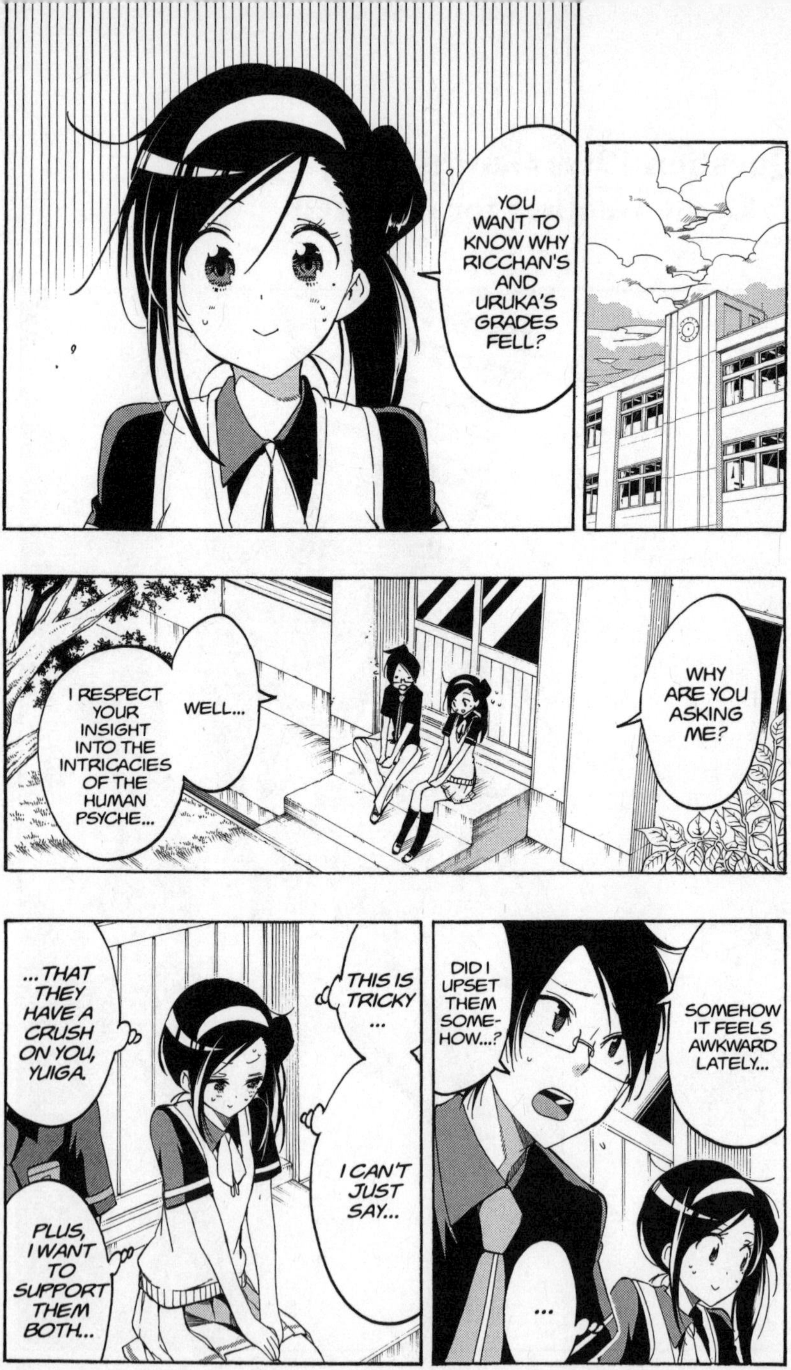
YOU WANT TO KNOW WHY RICCHAN'S AND URUKA'S GRADES FELL?
WHY ARE YOU ASKING ME?
WELL...
I RESPECT YOUR INSIGHT INTO THE INTRICACIES OF THE HUMAN PSYCHE...
SOMEHOW IT FEELS AWKWARD LATELY...
DID I UPSET THEM SOME-HOW...?
...
THIS IS TRICKY...
I CAN'T JUST SAY...
...THAT THEY HAVE A CRUSH ON YOU, YUIGA.
PLUS, I WANT TO SUPPORT THEM BOTH...

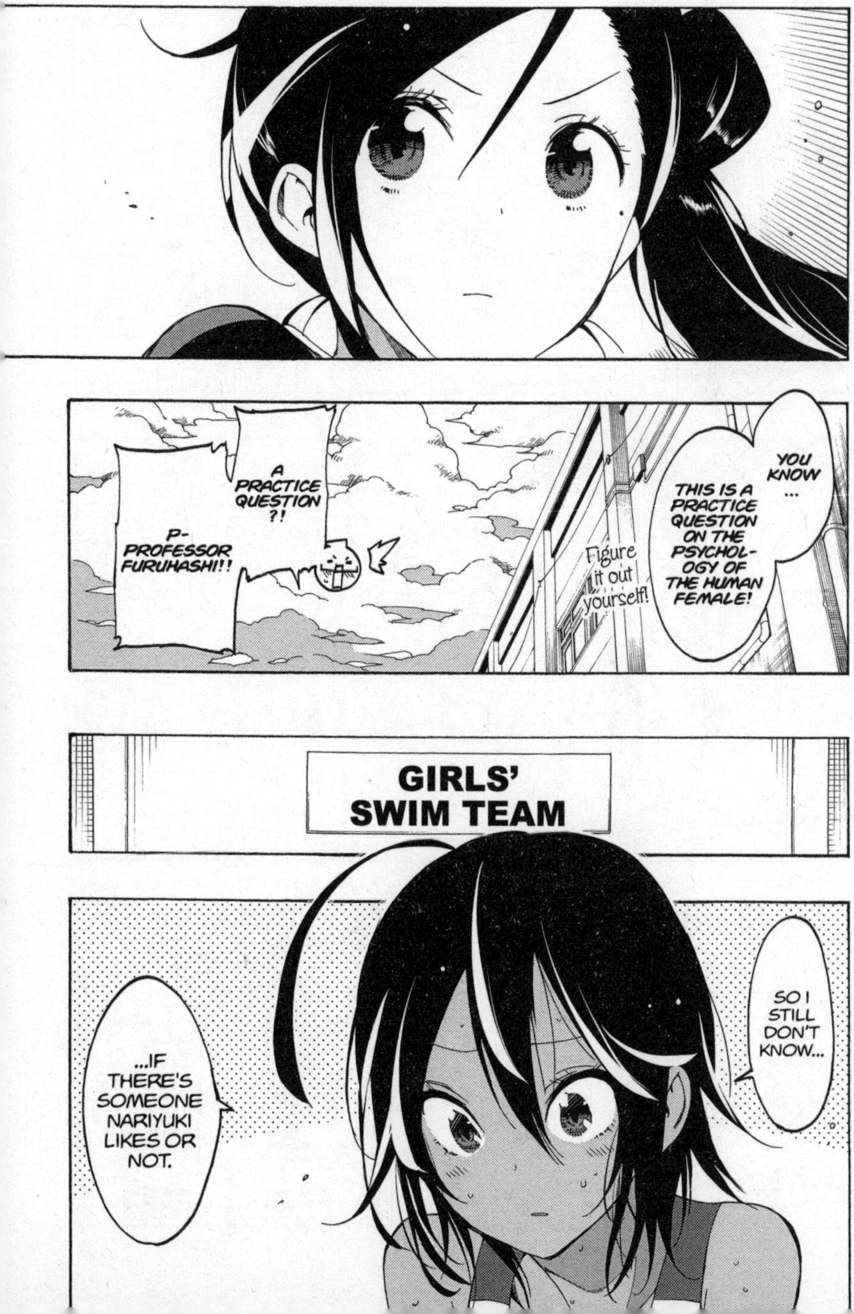
YOU KNOW ...
THIS IS A PRACTICE QUESTION ON THE PSYCHOLOGY OF THE HUMAN FEMALE!
Figure it out yourself!
A PRACTICE QUESTION?!
P-PROFESSOR FURUHASHI!!
GIRLS' SWIM TEAM
SO I STILL DON'T KNOW...
...IF THERE'S SOMEONE NARIYUKI LIKES OR NOT.

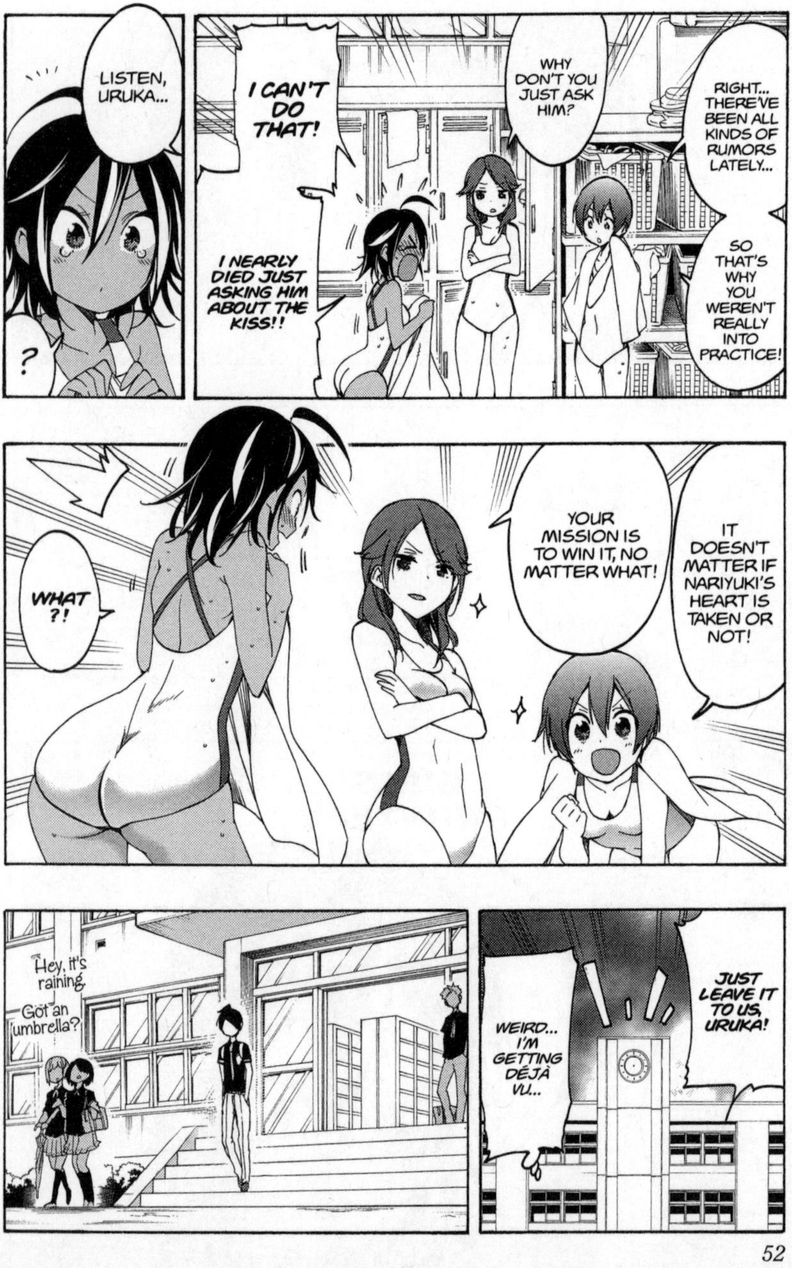
RIGHT... THERE'VE BEEN ALL KINDS OF RUMORS LATELY...
SO THAT'S WHY YOU WEREN'T REALLY INTO PRACTICE!
WHY DON'T YOU JUST ASK HIM?
I CAN'T DO THAT!
I NEARLY DIED JUST ASKING HIM ABOUT THE KISS!!
LISTEN, URUKA...
?
IT DOESN'T MATTER IF NARIYUKI'S HEART IS TAKEN OR NOT!
YOUR MISSION IS TO WIN IT, NO MATTER WHAT!
WHAT?!
JUST LEAVE IT TO US, URUKA!
WEIRD... I'M GETTING DÉJÀ VU...
Hey, it's raining.
Got an umbrella?

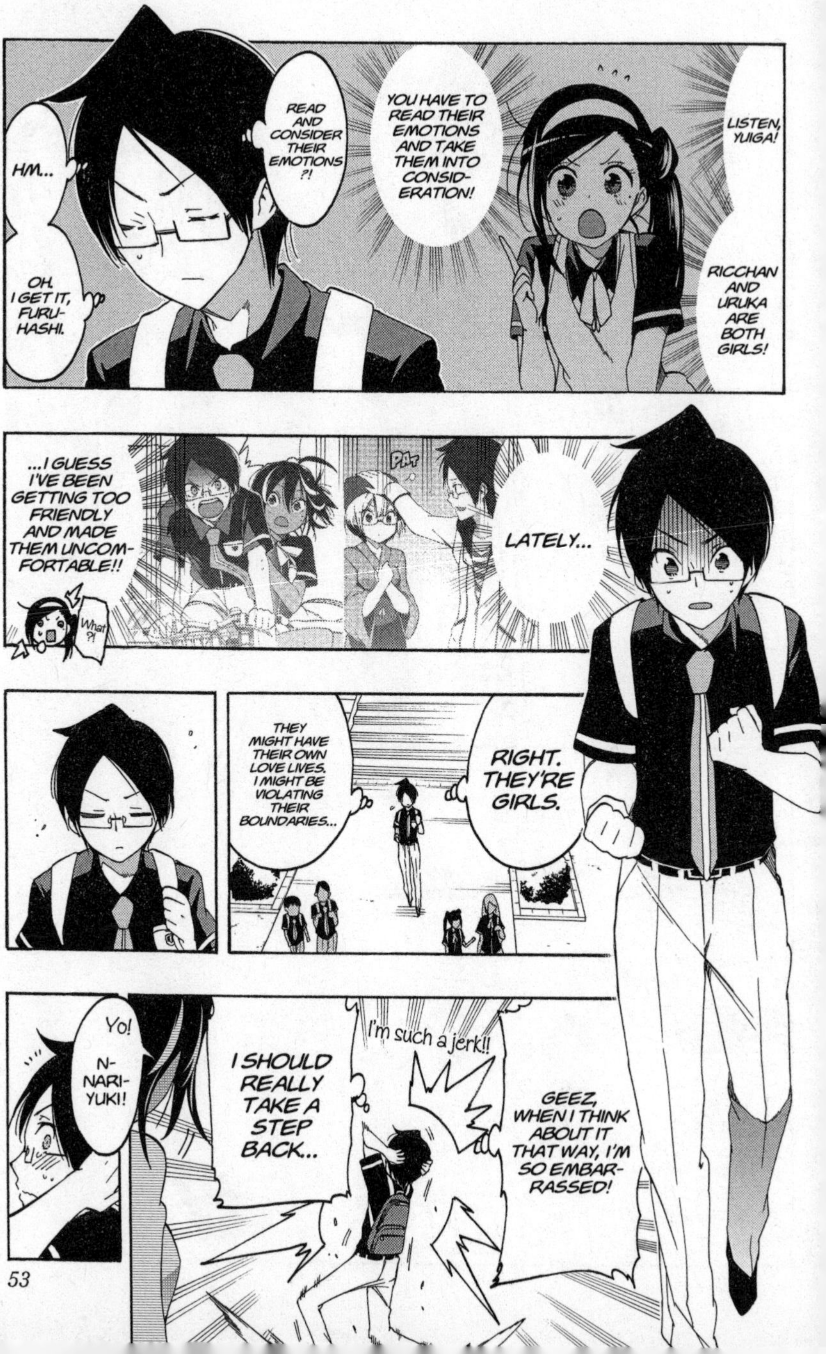
LISTEN, YUIGA!
RICCHAN AND URUKA ARE BOTH GIRLS!
YOU HAVE TO READ THEIR EMOTIONS AND TAKE THEM INTO CONSIDERATION!
READ AND CONSIDER THEIR EMOTIONS ?!
HM...
OH. I GET IT, FURUHASHI.
LATELY...
...I GUESS I'VE BEEN GETTING TOO FRIENDLY AND MADE THEM UNCOMFORTABLE!!
PAT
What ?!
RIGHT. THEY'RE GIRLS.
THEY MIGHT HAVE THEIR OWN LOVE LIVES. I MIGHT BE VIOLATING THEIR BOUNDARIES...
GEEZ, WHEN I THINK ABOUT IT THAT WAY, I'M SO EMBARRASSED!
I'm such a jerk!!
I SHOULD REALLY TAKE A STEP BACK...
Yo!
N-NARIYUKI!

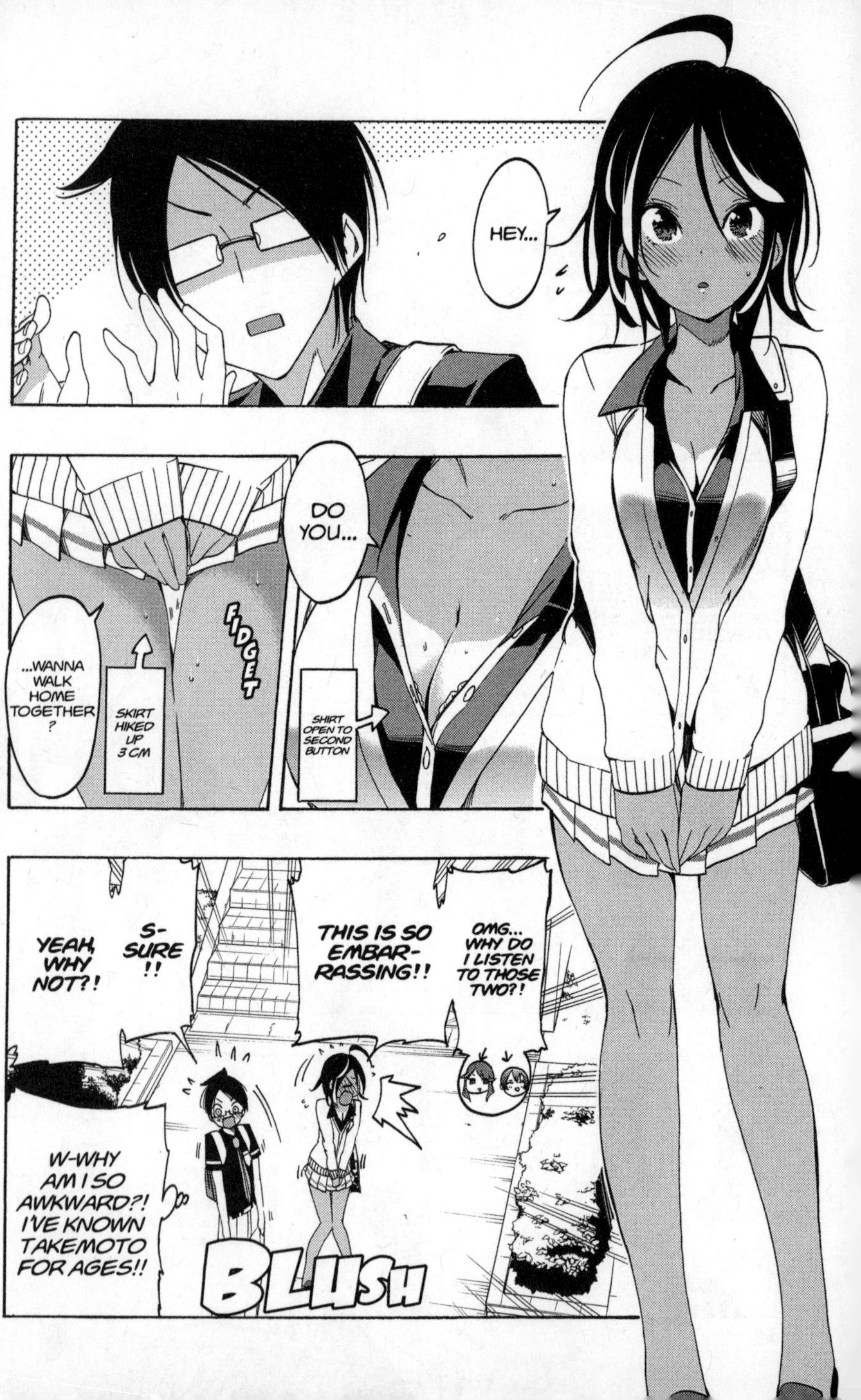
HEY...
DO YOU...
SHIRT OPEN TO SECOND BUTTON
FIDGET
SKIRT HIKED UP 3 CM
...WANNA WALK HOME TOGETHER?
OMG... WHY DO I LISTEN TO THOSE TWO?!
THIS IS SO EMBAR-RASSING!!
S-SURE!!
YEAH, WHY NOT?!
W-WHY AM I SO AWKWARD?! I'VE KNOWN TAKEMOTO FOR AGES!!
BLUSH

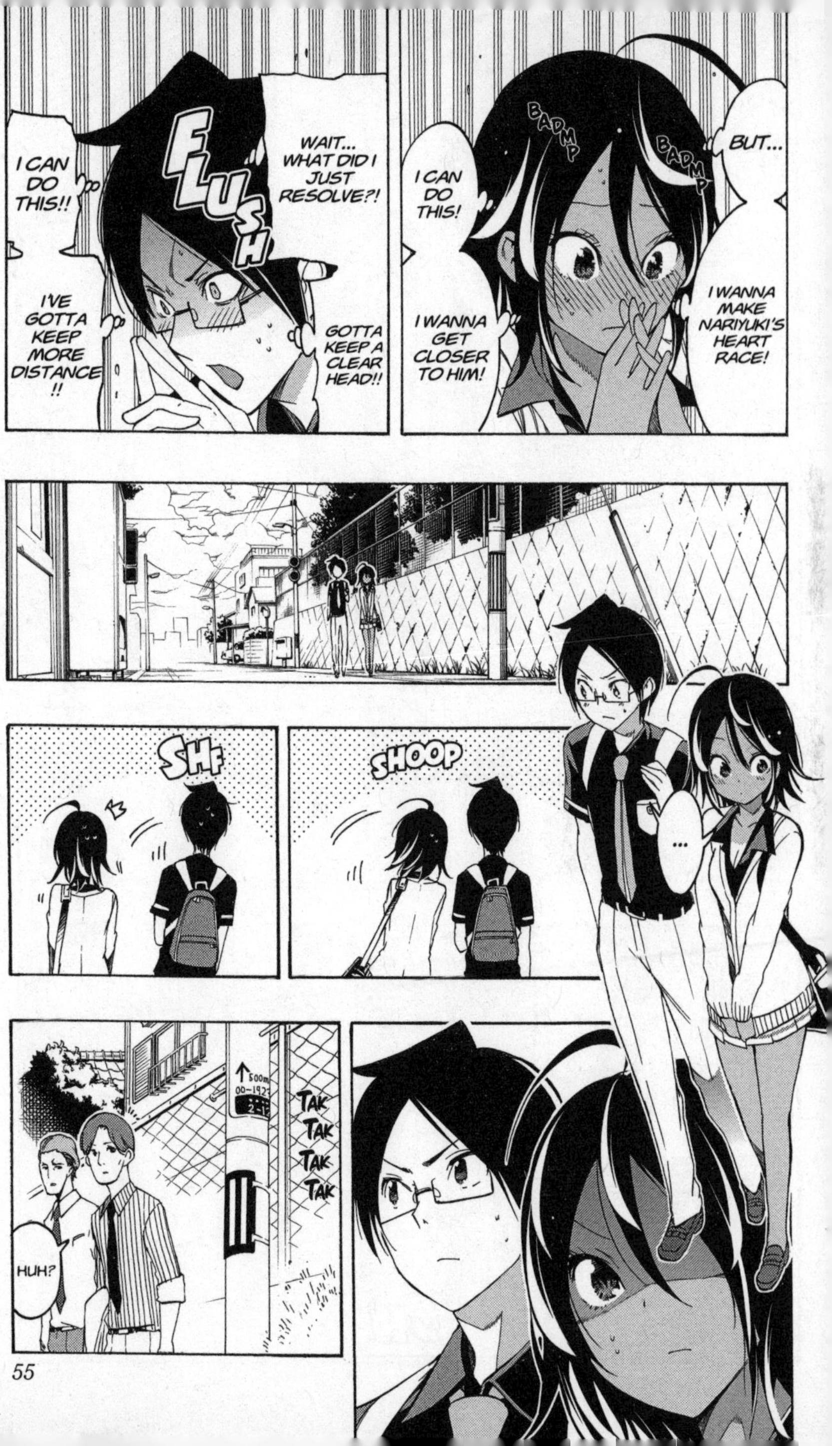

BADMP
BADMP
BUT...
I WANNA MAKE NARIYUKI'S HEART RACE!
I CAN DO THIS!
I WANNA GET CLOSER TO HIM!
WAIT... WHAT DID I JUST RESOLVE?!
FLUSH
GOTTA KEEP A CLEAR HEAD!!
I CAN DO THIS!!
I'VE GOTTA KEEP MORE DISTANCE!!
...
SHOOP
SHF
TAK TAK TAK TAK
HUH?

TMP TMP TMP TMP

?!

TAK TAK TAK TAK

RRMB-B

WHAT A WEIRD COUPLE...

TMP TMP TMP TMP

WHAT'S WITH THEM?

LET'S STOP BY!

OH, LOOK... A SHRINE!

I'M WAY TOO BEAT TO CLIMB THOSE STAIRS...

WHAT ARE YOU, NUTS?!

NOW WE'RE LOST...

Hff hff!

Huh

Wheez! Wheez!

56

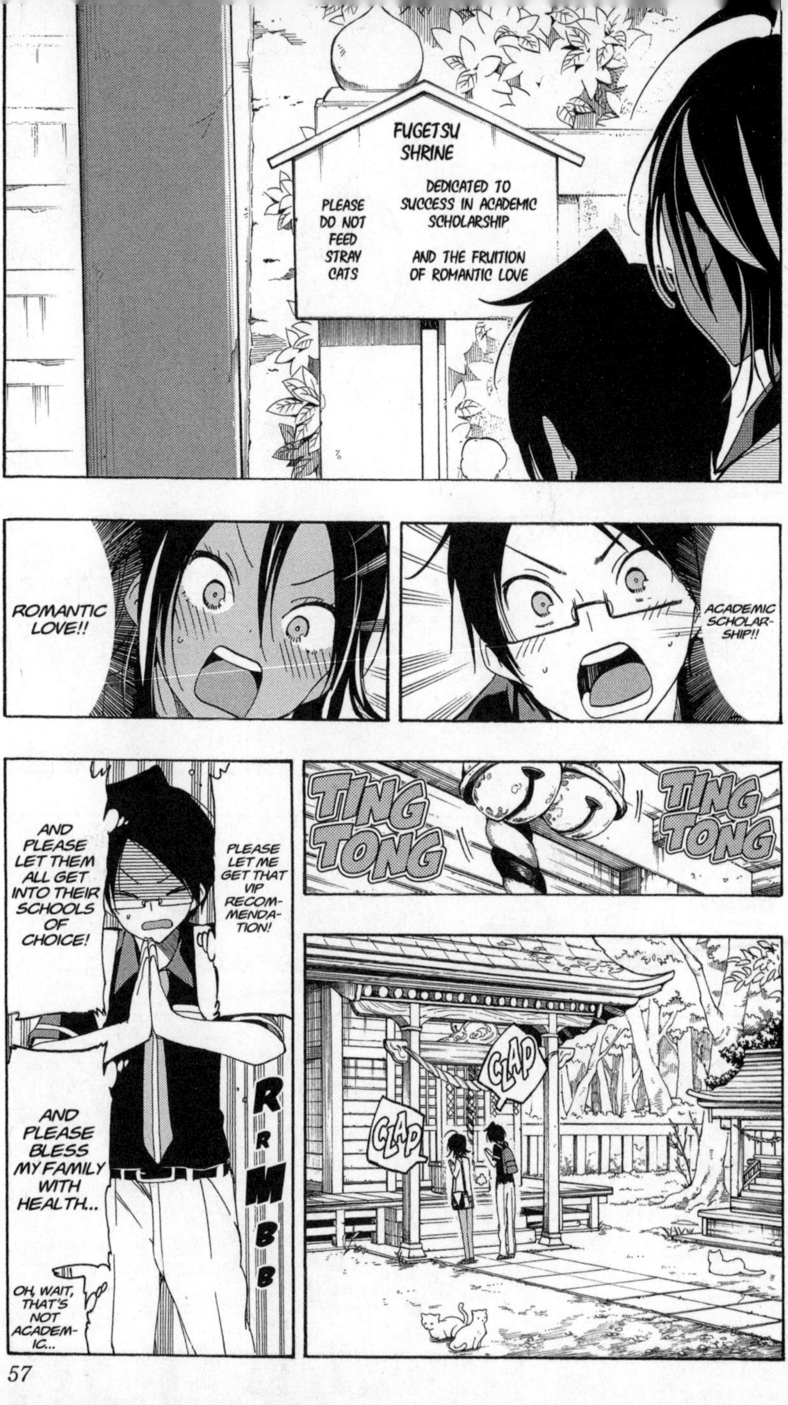
FUGETSU SHRINE
PLEASE DO NOT FEED STRAY CATS
DEDICATED TO SUCCESS IN ACADEMIC SCHOLARSHIP
AND THE FRUITION OF ROMANTIC LOVE
ACADEMIC SCHOLAR-SHIP!!
ROMANTIC LOVE!!
TING TONG
TING TONG
CLAP
CLAP
PLEASE LET ME GET THAT VIP RECOMMENDA-TION!
AND PLEASE LET THEM ALL GET INTO THEIR SCHOOLS OF CHOICE!
RRMBB
AND PLEASE BLESS MY FAMILY WITH HEALTH...
OH, WAIT, THAT'S NOT ACADEM-IC...

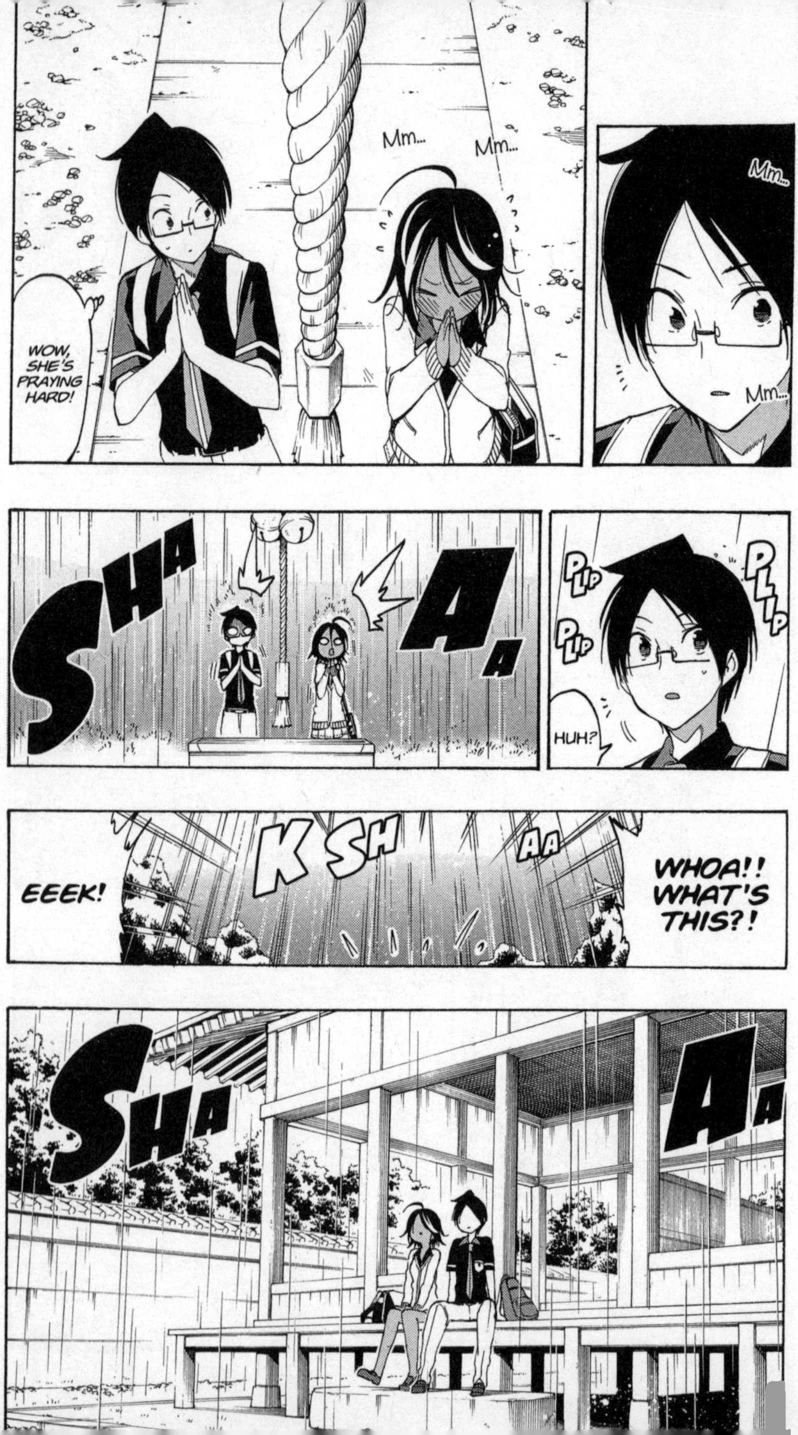
Mm...
Mm...
Mm...
Mm...
WOW, SHE'S PRAYING HARD!
PLIP
PLIP
PLIP
HUH?
SHA
AA
WHOA!! WHAT'S THIS?!
KSH
AA
EEEK!
SHA
AA

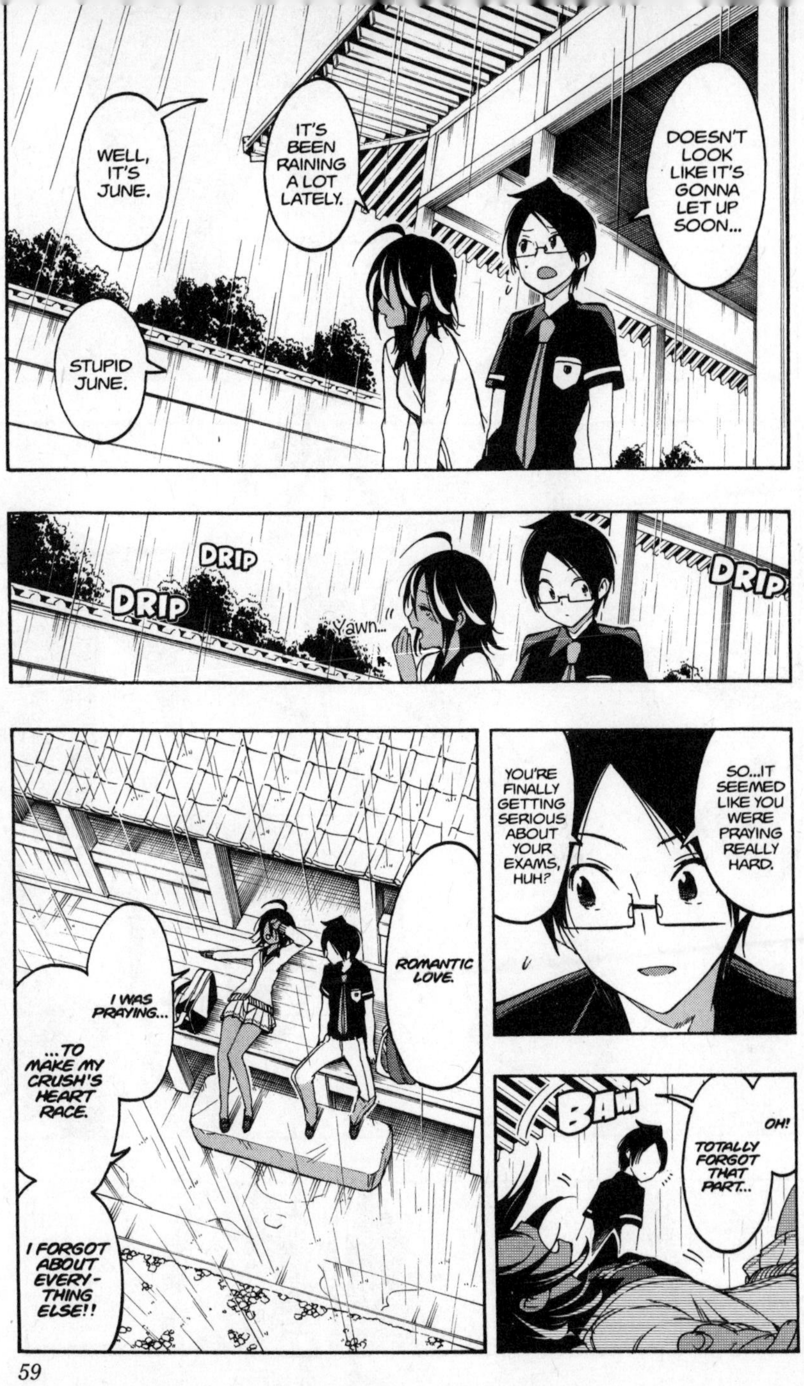
DOESN'T LOOK LIKE IT'S GONNA LET UP SOON...
IT'S BEEN RAINING A LOT LATELY.
WELL, IT'S JUNE.
STUPID JUNE.
DRIP
Yawn...
DRIP
DRIP
SO...IT SEEMED LIKE YOU WERE PRAYING REALLY HARD.
YOU'RE FINALLY GETTING SERIOUS ABOUT YOUR EXAMS, HUH?
OH!
TOTALLY FORGOT THAT PART...
BAM
ROMANTIC LOVE.
I WAS PRAYING...
...TO MAKE MY CRUSH'S HEART RACE.
I FORGOT ABOUT EVERYTHING ELSE!!

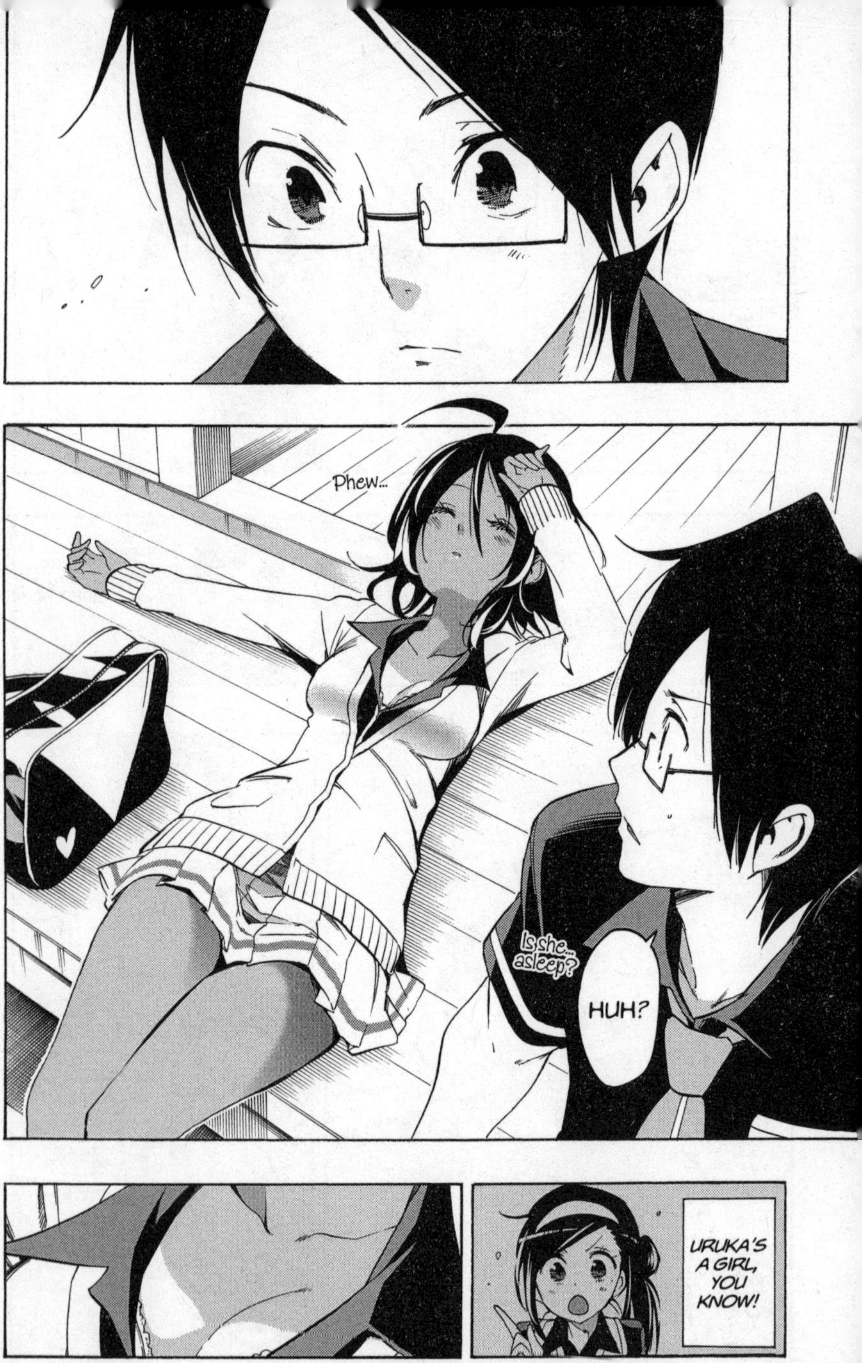
...
Phew...
HUH?
Is she... asleep?
URUKA'S A GIRL, YOU KNOW!

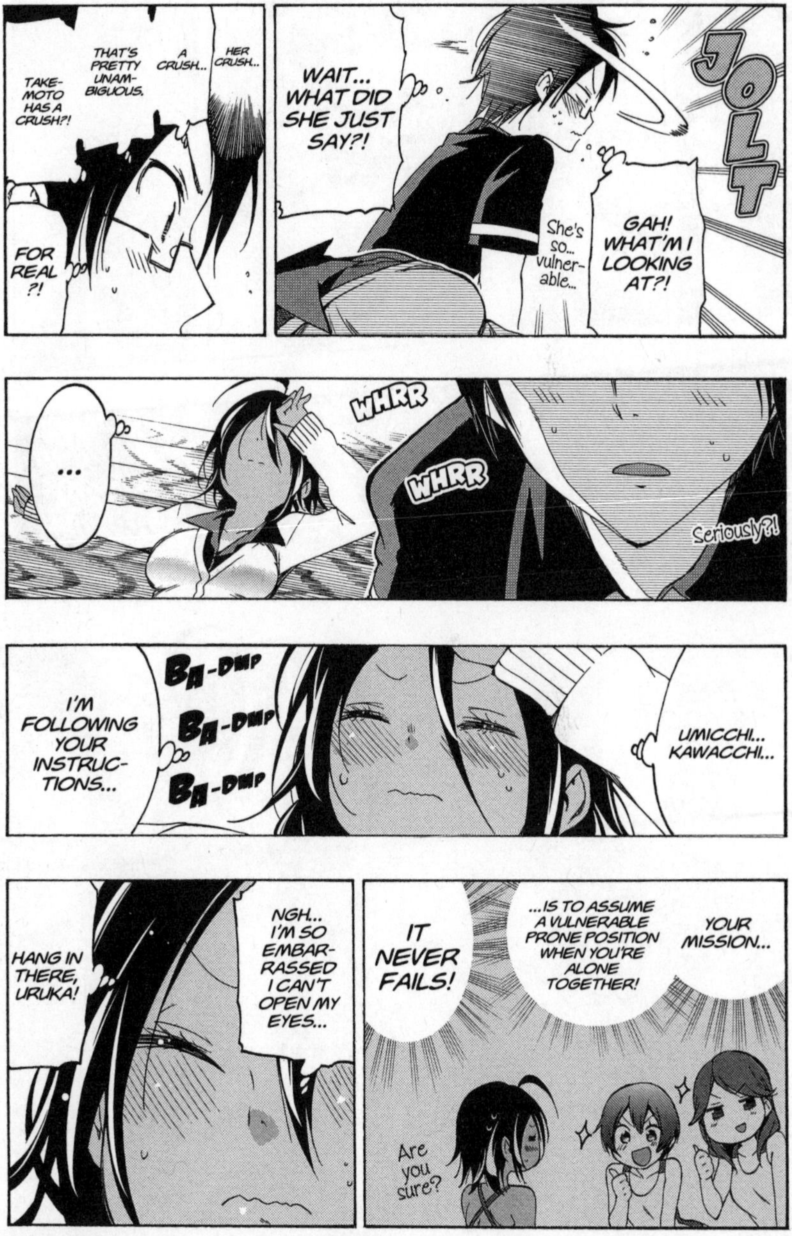
JOLT
WAIT... WHAT DID SHE JUST SAY?!
GAH! WHAT'M I LOOKING AT?!
She's so... vulnerable...
HER CRUSH...
A CRUSH...
THAT'S PRETTY UNAMBIGUOUS.
TAKEMOTO HAS A CRUSH?!
FOR REAL?!
Seriously?!
WHRR
WHRR
...
UMICCHI... KAWACCHI...
BA-DMP
BA-DMP
BA-DMP
I'M FOLLOWING YOUR INSTRUCTIONS...
YOUR MISSION...
...IS TO ASSUME A VULNERABLE PRONE POSITION WHEN YOU'RE ALONE TOGETHER!
IT NEVER FAILS!
Are you sure?
NGH... I'M SO EMBARRASSED I CAN'T OPEN MY EYES...
HANG IN THERE, URUKA!

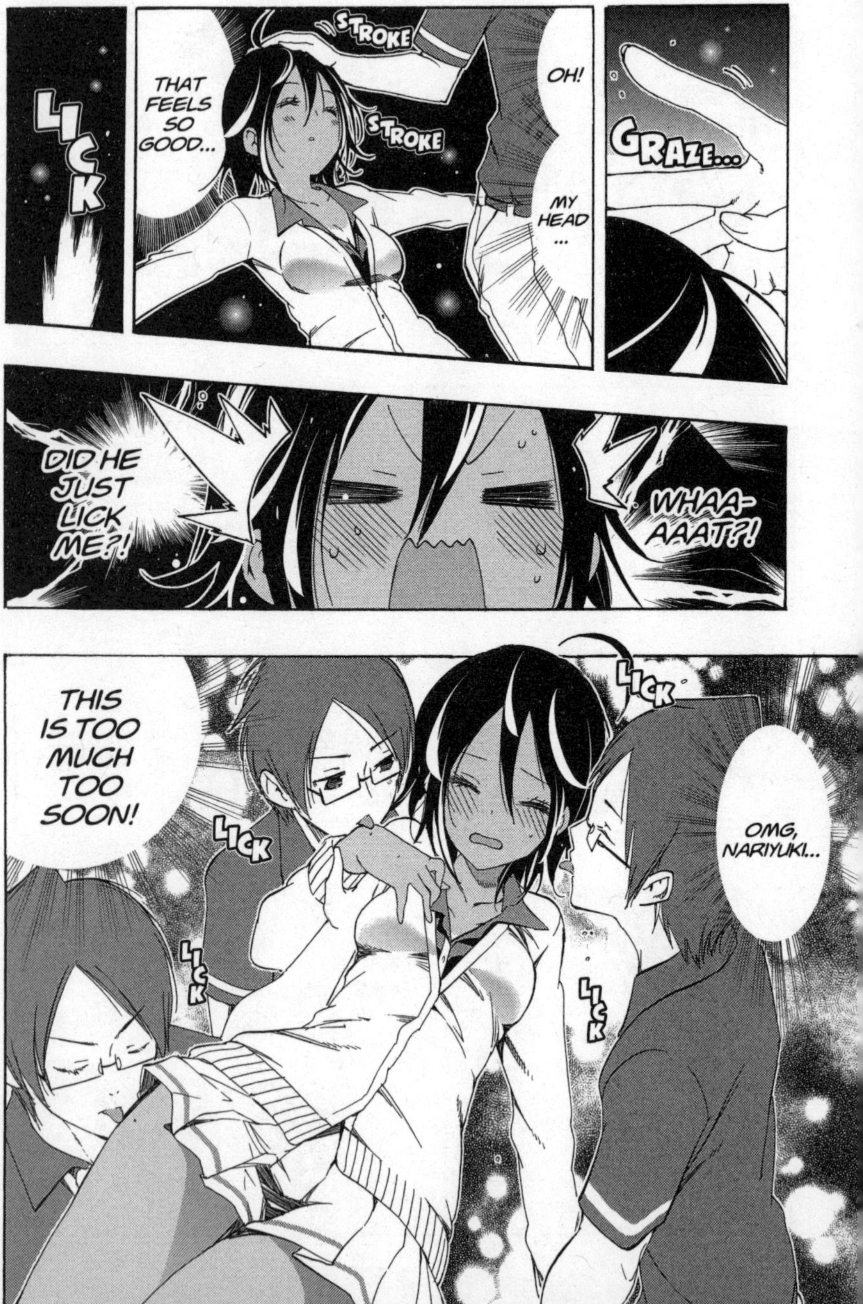
GRAZE...
OH!
MY HEAD...
STROKE
THAT FEELS SO GOOD...
STROKE
LICK
WHAAA-AAAT?!
DID HE JUST LICK ME?!
LICK
OMG, NARIYUKI...
LICK
THIS IS TOO MUCH TOO SOON!
LICK
LICK

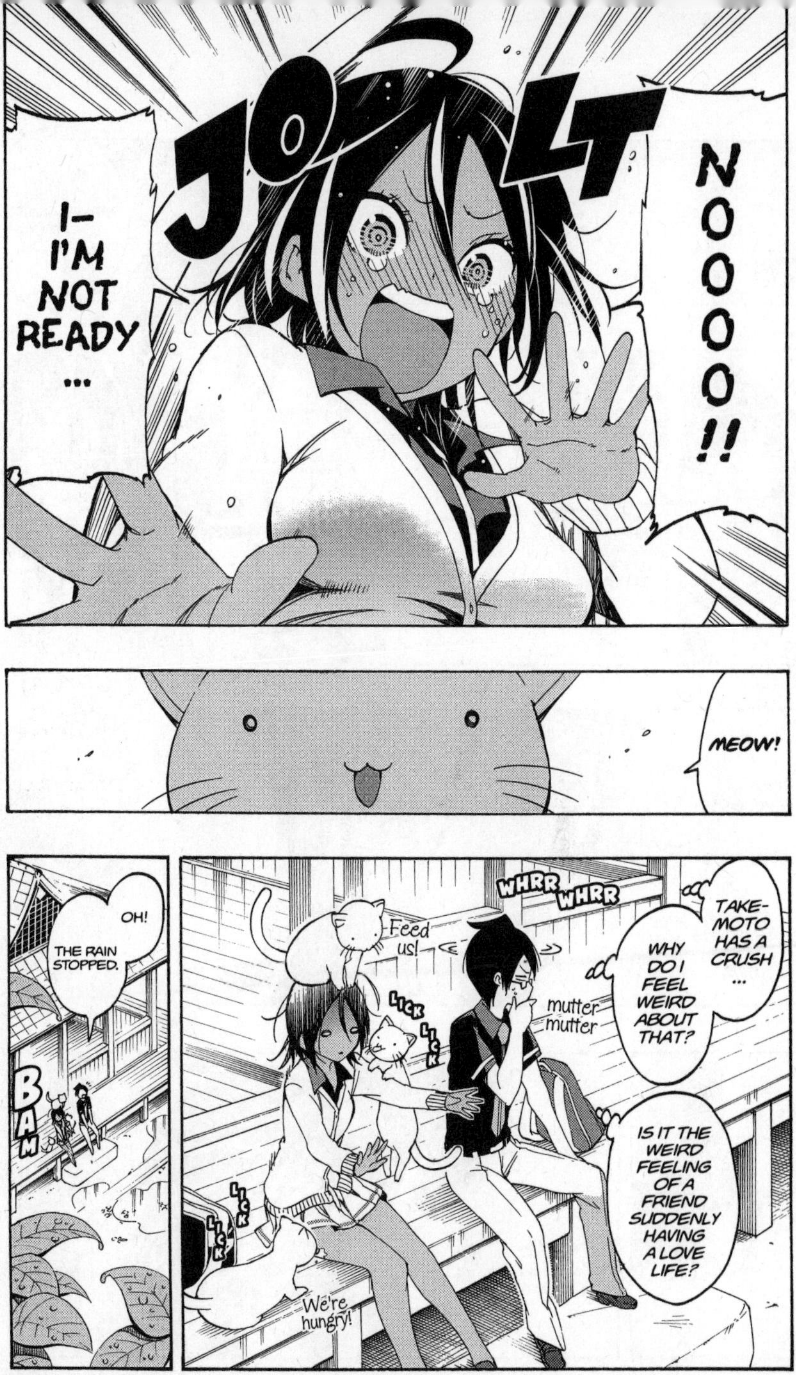
JOLT
NOOOO!!
I— I'M NOT READY ...
MEOW!
WHRR WHRR
TAKE-MOTO HAS A CRUSH ...
WHY DO I FEEL WEIRD ABOUT THAT?
Feed us!
LICK LICK
mutter mutter
IS IT THE WEIRD FEELING OF A FRIEND SUDDENLY HAVING A LOVE LIFE?
LICK LICK
We're hungry!
OH!
THE RAIN STOPPED.
BAM

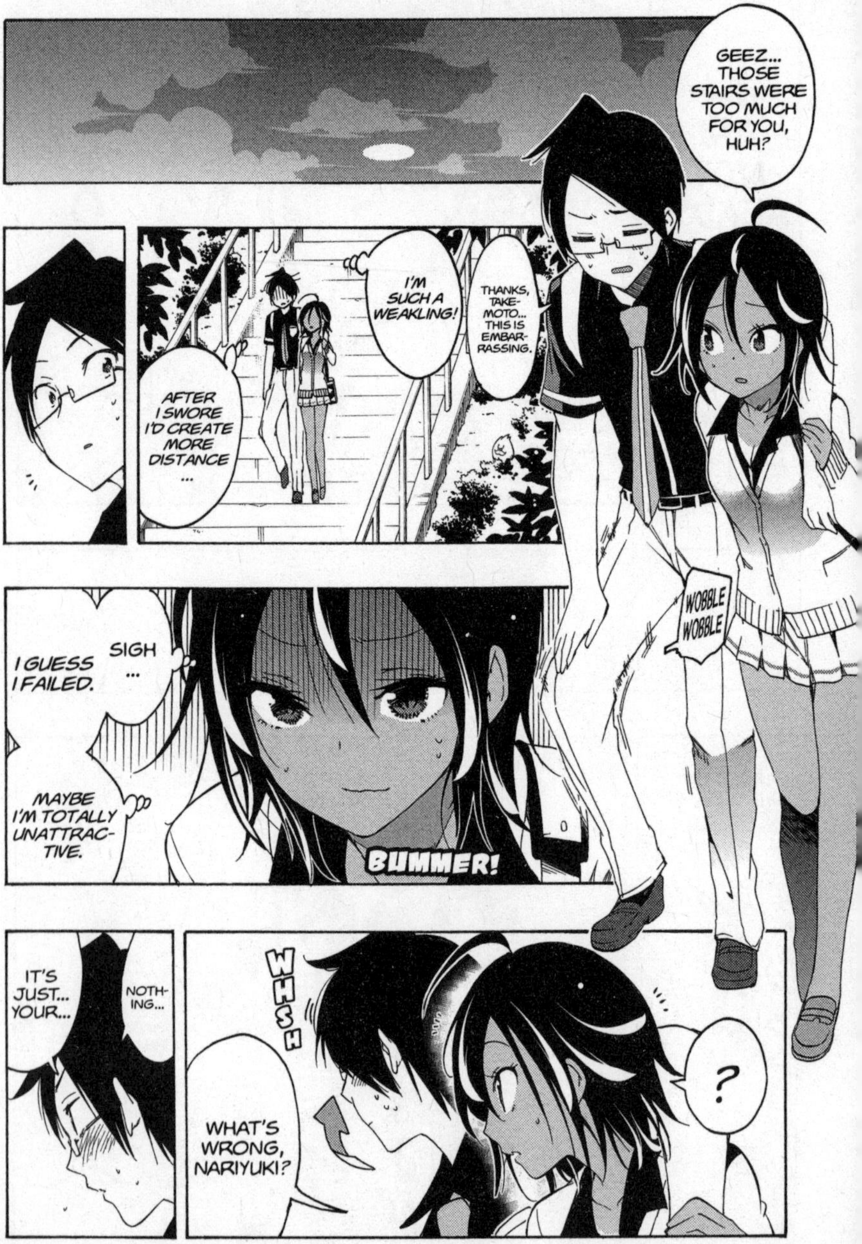
GEEZ... THOSE STAIRS WERE TOO MUCH FOR YOU, HUH?
THANKS, TAKEMOTO... THIS IS EMBARRASSING.
WOBBLE WOBBLE
I'M SUCH A WEAKLING!
AFTER I SWORE I'D CREATE MORE DISTANCE...
SIGH...
I GUESS I FAILED.
MAYBE I'M TOTALLY UNATTRACTIVE.
BUMMER!
?
WHSH
WHAT'S WRONG, NARIYUKI?
NOTHING...
IT'S JUST... YOUR...

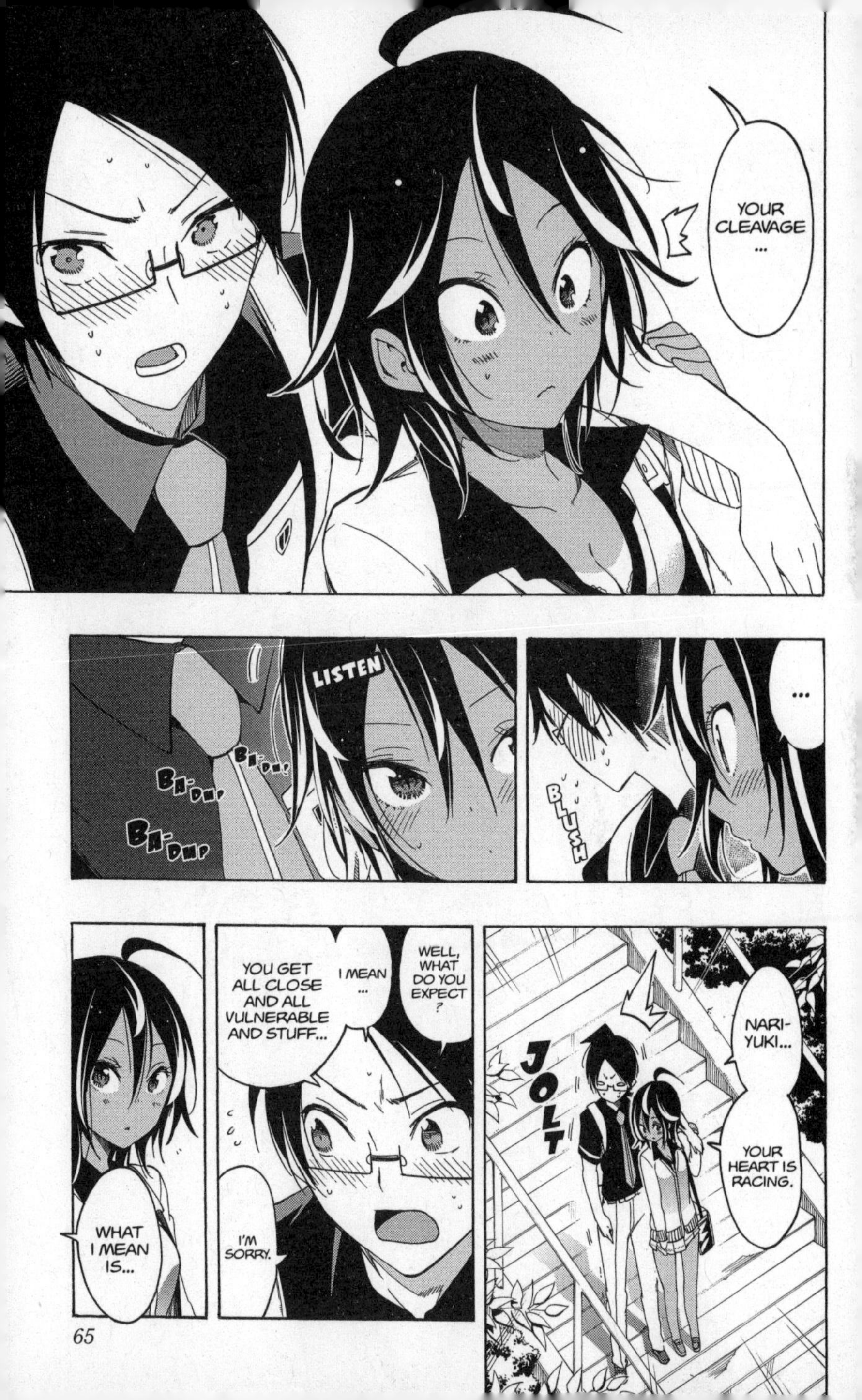
YOUR CLEAVAGE ...
...
BLUSH
LISTEN
BA-DMP
BA-DMP
BA-DMP
NARI-YUKI...
YOUR HEART IS RACING.
JOLT
WELL, WHAT DO YOU EXPECT?
I MEAN ...
YOU GET ALL CLOSE AND ALL VULNERABLE AND STUFF...
I'M SORRY.
WHAT I MEAN IS...

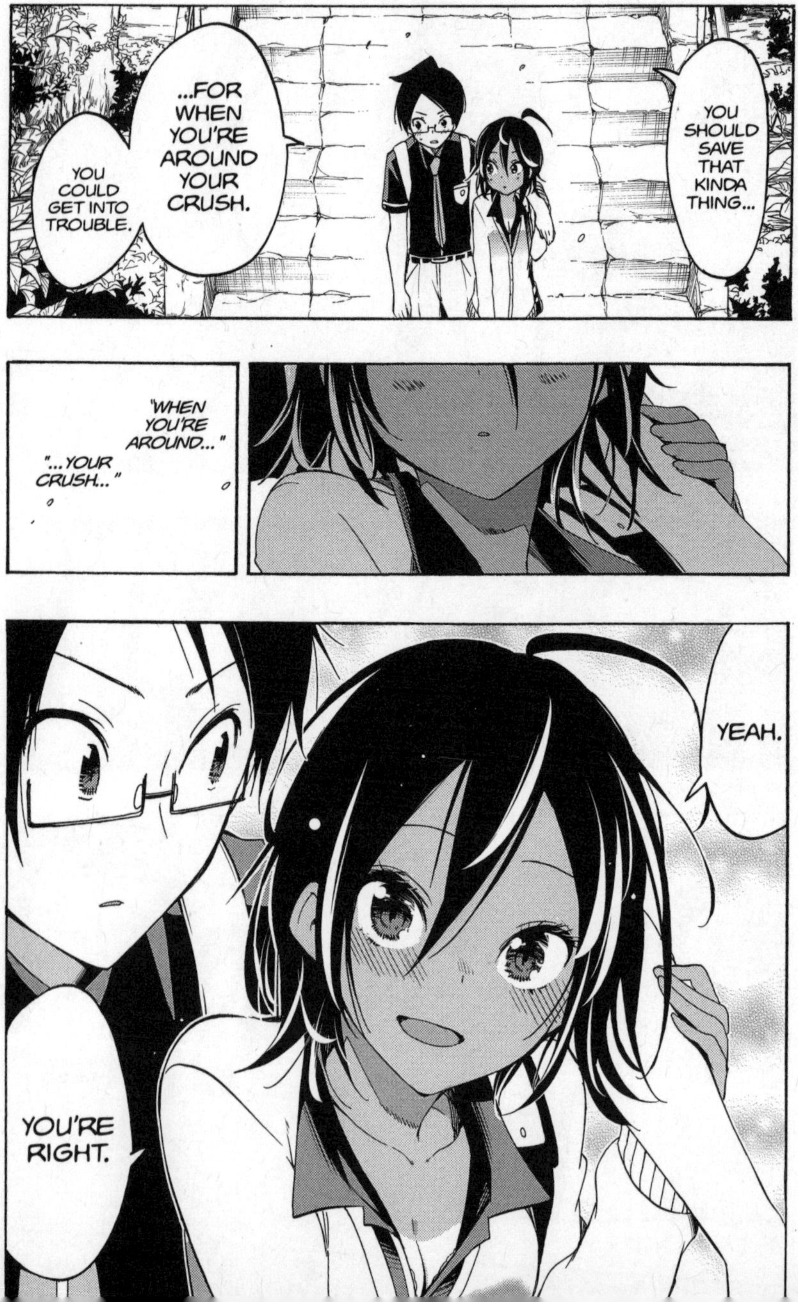
YOU SHOULD SAVE THAT KINDA THING...
...FOR WHEN YOU'RE AROUND YOUR CRUSH.
YOU COULD GET INTO TROUBLE.
"WHEN YOU'RE AROUND..."
"...YOUR CRUSH..."
YEAH.
YOU'RE RIGHT.

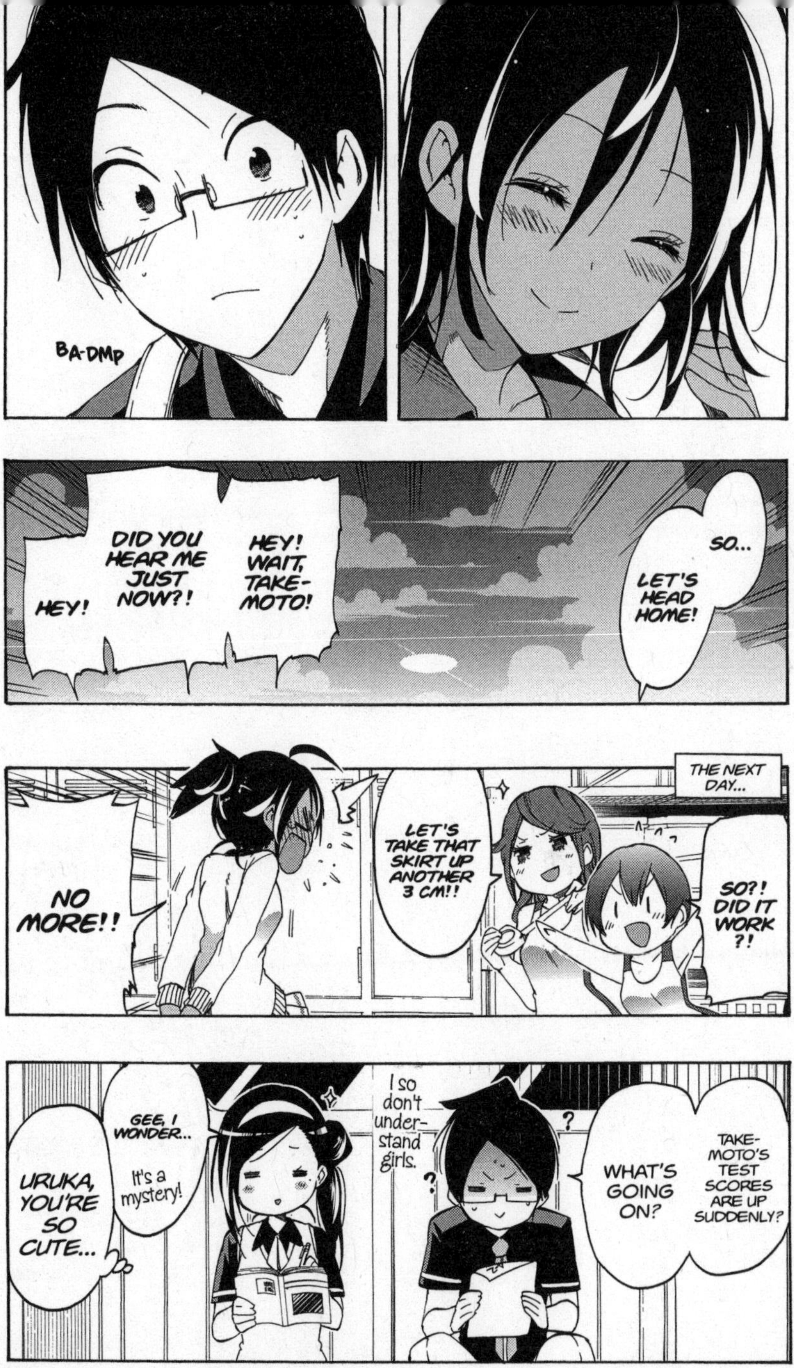

BA-DMP
SO... LET'S HEAD HOME!
HEY! WAIT, TAKE-MOTO!
DID YOU HEAR ME JUST NOW?!
HEY!
THE NEXT DAY...
SO?! DID IT WORK?!
LET'S TAKE THAT SKIRT UP ANOTHER 3 CM!!
NO MORE!!
TAKE-MOTO'S TEST SCORES ARE UP SUDDENLY?
WHAT'S GOING ON?
I so don't under-stand girls.
GEE, I WONDER...
It's a mystery!
URUKA, YOU'RE SO CUTE...

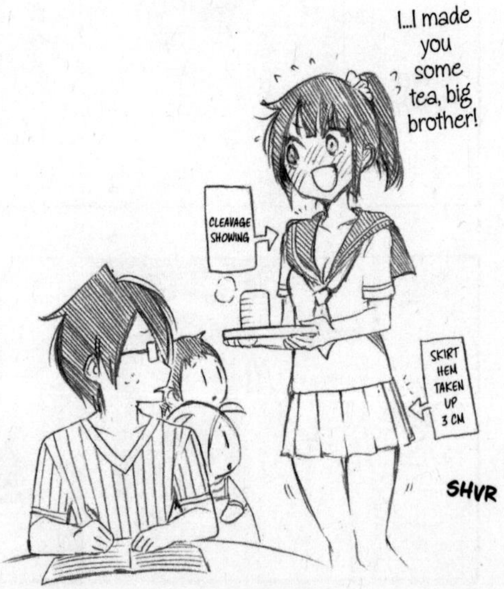
I...I made you some tea, big brother!
CLEAVAGE SHOWING
SKIRT HEM TAKEN UP 3 CM
SHVR

KRUNCH

OGATA UDON

SHAKA
SHAKA
SHAKA

YOU'RE BANNED FROM COMING WITHIN THREE METERS OF ME.

OH...

AND, DADDY...

...BUT I'LL HAVE TO USE THE OLD PAIR OF GLASSES I KEEP AS BACKUP.

I'D RATHER NOT...

WELL, IT IS WHAT IT IS.

WAAAAAAH!!

I...didn't mean to!..

DADDY JUST WANTED TO GIVE YOU A GOODBYE HUG...

I— I'M SO SORRY, RIZU-TAMA.

...

SHAKA
SHAKA
SHAKA

Question 20: A Genius Is Swayed by [X] in a Blurry World

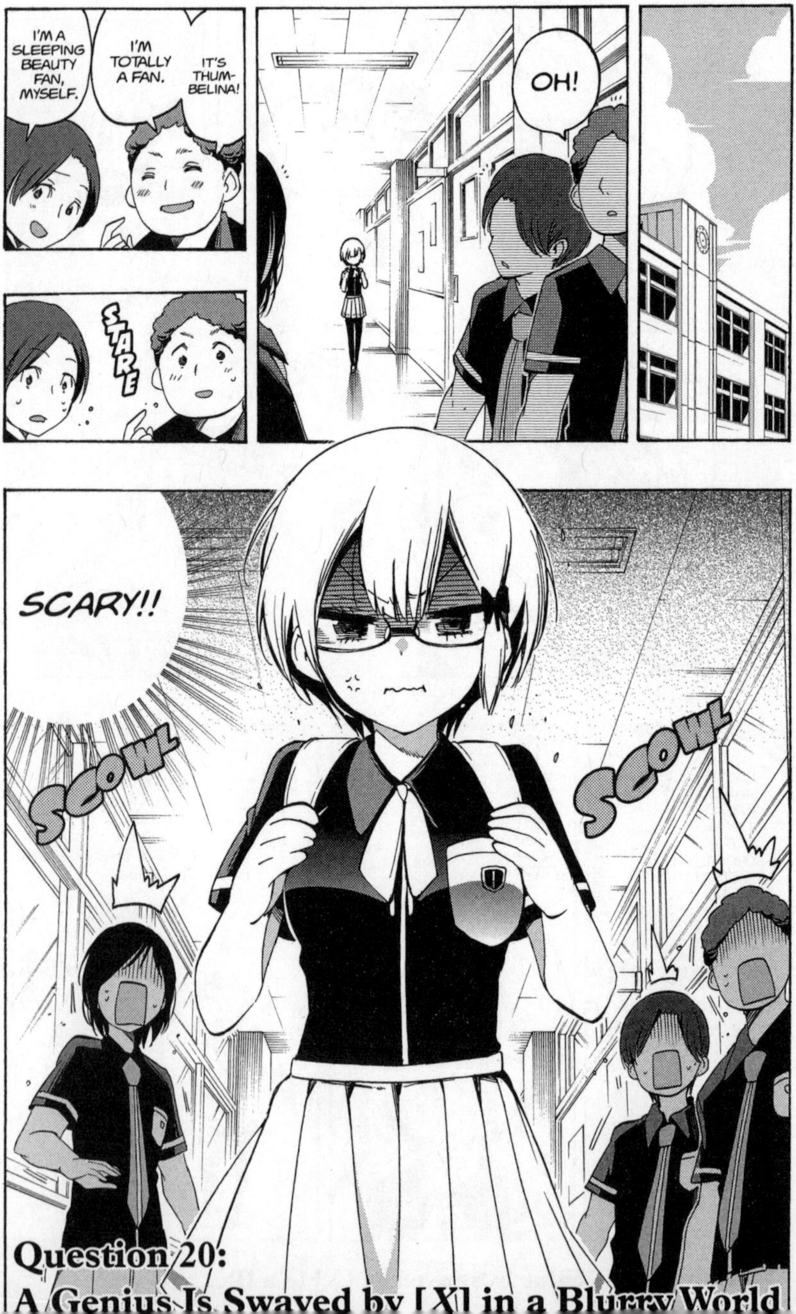
OH!
IT'S THUMBELINA!
I'M TOTALLY A FAN.
I'M A SLEEPING BEAUTY FAN, MYSELF.
STARE
SCARY!!
SCOWL
SCOWL

Question 20: A Genius Is Swayed by [X] in a Blurry World

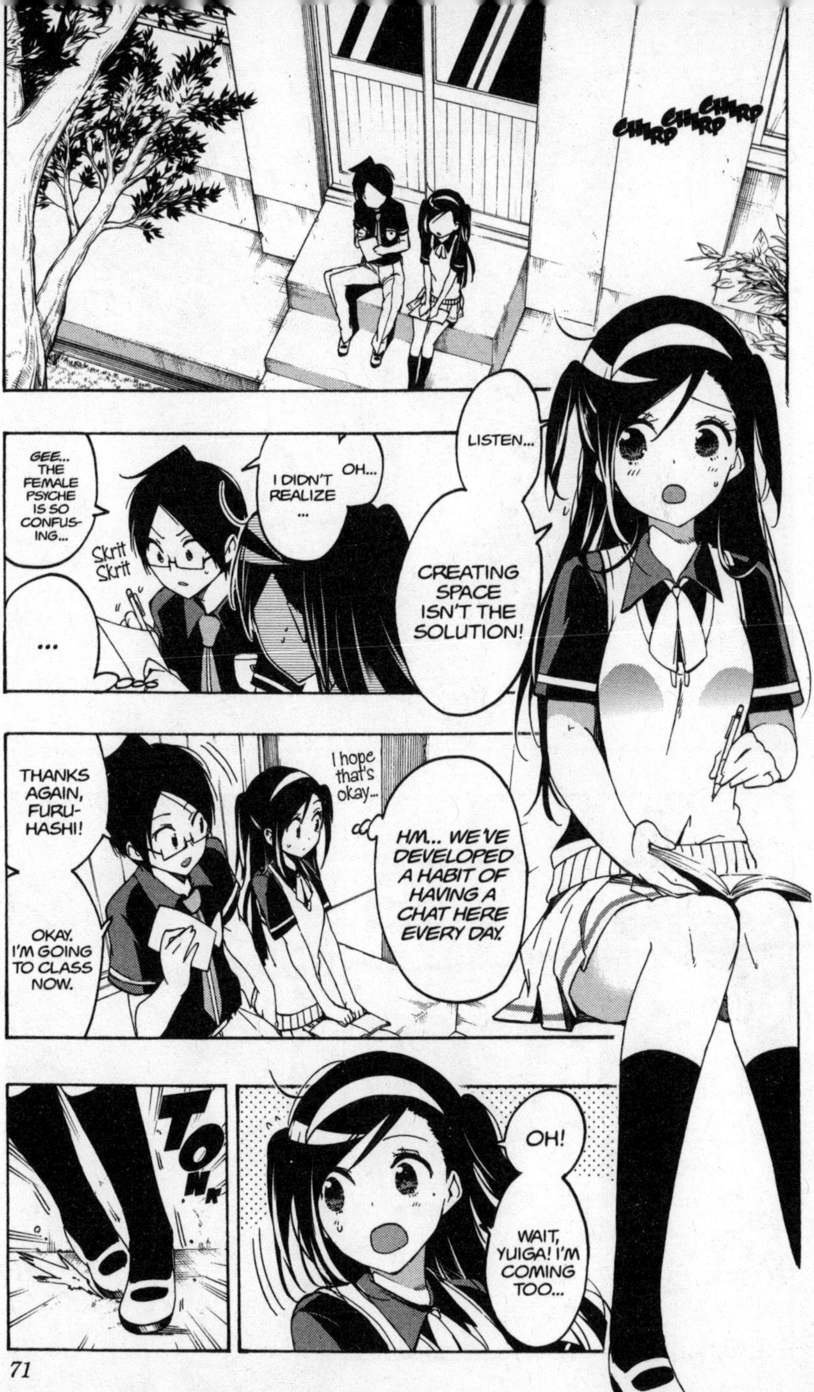
CHIRP CHIRP CHIRP
LISTEN...
CREATING SPACE ISN'T THE SOLUTION!
OH... I DIDN'T REALIZE...
GEE... THE FEMALE PSYCHE IS SO CONFUS-ING...
Skrit Skrit
...
HM... WE'VE DEVELOPED A HABIT OF HAVING A CHAT HERE EVERY DAY.
I hope that's okay...
THANKS AGAIN, FURU-HASHI!
OKAY. I'M GOING TO CLASS NOW.
OH!
WAIT, YUIGA! I'M COMING TOO...
TONK

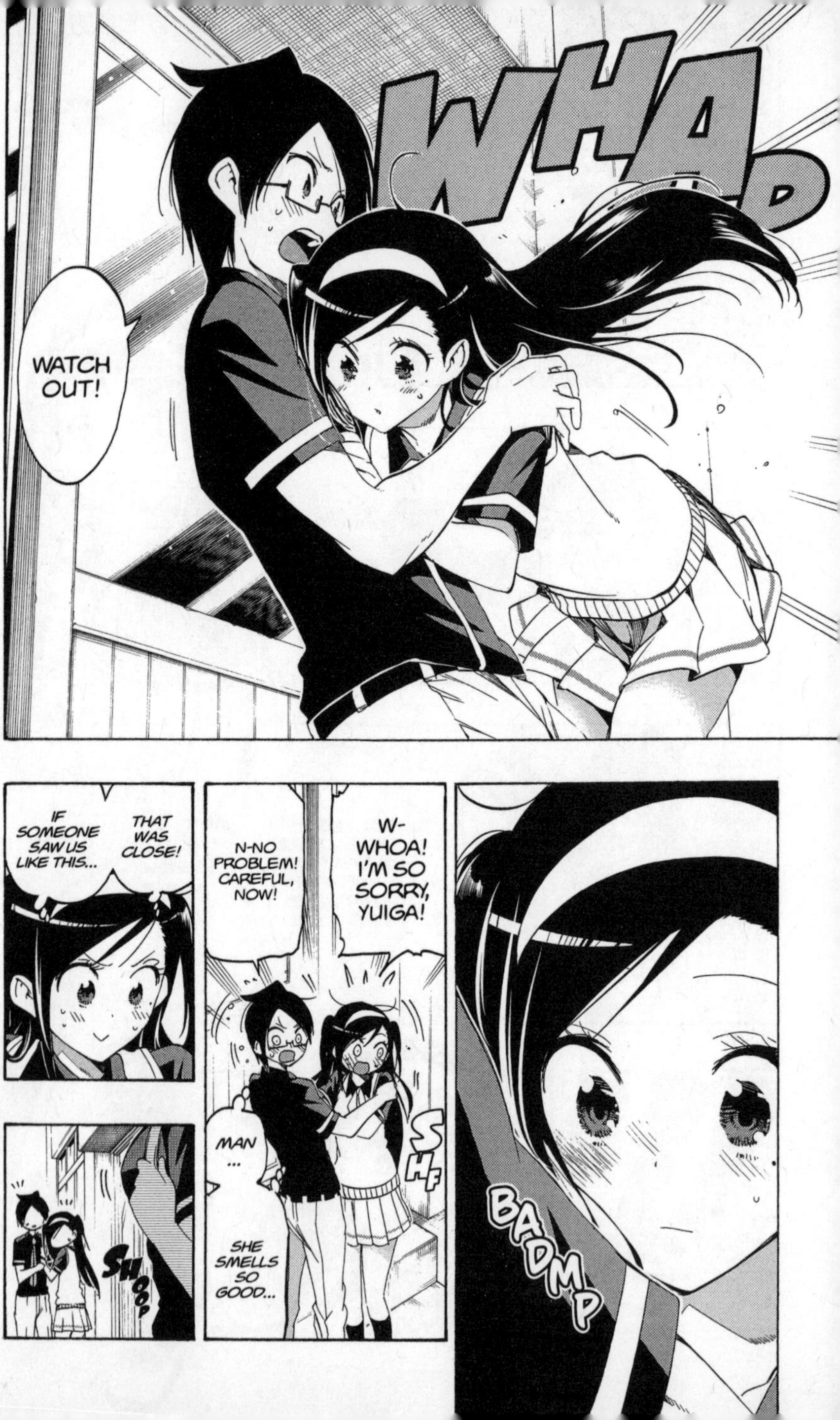
WHA
WATCH OUT!
BADMP
W-WHOA! I'M SO SORRY, YUIGA!
N-NO PROBLEM! CAREFUL, NOW!
SHF
MAN...
SHE SMELLS SO GOOD...
THAT WAS CLOSE!
IF SOMEONE SAW US LIKE THIS...
SHOOP

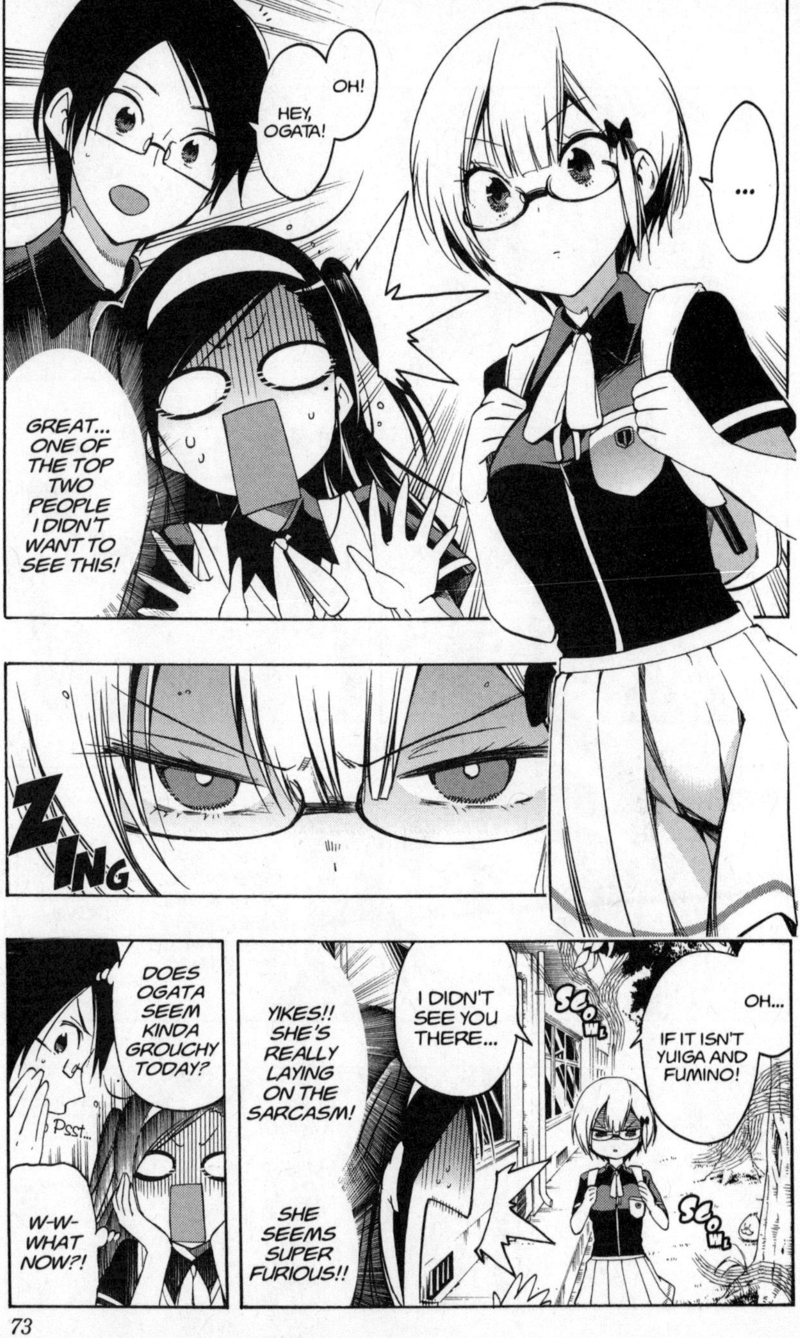

OH!
HEY, OGATA!
...
GREAT... ONE OF THE TOP TWO PEOPLE I DIDN'T WANT TO SEE THIS!
ZING
OH...
IF IT ISN'T YUIGA AND FUMINO!
SEOWL
I DIDN'T SEE YOU THERE...
SEOWL
YIKES!! SHE'S REALLY LAYING ON THE SARCASM!
SHE SEEMS SUPER FURIOUS!!
DOES OGATA SEEM KINDA GROUCHY TODAY?
Psst...
W-W-WHAT NOW?!

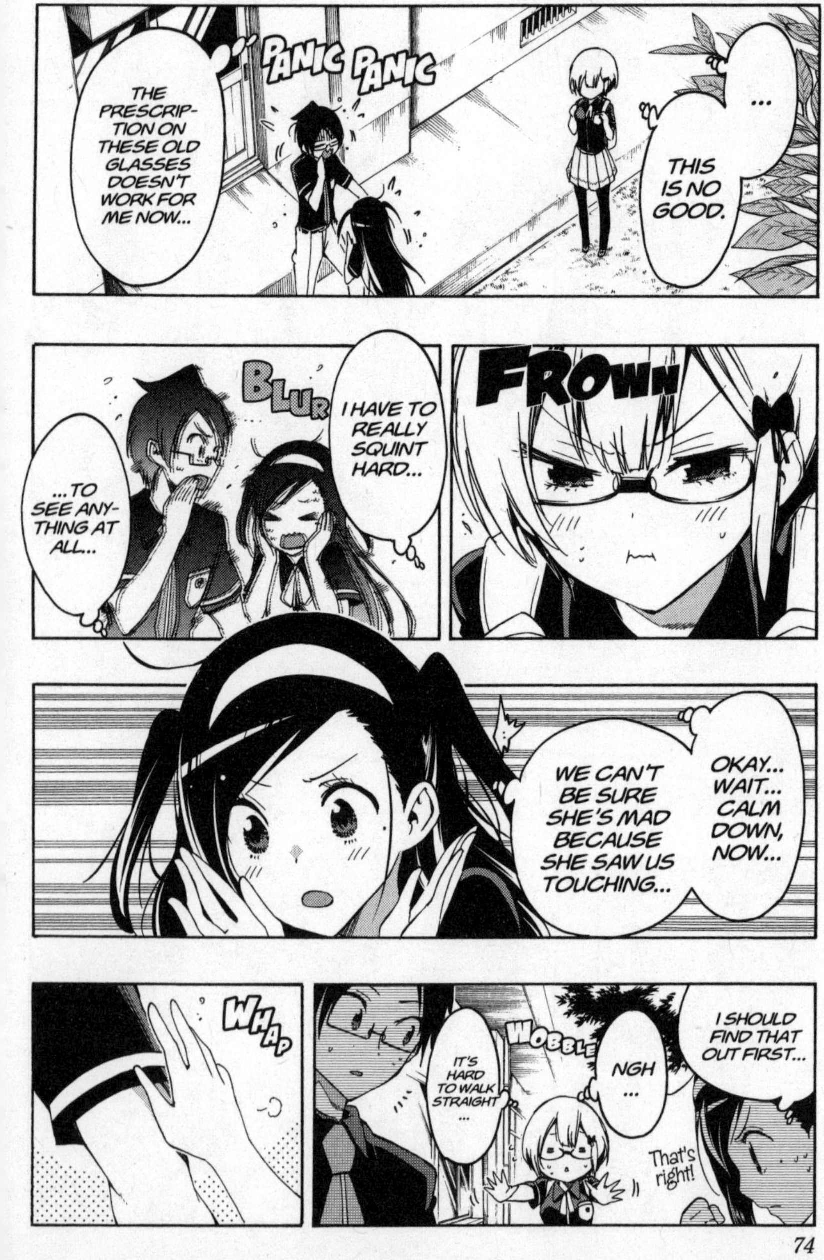
...
THIS IS NO GOOD.
PANIC PANIC
THE PRESCRIPTION ON THESE OLD GLASSES DOESN'T WORK FOR ME NOW...
FROWN
I HAVE TO REALLY SQUINT HARD...
BLUR
...TO SEE ANYTHING AT ALL...
OKAY... WAIT... CALM DOWN, NOW...
WE CAN'T BE SURE SHE'S MAD BECAUSE SHE SAW US TOUCHING...
I SHOULD FIND THAT OUT FIRST...
NGH ...
That's right!
WOBBLE
IT'S HARD TO WALK STRAIGHT ...
WHAP

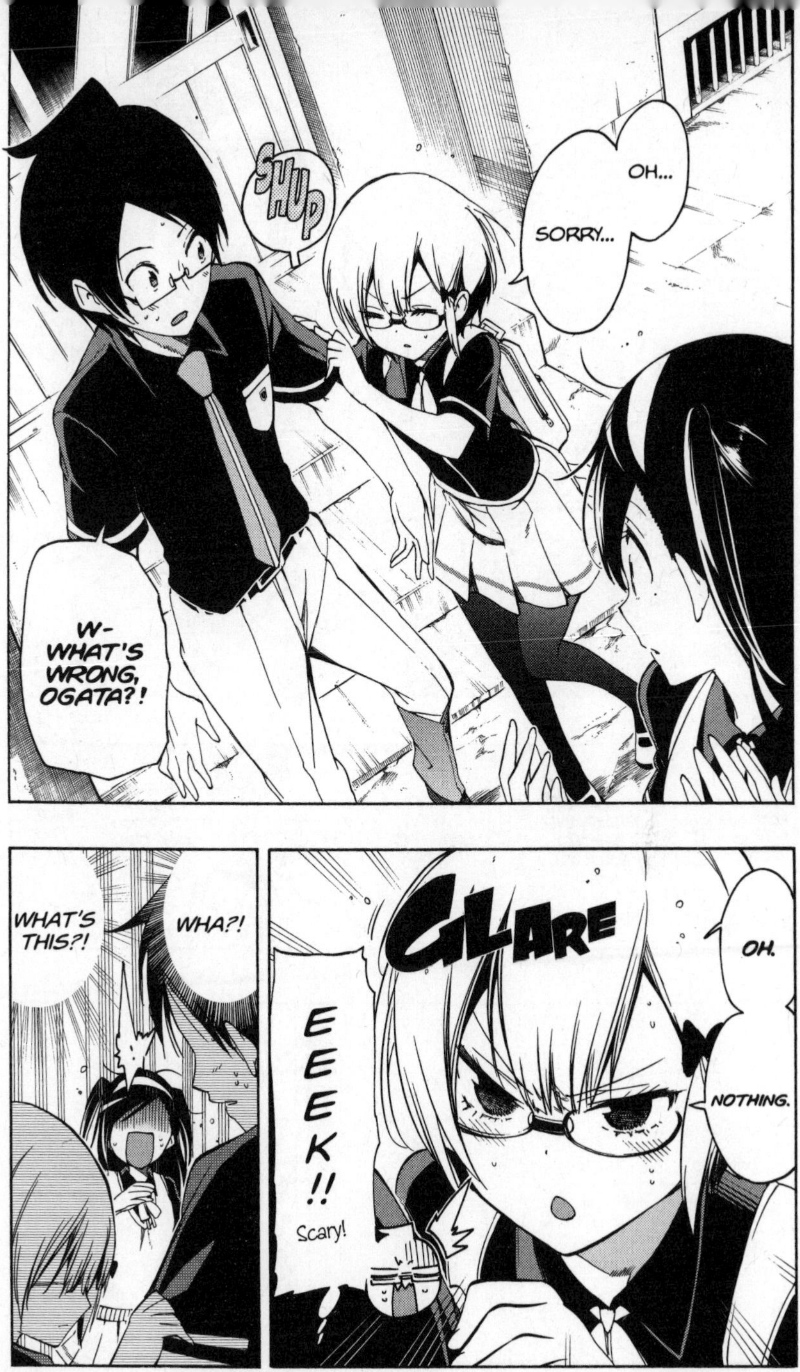
OH...
SORRY...
SHUP
W-WHAT'S WRONG, OGATA?!
OH.
NOTHING.
GLARE
EEEEK!!
Scary!
WHA?!
WHAT'S THIS?!

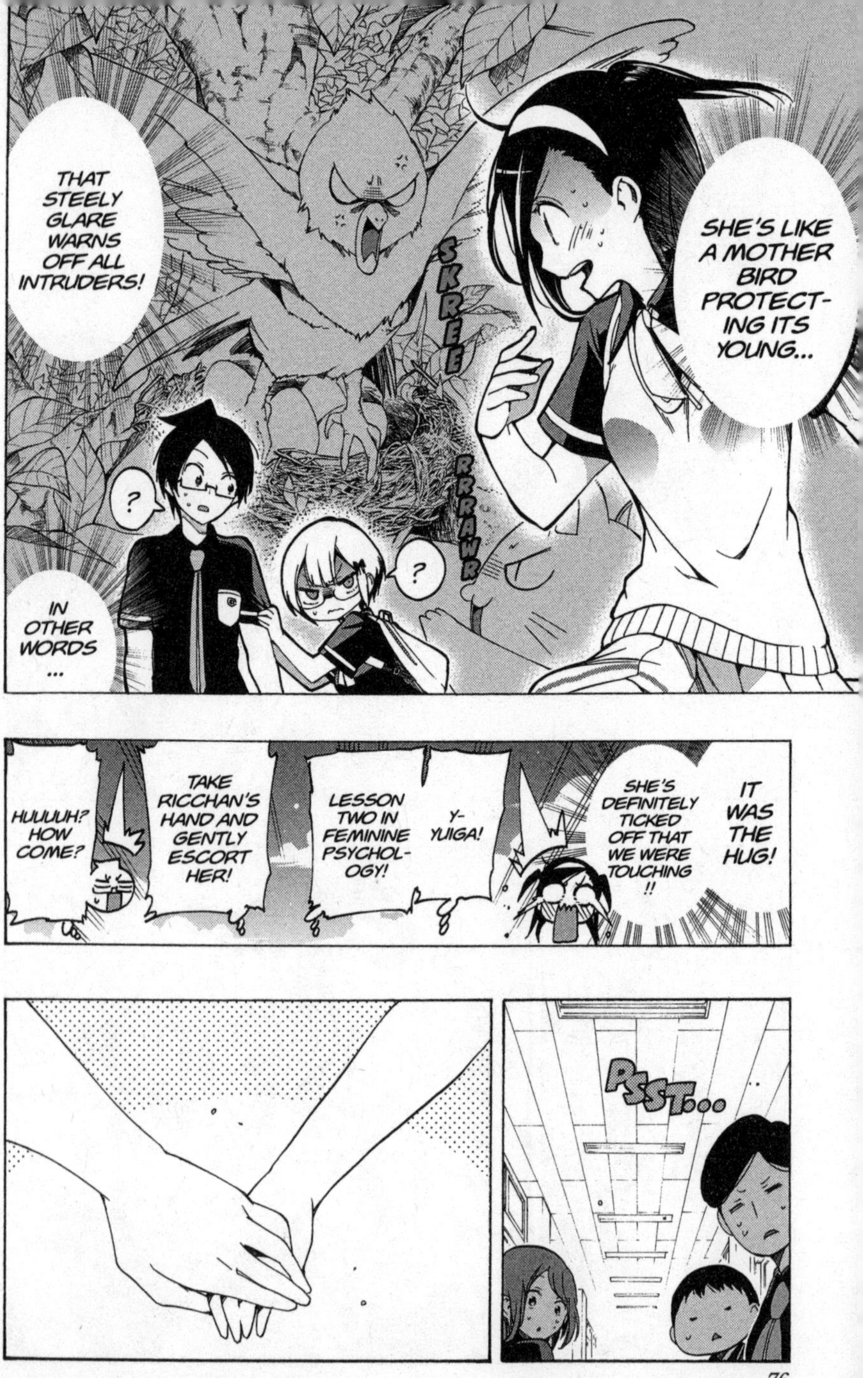
SHE'S LIKE A MOTHER BIRD PROTECTING ITS YOUNG...
SKREE
THAT STEELY GLARE WARNS OFF ALL INTRUDERS!
RRRAWR
?
?
IN OTHER WORDS...
IT WAS THE HUG!
SHE'S DEFINITELY TICKED OFF THAT WE WERE TOUCHING!!
Y-YUIGA!
LESSON TWO IN FEMININE PSYCHOLOGY!
TAKE RICCHAN'S HAND AND GENTLY ESCORT HER!
HUUUUH? HOW COME?
PSST...

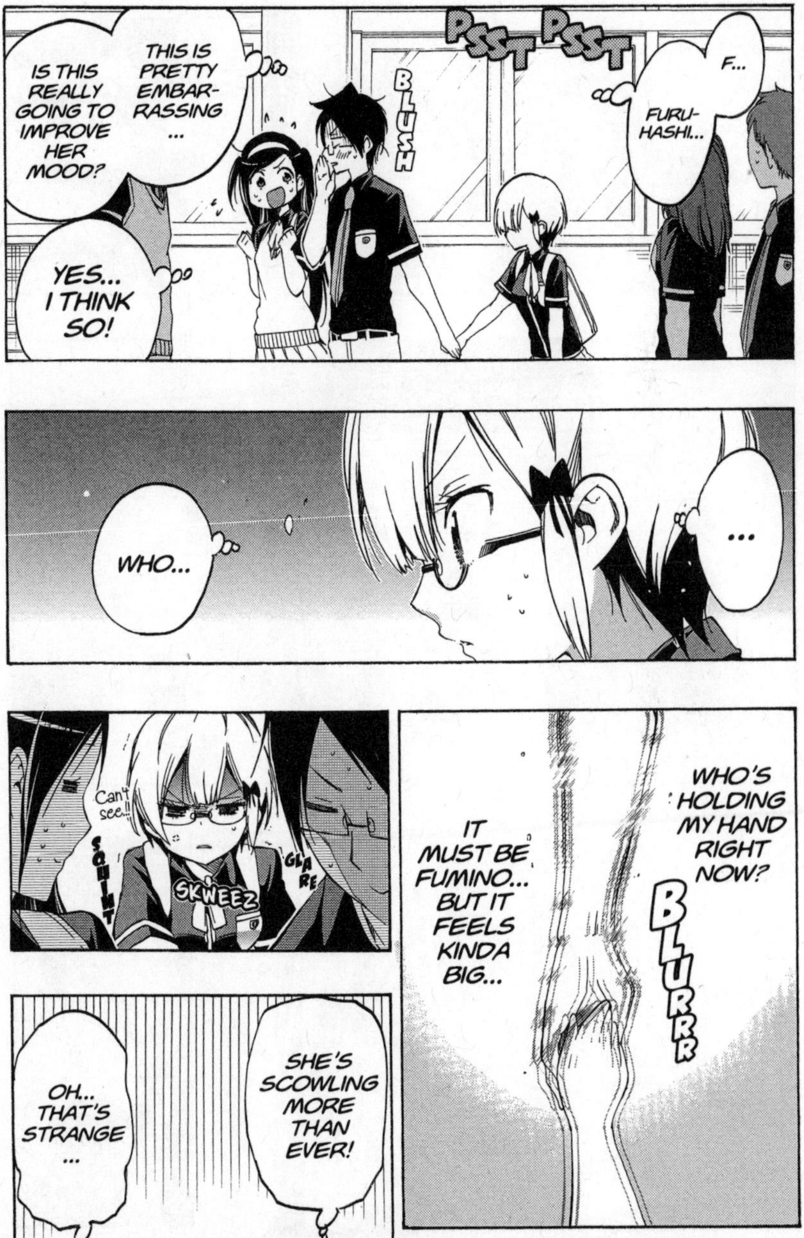
PSST PSST
F... FURU-HASHI...
BLUSH
THIS IS PRETTY EMBAR-RASSING...
IS THIS REALLY GOING TO IMPROVE HER MOOD?
YES... I THINK SO!
...
WHO...
WHO'S HOLDING MY HAND RIGHT NOW?
BLURRR
IT MUST BE FUMINO... BUT IT FEELS KINDA BIG...
GLARE
Can't see..!!
SQUINT
SKWEEZ
SHE'S SCOWLING MORE THAN EVER!
OH... THAT'S STRANGE...

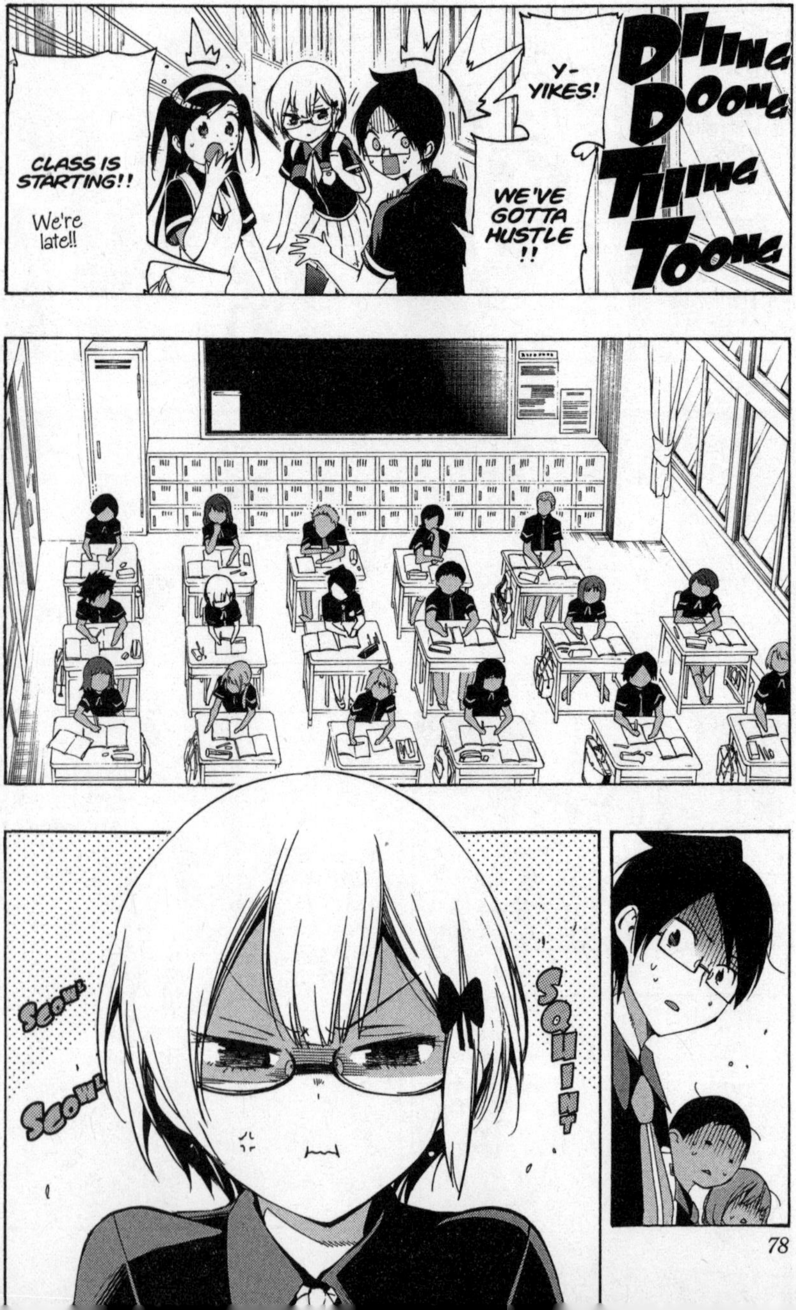
DIIING DOONG
TIIING TOONG
Y-YIKES!
WE'VE GOTTA HUSTLE!!
CLASS IS STARTING!!
We're late!!
SQUIINT
SCOWL
SCOWL

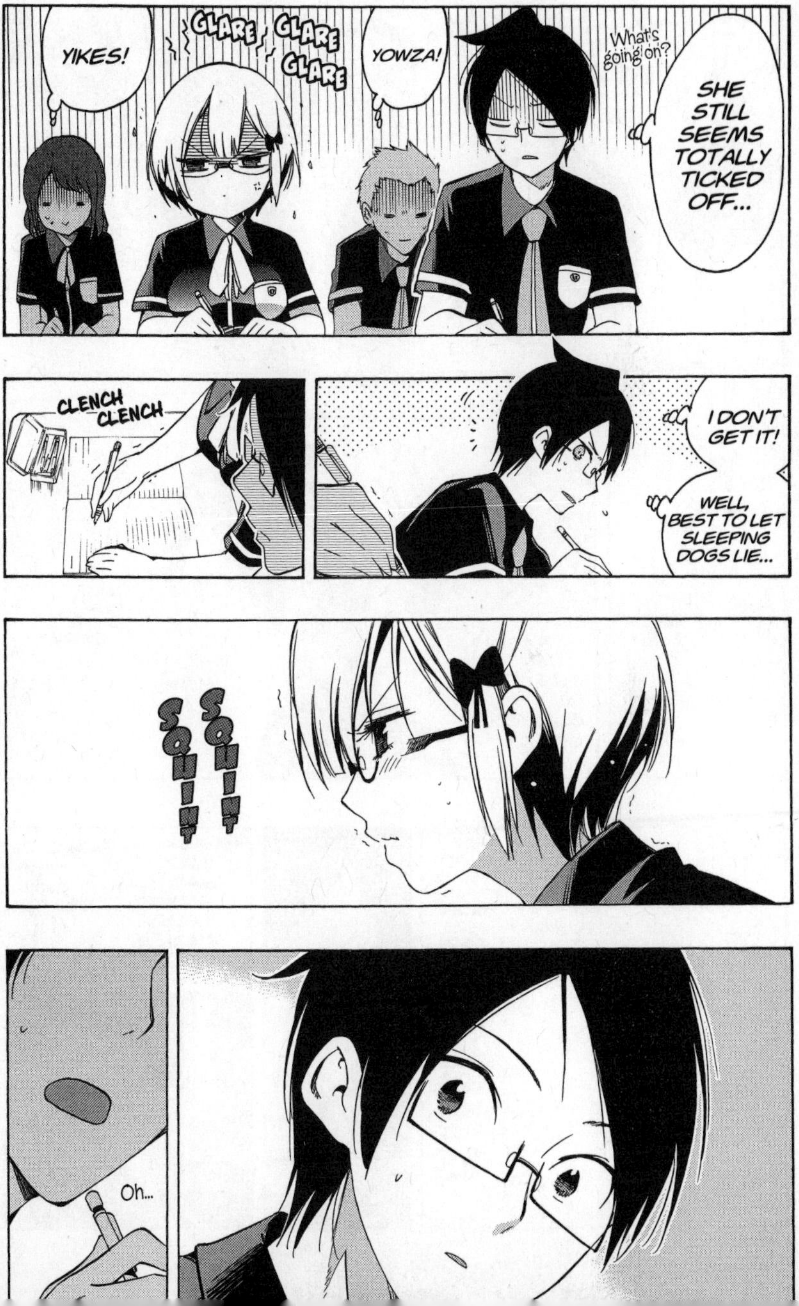
SHE STILL SEEMS TOTALLY TICKED OFF...
What's going on?
YOWZA!
GLARE
GLARE
GLARE
YIKES!
I DON'T GET IT!
WELL, BEST TO LET SLEEPING DOGS LIE...
CLENCH CLENCH
SQUINT
SQUINT
Oh...

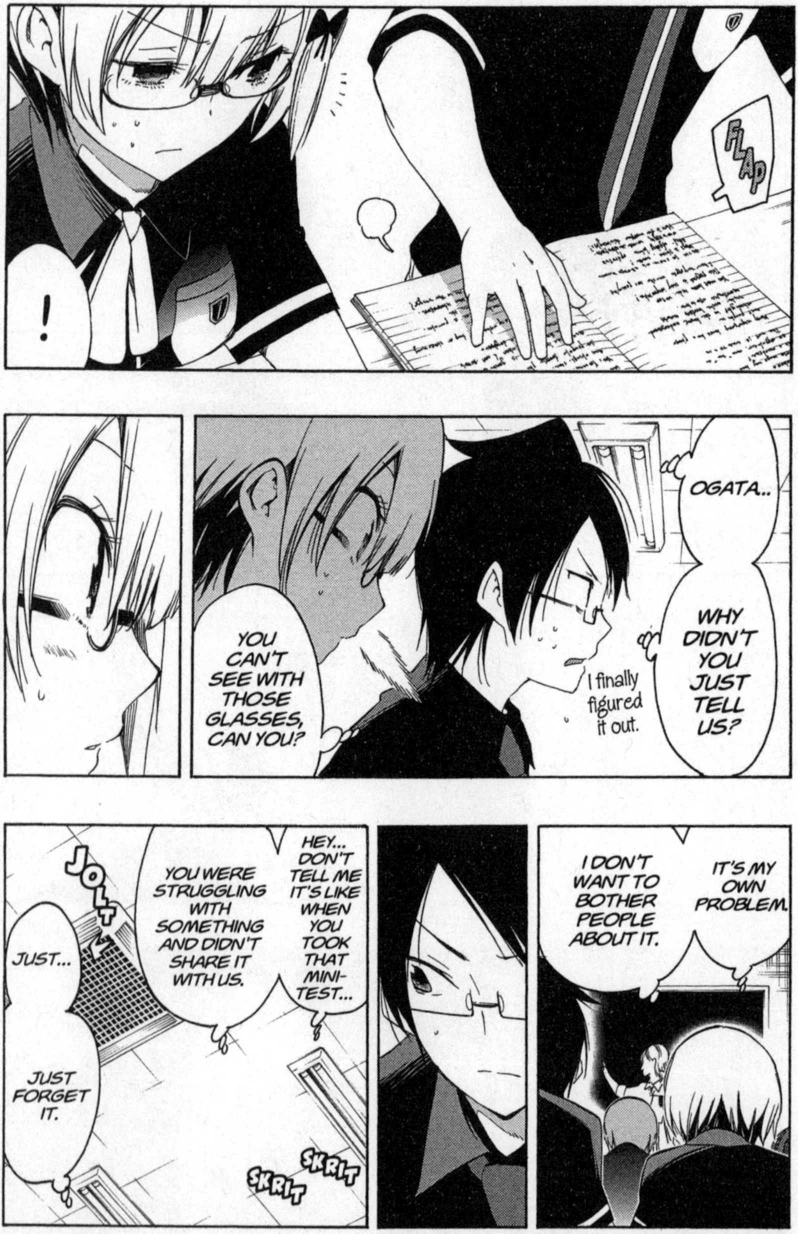
FLAP
!
OGATA...
WHY DIDN'T YOU JUST TELL US?
I finally figured it out.
YOU CAN'T SEE WITH THOSE GLASSES, CAN YOU?
IT'S MY OWN PROBLEM.
I DON'T WANT TO BOTHER PEOPLE ABOUT IT.
HEY... DON'T TELL ME IT'S LIKE WHEN YOU TOOK THAT MINI-TEST...
YOU WERE STRUGGLING WITH SOMETHING AND DIDN'T SHARE IT WITH US.
JOLT
JUST...
JUST FORGET IT.
SKRIT
SKRIT

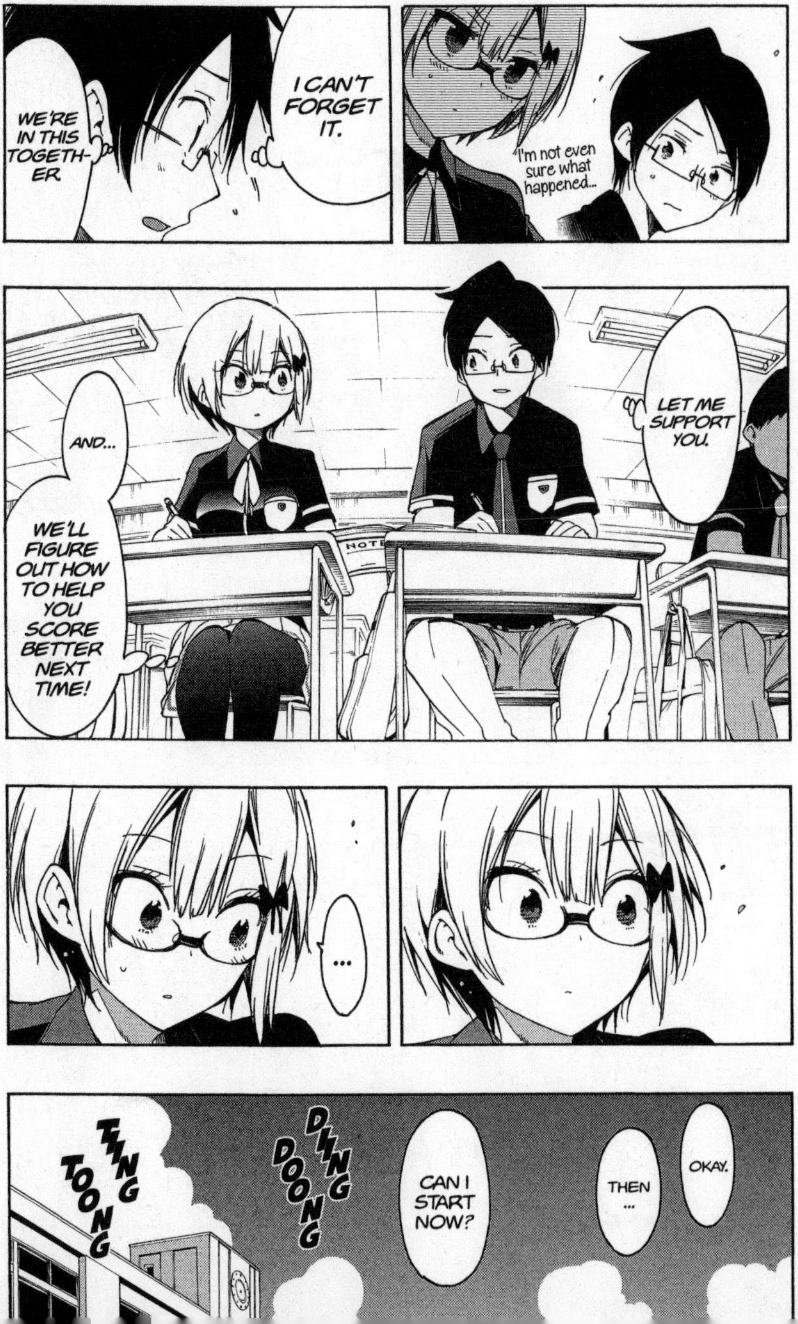
I'm not even sure what happened...
I CAN'T FORGET IT.
WE'RE IN THIS TOGETH-ER.
LET ME SUPPORT YOU.
AND...
WE'LL FIGURE OUT HOW TO HELP YOU SCORE BETTER NEXT TIME!
...
OKAY.
THEN ...
CAN I START NOW?
DING DONG
TING TONG

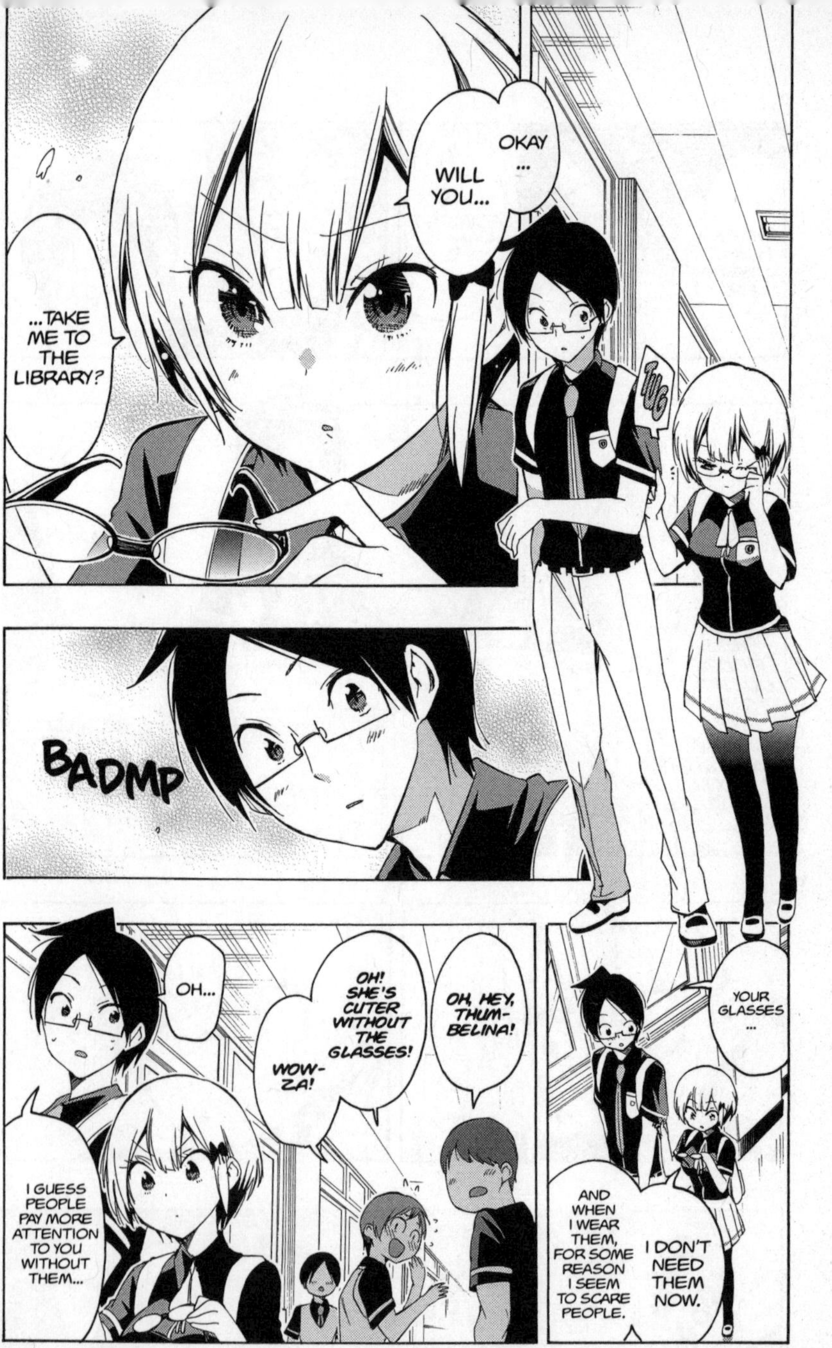
TUG
OKAY ...
WILL YOU...
...TAKE ME TO THE LIBRARY?
BADMP
YOUR GLASSES ...
I DON'T NEED THEM NOW.
AND WHEN I WEAR THEM, FOR SOME REASON I SEEM TO SCARE PEOPLE.
OH, HEY, THUMBELINA!
OH! SHE'S CUTER WITHOUT THE GLASSES!
WOW-ZA!
OH...
I GUESS PEOPLE PAY MORE ATTENTION TO YOU WITHOUT THEM...

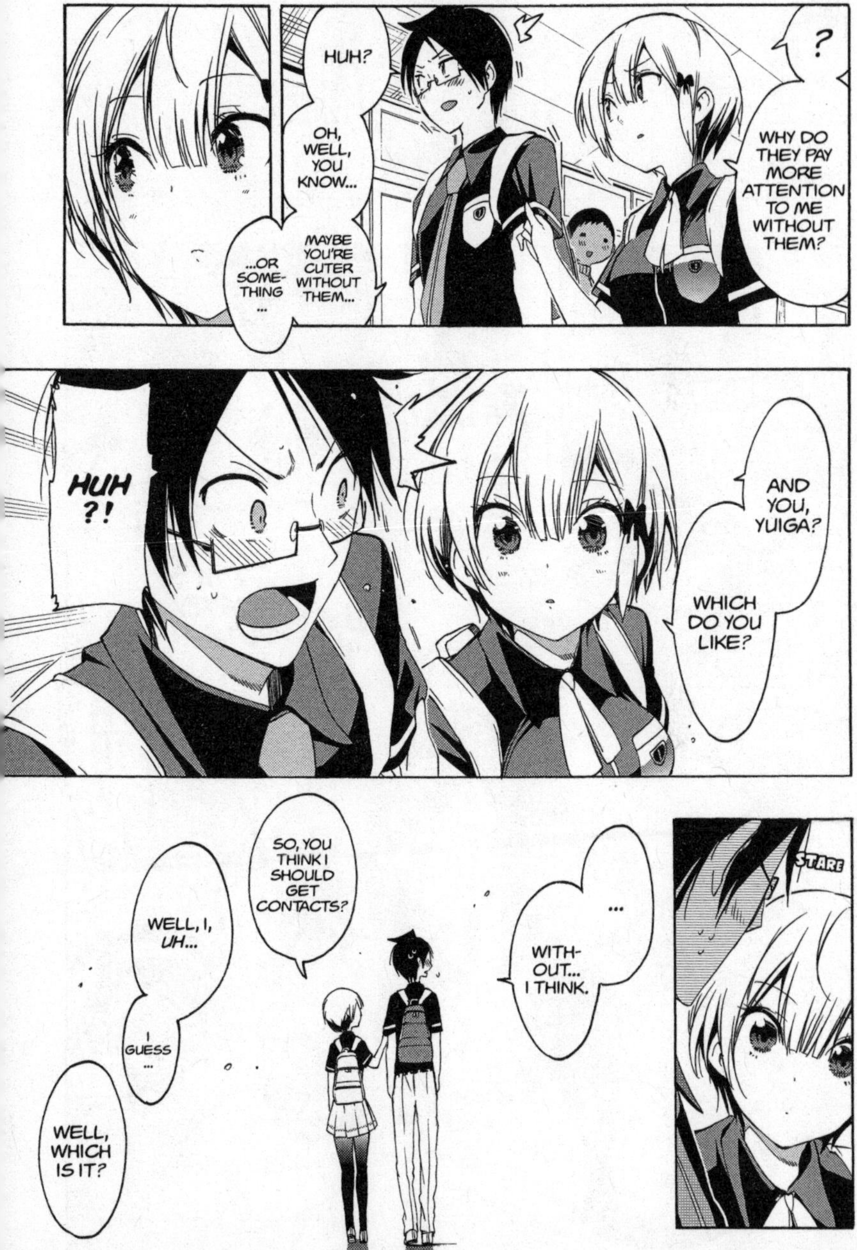
?
WHY DO THEY PAY MORE ATTENTION TO ME WITHOUT THEM?
HUH?
OH, WELL, YOU KNOW...
MAYBE YOU'RE CUTER WITHOUT THEM...
...OR SOME-THING...
AND YOU, YUIGA?
WHICH DO YOU LIKE?
HUH?!
STARE
...
WITH-OUT... I THINK.
SO, YOU THINK I SHOULD GET CONTACTS?
WELL, I, UH...
I GUESS...
WELL, WHICH IS IT?

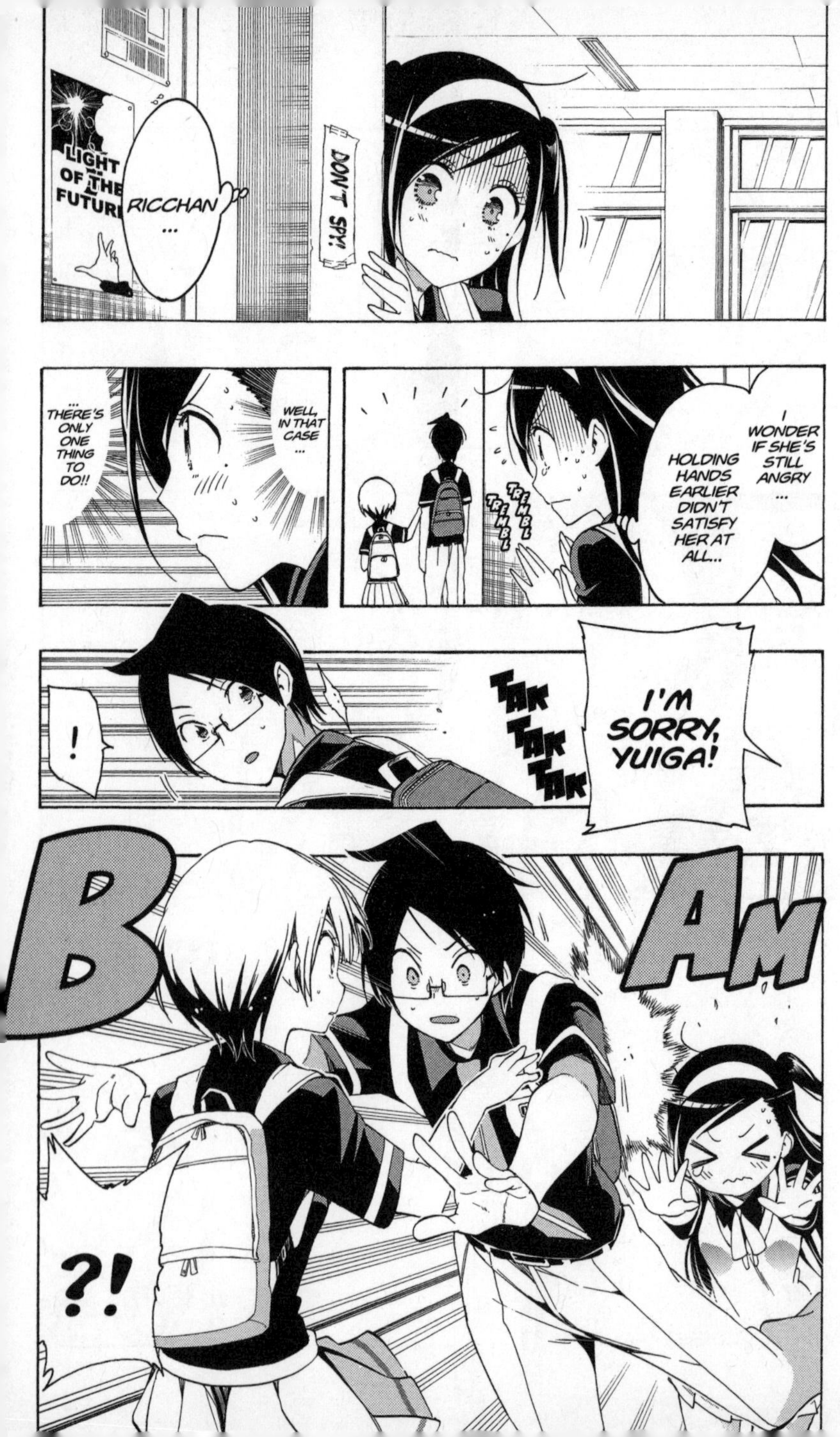
DON'T SPY!
RICCHAN ...
LIGHT OF THE FUTURE
I WONDER IF SHE'S STILL ANGRY ...
HOLDING HANDS EARLIER DIDN'T SATISFY HER AT ALL...
TREMBL TREMBL
WELL, IN THAT CASE ...
... THERE'S ONLY ONE THING TO DO!!
I'M SORRY, YUIGA!
TAK TAK TAK
!
BAM
?!

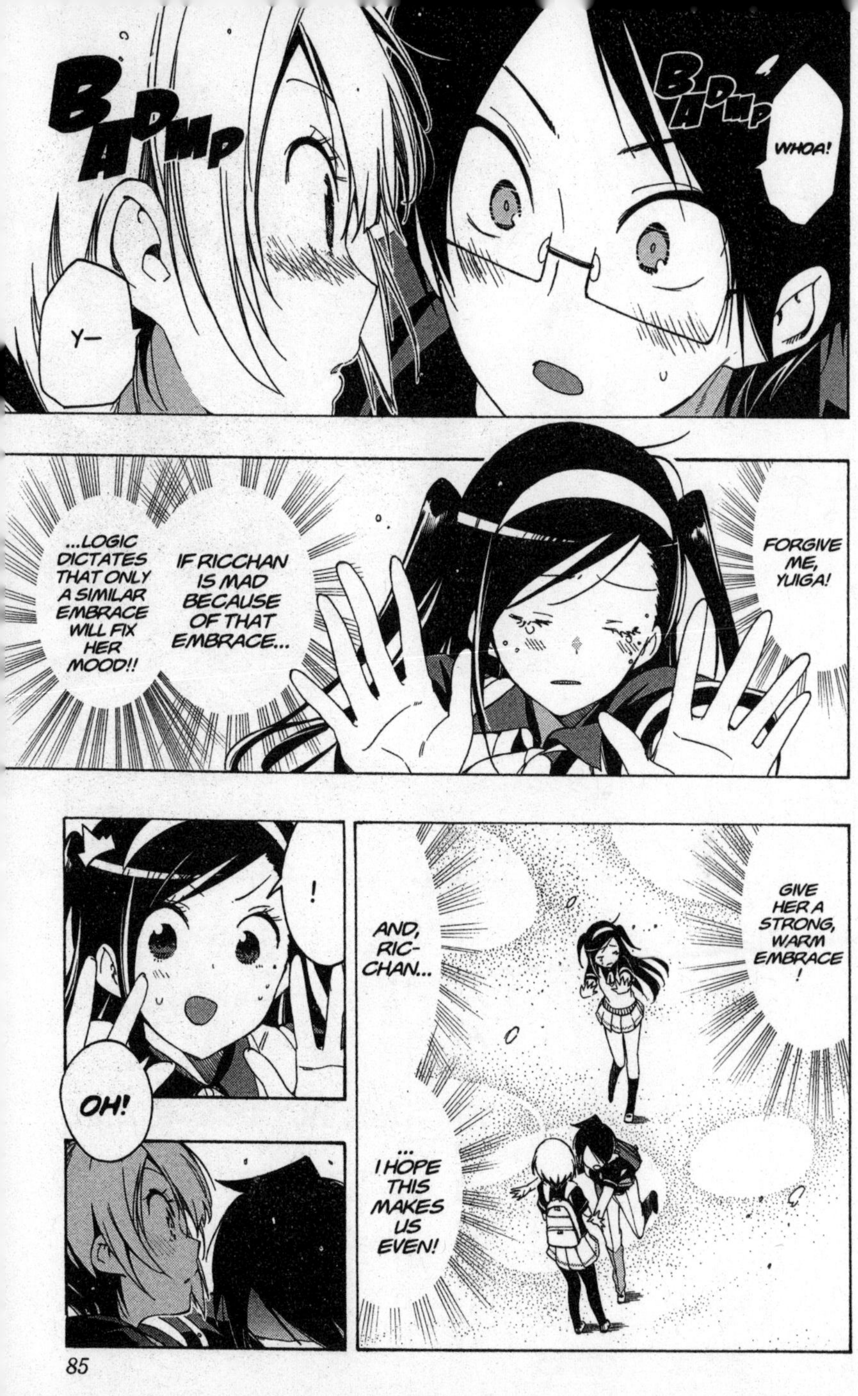
BADUMP
WHOA!
BADUMP
Y—
FORGIVE ME, YUIGA!
IF RICCHAN IS MAD BECAUSE OF THAT EMBRACE...
...LOGIC DICTATES THAT ONLY A SIMILAR EMBRACE WILL FIX HER MOOD!!
GIVE HER A STRONG, WARM EMBRACE!
AND, RIC-CHAN...
...I HOPE THIS MAKES US EVEN!
!
OH!

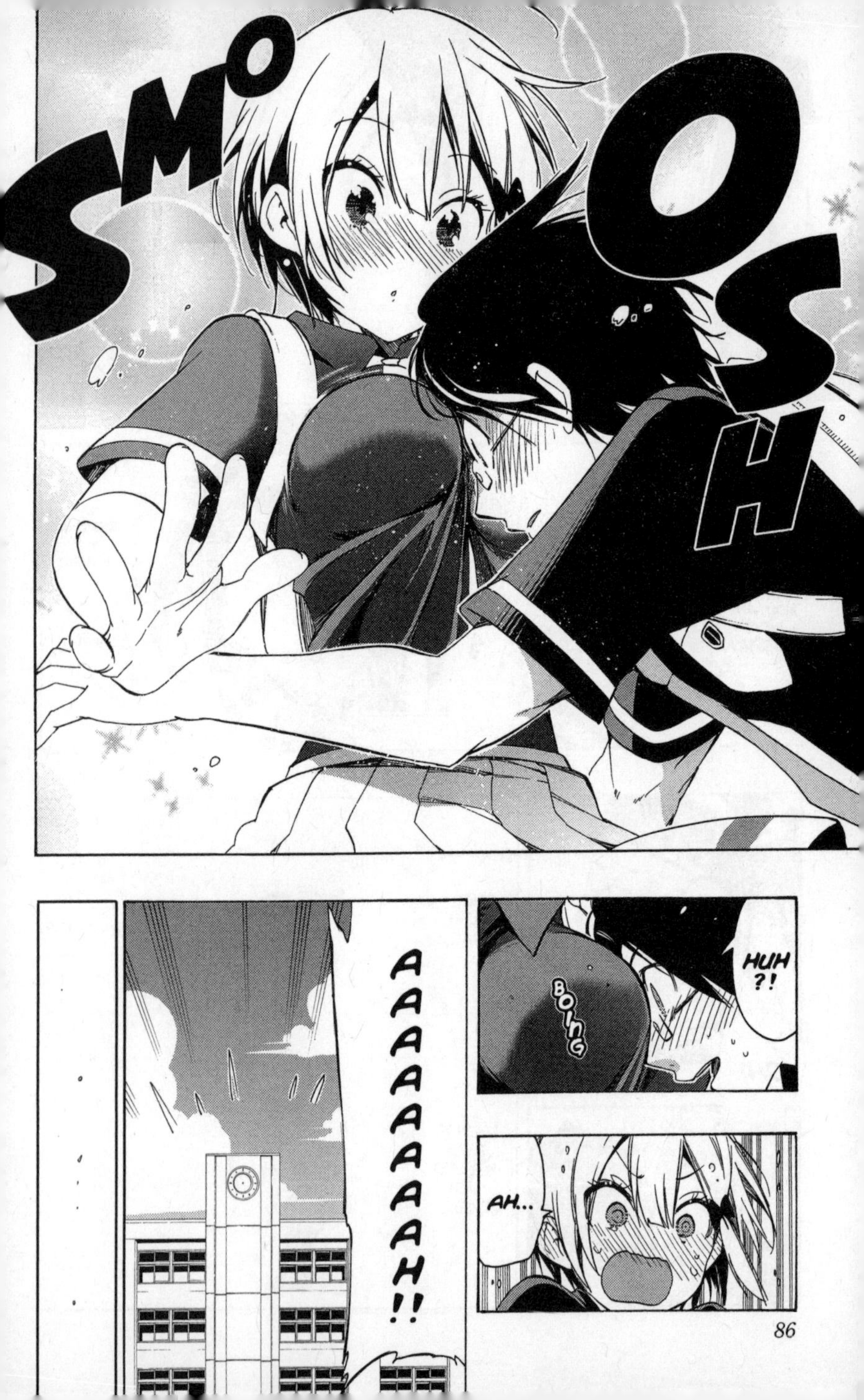
SMOOSH
BOING
HUH ?!
AH...
AAAAAAAAH!!

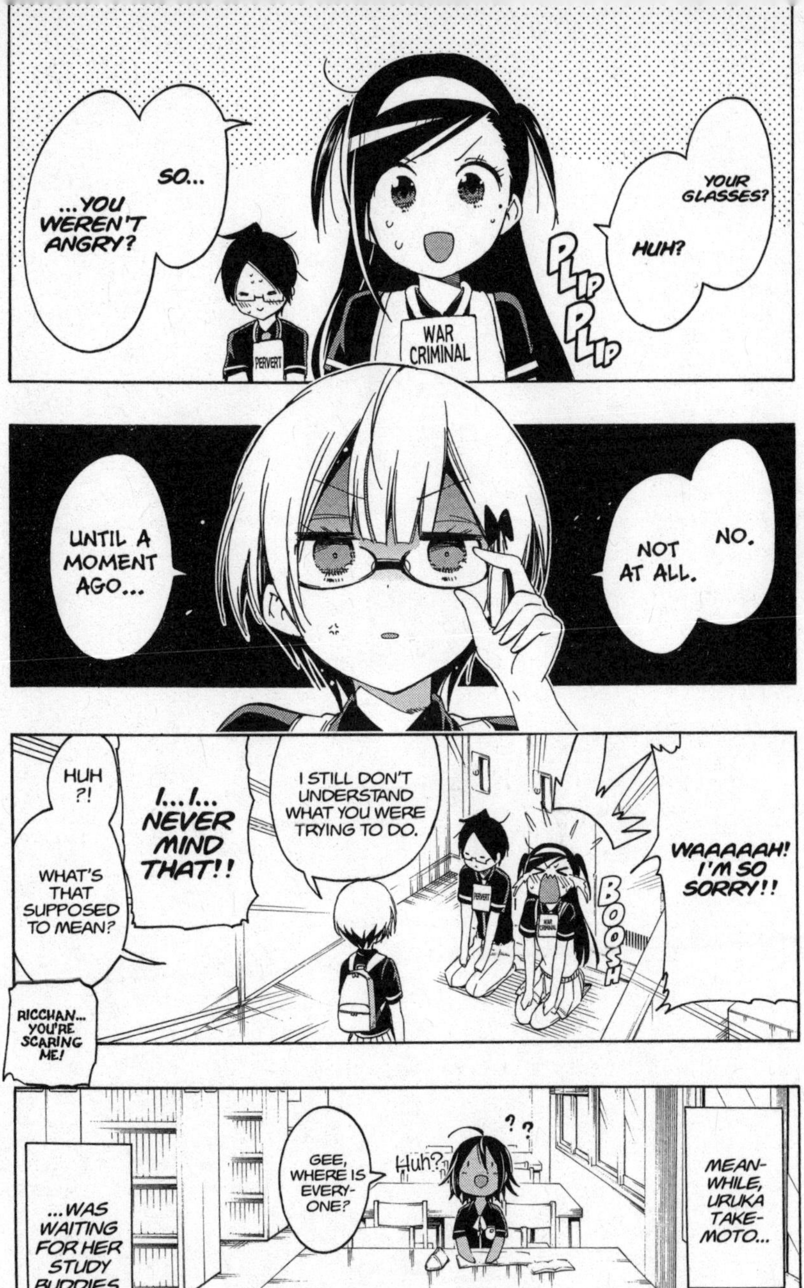
YOUR GLASSES? HUH?
PLIP PLIP
WAR CRIMINAL
PERVERT
SO... ...YOU WEREN'T ANGRY?
NO. NOT AT ALL.
UNTIL A MOMENT AGO...
WAAAAAH! I'M SO SORRY!!
BOOSH
PERVERT
WAR CRIMINAL
I STILL DON'T UNDERSTAND WHAT YOU WERE TRYING TO DO.
I...I... NEVER MIND THAT!!
HUH?! WHAT'S THAT SUPPOSED TO MEAN?
RICCHAN... YOU'RE SCARING ME!
MEAN-WHILE, URUKA TAKE-MOTO...
??
Huh?
GEE, WHERE IS EVERY-ONE?
...WAS WAITING FOR HER STUDY BUDDIES.

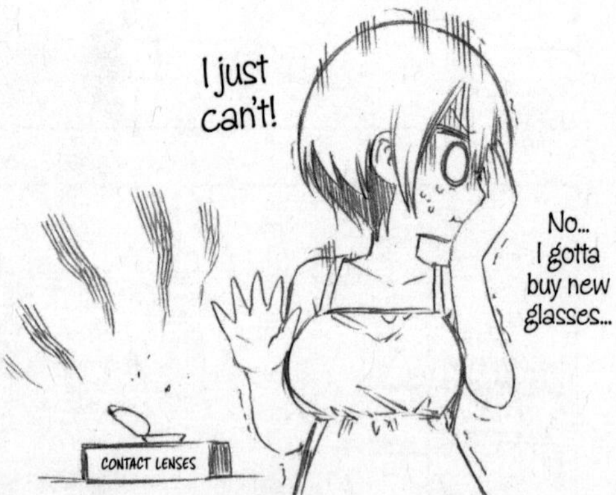
I just can't!
No... I gotta buy new glasses...
CONTACT LENSES

Question 21: The Forbidden Item That Connects an [X] Genius

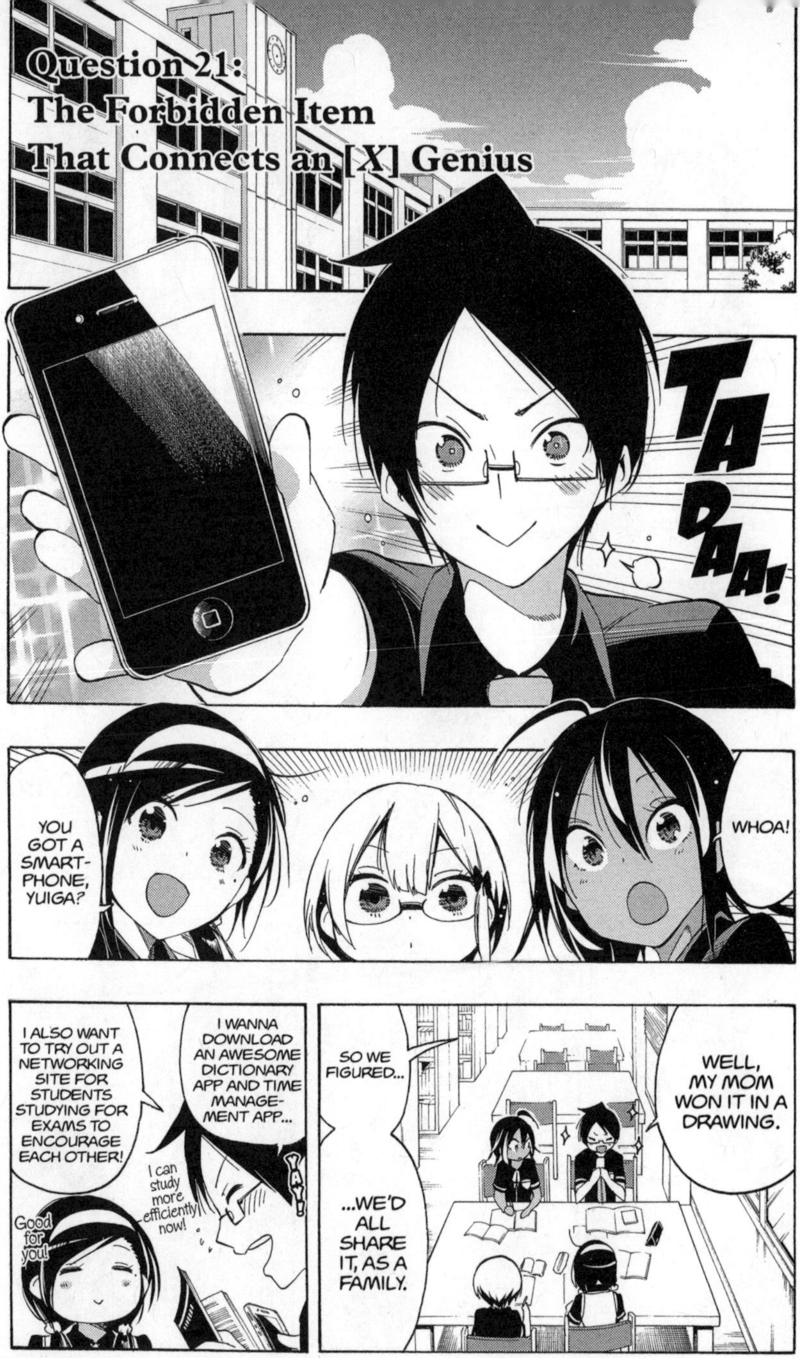
TA DAA!
WHOA!
YOU GOT A SMARTPHONE, YUIGA?
WELL, MY MOM WON IT IN A DRAWING.
SO WE FIGURED...
...WE'D ALL SHARE IT, AS A FAMILY.
I WANNA DOWNLOAD AN AWESOME DICTIONARY APP AND TIME MANAGEMENT APP...
I ALSO WANT TO TRY OUT A NETWORKING SITE FOR STUDENTS STUDYING FOR EXAMS TO ENCOURAGE EACH OTHER!
YAY!
I can study more efficiently now!
Good for you!

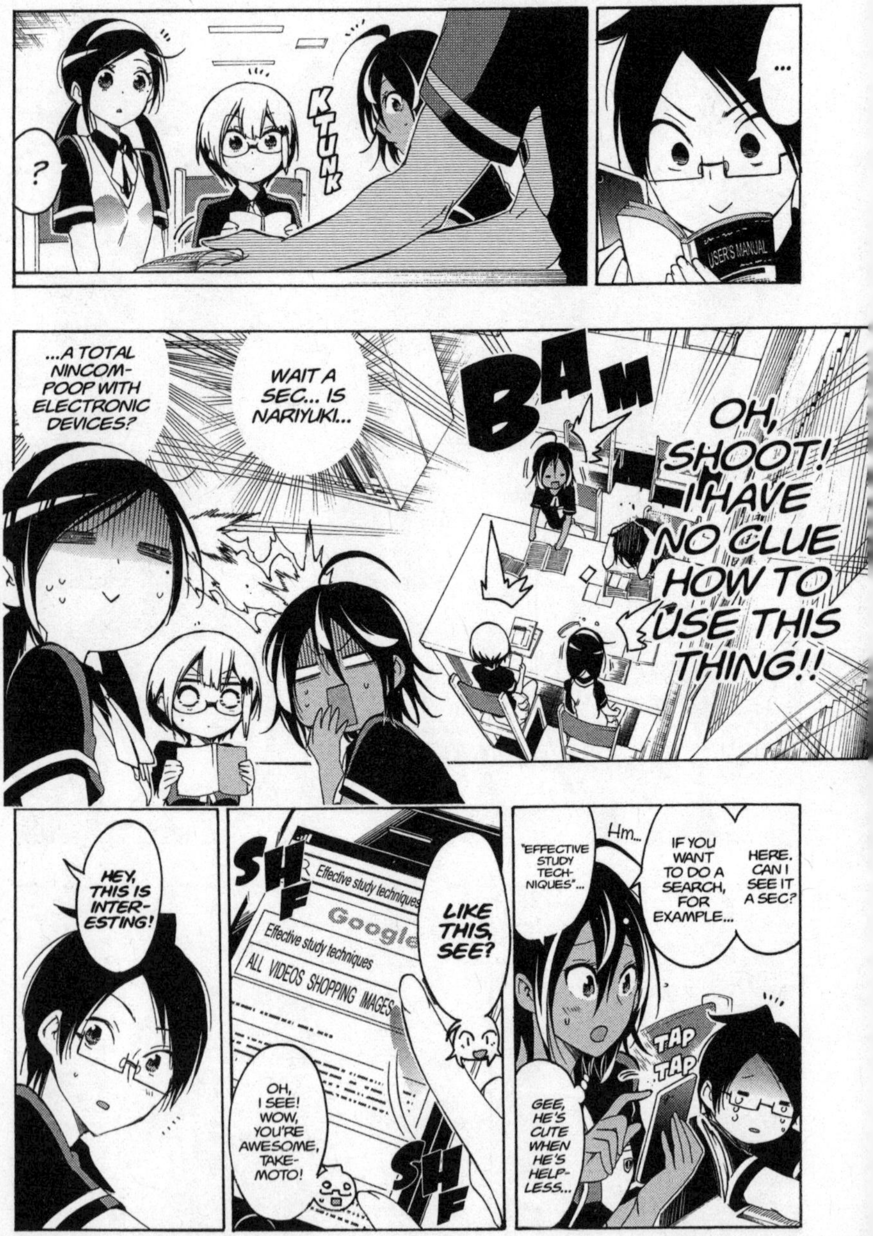
...
KTUNK
?
BAM
OH, SHOOT! I HAVE NO CLUE HOW TO USE THIS THING!!
WAIT A SEC... IS NARIYUKI...
...A TOTAL NINCOMPOOP WITH ELECTRONIC DEVICES?
HERE. CAN I SEE IT A SEC?
IF YOU WANT TO DO A SEARCH, FOR EXAMPLE...
Hm...
"EFFECTIVE STUDY TECHNIQUES"...
TAP TAP
GEE, HE'S CUTE WHEN HE'S HELPLESS...
SHF
Effective study techniques
Google
Effective study techniques
ALL VIDEOS SHOPPING IMAGES
LIKE THIS, SEE?
OH, I SEE! WOW, YOU'RE AWESOME, TAKEMOTO!
SHF
HEY, THIS IS INTERESTING!

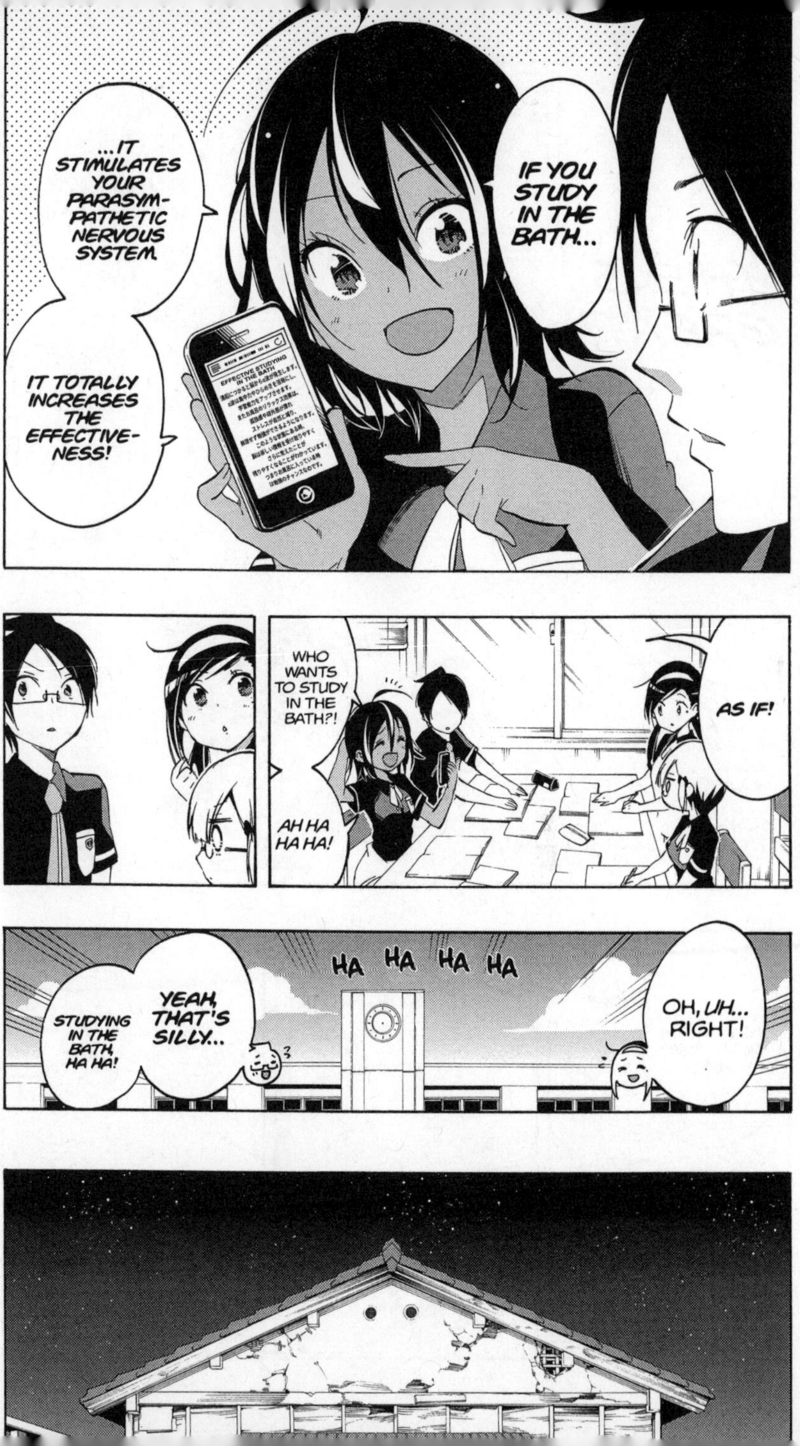
IF YOU STUDY IN THE BATH...
...IT STIMULATES YOUR PARASYM-PATHETIC NERVOUS SYSTEM.
EFFECTIVE STUDYING IN THE BATH
IT TOTALLY INCREASES THE EFFECTIVE-NESS!
AS IF!
WHO WANTS TO STUDY IN THE BATH?!
AH HA HA HA!
HA HA HA HA
OH, UH... RIGHT!
YEAH, THAT'S SILLY...
STUDYING IN THE BATH, HA HA!

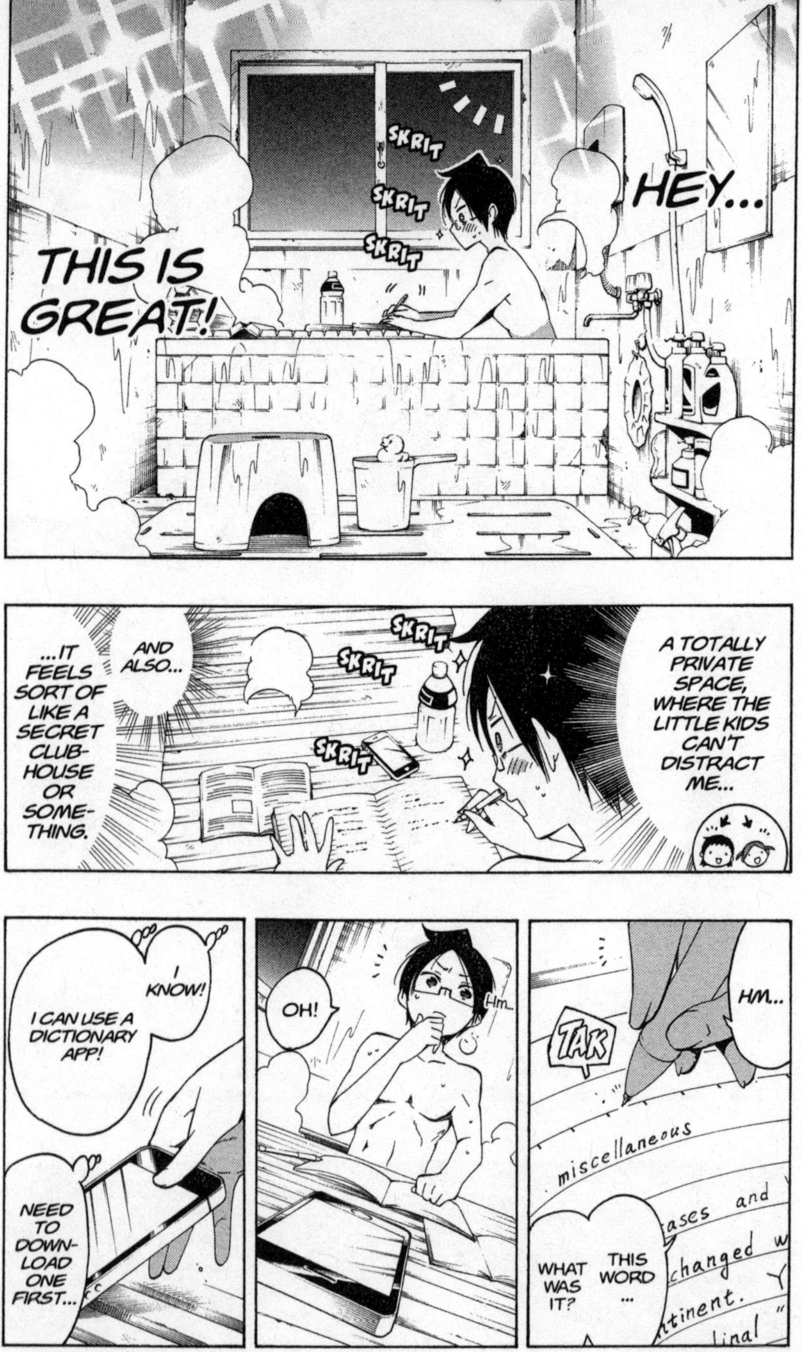
HEY...
SKRIT
SKRIT
SKRIT
THIS IS GREAT!
A TOTALLY PRIVATE SPACE, WHERE THE LITTLE KIDS CAN'T DISTRACT ME...
SKRIT
SKRIT
SKRIT
AND ALSO...
...IT FEELS SORT OF LIKE A SECRET CLUBHOUSE OR SOMETHING.
HM...
TAK
miscellaneous
THIS WORD...
WHAT WAS IT?
Hm...
OH!
I KNOW!
I CAN USE A DICTIONARY APP!
NEED TO DOWNLOAD ONE FIRST...

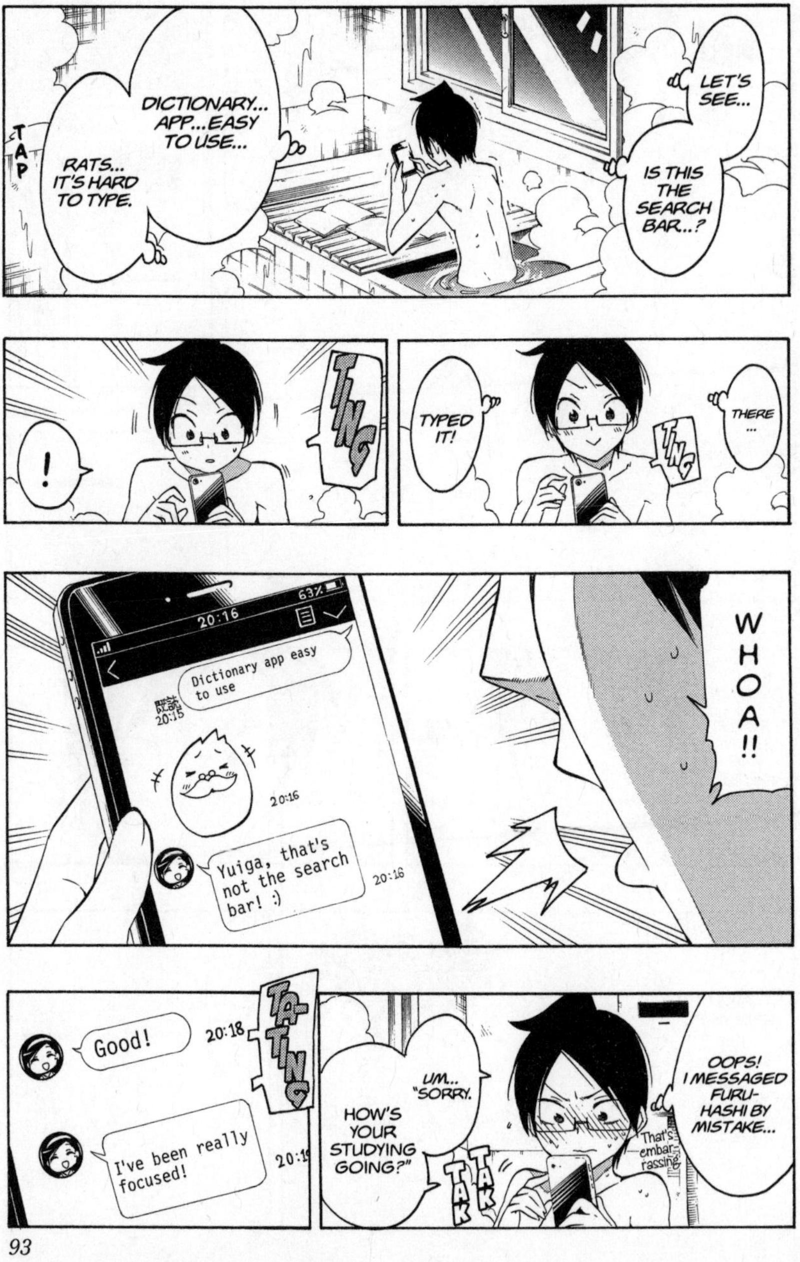
LET'S SEE...
IS THIS THE SEARCH BAR...?
DICTIONARY... APP...EASY TO USE...
RATS... IT'S HARD TO TYPE.
TAP
THERE ...
TING
TYPED IT!
TING
!
WHOA!!
63%
20:16
Dictionary app easy to use
既読
20:15
20:16
Yuiga, that's not the search bar! :)
20:16
OOPS! I MESSAGED FURU-HASHI BY MISTAKE...
That's embarrassing
UM... "SORRY.
HOW'S YOUR STUDYING GOING?"
TAK TAK
TA-TING
20:18
Good!
I've been really focused!
20:1

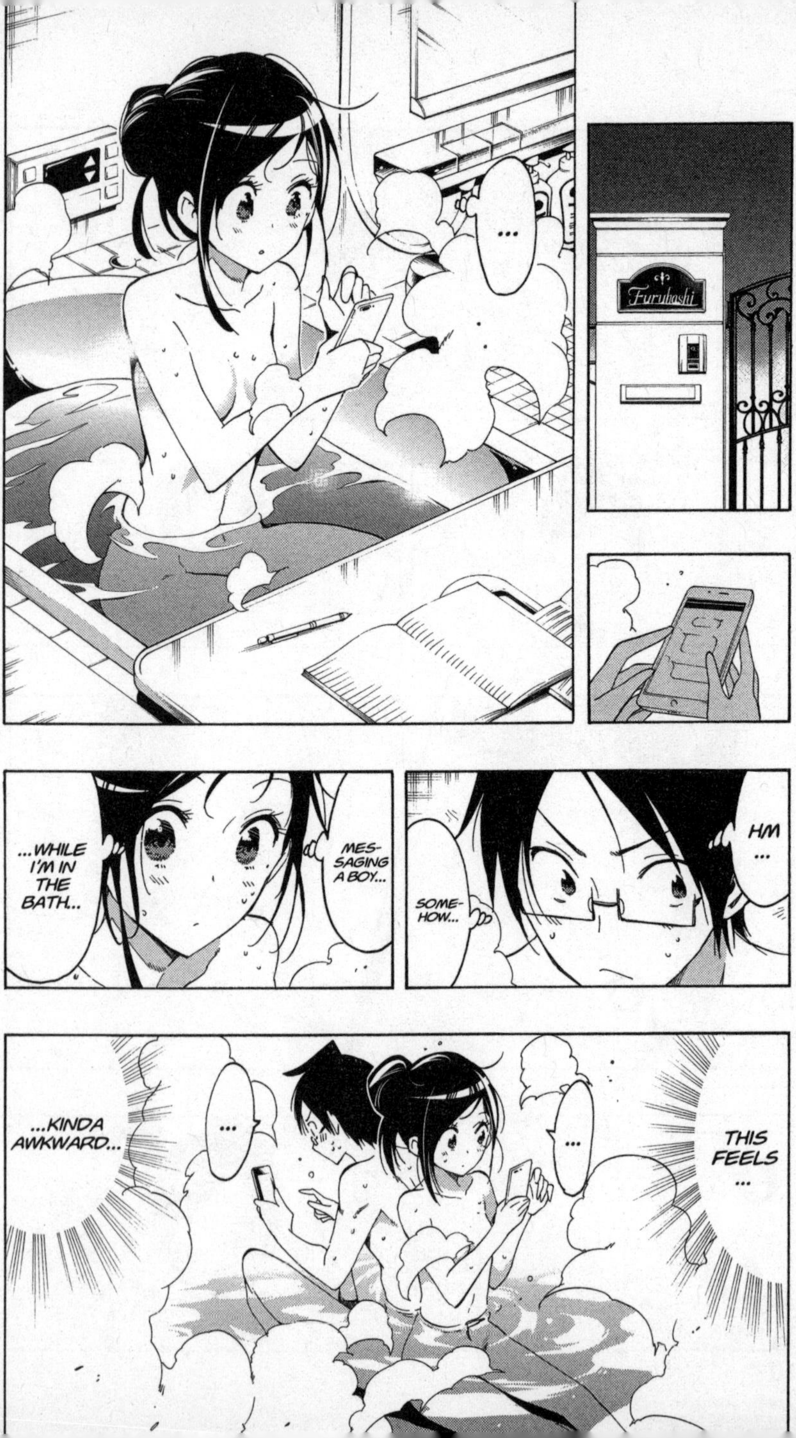
Furuhashi
...
HM ...
SOME-HOW...
MES-SAGING A BOY...
...WHILE I'M IN THE BATH...
THIS FEELS ...
...
...
...KINDA AWKWARD...

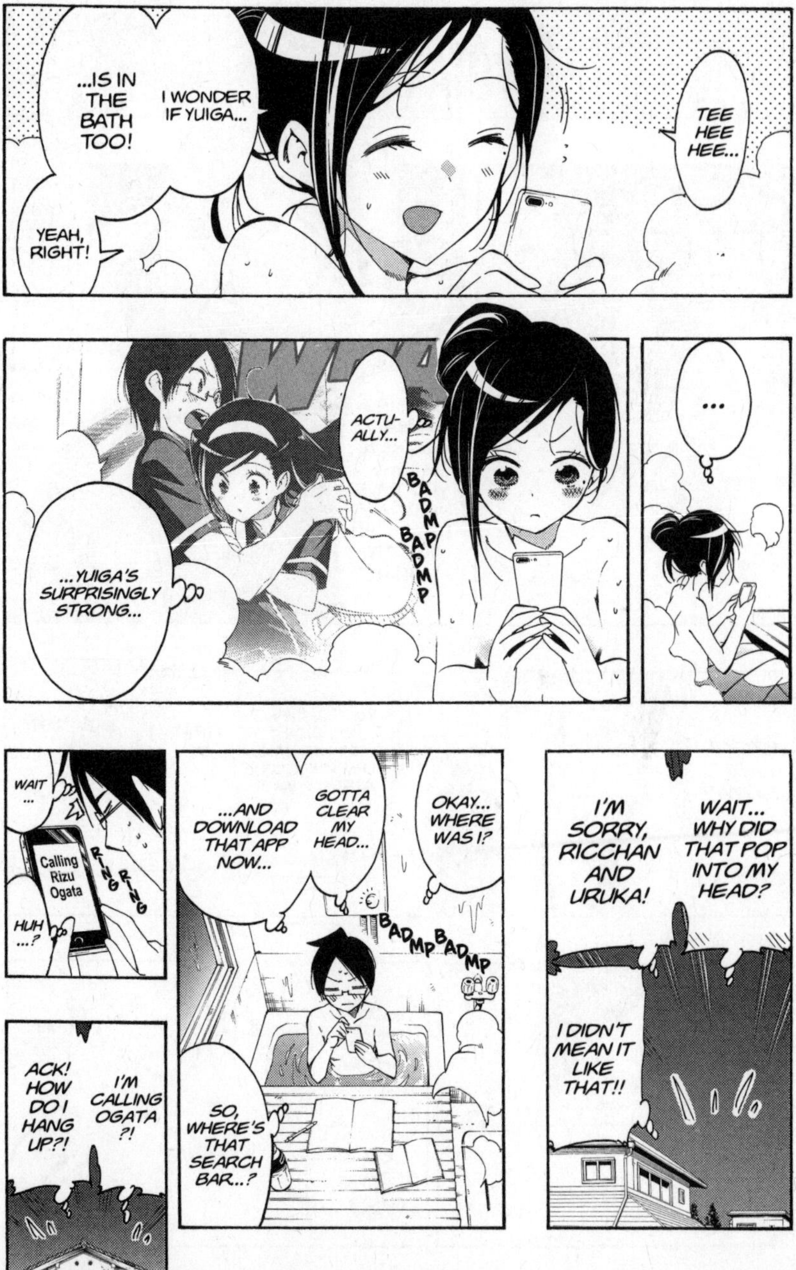
TEE HEE HEE...
I WONDER IF YUIGA...
...IS IN THE BATH TOO!
YEAH, RIGHT!
...
ACTU-ALLY...
BADMP BADMP
...YUIGA'S SURPRISINGLY STRONG...
WAIT... WHY DID THAT POP INTO MY HEAD?
I'M SORRY, RICCHAN AND URUKA!
I DIDN'T MEAN IT LIKE THAT!!
OKAY... WHERE WAS I?
GOTTA CLEAR MY HEAD...
...AND DOWNLOAD THAT APP NOW...
BADMP BADMP
SO, WHERE'S THAT SEARCH BAR...?
WAIT ...
Calling Rizu Ogata
RING RING
HUH ...?
I'M CALLING OGATA ?!
ACK! HOW DO I HANG UP?!

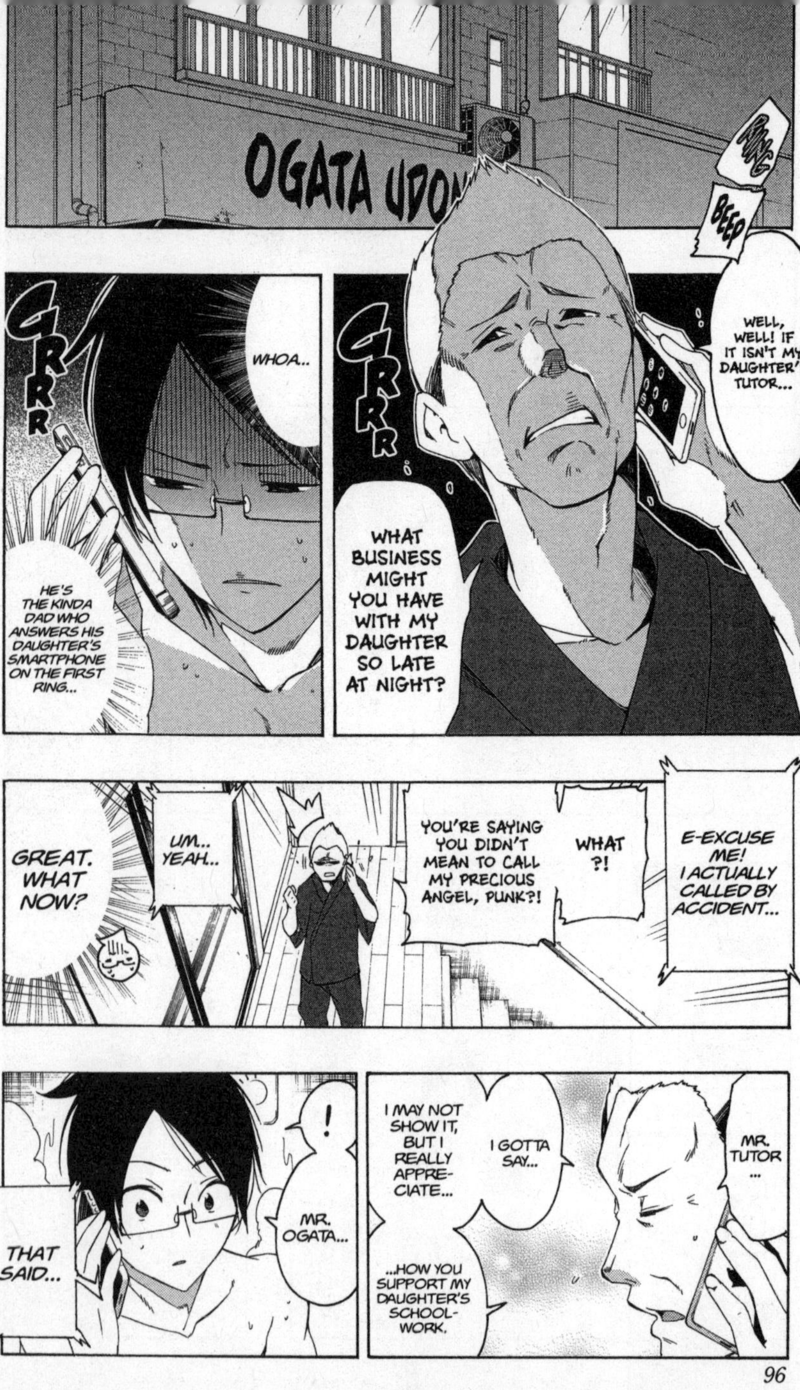
OGATA UDON
RING
BEEP
GRRR
WELL, WELL! IF IT ISN'T MY DAUGHTER'S TUTOR...
WHAT BUSINESS MIGHT YOU HAVE WITH MY DAUGHTER SO LATE AT NIGHT?
GRRR
WHOA..
HE'S THE KINDA DAD WHO ANSWERS HIS DAUGHTER'S SMARTPHONE ON THE FIRST RING...
E-EXCUSE ME! I ACTUALLY CALLED BY ACCIDENT...
WHAT?!
YOU'RE SAYING YOU DIDN'T MEAN TO CALL MY PRECIOUS ANGEL, PUNK?!
UM.. YEAH..
GREAT. WHAT NOW?
MR. TUTOR...
I GOTTA SAY...
I MAY NOT SHOW IT, BUT I REALLY APPRECIATE...
...HOW YOU SUPPORT MY DAUGHTER'S SCHOOLWORK.
!
MR. OGATA...
THAT SAID...

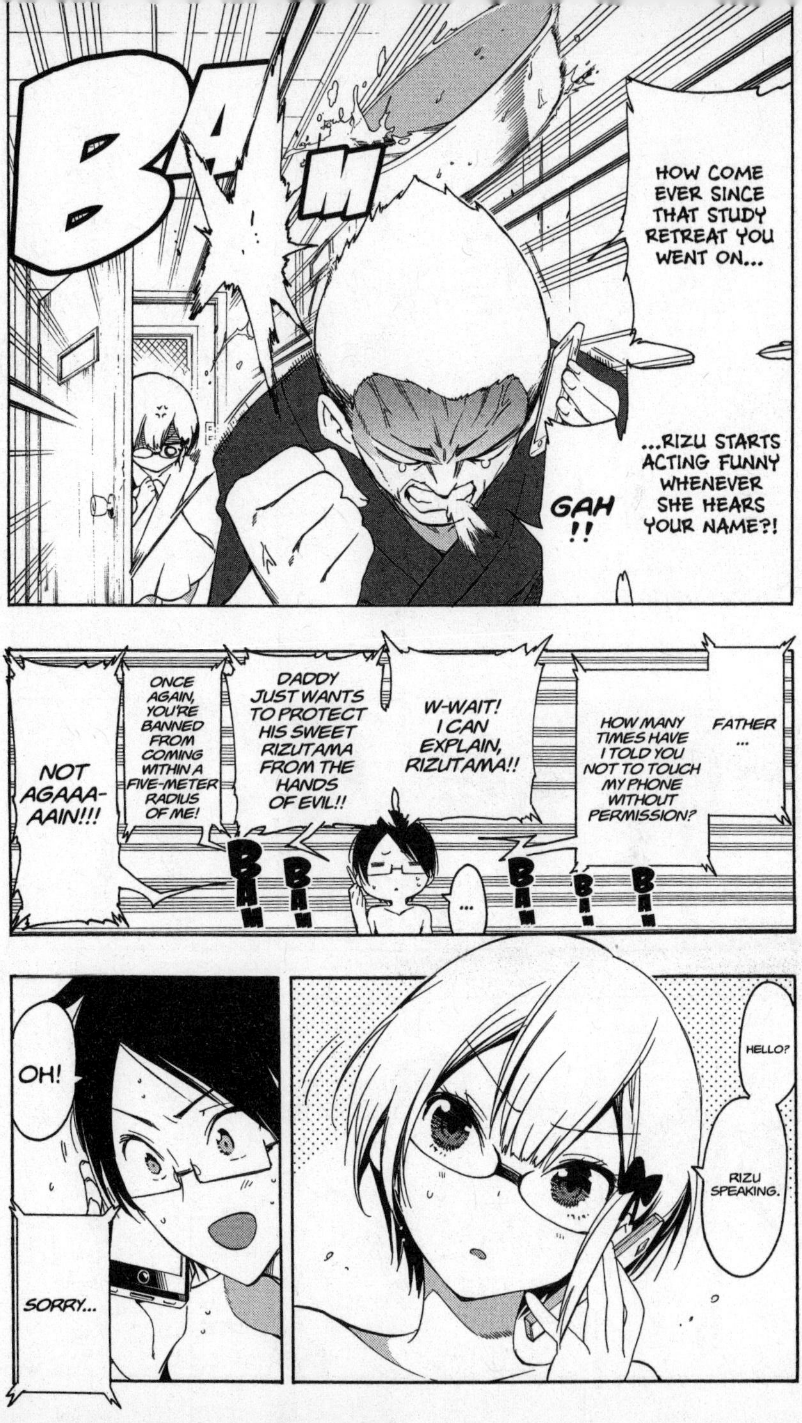
HOW COME EVER SINCE THAT STUDY RETREAT YOU WENT ON...
BAM
...RIZU STARTS ACTING FUNNY WHENEVER SHE HEARS YOUR NAME?!
GAH!!
FATHER...
HOW MANY TIMES HAVE I TOLD YOU NOT TO TOUCH MY PHONE WITHOUT PERMISSION?
BAM
BAM
W-WAIT! I CAN EXPLAIN, RIZUTAMA!!
...
DADDY JUST WANTS TO PROTECT HIS SWEET RIZUTAMA FROM THE HANDS OF EVIL!!
ONCE AGAIN, YOU'RE BANNED FROM COMING WITHIN A FIVE-METER RADIUS OF ME!
BAM
BAM
NOT AGAAAA-AAIN!!!
HELLO?
RIZU SPEAKING.
OH!
SORRY...

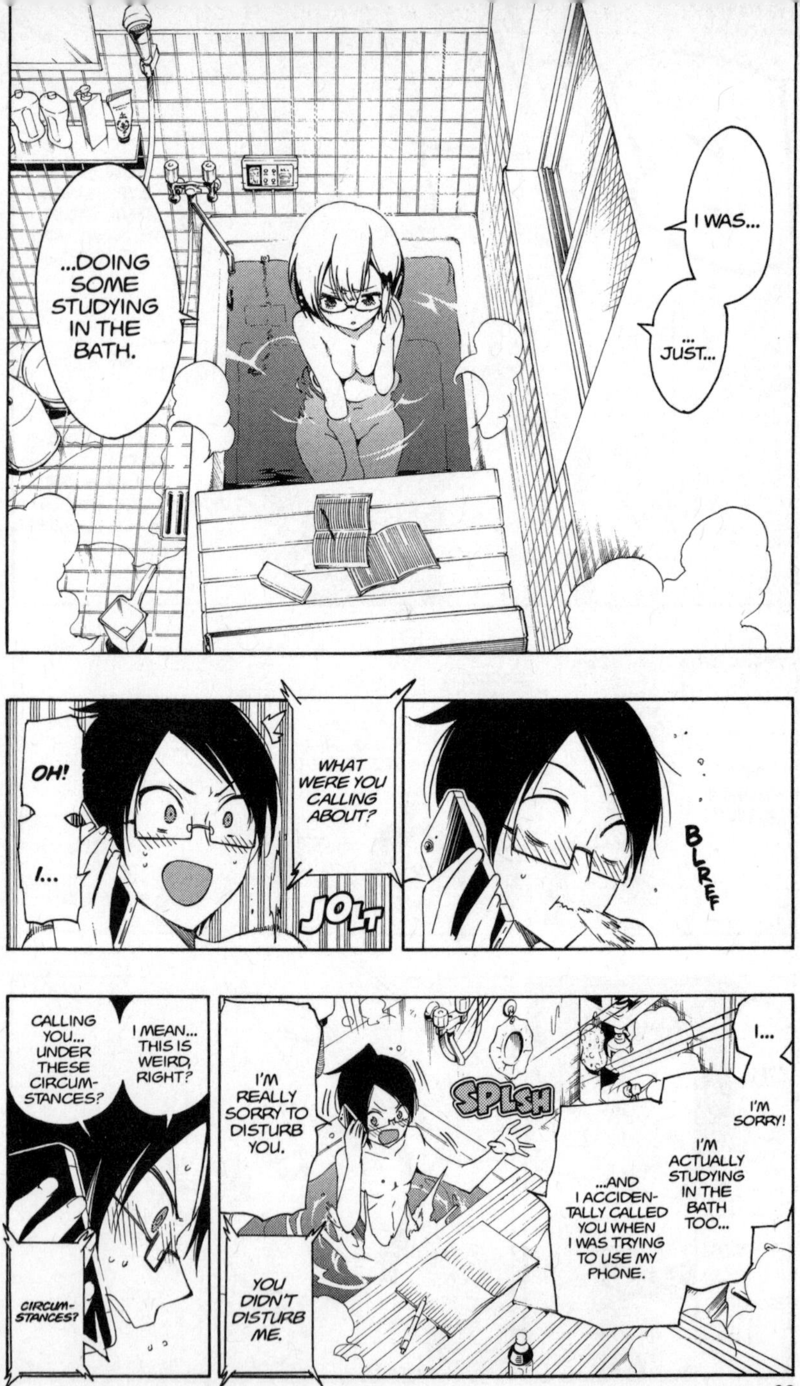
I WAS...
...JUST...
...DOING SOME STUDYING IN THE BATH.
BLREFF
WHAT WERE YOU CALLING ABOUT?
JOLT
OH!
I...
I...
I'M SORRY!
I'M ACTUALLY STUDYING IN THE BATH TOO...
...AND I ACCIDENTALLY CALLED YOU WHEN I WAS TRYING TO USE MY PHONE.
SPLSH
I'M REALLY SORRY TO DISTURB YOU.
YOU DIDN'T DISTURB ME.
I MEAN... THIS IS WEIRD, RIGHT?
CALLING YOU... UNDER THESE CIRCUMSTANCES?
CIRCUMSTANCES?

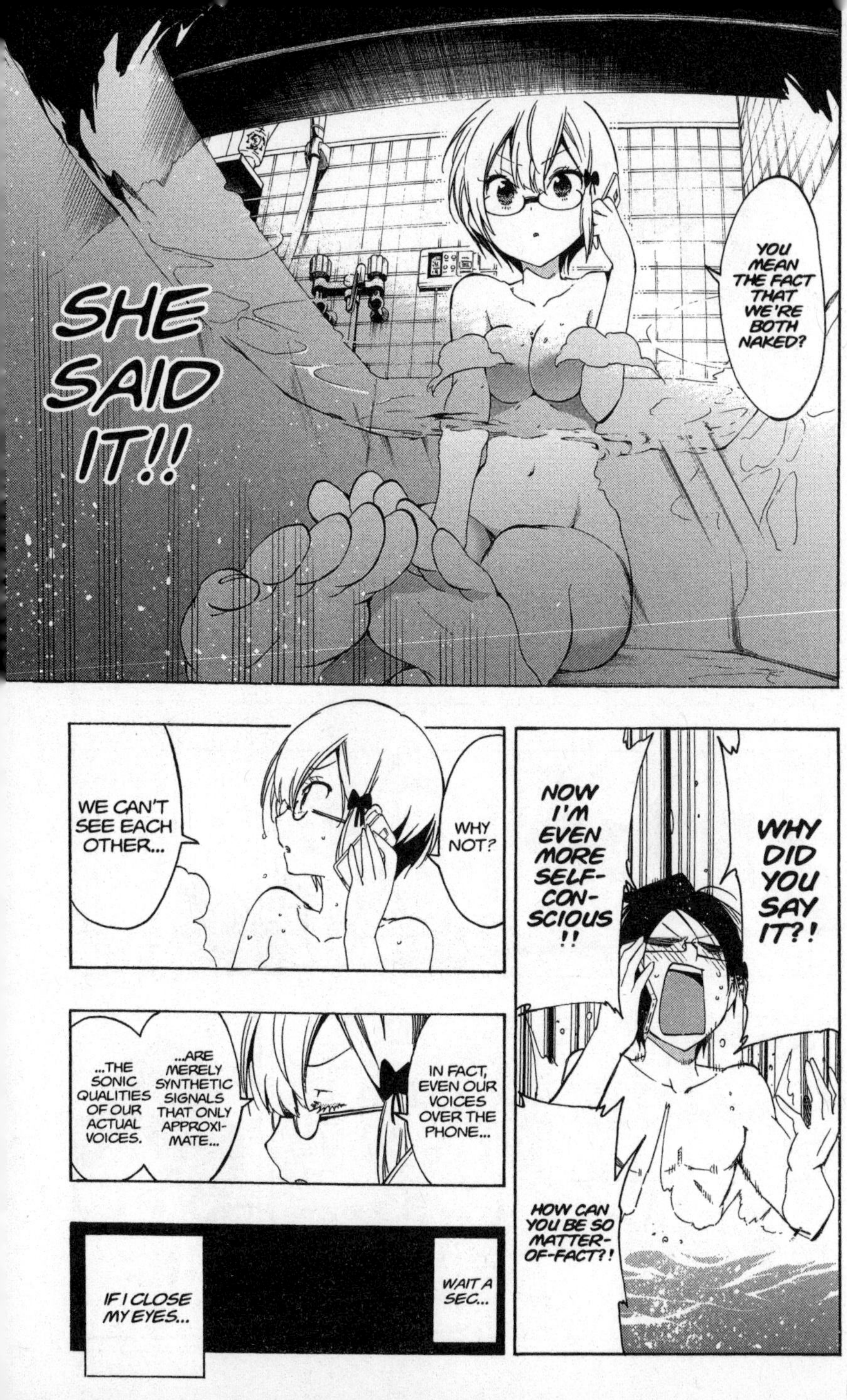

YOU MEAN THE FACT THAT WE'RE BOTH NAKED?
SHE SAID IT!!
WHY DID YOU SAY IT?!
NOW I'M EVEN MORE SELF-CONSCIOUS!!
HOW CAN YOU BE SO MATTER-OF-FACT?!
WHY NOT?
WE CAN'T SEE EACH OTHER...
IN FACT, EVEN OUR VOICES OVER THE PHONE...
...ARE MERELY SYNTHETIC SIGNALS THAT ONLY APPROXI-MATE...
...THE SONIC QUALITIES OF OUR ACTUAL VOICES.
WAIT A SEC...
IF I CLOSE MY EYES...

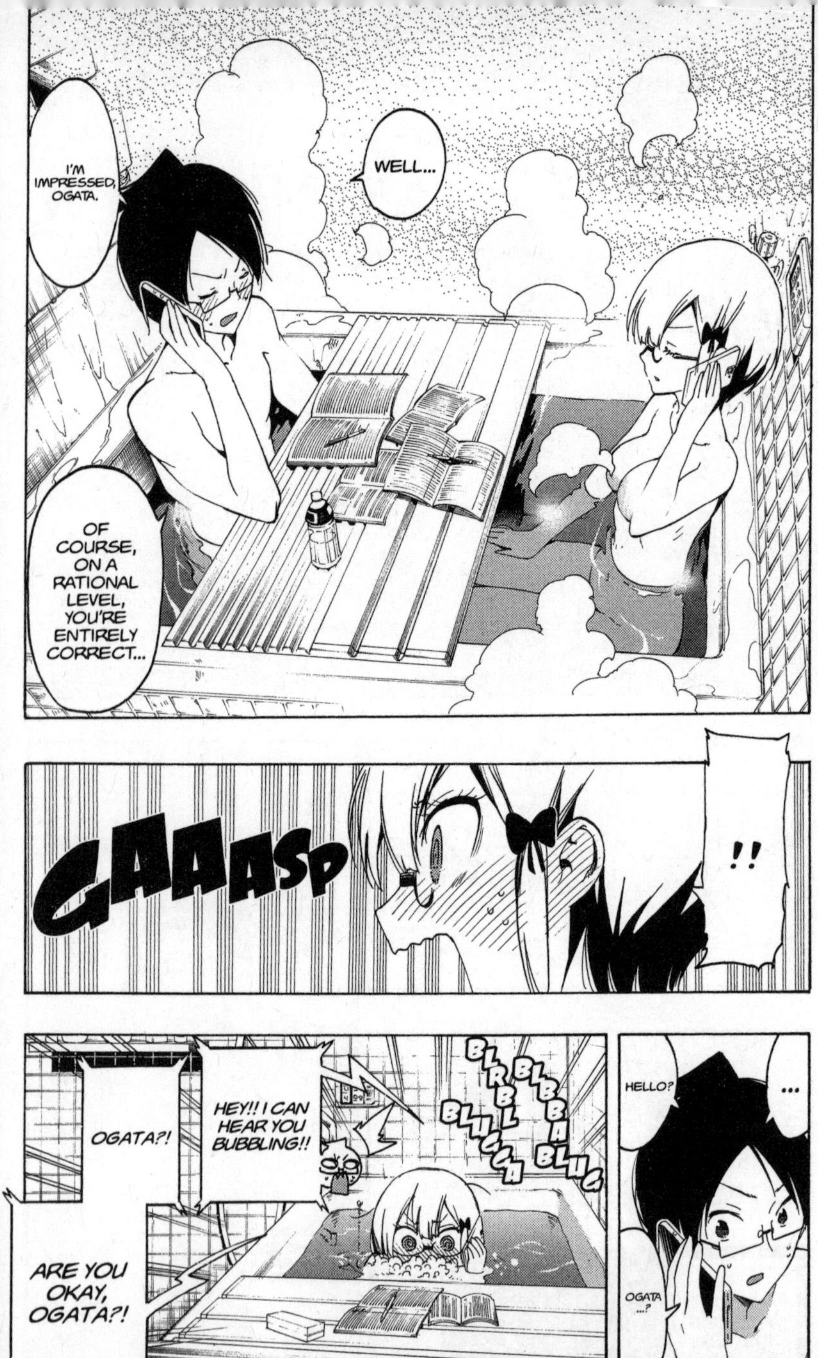
I'M IMPRESSED, OGATA.
WELL...
OF COURSE, ON A RATIONAL LEVEL, YOU'RE ENTIRELY CORRECT...
!!
GAAASP
...
HELLO?
OGATA ...?
BLBBABLUG
BLRBLBLUGGA
HEY!! I CAN HEAR YOU BUBBLING!!
OGATA?!
ARE YOU OKAY, OGATA?!

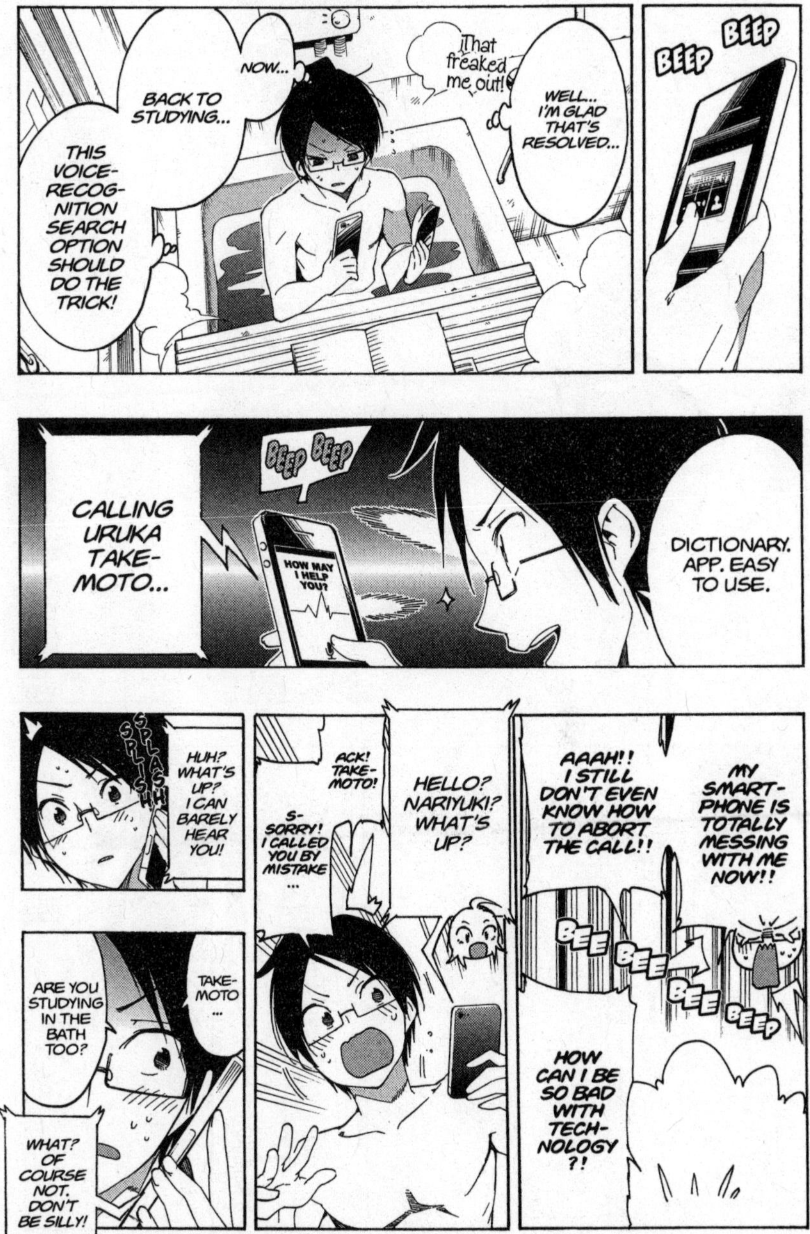
BEEP BEEP
WELL... I'M GLAD THAT'S RESOLVED...
That freaked me out!
NOW...
BACK TO STUDYING...
THIS VOICE-RECOGNITION SEARCH OPTION SHOULD DO THE TRICK!
DICTIONARY. APP. EASY TO USE.
BEEP BEEP
HOW MAY I HELP YOU?
CALLING URUKA TAKEMOTO...
MY SMARTPHONE IS TOTALLY MESSING WITH ME NOW!!
AAAH!! I STILL DON'T EVEN KNOW HOW TO ABORT THE CALL!!
BEE BEE BEE BEEP
HOW CAN I BE SO BAD WITH TECHNOLOGY?!
HELLO? NARIYUKI? WHAT'S UP?
ACK! TAKEMOTO!
S-SORRY! I CALLED YOU BY MISTAKE...
SPLISH SPLASH
HUH? WHAT'S UP? I CAN BARELY HEAR YOU!
TAKEMOTO...
ARE YOU STUDYING IN THE BATH TOO?
WHAT? OF COURSE NOT. DON'T BE SILLY!

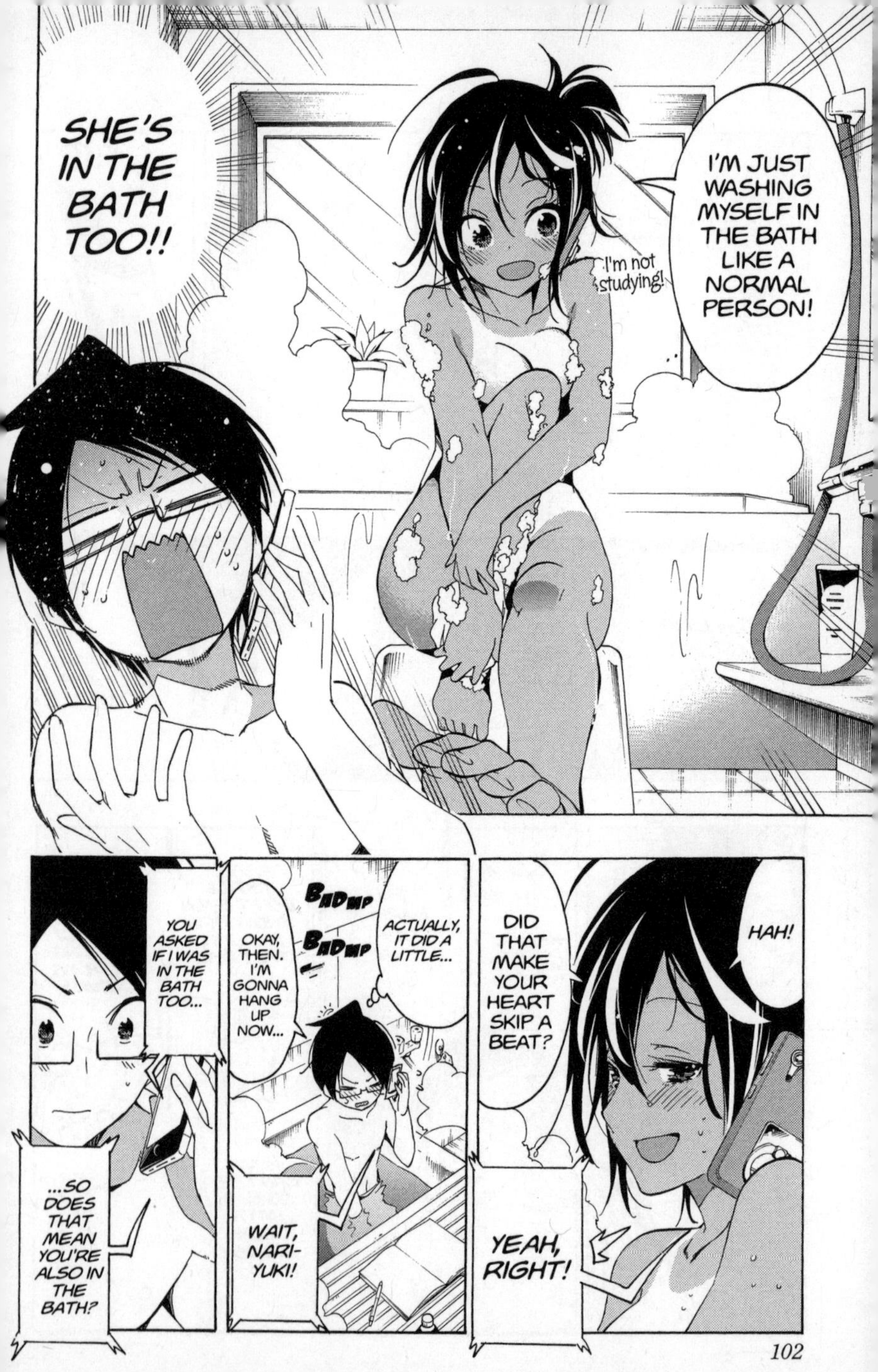
I'M JUST WASHING MYSELF IN THE BATH LIKE A NORMAL PERSON!
I'm not studying!
SHE'S IN THE BATH TOO!!
HAH!
DID THAT MAKE YOUR HEART SKIP A BEAT?
YEAH, RIGHT!
ACTUALLY, IT DID A LITTLE...
BADUMP
BADUMP
OKAY, THEN. I'M GONNA HANG UP NOW...
WAIT, NARI-YUKI!
YOU ASKED IF I WAS IN THE BATH TOO...
...SO DOES THAT MEAN YOU'RE ALSO IN THE BATH?

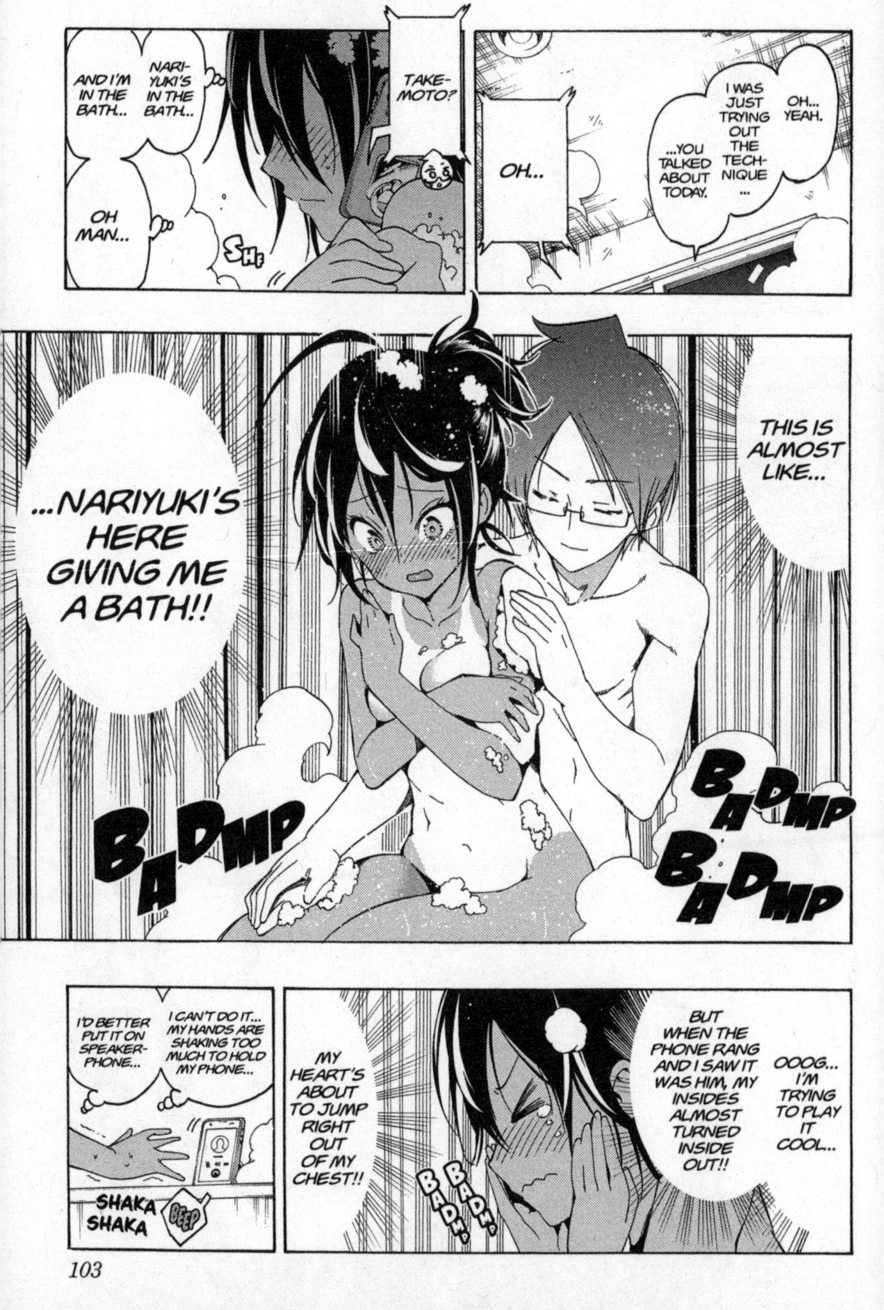
OH... YEAH.
I WAS JUST TRYING OUT THE TECHNIQUE...
...YOU TALKED ABOUT TODAY.
OH...
TAKE-MOTO?
NARI-YUKI'S IN THE BATH...
AND I'M IN THE BATH...
OH MAN...
SHF
THIS IS ALMOST LIKE...
...NARIYUKI'S HERE GIVING ME A BATH!!
BADMP
BADMP
BADMP
OOOG... I'M TRYING TO PLAY IT COOL...
BUT WHEN THE PHONE RANG AND I SAW IT WAS HIM, MY INSIDES ALMOST TURNED INSIDE OUT!!
MY HEART'S ABOUT TO JUMP RIGHT OUT OF MY CHEST!!
BADMP
BADMP
I CAN'T DO IT... MY HANDS ARE SHAKING TOO MUCH TO HOLD MY PHONE...
I'D BETTER PUT IT ON SPEAKER-PHONE...
BEEP
SHAKA SHAKA

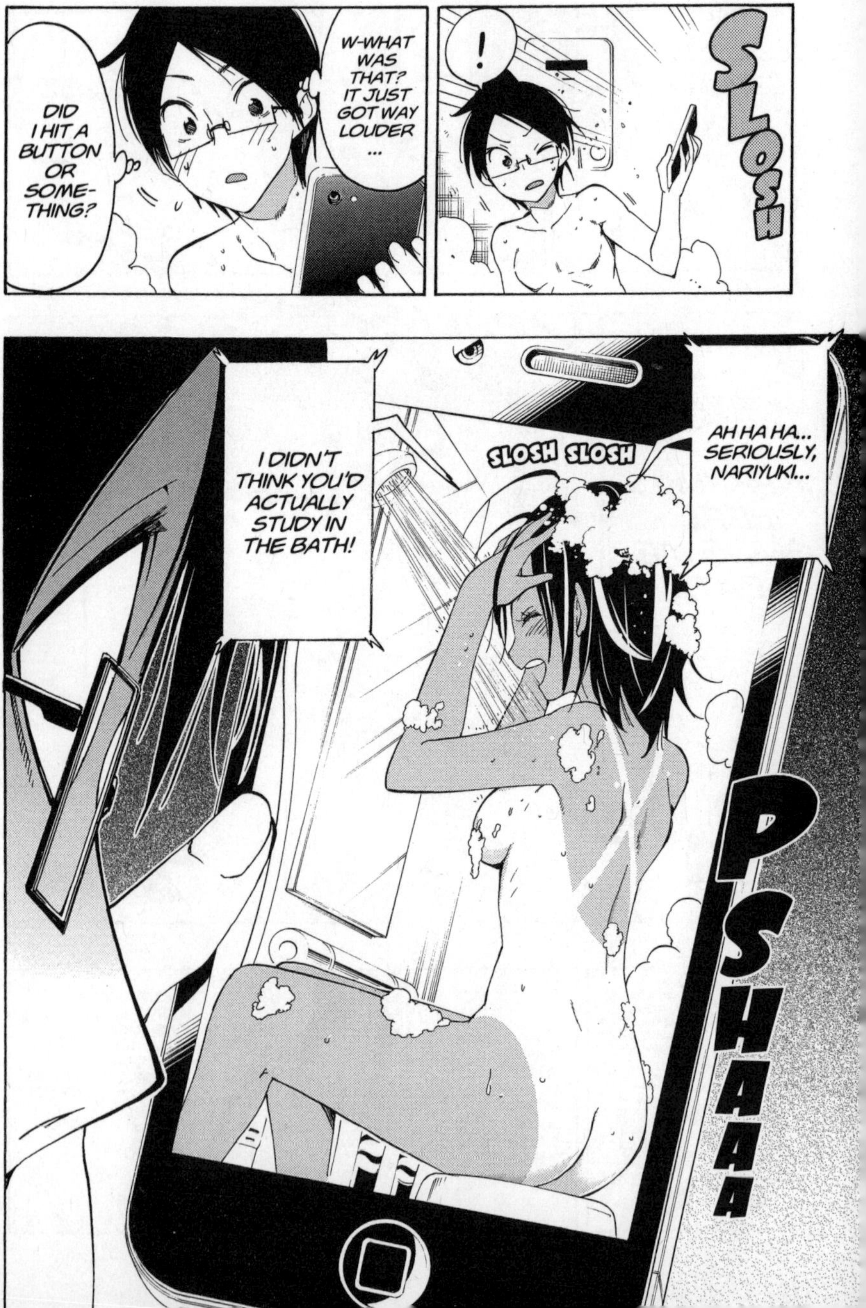
!
SLOSH
W-WHAT WAS THAT? IT JUST GOT WAY LOUDER ...
DID I HIT A BUTTON OR SOMETHING?
AH HA HA... SERIOUSLY, NARIYUKI...
SLOSH SLOSH
I DIDN'T THINK YOU'D ACTUALLY STUDY IN THE BATH!
PSHAAA

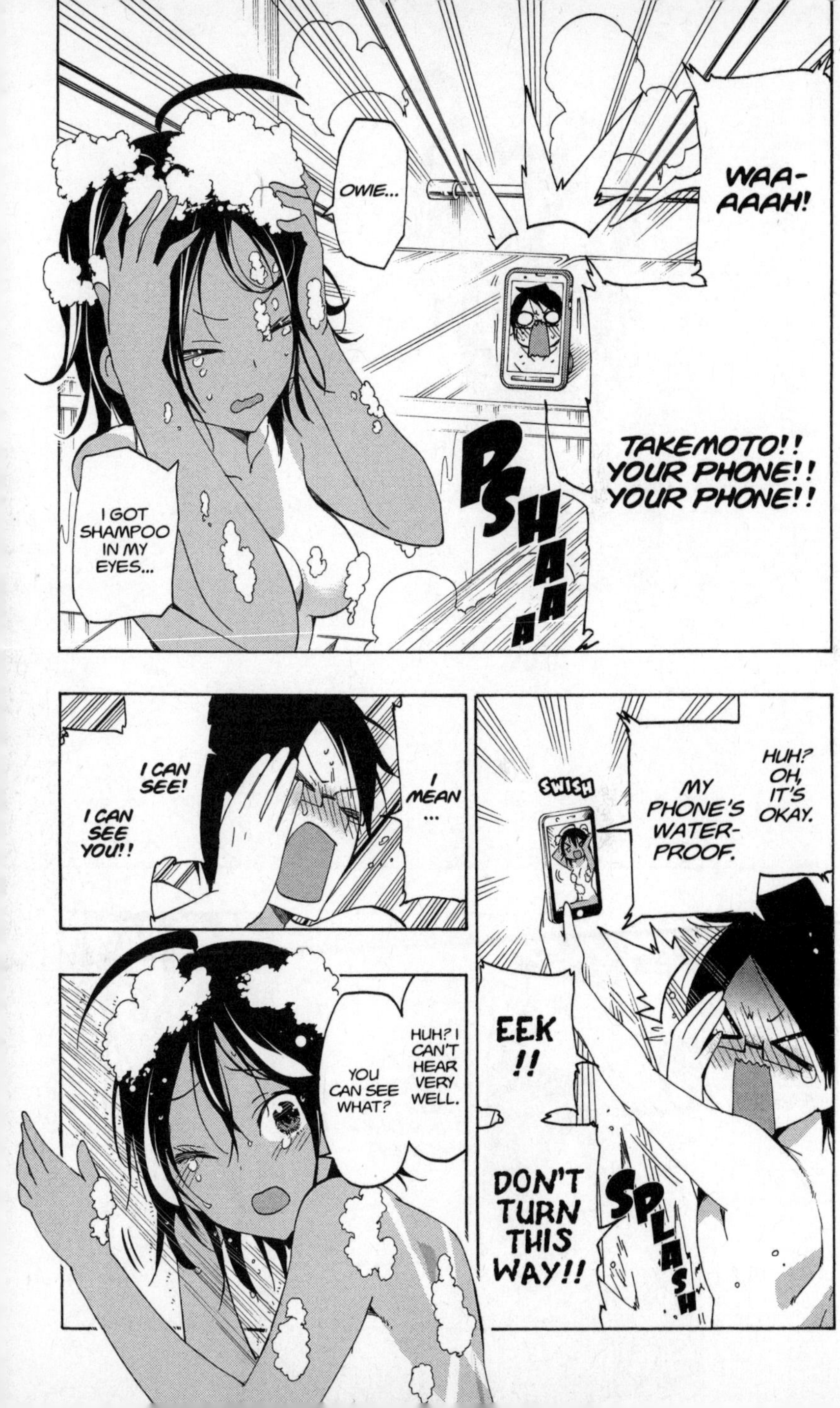
WAA-AAAH!
OWIE...
TAKEMOTO!! YOUR PHONE!! YOUR PHONE!!
PSHAAAA
I GOT SHAMPOO IN MY EYES...
HUH? OH, IT'S OKAY.
MY PHONE'S WATER-PROOF.
SWISH
EEK!!
DON'T TURN THIS WAY!!
SPLASH
I MEAN...
I CAN SEE!
I CAN SEE YOU!!
HUH? I CAN'T HEAR VERY WELL.
YOU CAN SEE WHAT?

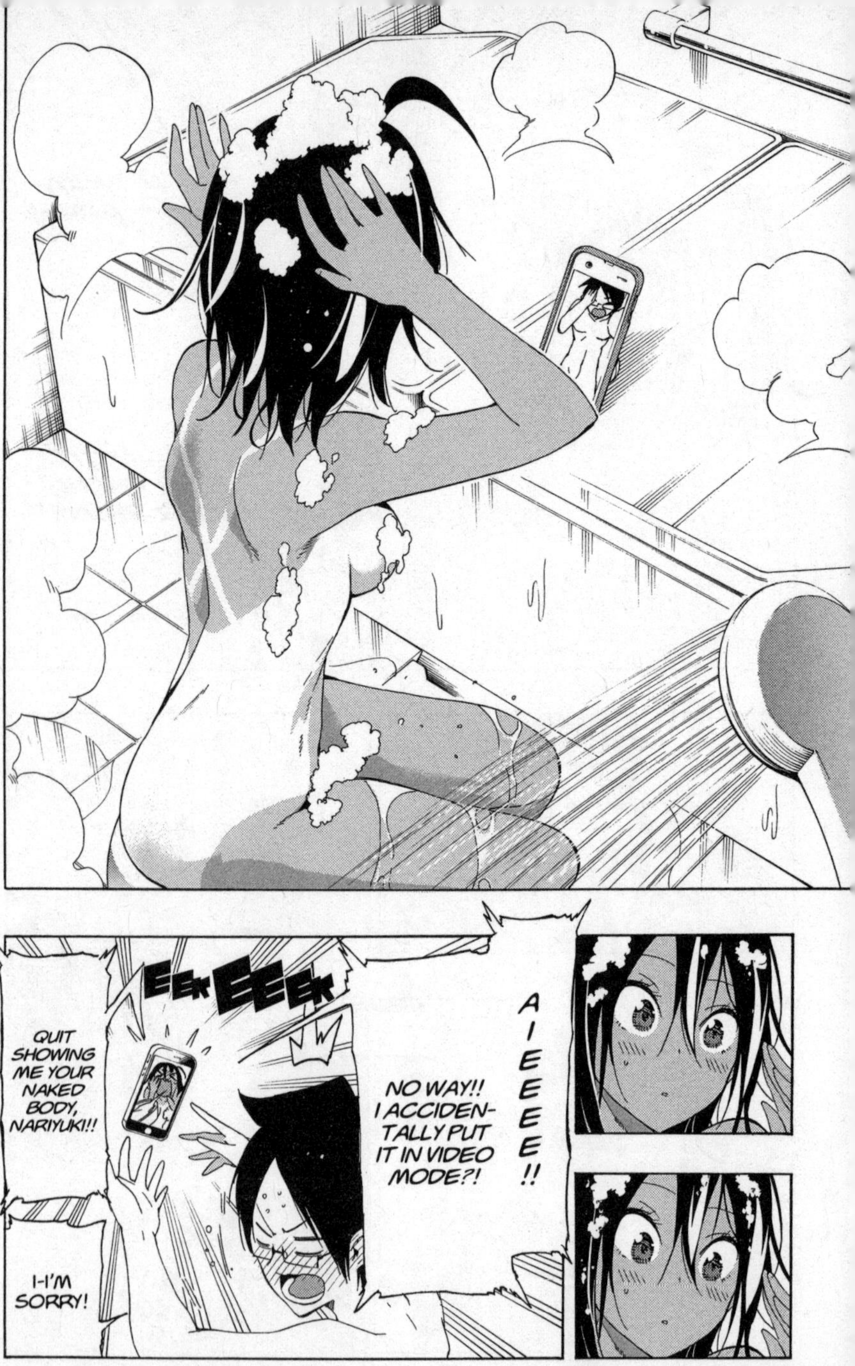
AIEEEEE!!
EEK EEEK
NO WAY!! I ACCIDEN-TALLY PUT IT IN VIDEO MODE?!
QUIT SHOWING ME YOUR NAKED BODY, NARIYUKI!!
I-I'M SORRY!

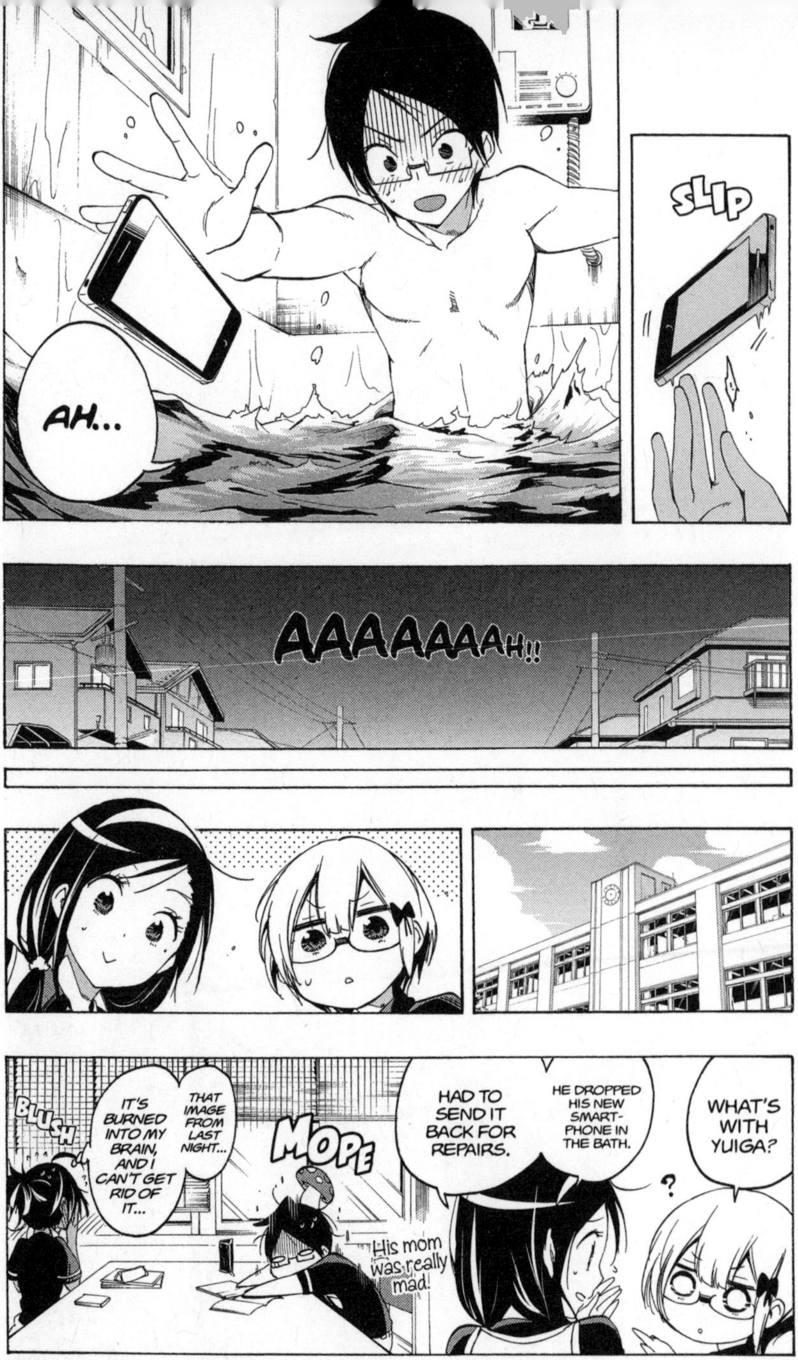
SLIP
AH...
AAAAAAAH!!
WHAT'S WITH YUIGA?
?
HE DROPPED HIS NEW SMART-PHONE IN THE BATH.
HAD TO SEND IT BACK FOR REPAIRS.
His mom was really mad!
MOPE
THAT IMAGE FROM LAST NIGHT...
IT'S BURNED INTO MY BRAIN, AND I CAN'T GET RID OF IT...
BLUSH

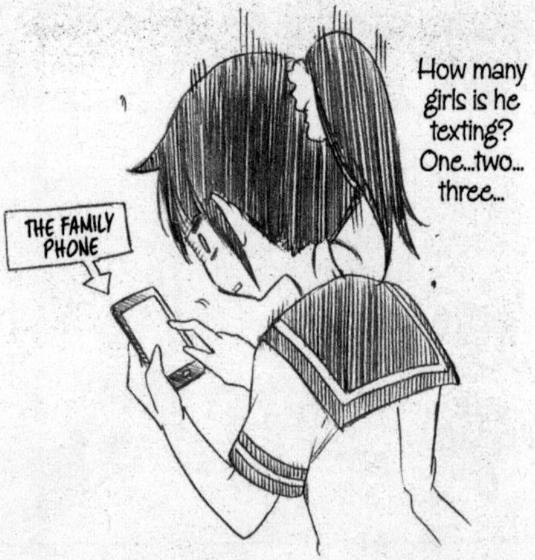
How many girls is he texting? One...two... three...
THE FAMILY PHONE

Question 22:
A Former Tutor's Secret Spot Is [*X*]

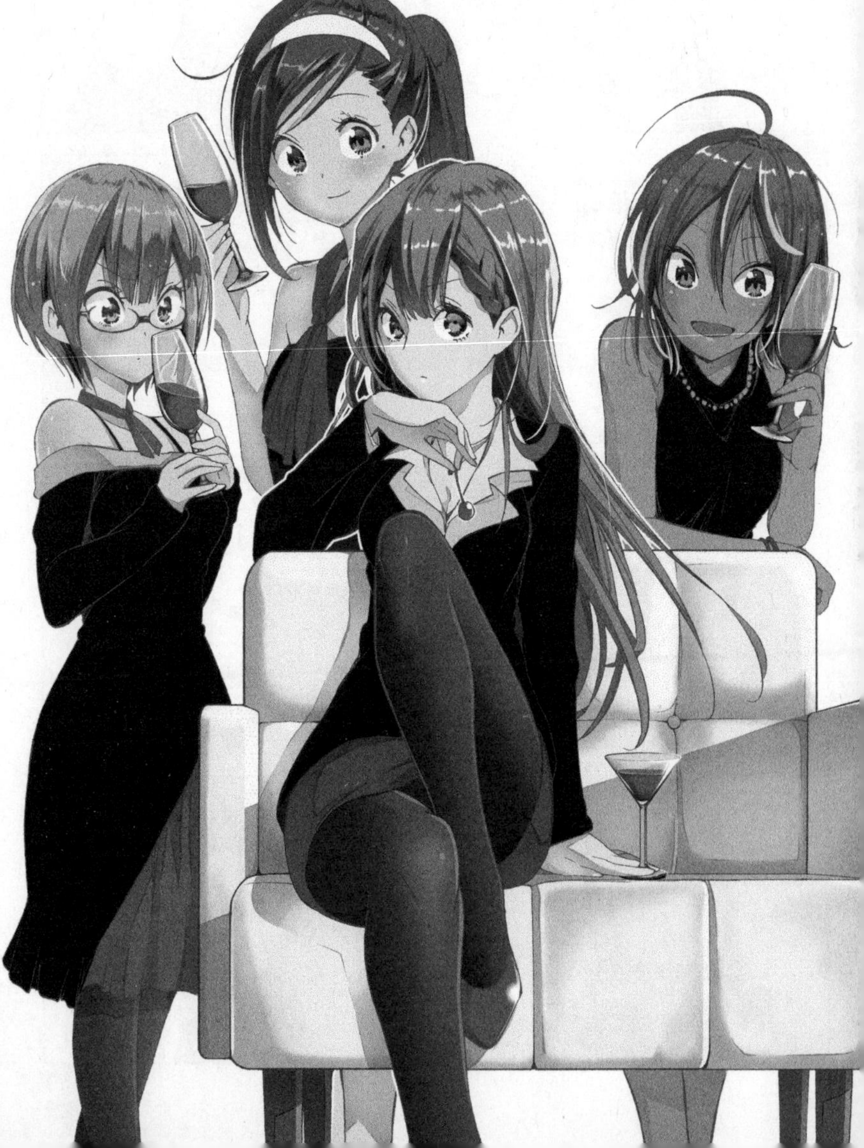

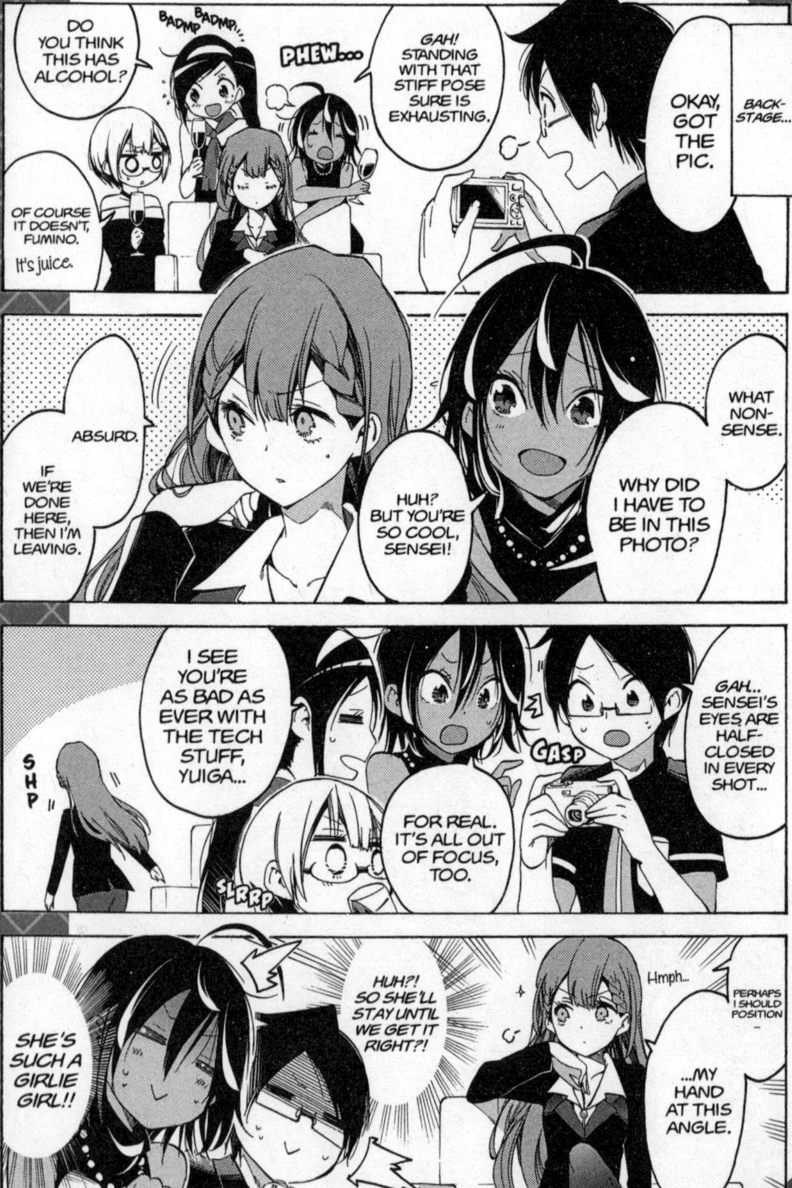
BACKSTAGE...
OKAY, GOT THE PIC.
GAH! STANDING WITH THAT STIFF POSE SURE IS EXHAUSTING.
PHEW...
BADMP BADMP
DO YOU THINK THIS HAS ALCOHOL?
OF COURSE IT DOESN'T, FUMINO.
It's juice.
WHAT NONSENSE.
WHY DID I HAVE TO BE IN THIS PHOTO?
HUH? BUT YOU'RE SO COOL, SENSEI!
ABSURD.
IF WE'RE DONE HERE, THEN I'M LEAVING.
GAH... SENSEI'S EYES ARE HALF-CLOSED IN EVERY SHOT...
GASP
I SEE YOU'RE AS BAD AS EVER WITH THE TECH STUFF, YUIGA...
FOR REAL. IT'S ALL OUT OF FOCUS, TOO.
SLRRP
SHP
PERHAPS I SHOULD POSITION...
...MY HAND AT THIS ANGLE.
Hmph...
HUH?! SO SHE'LL STAY UNTIL WE GET IT RIGHT?!
SHE'S SUCH A GIRLIE GIRL!!

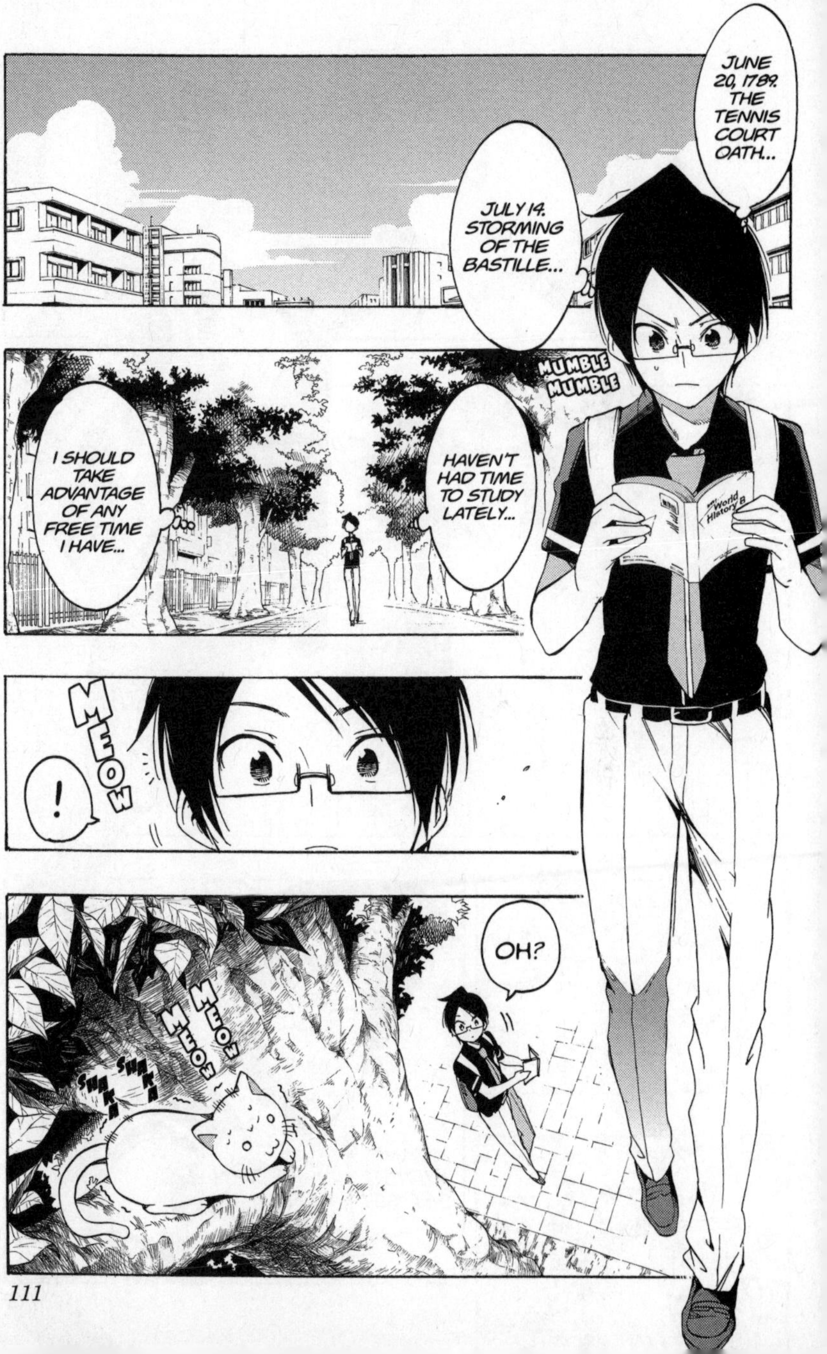

JUNE 20, 1789. THE TENNIS COURT OATH...
JULY 14. STORMING OF THE BASTILLE...
MUMBLE MUMBLE
World History B
HAVEN'T HAD TIME TO STUDY LATELY...
I SHOULD TAKE ADVANTAGE OF ANY FREE TIME I HAVE...
MEOW
!
OH?
MEOW MEOW
SHAKA SHAKA

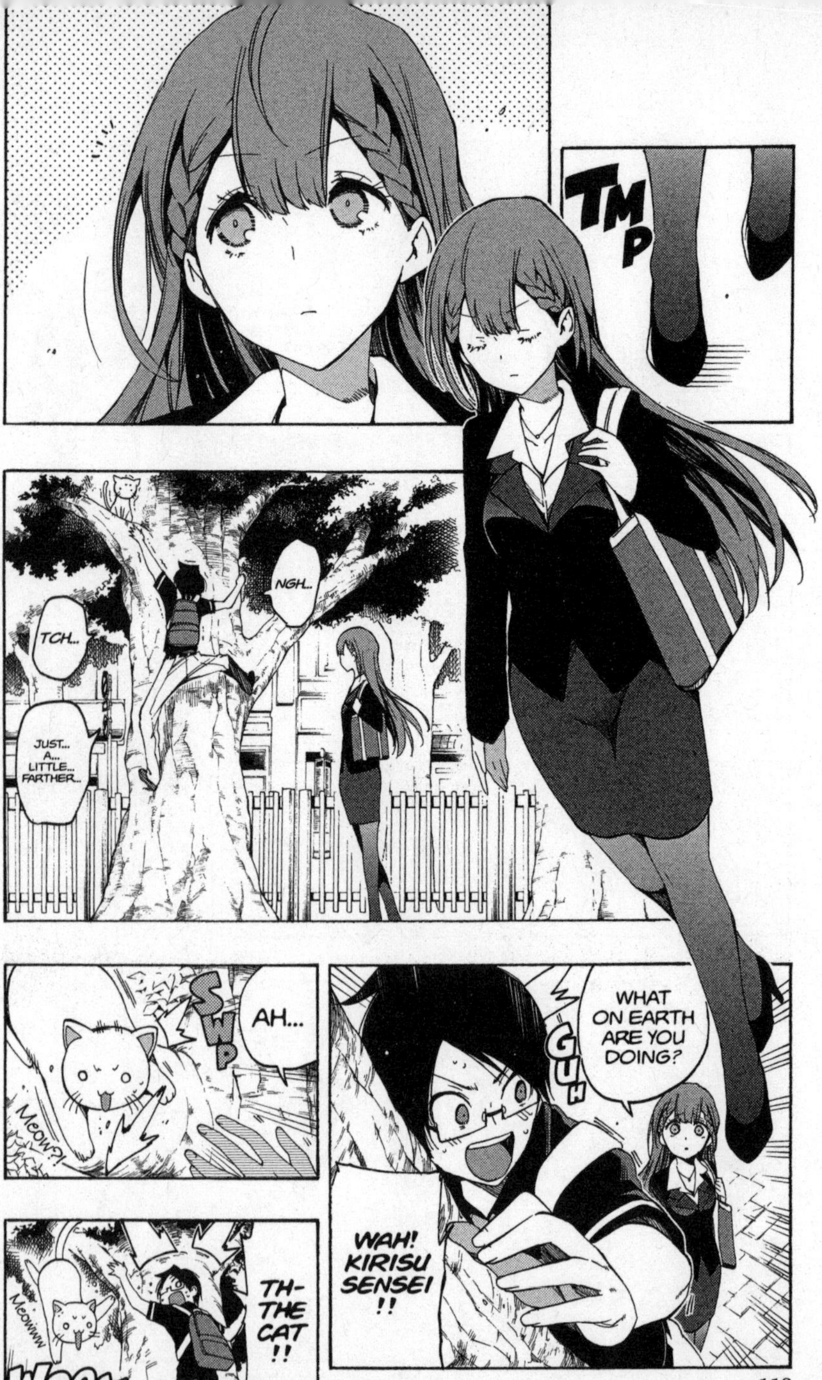
TMP
NGH..
TCH..
JUST... A... LITTLE... FARTHER..
WHAT ON EARTH ARE YOU DOING?
GUH
WAH! KIRISU SENSEI!!
AH...
SWP
Meeow?!
TH-THE CAT!!
Meowww
WOOSH

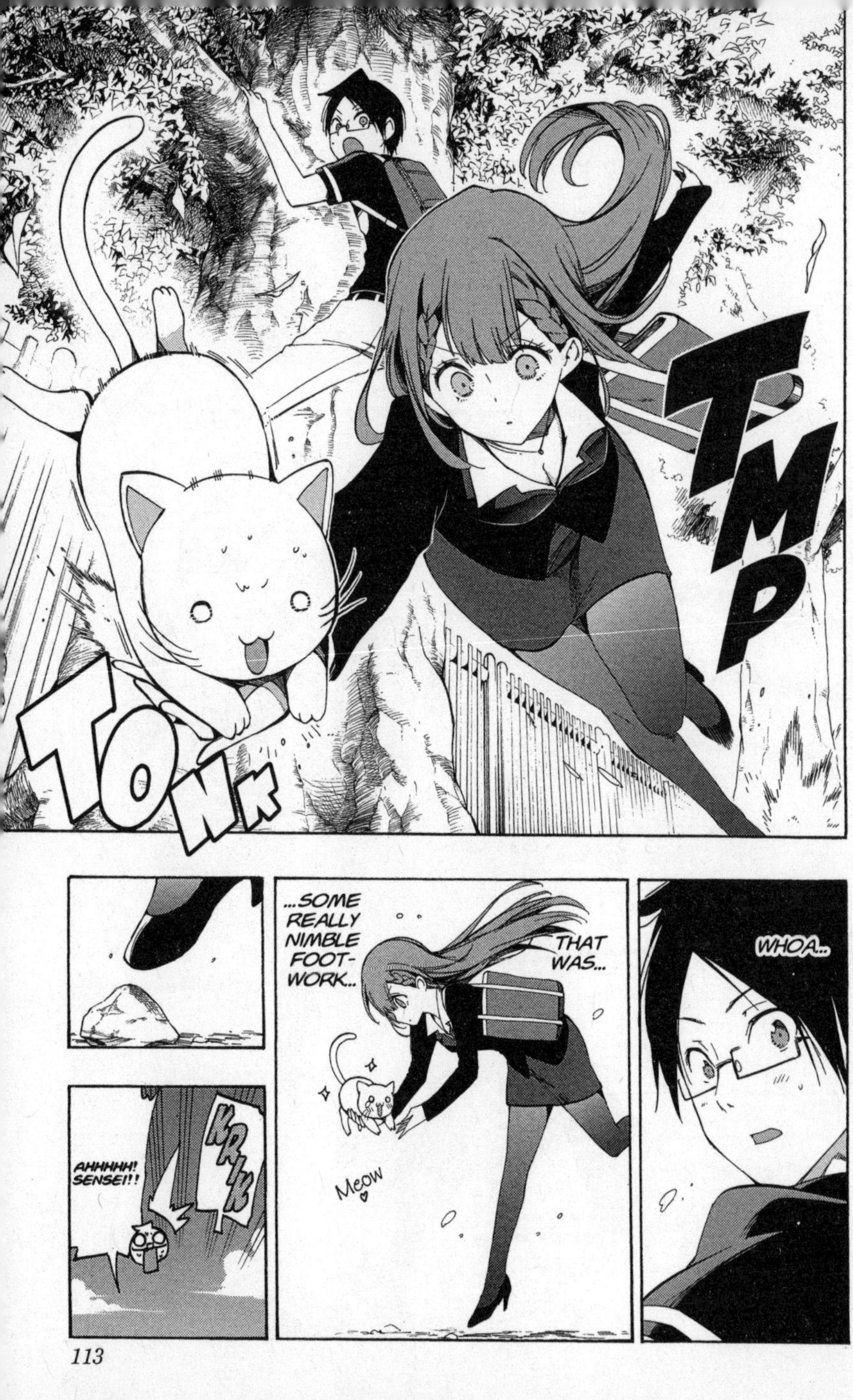
TMP
TONK
WHOA...
THAT WAS...
...SOME REALLY NIMBLE FOOT-WORK...
Meow
KRIK
AHHHHH! SENSEI!!

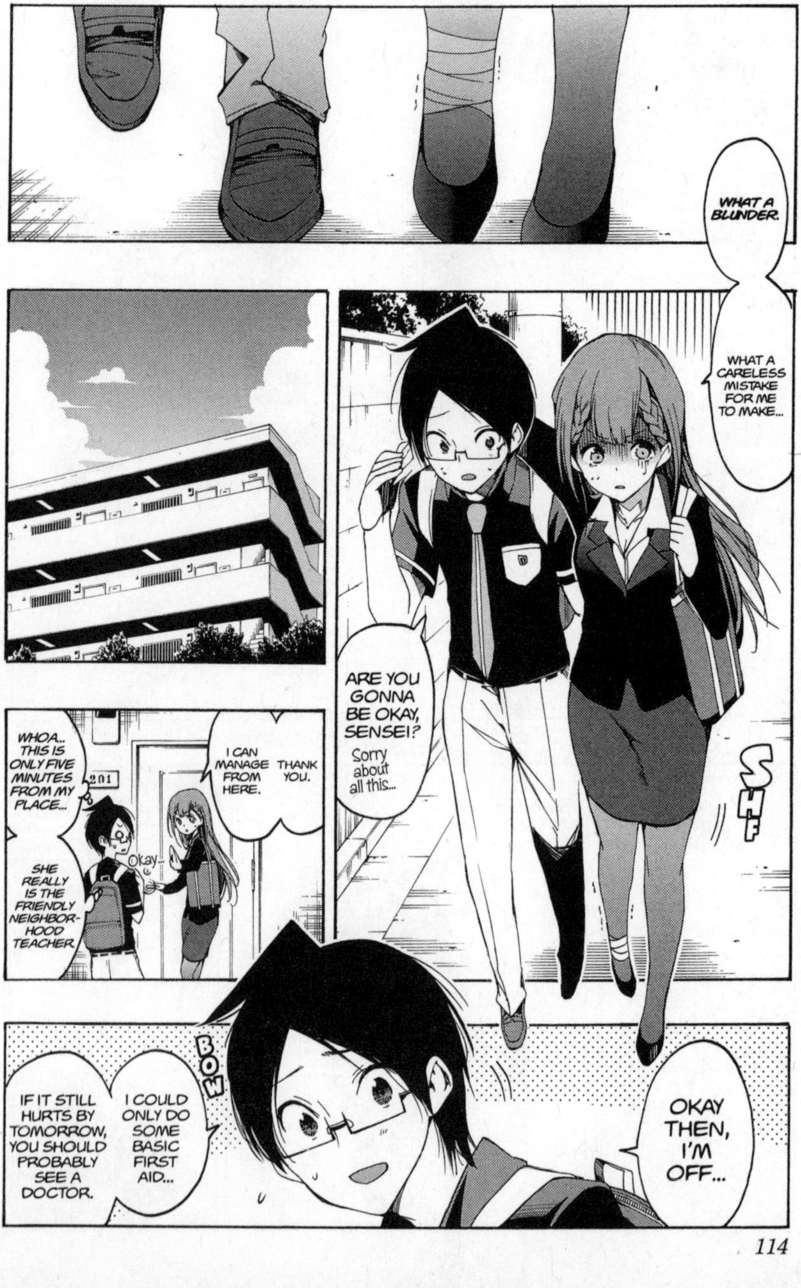
WHAT A BLUNDER.
WHAT A CARELESS MISTAKE FOR ME TO MAKE...
ARE YOU GONNA BE OKAY, SENSEI?
Sorry about all this...
SHF
I CAN MANAGE FROM HERE. THANK YOU.
Okay...
WHOA... THIS IS ONLY FIVE MINUTES FROM MY PLACE...
SHE REALLY IS THE FRIENDLY NEIGHBOR-HOOD TEACHER.
201
OKAY THEN, I'M OFF...
BOW
I COULD ONLY DO SOME BASIC FIRST AID...
IF IT STILL HURTS BY TOMORROW, YOU SHOULD PROBABLY SEE A DOCTOR.

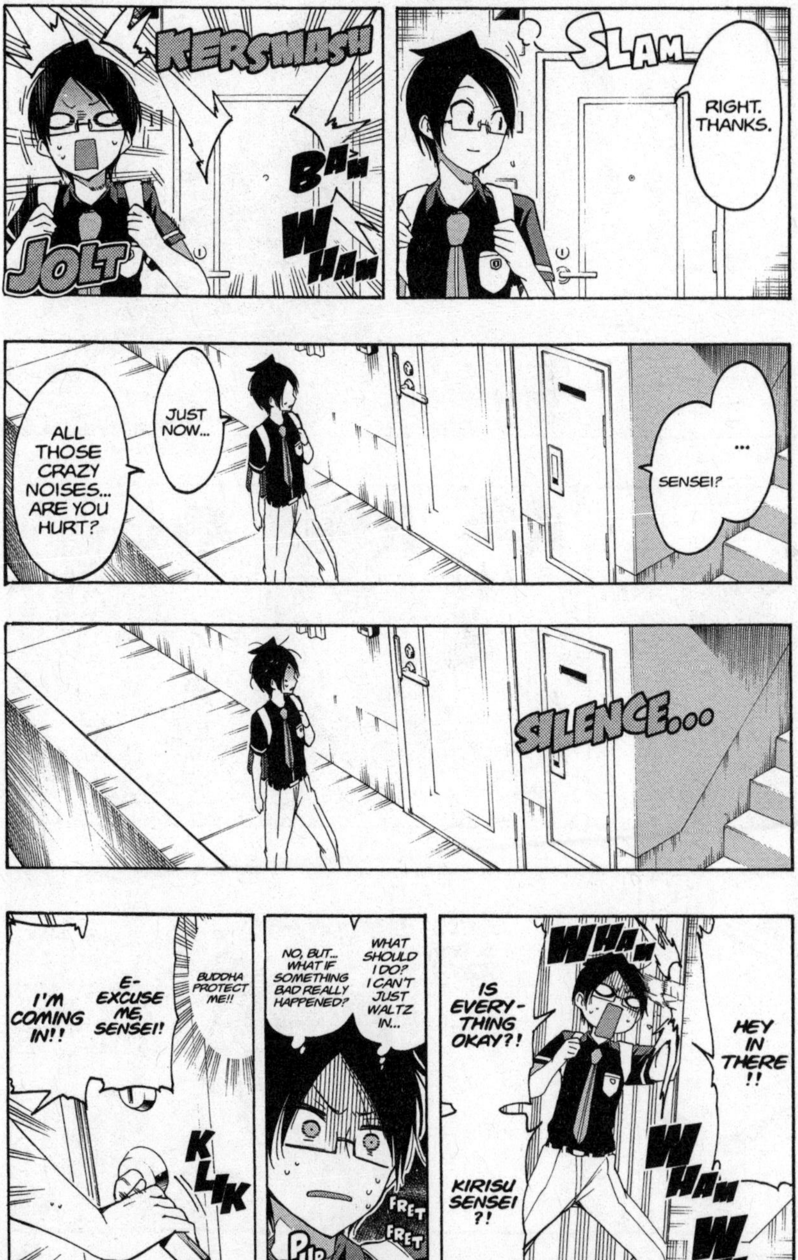
SLAM
RIGHT. THANKS.
KERSMASH
BAM
WHAM
JOLT
...
SENSEI?
JUST NOW...
ALL THOSE CRAZY NOISES... ARE YOU HURT?
SILENCE...
WHAM
HEY IN THERE!!
IS EVERY-THING OKAY?!
KIRISU SENSEI?!
WHAM
WHAM
WHAT SHOULD I DO? I CAN'T JUST WALTZ IN...
NO, BUT... WHAT IF SOMETHING BAD REALLY HAPPENED?
FRET FRET
PLIP PLIP
BUDDHA PROTECT ME!!
E-EXCUSE ME, SENSEI!
I'M COMING IN!!
KLIK

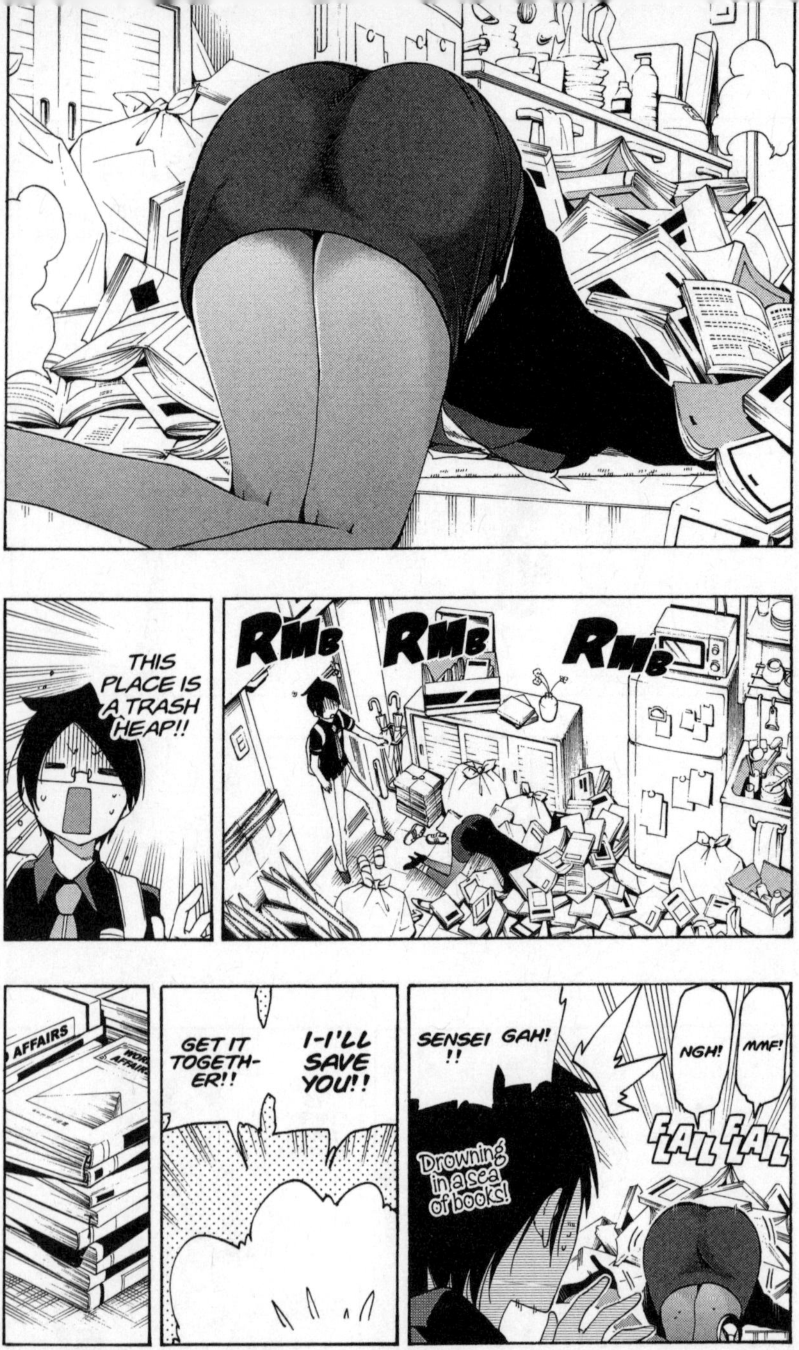
RMB
RMB
RMB
THIS PLACE IS A TRASH HEAP!!
MMF!
NGH!
GAH!
SENSEI!!
FLAIL FLAIL
Drowning in a sea of books!
I-I'LL SAVE YOU!!
GET IT TOGETHER!!
AFFAIRS

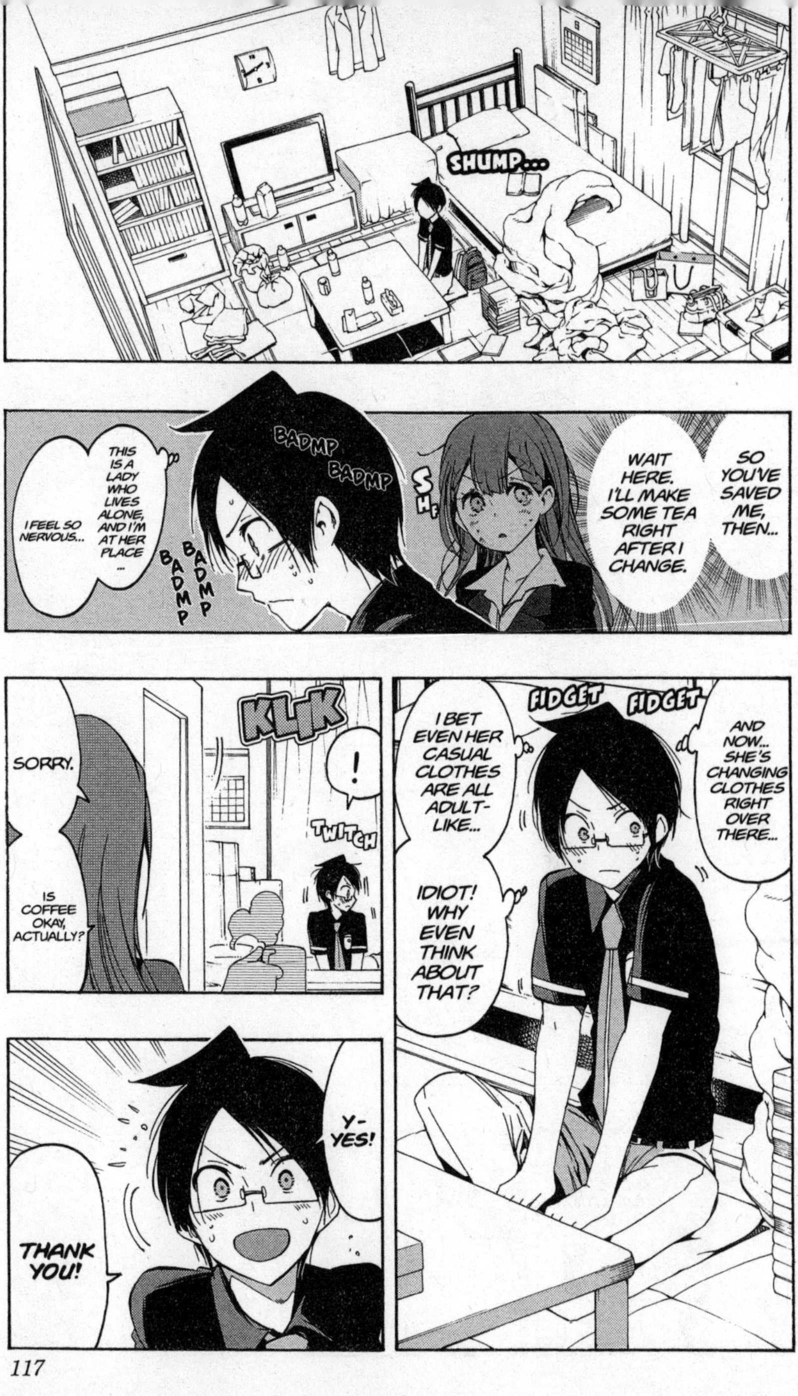
SHUMP...
SO YOU'VE SAVED ME, THEN...
WAIT HERE. I'LL MAKE SOME TEA RIGHT AFTER I CHANGE.
SHF
BADMP BADMP
BADMP BADMP
THIS IS A LADY WHO LIVES ALONE, AND I'M AT HER PLACE...
I FEEL SO NERVOUS...
FIDGET FIDGET
AND NOW... SHE'S CHANGING CLOTHES RIGHT OVER THERE...
I BET EVEN HER CASUAL CLOTHES ARE ALL ADULT-LIKE...
IDIOT! WHY EVEN THINK ABOUT THAT?
KLIK
!
TWITCH
SORRY.
IS COFFEE OKAY, ACTUALLY?
Y-YES!
THANK YOU!

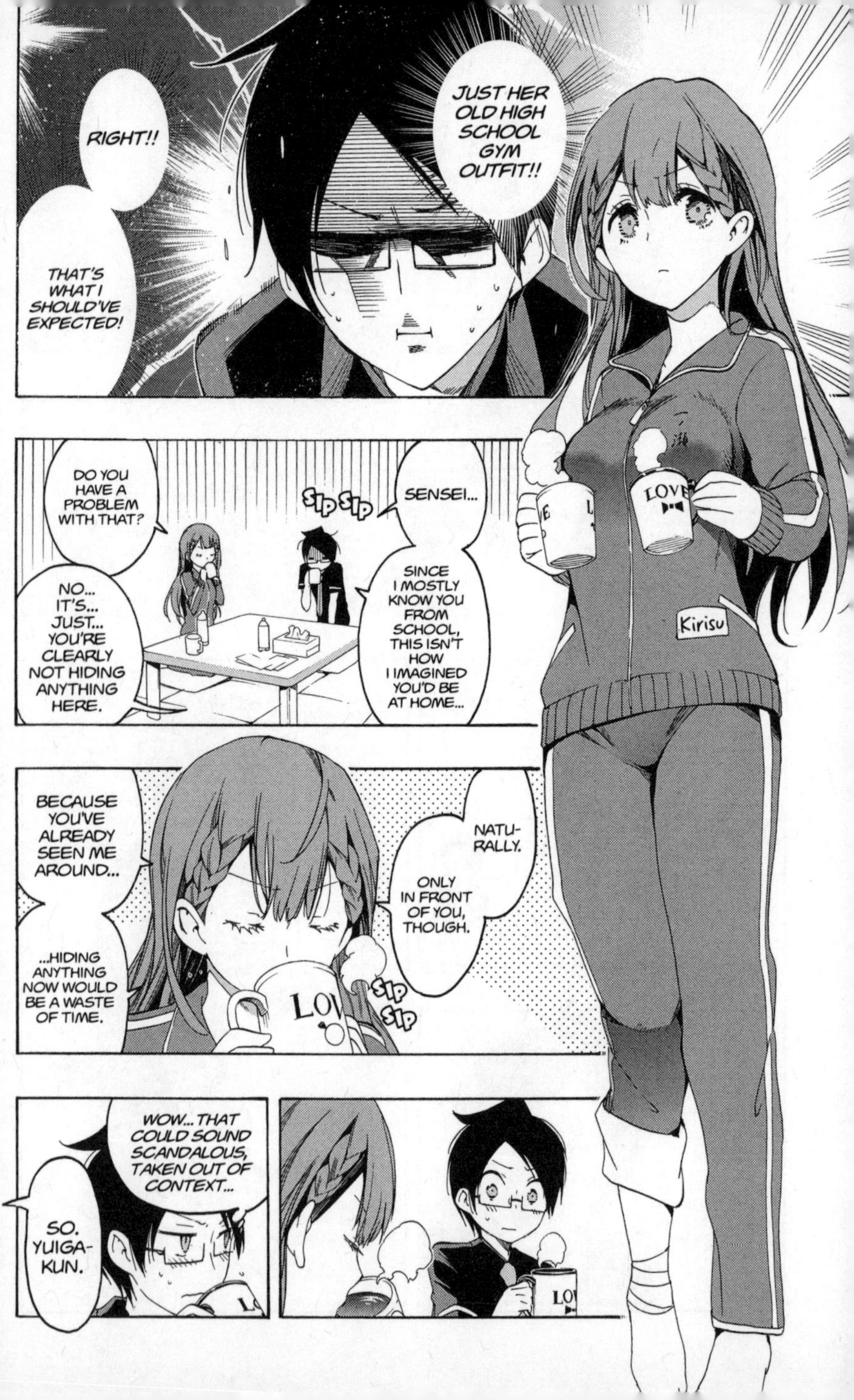

LOVE
Kirisu
JUST HER OLD HIGH SCHOOL GYM OUTFIT!!
RIGHT!!
THAT'S WHAT I SHOULD'VE EXPECTED!
SENSEI...
SIP SIP
DO YOU HAVE A PROBLEM WITH THAT?
SINCE I MOSTLY KNOW YOU FROM SCHOOL, THIS ISN'T HOW I IMAGINED YOU'D BE AT HOME...
NO... IT'S... JUST... YOU'RE CLEARLY NOT HIDING ANYTHING HERE.
NATU-RALLY.
ONLY IN FRONT OF YOU, THOUGH.
BECAUSE YOU'VE ALREADY SEEN ME AROUND...
SIP SIP
...HIDING ANYTHING NOW WOULD BE A WASTE OF TIME.
WOW... THAT COULD SOUND SCANDALOUS, TAKEN OUT OF CONTEXT...
SO. YUIGA-KUN.

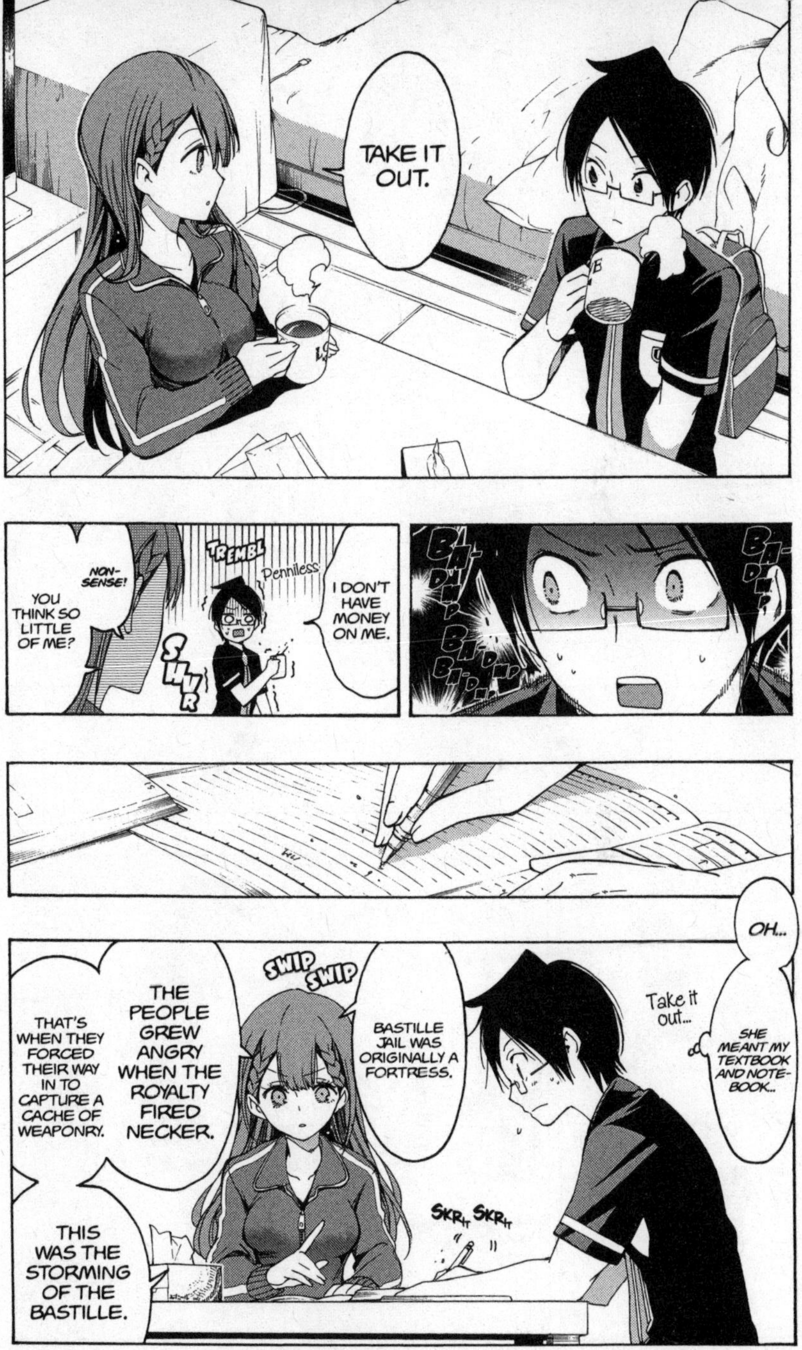
TAKE IT OUT.
BA-DMP
BA-DMP BA-DMP BA-DMP
I DON'T HAVE MONEY ON ME.
Penniless
TREMBL
SHVR
NON-SENSE!
YOU THINK SO LITTLE OF ME?
OH...
Take it out...
SHE MEANT MY TEXTBOOK AND NOTE-BOOK...
SKRITT SKRITT
SWIP SWIP
BASTILLE JAIL WAS ORIGINALLY A FORTRESS.
THE PEOPLE GREW ANGRY WHEN THE ROYALTY FIRED NECKER.
THAT'S WHEN THEY FORCED THEIR WAY IN TO CAPTURE A CACHE OF WEAPONRY.
THIS WAS THE STORMING OF THE BASTILLE.

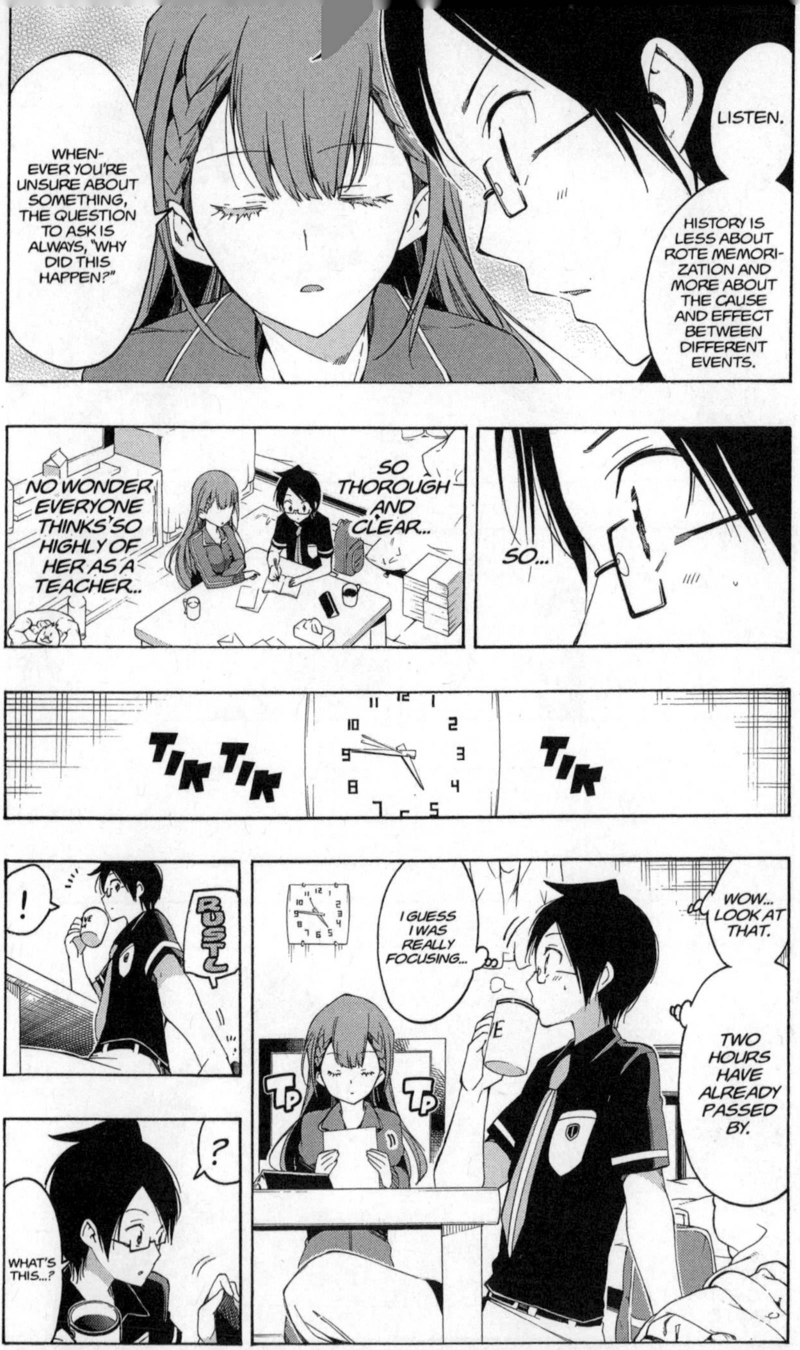
LISTEN.
HISTORY IS LESS ABOUT ROTE MEMORIZATION AND MORE ABOUT THE CAUSE AND EFFECT BETWEEN DIFFERENT EVENTS.
WHENEVER YOU'RE UNSURE ABOUT SOMETHING, THE QUESTION TO ASK IS ALWAYS, "WHY DID THIS HAPPEN?"
SO...
SO THOROUGH AND CLEAR...
NO WONDER EVERYONE THINKS SO HIGHLY OF HER AS A TEACHER...
TIK TIK
TIK
WOW... LOOK AT THAT.
TWO HOURS HAVE ALREADY PASSED BY.
I GUESS I WAS REALLY FOCUSING...
TP
TP
!
RUSTL
?
WHAT'S THIS...?

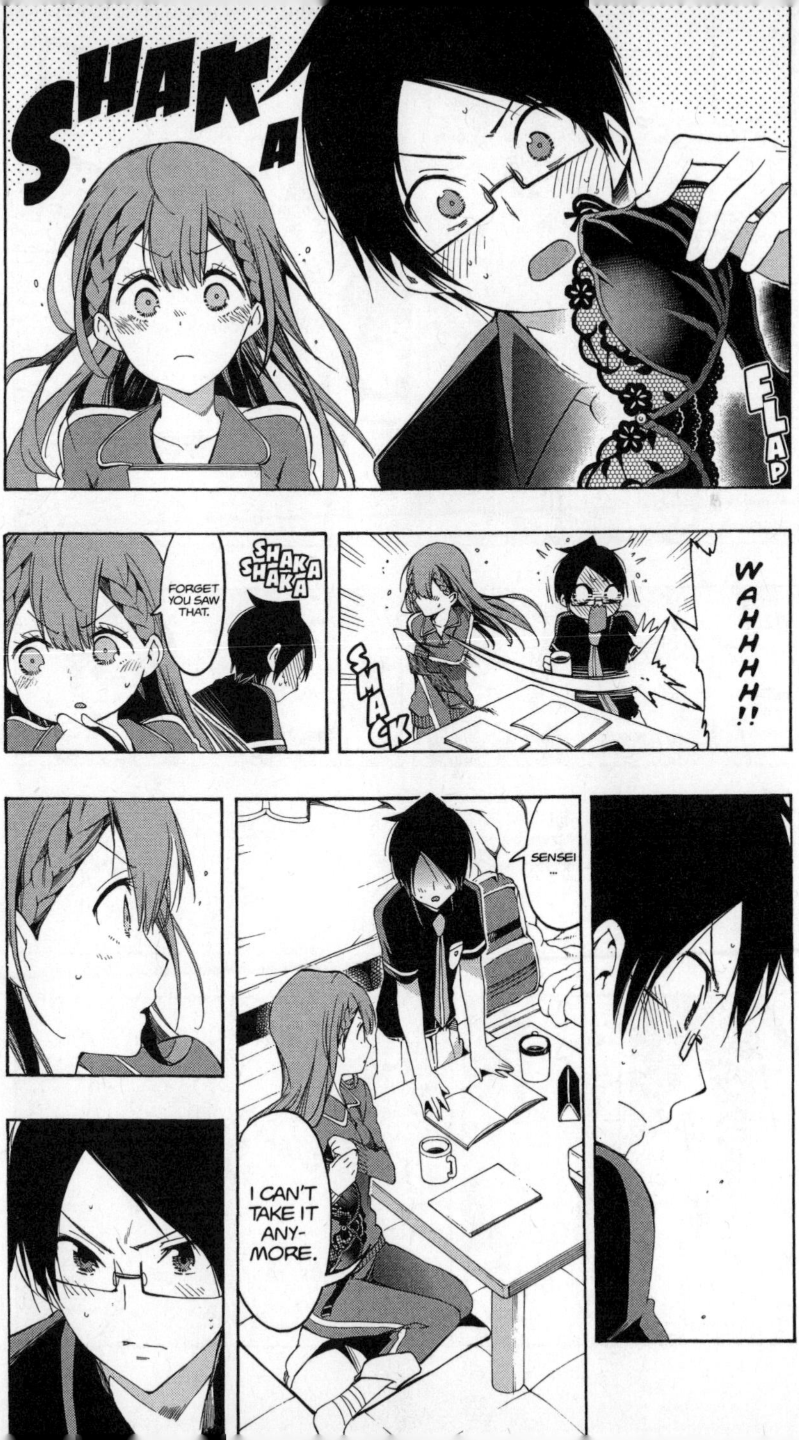
SHAKA
FLAP
WAHHHHH!!
SMACK
SHAKA SHAKA
FORGET YOU SAW THAT.
SENSEI ...
I CAN'T TAKE IT ANY-MORE.

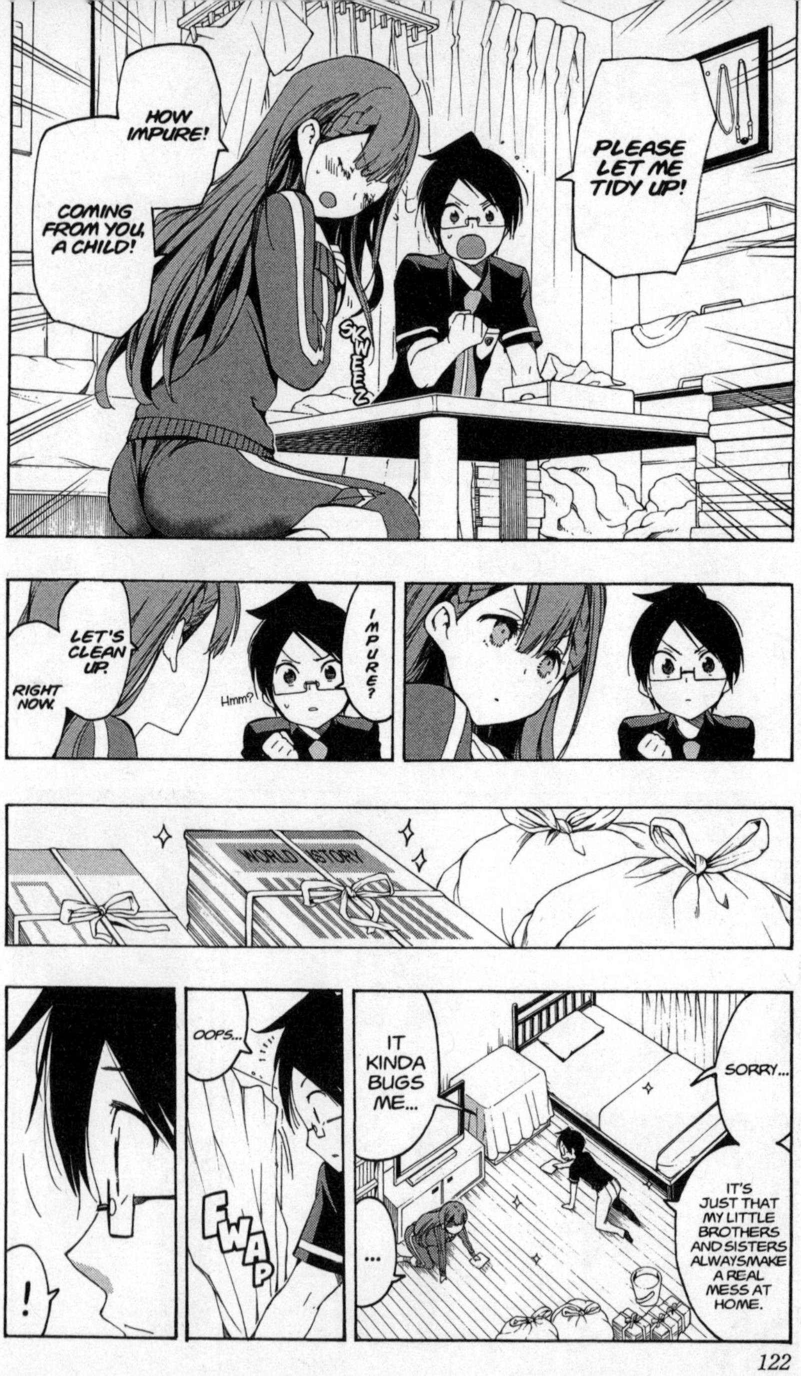

PLEASE LET ME TIDY UP!
HOW IMPURE!
COMING FROM YOU, A CHILD!
SKWEEZ
IMPURE?
Hmm?
LET'S CLEAN UP.
RIGHT NOW.
WORLD HISTORY
SORRY...
IT'S JUST THAT MY LITTLE BROTHERS AND SISTERS ALWAYSMAKE A REAL MESS AT HOME.
IT KINDA BUGS ME...
OOPS...
FWAP
...
!

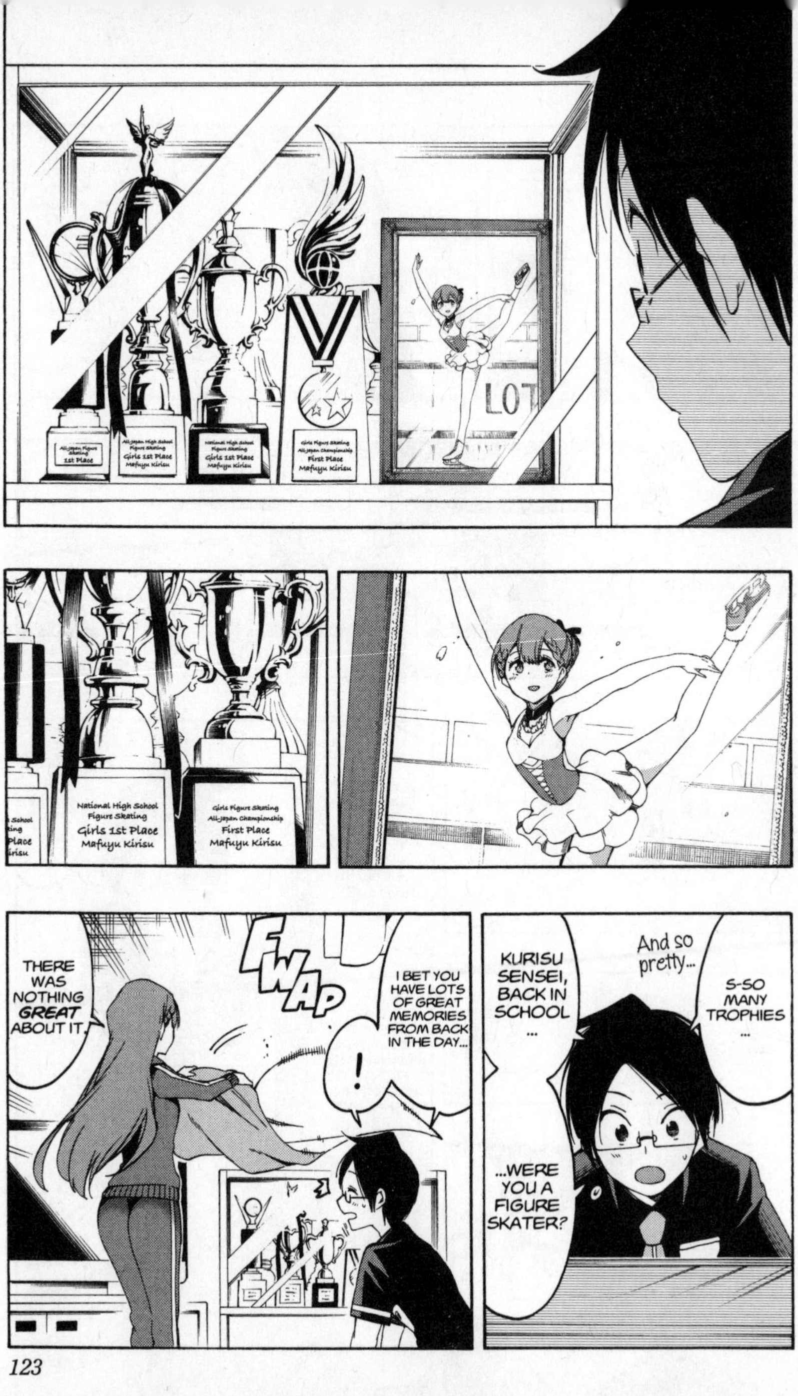
All-Japan Figure Skating 1st Place
All-Japan High School Figure Skating Girls 1st Place Mafuyu Kirisu
National High School Figure Skating Girls 1st Place Mafuyu Kirisu
Girls Figure Skating All-Japan Championship First Place Mafuyu Kirisu
LOT
National High School Figure Skating Girls 1st Place Mafuyu Kirisu
Girls Figure Skating All-Japan Championship First Place Mafuyu Kirisu
S-SO MANY TROPHIES ...
And so pretty...
KURISU SENSEI, BACK IN SCHOOL ...
...WERE YOU A FIGURE SKATER?
I BET YOU HAVE LOTS OF GREAT MEMORIES FROM BACK IN THE DAY...
!
FWAP
THERE WAS NOTHING GREAT ABOUT IT.

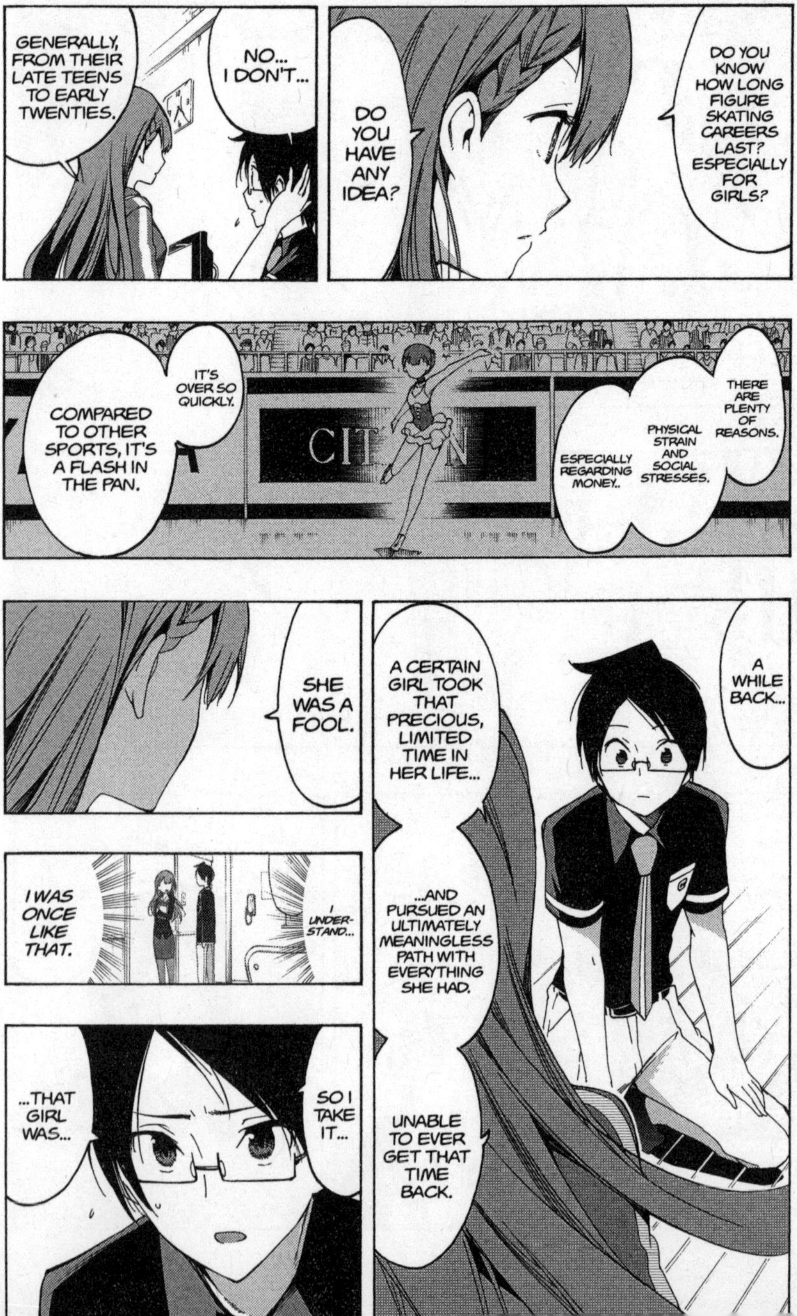
DO YOU KNOW HOW LONG FIGURE SKATING CAREERS LAST? ESPECIALLY FOR GIRLS?
DO YOU HAVE ANY IDEA?
NO... I DON'T...
GENERALLY, FROM THEIR LATE TEENS TO EARLY TWENTIES.
THERE ARE PLENTY OF REASONS.
PHYSICAL STRAIN AND SOCIAL STRESSES.
ESPECIALLY REGARDING MONEY..
IT'S OVER SO QUICKLY.
COMPARED TO OTHER SPORTS, IT'S A FLASH IN THE PAN.
A WHILE BACK...
A CERTAIN GIRL TOOK THAT PRECIOUS, LIMITED TIME IN HER LIFE...
...AND PURSUED AN ULTIMATELY MEANINGLESS PATH WITH EVERYTHING SHE HAD.
UNABLE TO EVER GET THAT TIME BACK.
SHE WAS A FOOL.
I UNDER-STAND...
I WAS ONCE LIKE THAT.
SO I TAKE IT...
...THAT GIRL WAS...

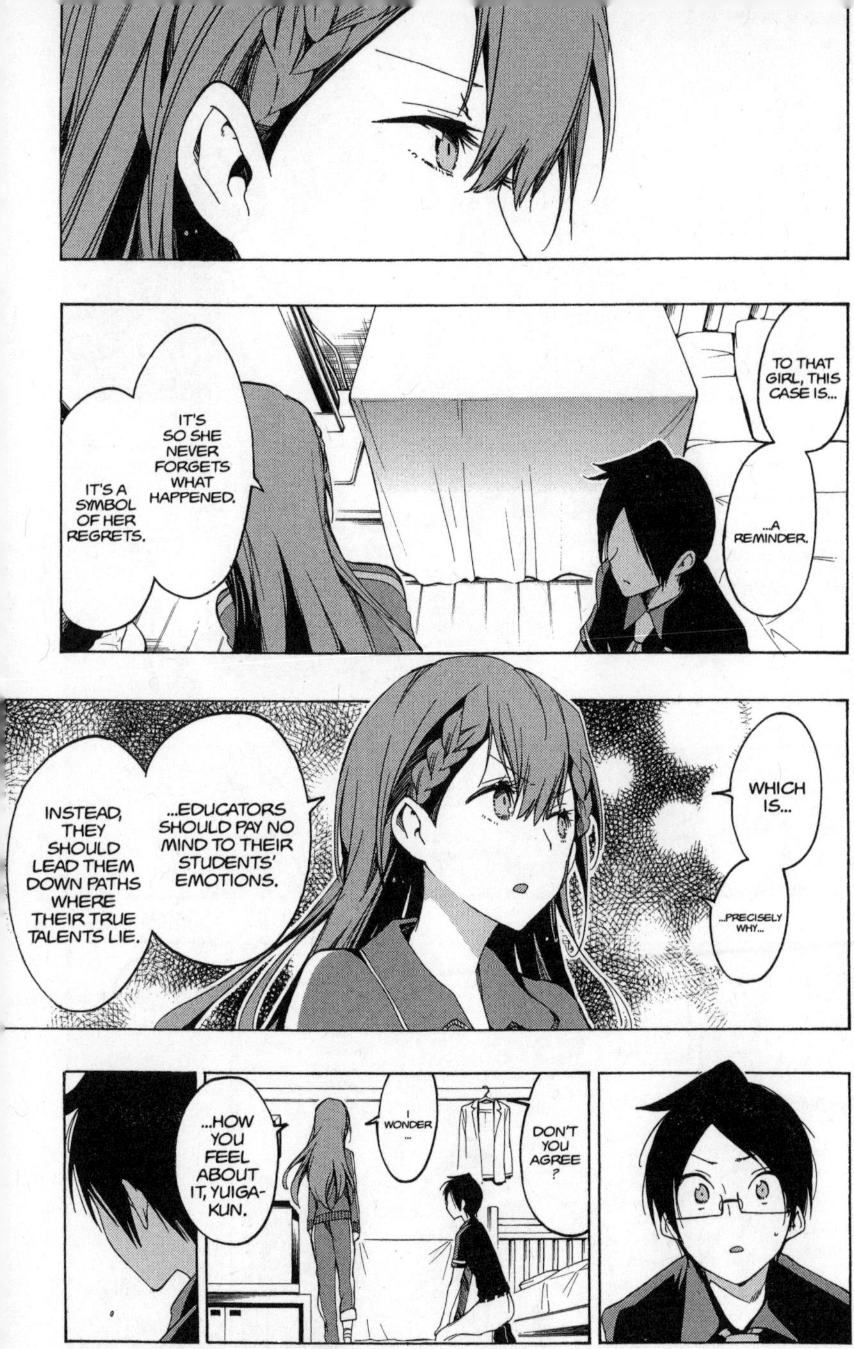
TO THAT GIRL, THIS CASE IS...
...A REMINDER.
IT'S SO SHE NEVER FORGETS WHAT HAPPENED.
IT'S A SYMBOL OF HER REGRETS.
WHICH IS...
...PRECISELY WHY...
...EDUCATORS SHOULD PAY NO MIND TO THEIR STUDENTS' EMOTIONS.
INSTEAD, THEY SHOULD LEAD THEM DOWN PATHS WHERE THEIR TRUE TALENTS LIE.
DON'T YOU AGREE?
I WONDER...
...HOW YOU FEEL ABOUT IT, YUIGA-KUN.

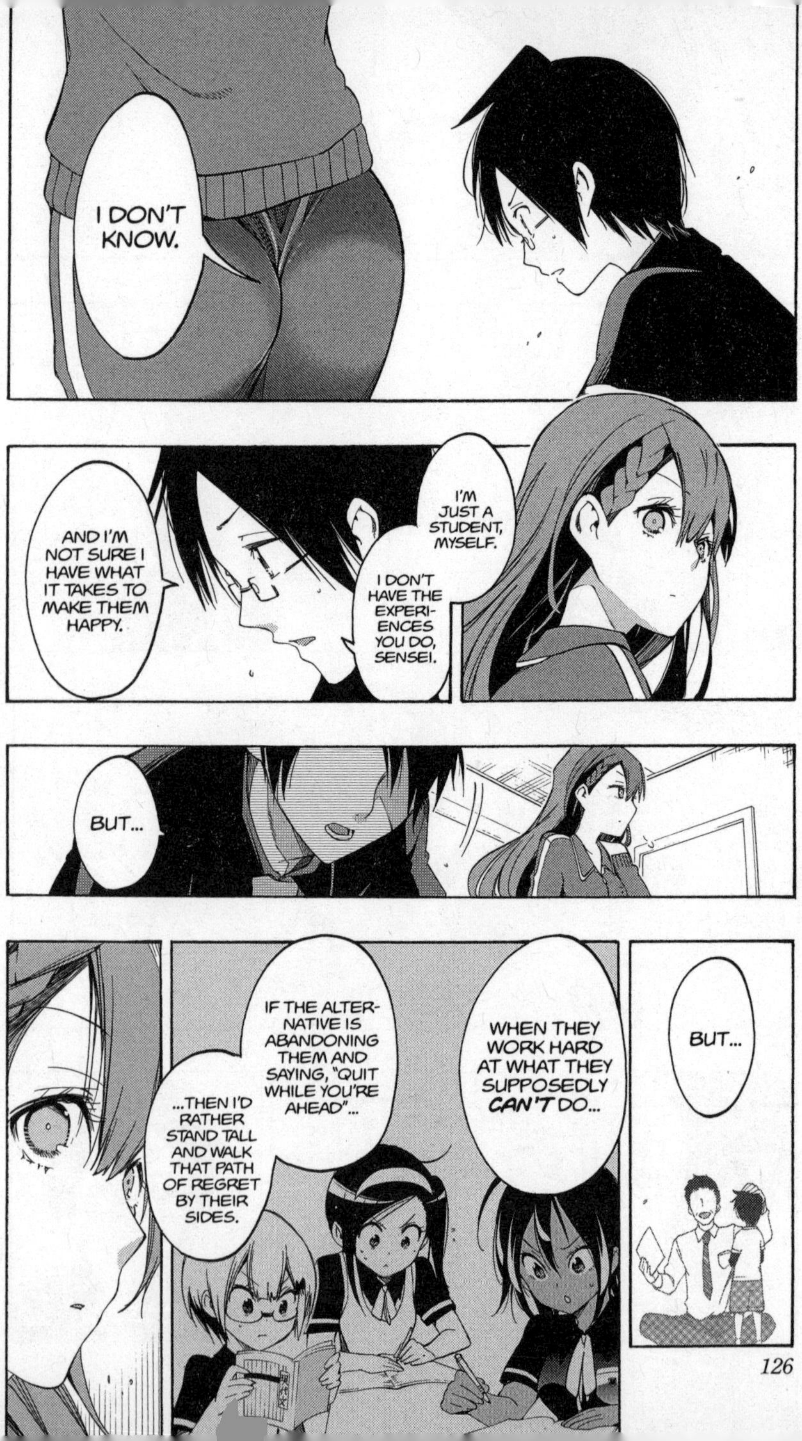
I DON'T KNOW.
I'M JUST A STUDENT, MYSELF.
I DON'T HAVE THE EXPERI-ENCES YOU DO, SENSEI.
AND I'M NOT SURE I HAVE WHAT IT TAKES TO MAKE THEM HAPPY.
BUT...
BUT...
WHEN THEY WORK HARD AT WHAT THEY SUPPOSEDLY *CAN'T* DO...
IF THE ALTER-NATIVE IS ABANDONING THEM AND SAYING, "QUIT WHILE YOU'RE AHEAD"...
...THEN I'D RATHER STAND TALL AND WALK THAT PATH OF REGRET BY THEIR SIDES.

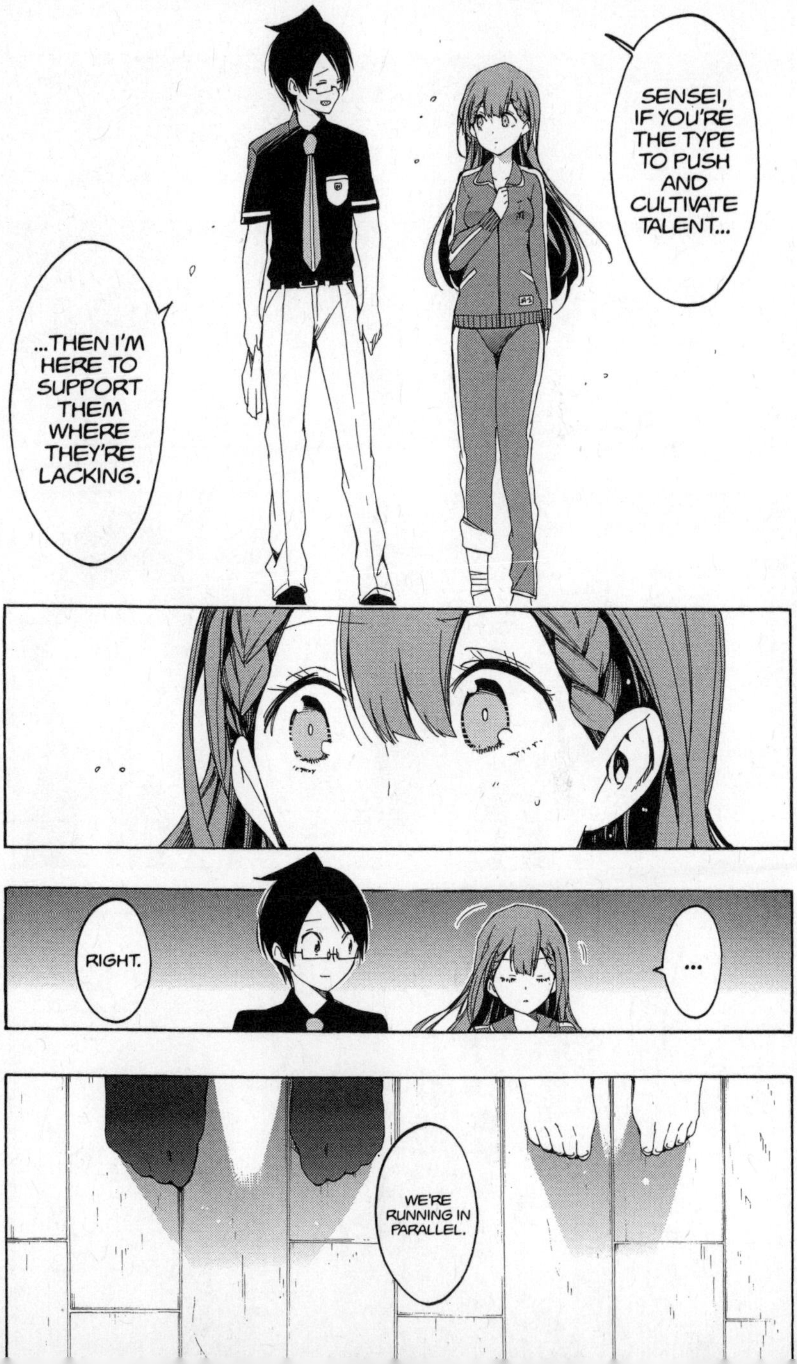
SENSEI, IF YOU'RE THE TYPE TO PUSH AND CULTIVATE TALENT...
...THEN I'M HERE TO SUPPORT THEM WHERE THEY'RE LACKING.
...
RIGHT.
WE'RE RUNNING IN PARALLEL.

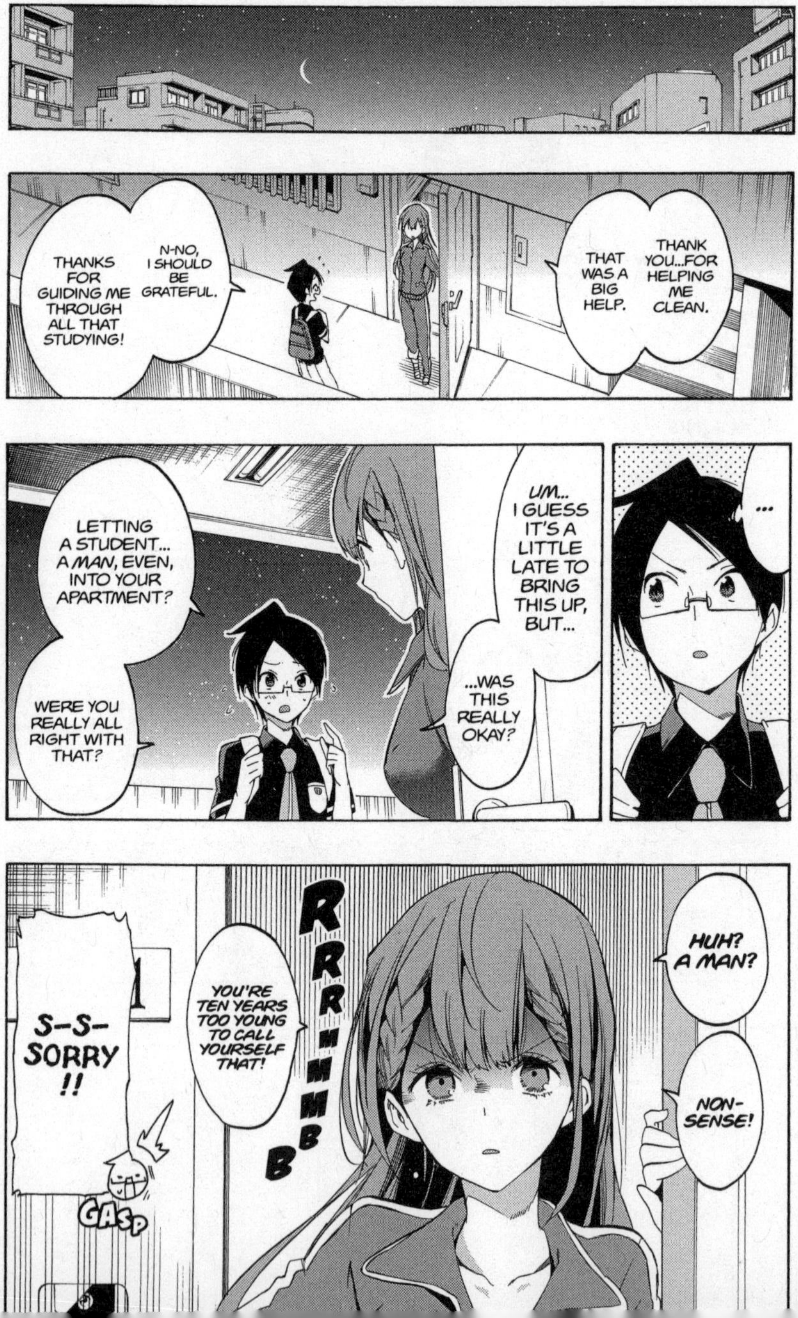
THANK YOU...FOR HELPING ME CLEAN.
THAT WAS A BIG HELP.
N-NO, I SHOULD BE GRATEFUL.
THANKS FOR GUIDING ME THROUGH ALL THAT STUDYING!
...
UM... I GUESS IT'S A LITTLE LATE TO BRING THIS UP, BUT...
...WAS THIS REALLY OKAY?
LETTING A STUDENT... A MAN, EVEN, INTO YOUR APARTMENT?
WERE YOU REALLY ALL RIGHT WITH THAT?
HUH? A MAN?
NON-SENSE!
RRRMMBB
YOU'RE TEN YEARS TOO YOUNG TO CALL YOURSELF THAT!
S-S-SORRY!!
GASP

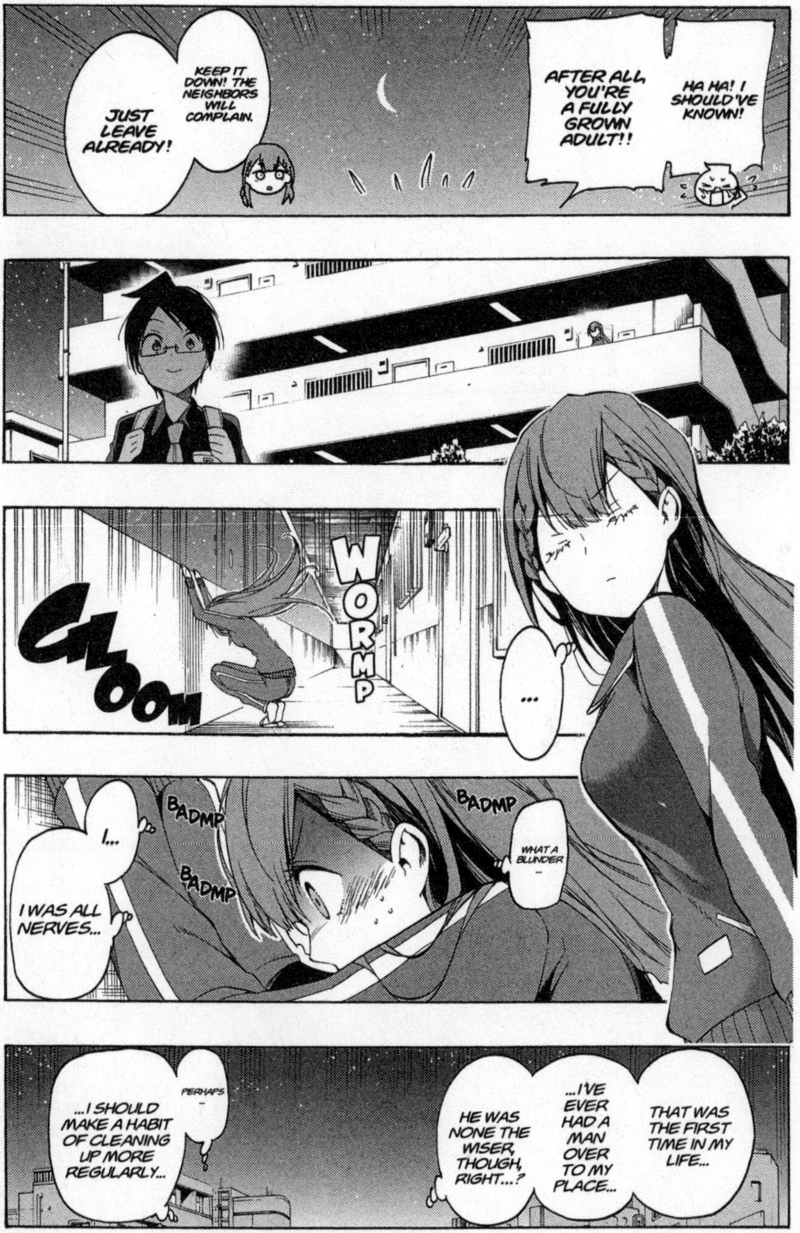
HA HA! I SHOULD'VE KNOWN!
AFTER ALL, YOU'RE A FULLY GROWN ADULT!!
KEEP IT DOWN! THE NEIGHBORS WILL COMPLAIN.
JUST LEAVE ALREADY!
...
WORMP
GLOOM
BADMP
WHAT A BLUNDER...
BADMP
BADMP
I...
I WAS ALL NERVES...
THAT WAS THE FIRST TIME IN MY LIFE...
...I'VE EVER HAD A MAN OVER TO MY PLACE...
HE WAS NONE THE WISER, THOUGH, RIGHT...?
PERHAPS...
...I SHOULD MAKE A HABIT OF CLEANING UP MORE REGULARLY...

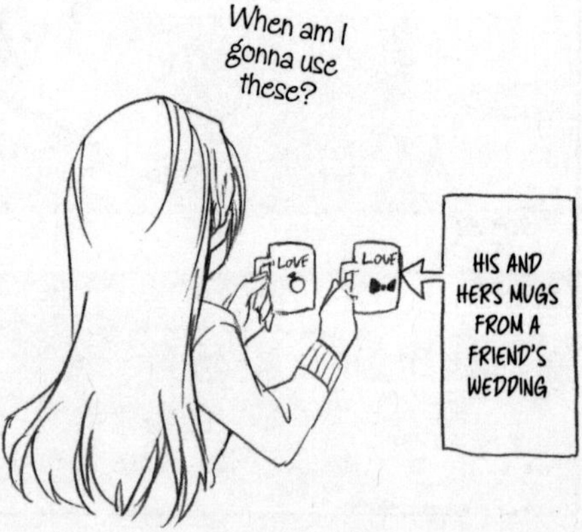
When am I gonna use these?
LOVE
LOVE
HIS AND HERS MUGS FROM A FRIEND'S WEDDING

Question 23: [X] Is Indispensible in a Genius's Flower Garden

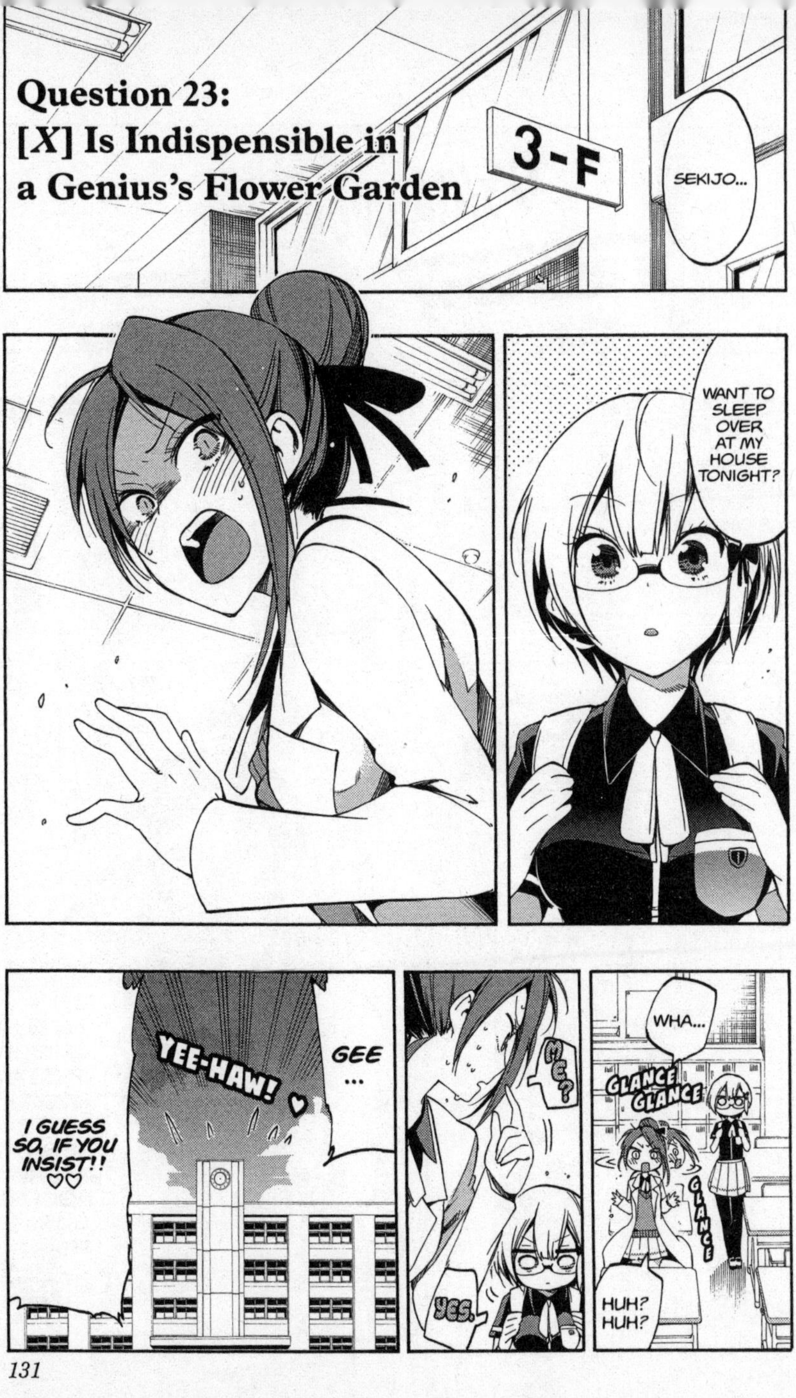
3-F
SEKIJO...
WANT TO SLEEP OVER AT MY HOUSE TONIGHT?
WHA...
GLANCE GLANCE
GLANCE
HUH? HUH?
ME?
YES.
GEE ...
YEE-HAW! ♥
I GUESS SO, IF YOU INSIST!! ♡♡

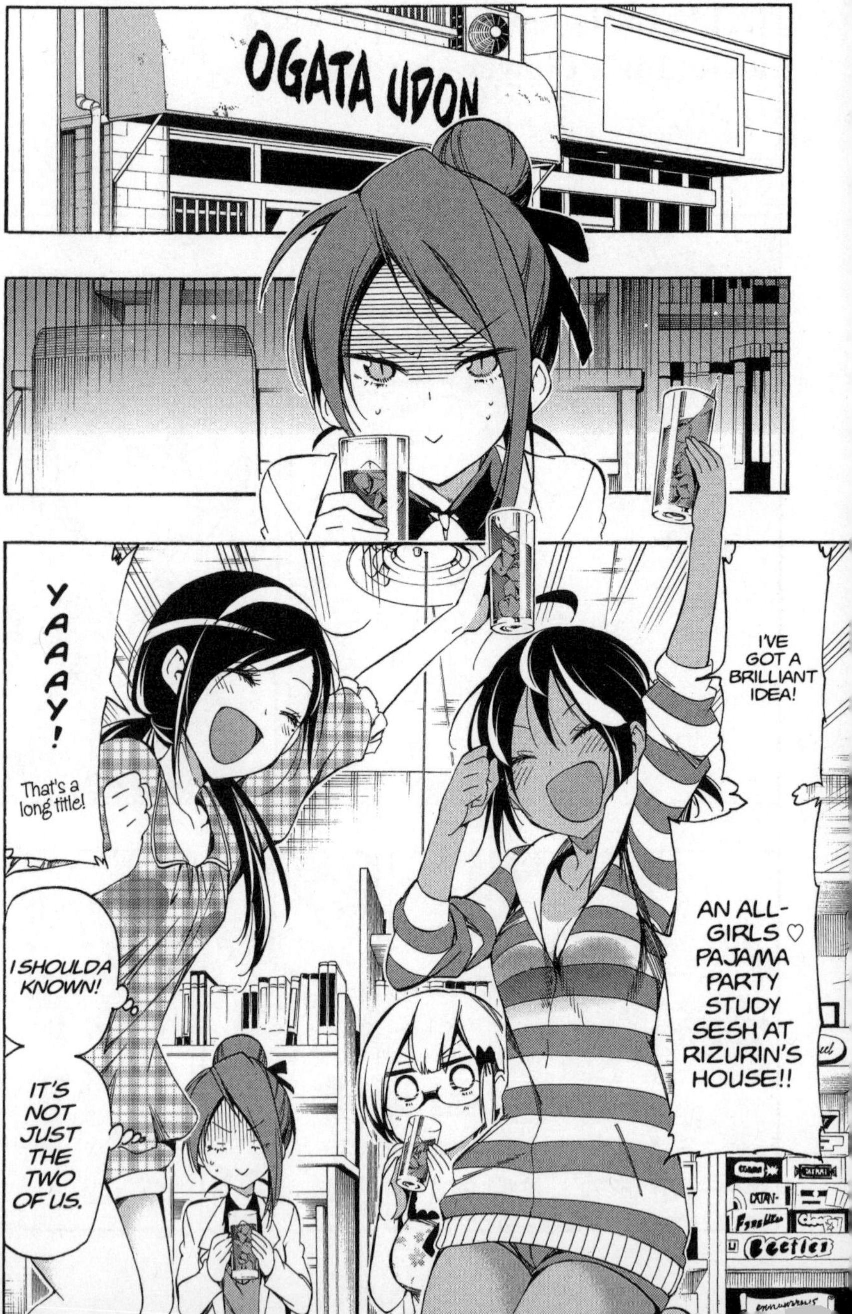

OGATA UDON
I'VE GOT A BRILLIANT IDEA!
AN ALL-GIRLS ♡ PAJAMA PARTY STUDY SESH AT RIZURIN'S HOUSE!!
YAAAAY!
That's a long title!
I SHOULDA KNOWN!
IT'S NOT JUST THE TWO OF US.

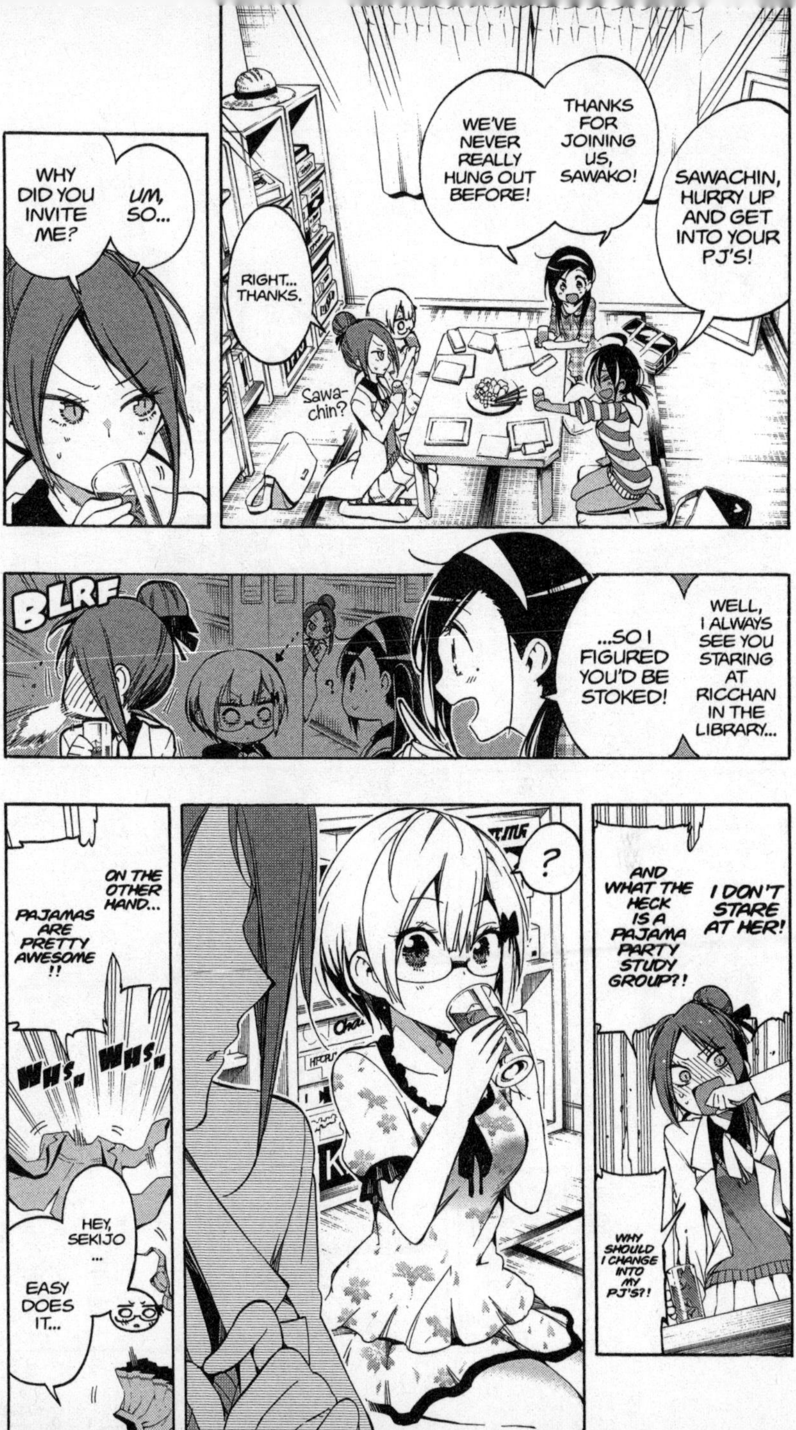
SAWACHIN, HURRY UP AND GET INTO YOUR PJ'S!
THANKS FOR JOINING US, SAWAKO!
WE'VE NEVER REALLY HUNG OUT BEFORE!
RIGHT... THANKS.
Sawa-chin?
UM, SO...
WHY DID YOU INVITE ME?
WELL, I ALWAYS SEE YOU STARING AT RICCHAN IN THE LIBRARY...
...SO I FIGURED YOU'D BE STOKED!
BLRF
I DON'T STARE AT HER!
AND WHAT THE HECK IS A PAJAMA PARTY STUDY GROUP?!
WHY SHOULD I CHANGE INTO MY PJ'S?!
?
ON THE OTHER HAND...
PAJAMAS ARE PRETTY AWESOME!!
WHSH WHSH
HEY, SEKIJO ... EASY DOES IT...

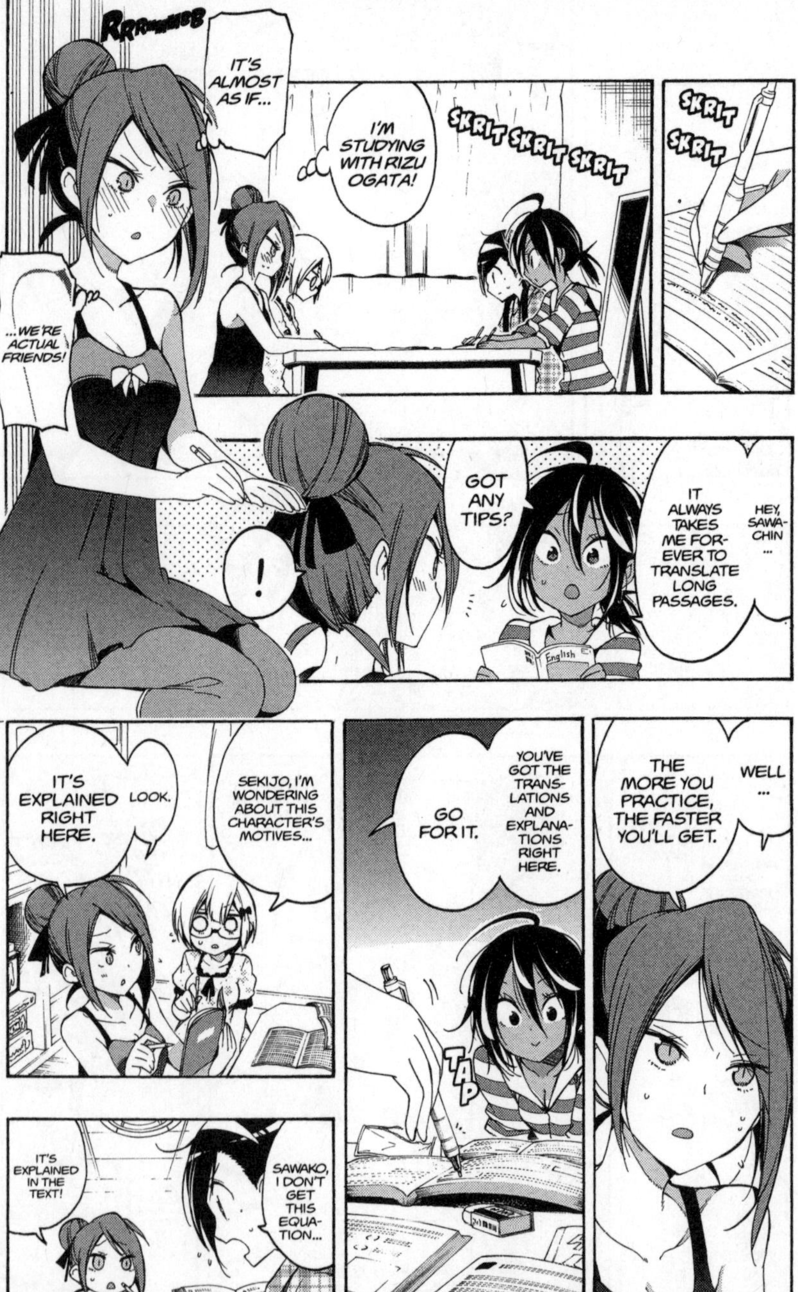
SKRIT
SKRIT
I'M STUDYING WITH RIZU OGATA!
SKRIT SKRIT SKRIT
RRRUMMBB
IT'S ALMOST AS IF...
HEY, SAWA-CHIN...
IT ALWAYS TAKES ME FOREVER TO TRANSLATE LONG PASSAGES.
GOT ANY TIPS?
!
...WE'RE ACTUAL FRIENDS!
WELL...
THE MORE YOU PRACTICE, THE FASTER YOU'LL GET.
YOU'VE GOT THE TRANSLATIONS AND EXPLANATIONS RIGHT HERE.
GO FOR IT.
TAP
SEKIJO, I'M WONDERING ABOUT THIS CHARACTER'S MOTIVES...
LOOK.
IT'S EXPLAINED RIGHT HERE.
SAWAKO, I DON'T GET THIS EQUATION...
IT'S EXPLAINED IN THE TEXT!
English

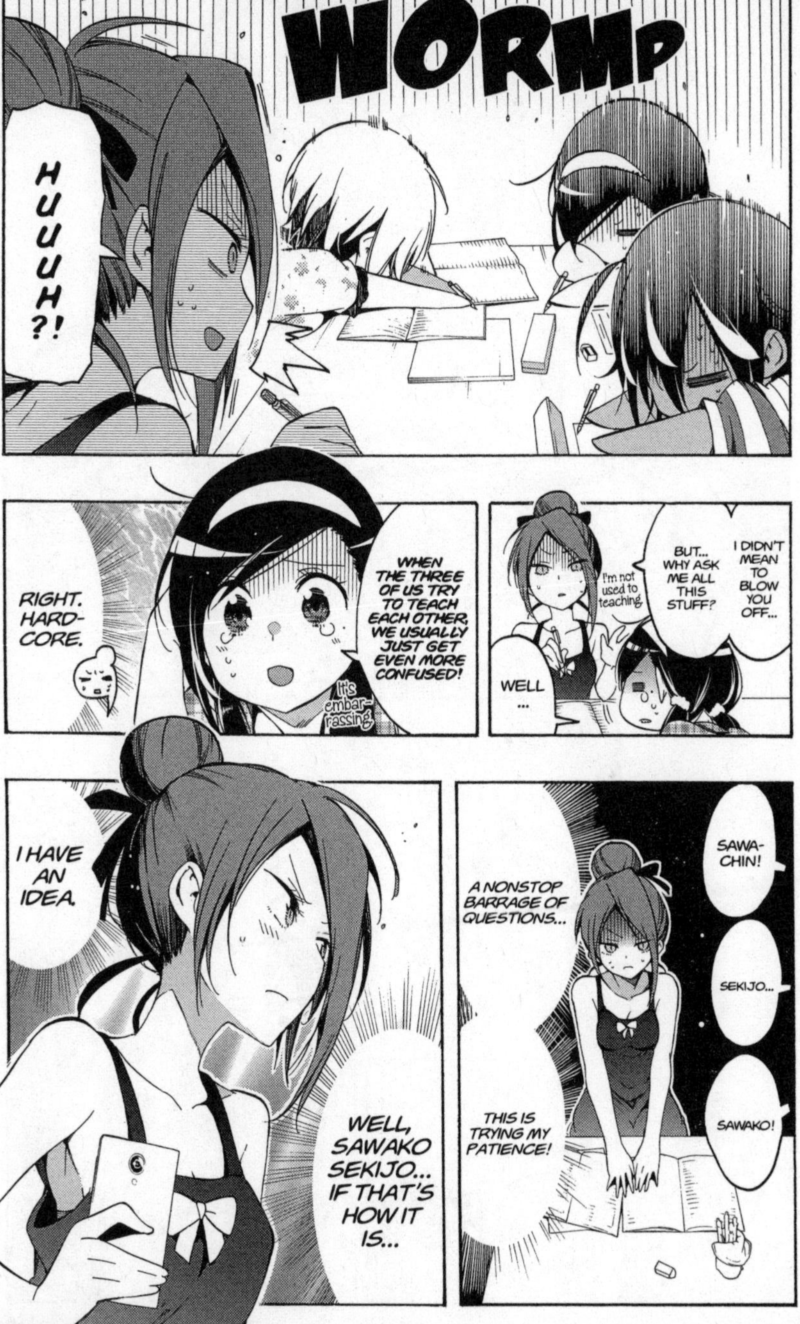
WORMP
HUUUUH?!
I DIDN'T MEAN TO BLOW YOU OFF...
BUT... WHY ASK ME ALL THIS STUFF?
I'm not used to teaching
WELL ...
WHEN THE THREE OF US TRY TO TEACH EACH OTHER, WE USUALLY JUST GET EVEN MORE CONFUSED!
It's embar-rassing
RIGHT. HARD-CORE.
SAWA-CHIN!
SEKIJO...
SAWAKO!
A NONSTOP BARRAGE OF QUESTIONS...
THIS IS TRYING MY PATIENCE!
WELL, SAWAKO SEKIJO... IF THAT'S HOW IT IS...
I HAVE AN IDEA.

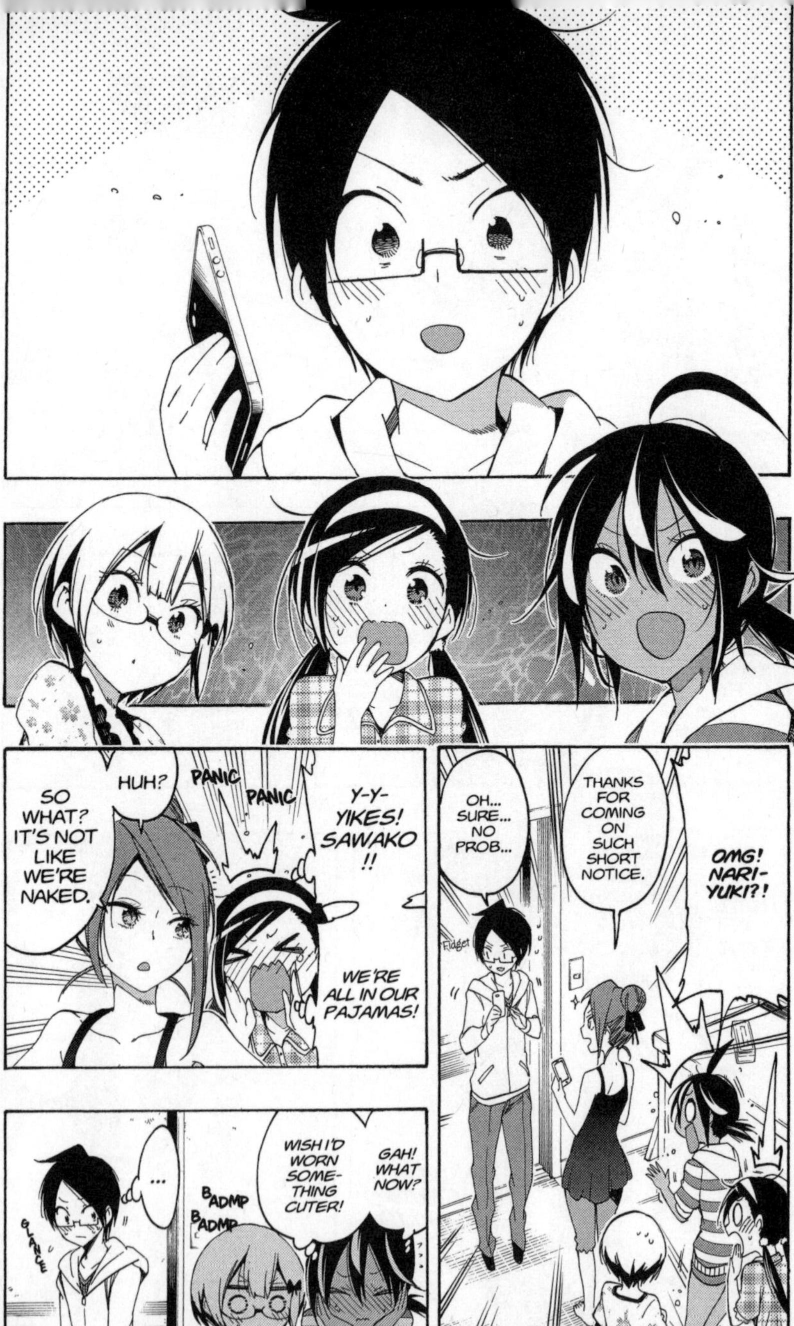
OMG! NARI-YUKI?!
THANKS FOR COMING ON SUCH SHORT NOTICE.
OH... SURE... NO PROB...
Fidget
Y-Y-YIKES! SAWAKO!!
WE'RE ALL IN OUR PAJAMAS!
PANIC
PANIC
HUH?
SO WHAT? IT'S NOT LIKE WE'RE NAKED.
GAH! WHAT NOW?
WISH I'D WORN SOMETHING CUTER!
BADMP
BADMP
...
GLANCE

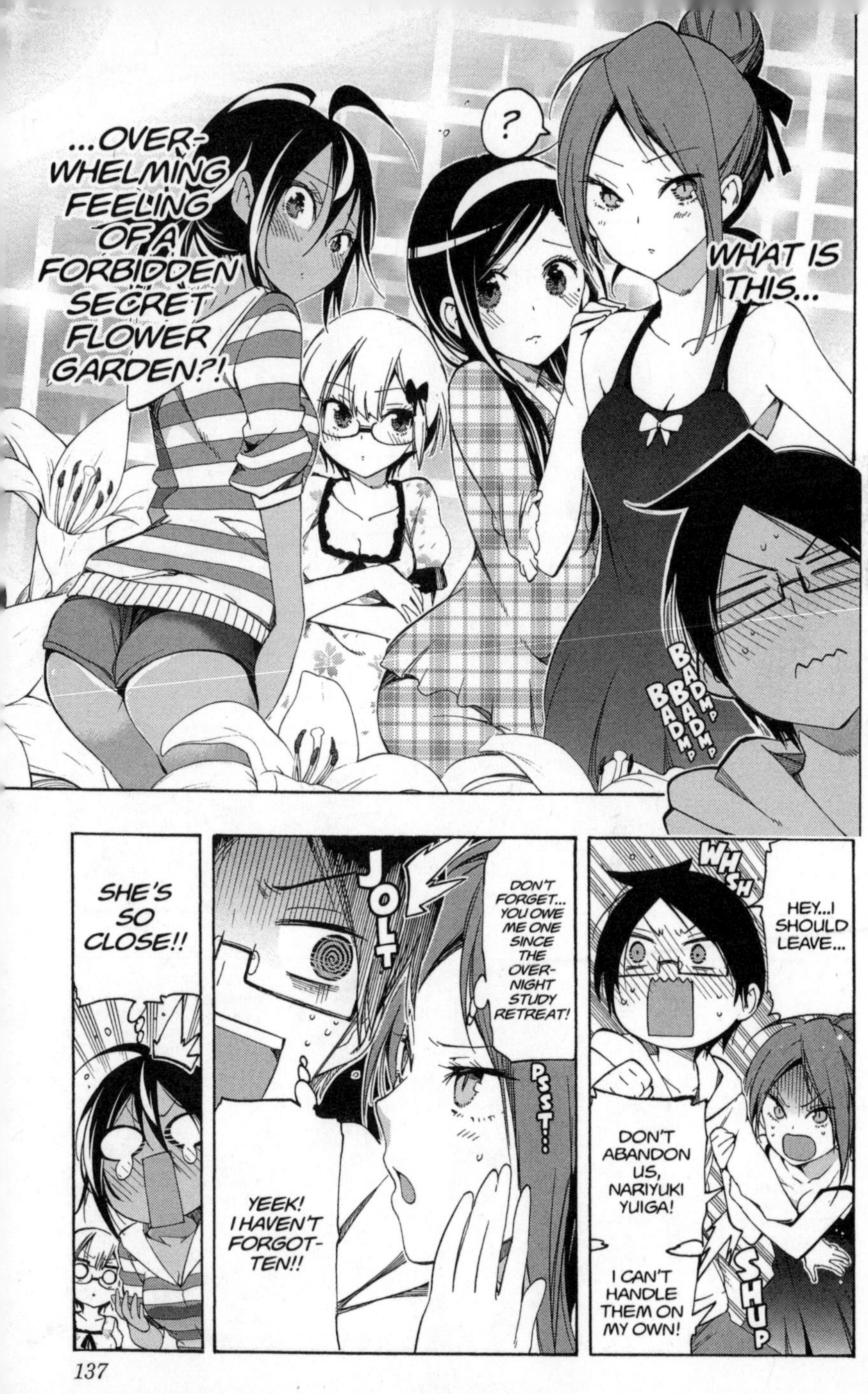
?
WHAT IS THIS...
...OVER-WHELMING FEELING OF A FORBIDDEN SECRET FLOWER GARDEN?!
BADMP BADMP BADMP
WHSH
HEY...I SHOULD LEAVE...
DON'T ABANDON US, NARIYUKI YUIGA!
I CAN'T HANDLE THEM ON MY OWN!
SHUP
DON'T FORGET... YOU OWE ME ONE SINCE THE OVER-NIGHT STUDY RETREAT!
JOLT
PSST...
YEEK! I HAVEN'T FORGOT-TEN!!
SHE'S SO CLOSE!!

WEIRD... MY STOMACH FEELS FUNNY ALL OF A SUDDEN...

HUH? TAKE-MOTO?

SINCE WHEN HAVE YOU BEEN SO EAGER TO STUDY?!

STARE

TUG

KNOCKA KNOCKA

YANK YANK

SHE'S RIGHT! SO WHAT IF WE'RE IN OUR PJ'S?!

YANK

C'MON, NARIYUKI! LET'S GET STUDYING!

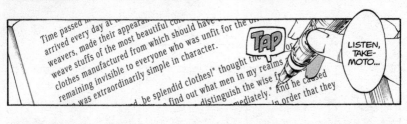

Time passed... arrived every day at t... weavers, made their appearan... weave stuffs of the most beautiful col... clothes manufactured from which should have... remaining invisible to everyone who was unfit for the o... was extraordinarily simple in character.

...be splendid clothes!" thought the... ...to find out what men in my realms... ...distinguish the wise f... ...mediately." And he c... ...in order that they...

TAP

LISTEN, TAKE-MOTO...

FOCUSED READING IS ESSENTIAL TO TRANSLATE A SHORT ENGLISH PASSAGE INTO JAPANESE.

HOWEVER, WHEN IT COMES TO LONGER TEXTS...

THAT'S AN IMPORTANT SKILL.

...THE SKILL SET IS SOMEWHAT DIFFERENT.

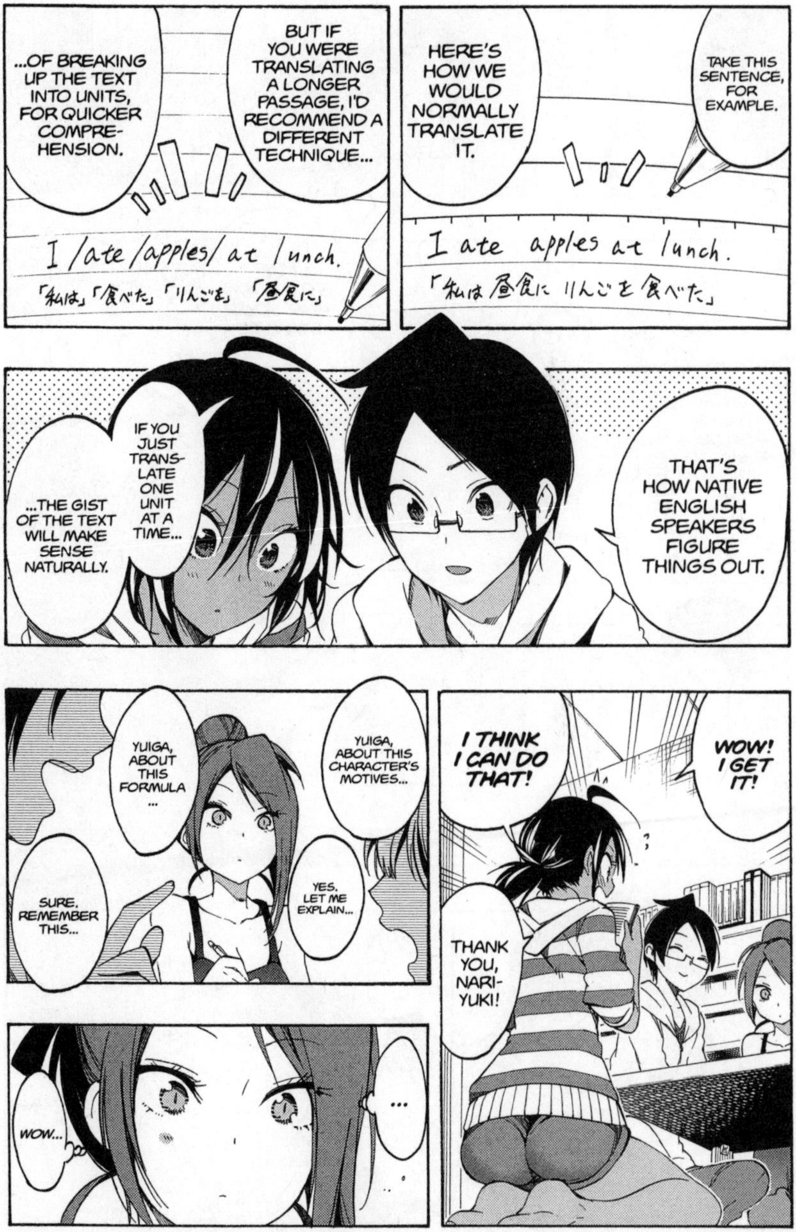
TAKE THIS SENTENCE, FOR EXAMPLE.
HERE'S HOW WE WOULD NORMALLY TRANSLATE IT.
I ate apples at lunch.
「私は昼食にりんごを食べた」
BUT IF YOU WERE TRANSLATING A LONGER PASSAGE, I'D RECOMMEND A DIFFERENT TECHNIQUE...
...OF BREAKING UP THE TEXT INTO UNITS, FOR QUICKER COMPRE-HENSION.
I /ate /apples/ at lunch.
「私は」「食べた」「りんごを」「昼食に」
THAT'S HOW NATIVE ENGLISH SPEAKERS FIGURE THINGS OUT.
IF YOU JUST TRANS-LATE ONE UNIT AT A TIME...
...THE GIST OF THE TEXT WILL MAKE SENSE NATURALLY.
WOW! I GET IT!
I THINK I CAN DO THAT!
THANK YOU, NARI-YUKI!
YUIGA, ABOUT THIS CHARACTER'S MOTIVES...
YUIGA, ABOUT THIS FORMULA ...
YES. LET ME EXPLAIN...
SURE. REMEMBER THIS...
...
WOW...

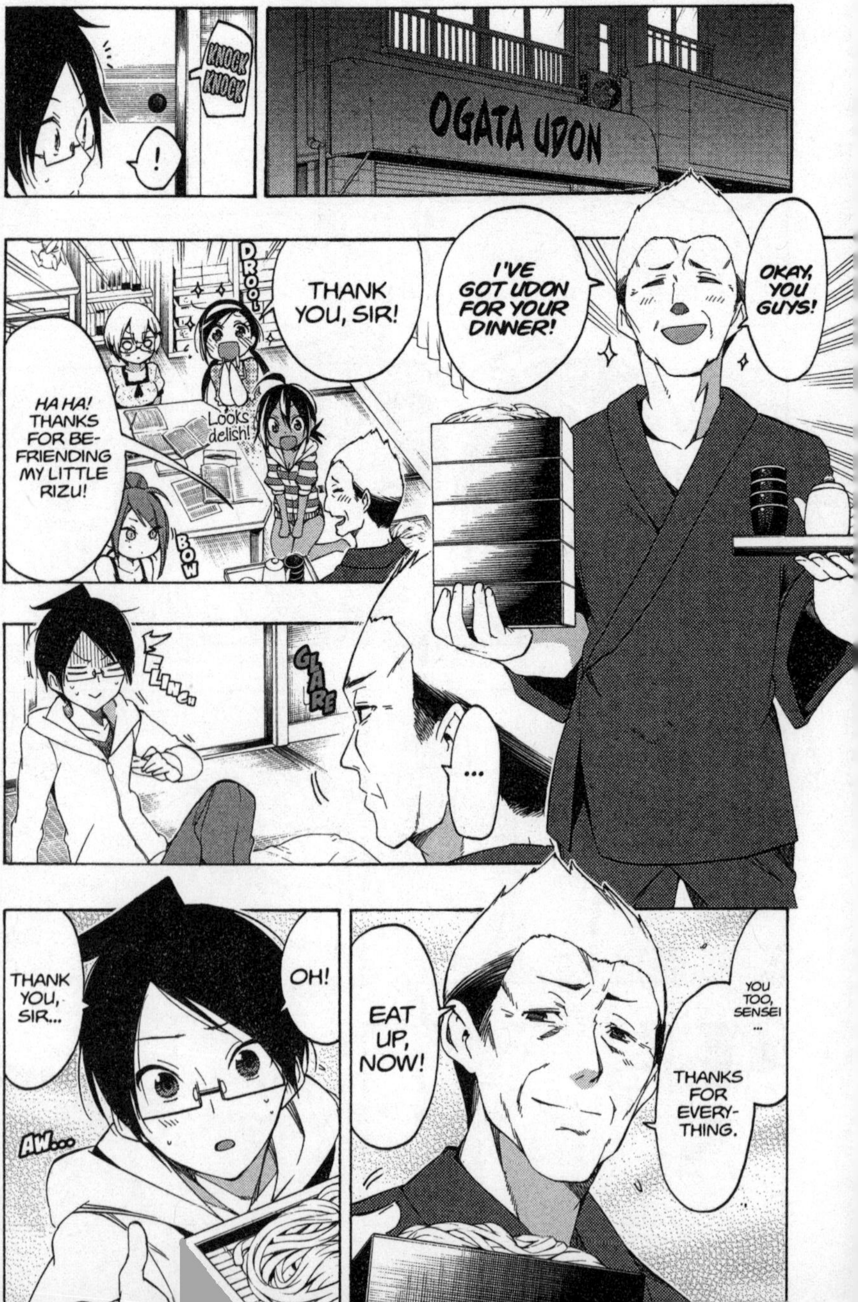
OGATA UDON
KNOCK KNOCK
!
OKAY, YOU GUYS!
I'VE GOT UDON FOR YOUR DINNER!
THANK YOU, SIR!
DROOL
Looks delish!
HA HA! THANKS FOR BE-FRIENDING MY LITTLE RIZU!
BOW
GLARE
FLINCH
...
YOU TOO, SENSEI...
THANKS FOR EVERYTHING.
EAT UP, NOW!
OH!
THANK YOU, SIR...
AW...

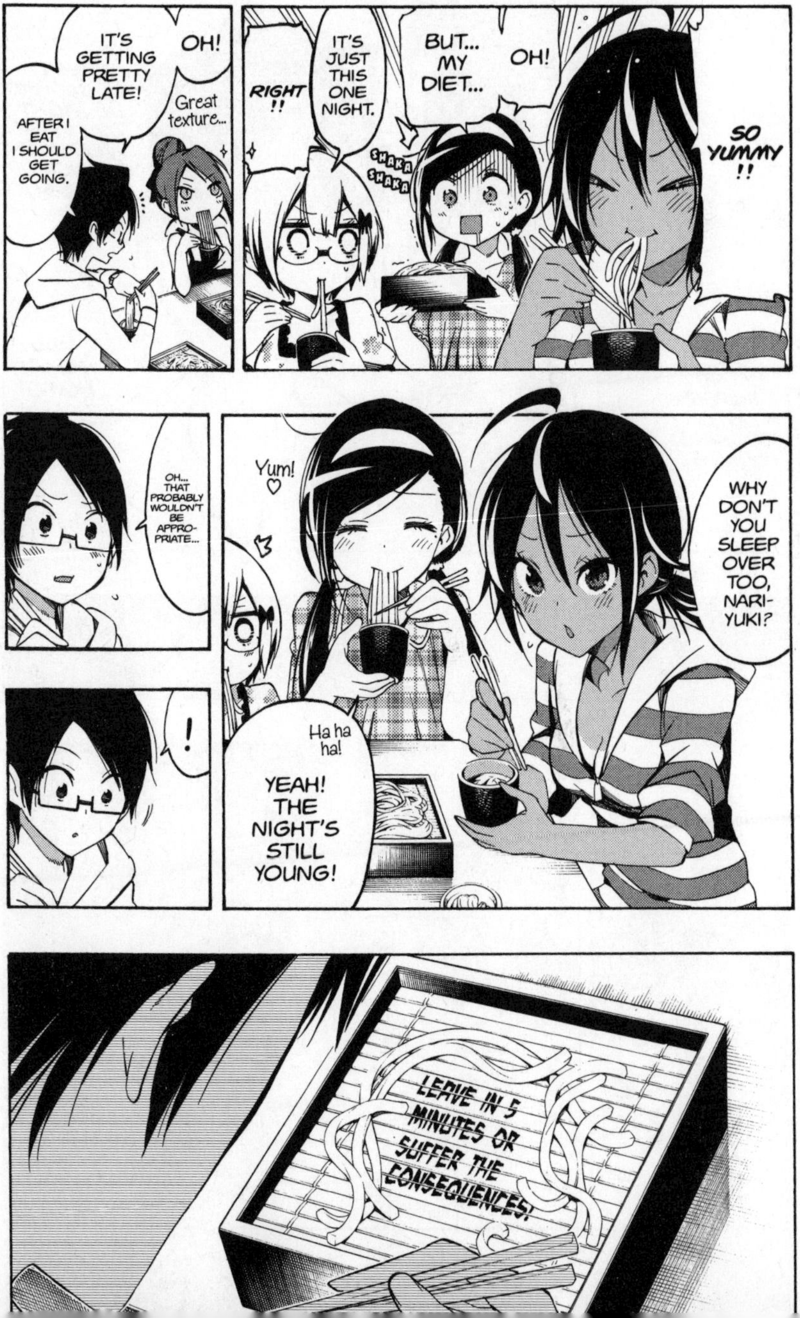
SO YUMMY!!
OH!
BUT... MY DIET...
SHAKA SHAKA
IT'S JUST THIS ONE NIGHT.
RIGHT!!
OH!
IT'S GETTING PRETTY LATE!
Great texture...
AFTER I EAT I SHOULD GET GOING.
WHY DON'T YOU SLEEP OVER TOO, NARI-YUKI?
Yum! ♡
Ha ha ha!
YEAH! THE NIGHT'S STILL YOUNG!
OH... THAT PROBABLY WOULDN'T BE APPRO-PRIATE...
!
LEAVE IN 5 MINUTES OR SUFFER THE CONSEQUENCES!

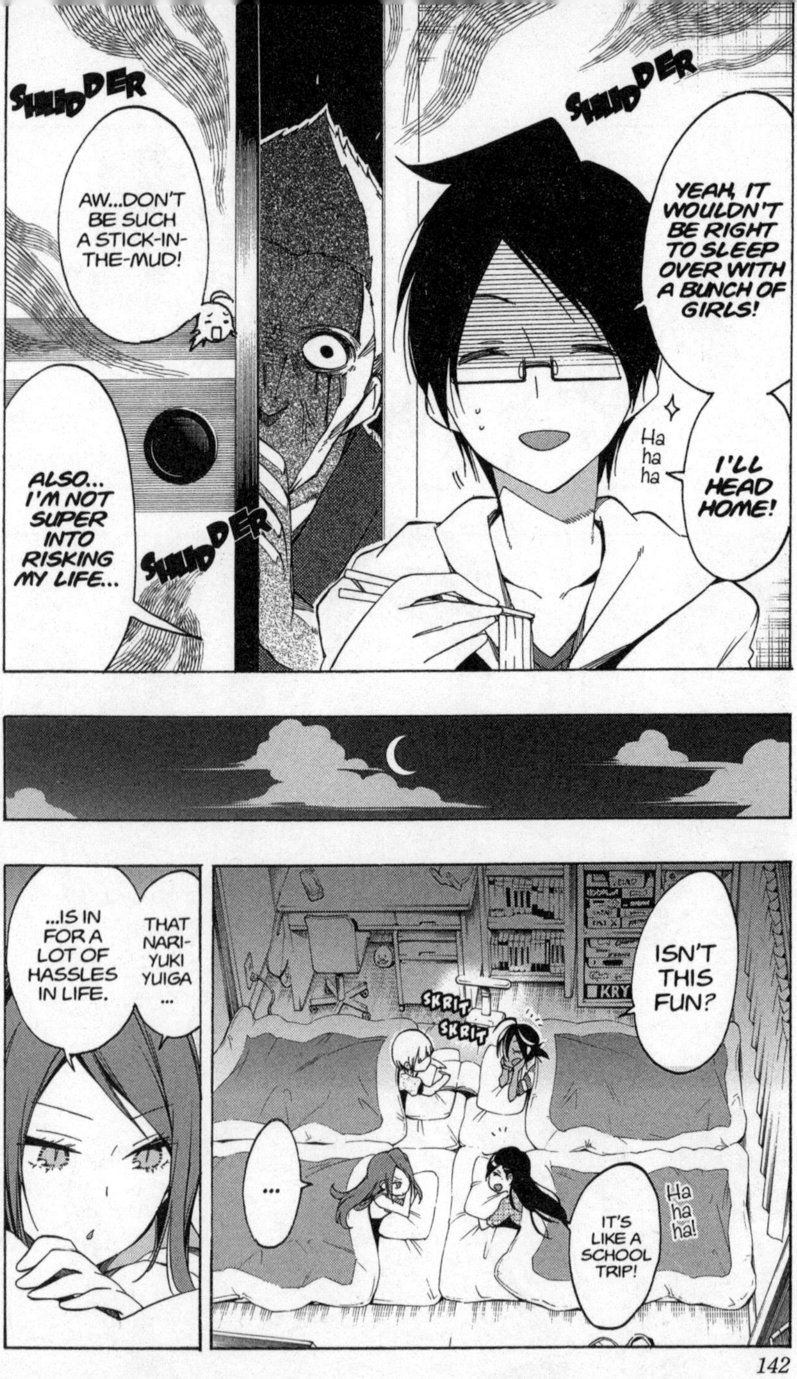
SHUDDER
YEAH, IT WOULDN'T BE RIGHT TO SLEEP OVER WITH A BUNCH OF GIRLS!
Ha ha ha
I'LL HEAD HOME!
SHUDDER
AW...DON'T BE SUCH A STICK-IN-THE-MUD!
ALSO... I'M NOT SUPER INTO RISKING MY LIFE...
SHUDDER
ISN'T THIS FUN?
SKRIT SKRIT
Ha ha ha!
IT'S LIKE A SCHOOL TRIP!
...
THAT NARI-YUKI YUIGA ...
...IS IN FOR A LOT OF HASSLES IN LIFE.

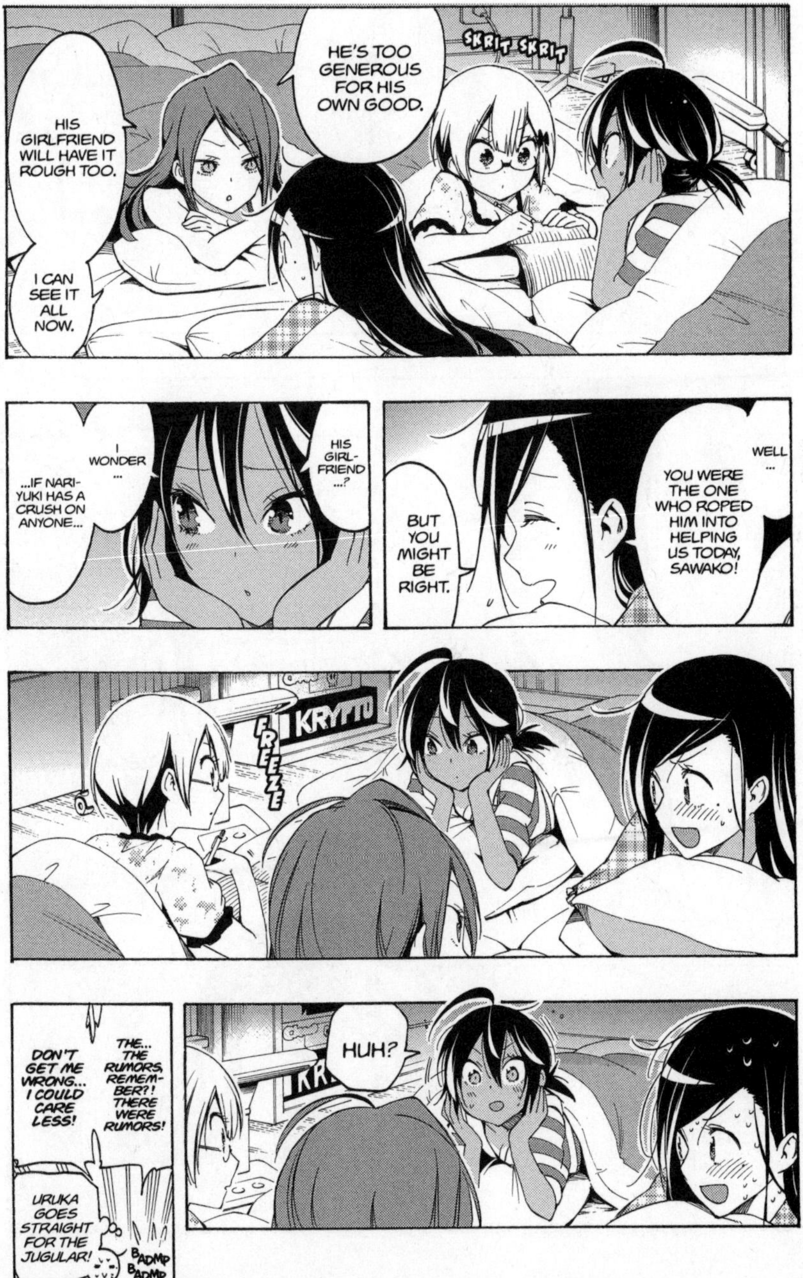
SKRIT SKRIT
HE'S TOO GENEROUS FOR HIS OWN GOOD.
HIS GIRLFRIEND WILL HAVE IT ROUGH TOO.
I CAN SEE IT ALL NOW.
WELL ...
YOU WERE THE ONE WHO ROPED HIM INTO HELPING US TODAY, SAWAKO!
BUT YOU MIGHT BE RIGHT.
HIS GIRL-FRIEND ...?
I WONDER ...
...IF NARI-YUKI HAS A CRUSH ON ANYONE...
KRYPTO
FREEZE
HUH?
THE... THE RUMORS, REMEM-BER?! THERE WERE RUMORS!
DON'T GET ME WRONG... I COULD CARE LESS!
URUKA GOES STRAIGHT FOR THE JUGULAR!
BADMP BADMP

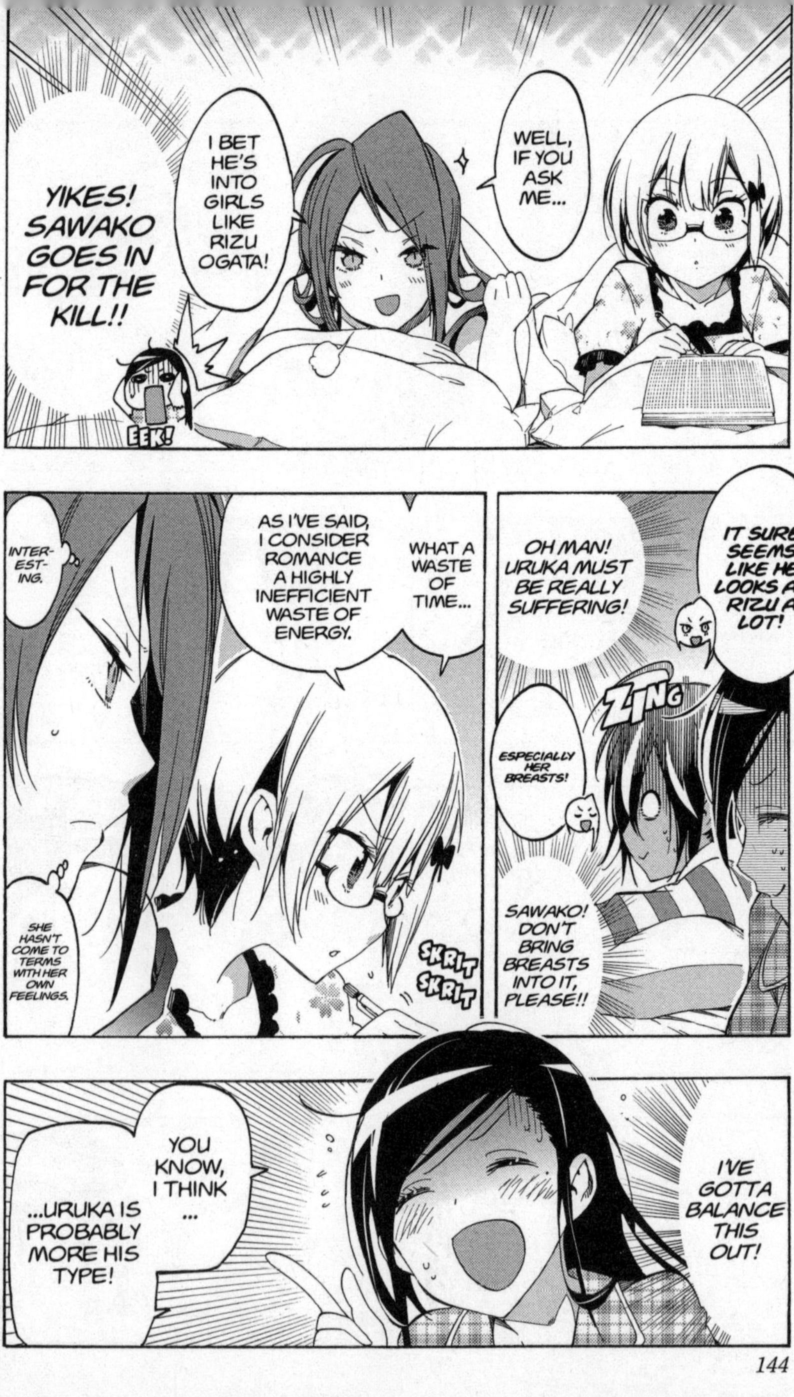
WELL, IF YOU ASK ME...
I BET HE'S INTO GIRLS LIKE RIZU OGATA!
YIKES! SAWAKO GOES IN FOR THE KILL!!
EEK!
IT SURE SEEMS LIKE HE LOOKS AT RIZU A LOT!
OH MAN! URUKA MUST BE REALLY SUFFERING!
ZING
ESPECIALLY HER BREASTS!
SAWAKO! DON'T BRING BREASTS INTO IT, PLEASE!!
WHAT A WASTE OF TIME...
AS I'VE SAID, I CONSIDER ROMANCE A HIGHLY INEFFICIENT WASTE OF ENERGY.
INTER-EST-ING.
SKRIT SKRIT
SHE HASN'T COME TO TERMS WITH HER OWN FEELINGS.
I'VE GOTTA BALANCE THIS OUT!
YOU KNOW, I THINK ...
...URUKA IS PROBABLY MORE HIS TYPE!

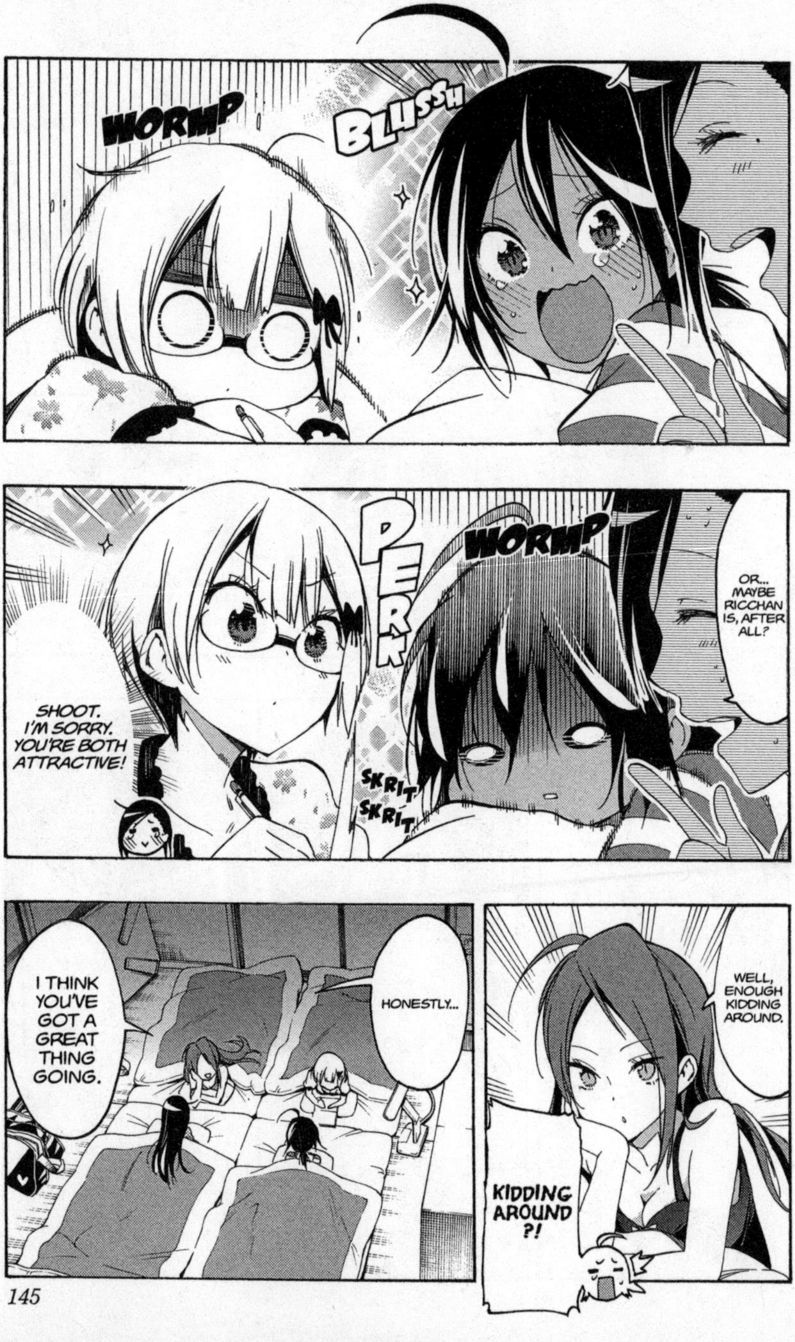
BLUSSH
WORMP
OR... MAYBE RICCHAN IS, AFTER ALL?
WORMP
PERK
SHOOT. I'M SORRY. YOU'RE BOTH ATTRACTIVE!
SKRIT SKRIT
WELL, ENOUGH KIDDING AROUND.
KIDDING AROUND?!
HONESTLY...
I THINK YOU'VE GOT A GREAT THING GOING.

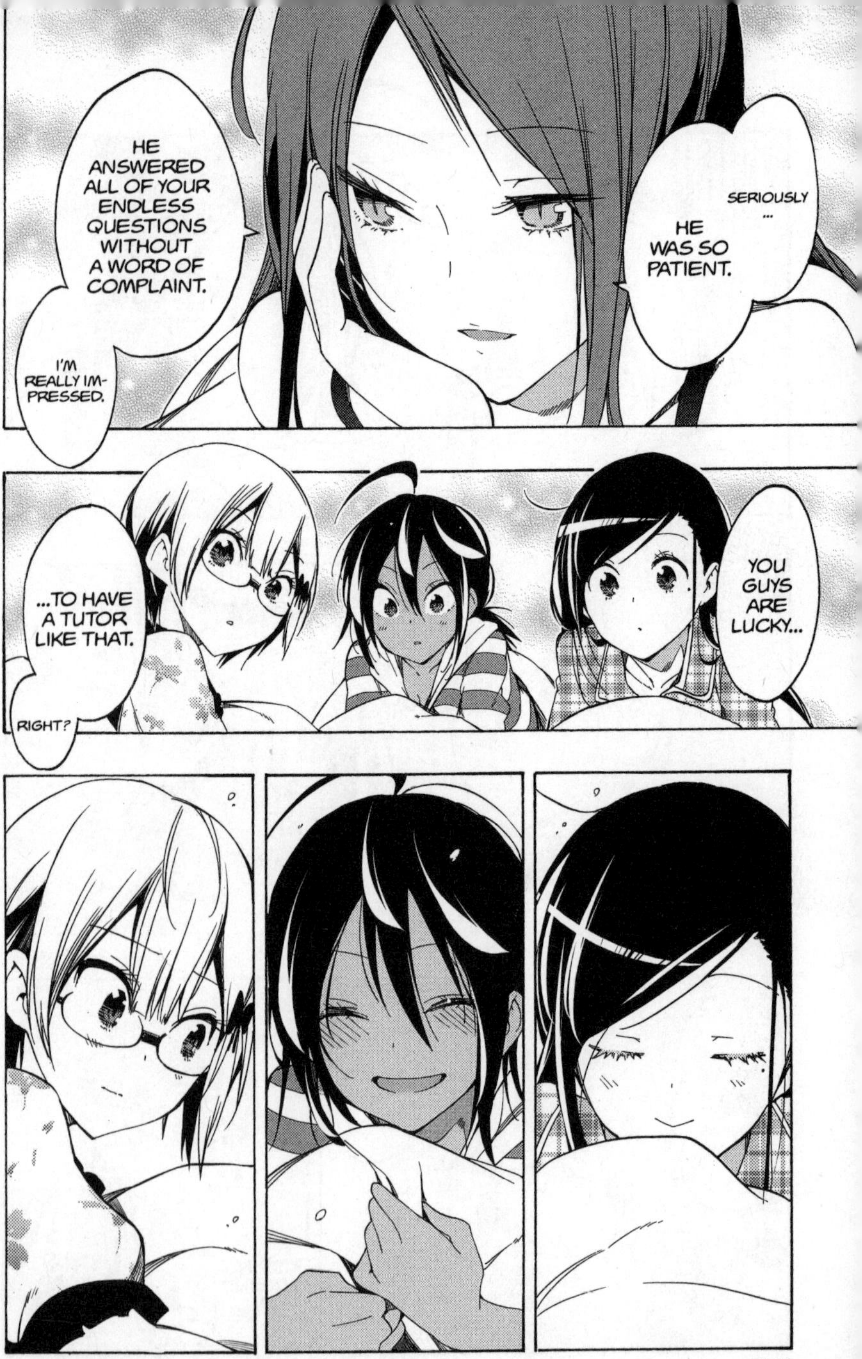
SERIOUSLY...
HE WAS SO PATIENT.
HE ANSWERED ALL OF YOUR ENDLESS QUESTIONS WITHOUT A WORD OF COMPLAINT.
I'M REALLY IM-PRESSED.
YOU GUYS ARE LUCKY...
...TO HAVE A TUTOR LIKE THAT.
RIGHT?

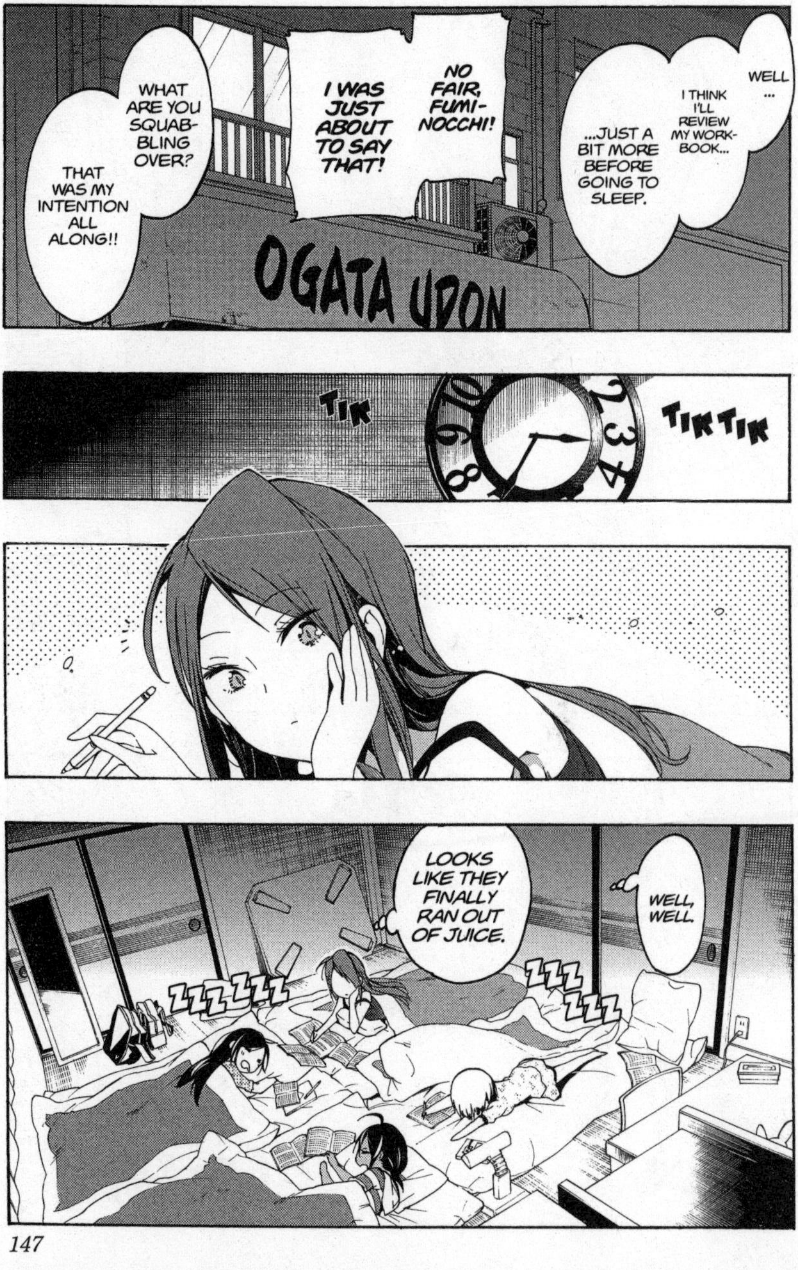
WELL ...
I THINK I'LL REVIEW MY WORK-BOOK...
...JUST A BIT MORE BEFORE GOING TO SLEEP.
NO FAIR, FUMI-NOCCHI!
I WAS JUST ABOUT TO SAY THAT!
WHAT ARE YOU SQUAB-BLING OVER?
THAT WAS MY INTENTION ALL ALONG!!
OGATA UDON
TIK TIK
TIK
WELL, WELL.
LOOKS LIKE THEY FINALLY RAN OUT OF JUICE.
ZZZ ZZZ
ZZZZZZ

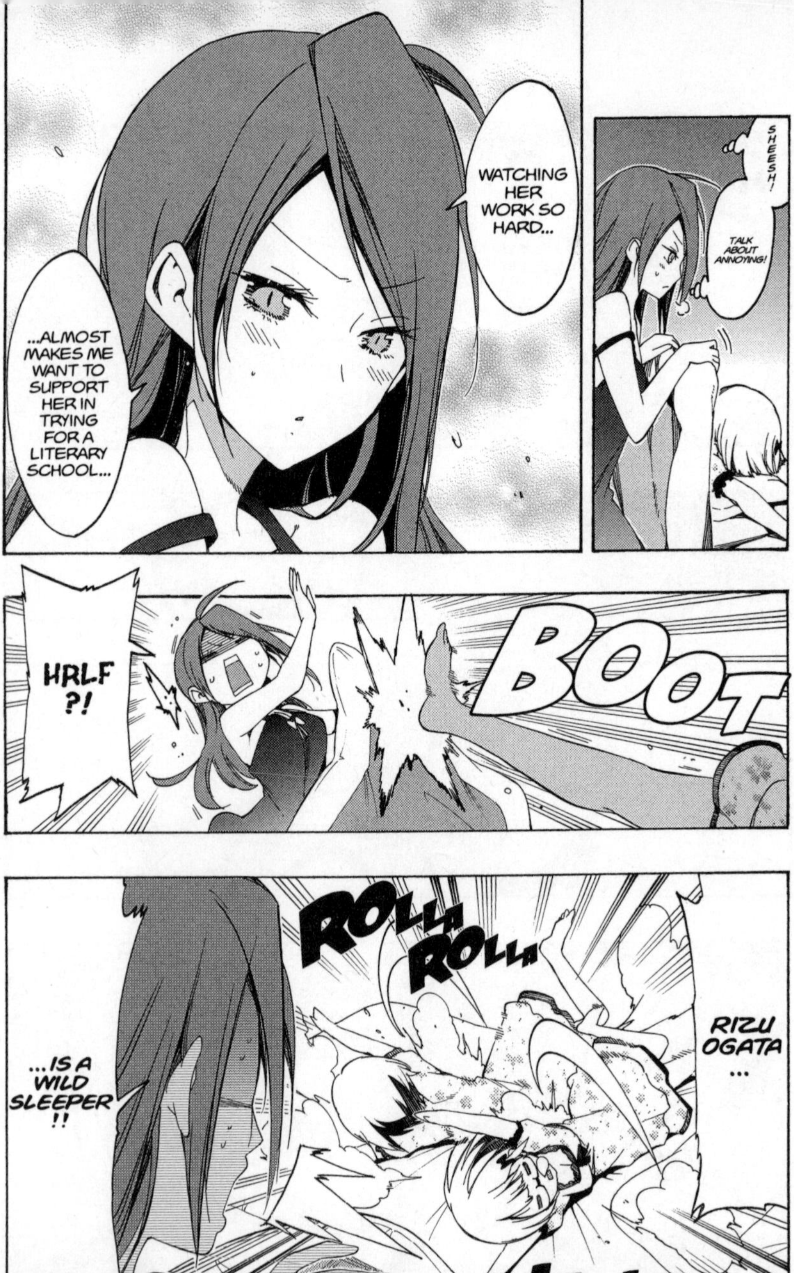
SHEESH!
TALK ABOUT ANNOYING!
WATCHING HER WORK SO HARD...
...ALMOST MAKES ME WANT TO SUPPORT HER IN TRYING FOR A LITERARY SCHOOL...
BOOT
HRLF ?!
RIZU OGATA ...
...IS A WILD SLEEPER !!
ROLLA ROLLA
FLAIL FLAIL

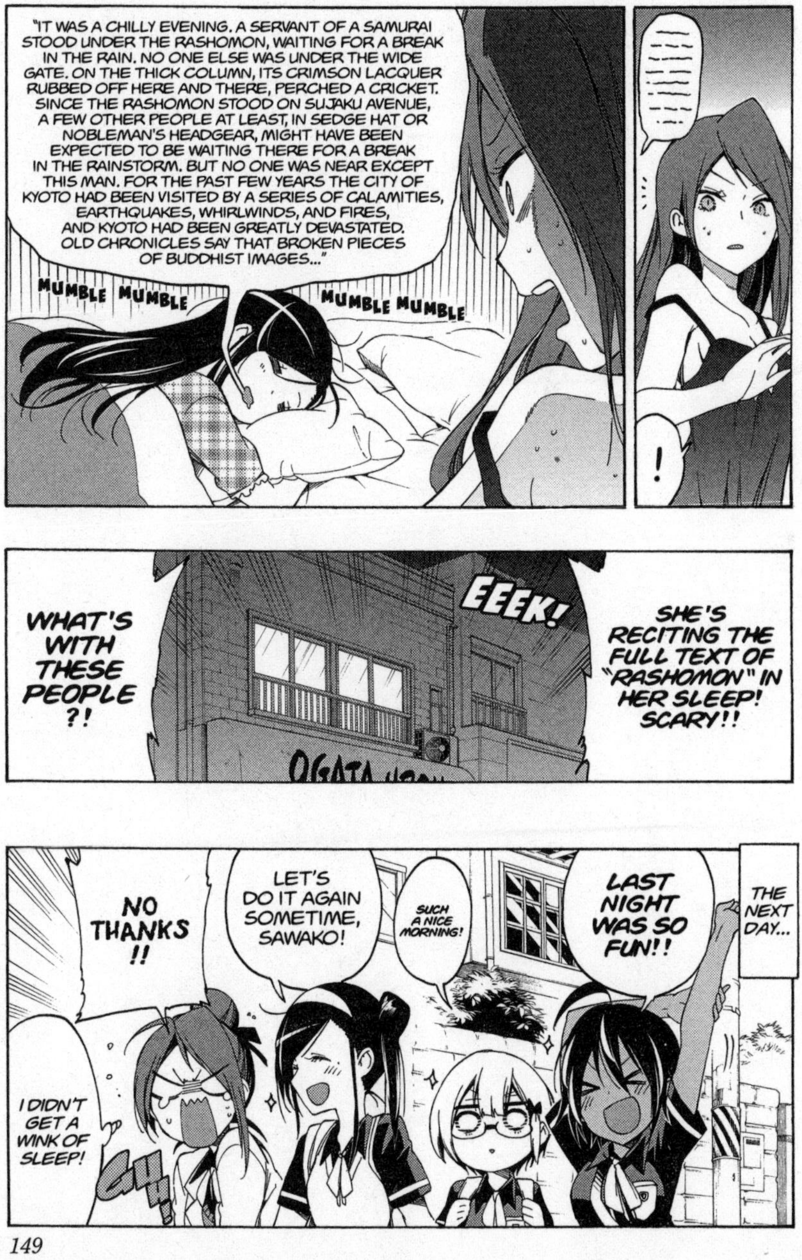
......
!
"IT WAS A CHILLY EVENING. A SERVANT OF A SAMURAI STOOD UNDER THE RASHOMON, WAITING FOR A BREAK IN THE RAIN. NO ONE ELSE WAS UNDER THE WIDE GATE. ON THE THICK COLUMN, ITS CRIMSON LACQUER RUBBED OFF HERE AND THERE, PERCHED A CRICKET. SINCE THE RASHOMON STOOD ON SUJAKU AVENUE, A FEW OTHER PEOPLE AT LEAST, IN SEDGE HAT OR NOBLEMAN'S HEADGEAR, MIGHT HAVE BEEN EXPECTED TO BE WAITING THERE FOR A BREAK IN THE RAINSTORM. BUT NO ONE WAS NEAR EXCEPT THIS MAN. FOR THE PAST FEW YEARS THE CITY OF KYOTO HAD BEEN VISITED BY A SERIES OF CALAMITIES, EARTHQUAKES, WHIRLWINDS, AND FIRES, AND KYOTO HAD BEEN GREATLY DEVASTATED. OLD CHRONICLES SAY THAT BROKEN PIECES OF BUDDHIST IMAGES..."
MUMBLE MUMBLE
MUMBLE MUMBLE
SHE'S RECITING THE FULL TEXT OF "RASHOMON" IN HER SLEEP! SCARY!!
EEEK!
WHAT'S WITH THESE PEOPLE?!
THE NEXT DAY...
LAST NIGHT WAS SO FUN!!
SUCH A NICE MORNING!
LET'S DO IT AGAIN SOMETIME, SAWAKO!
NO THANKS!!
I DIDN'T GET A WINK OF SLEEP!

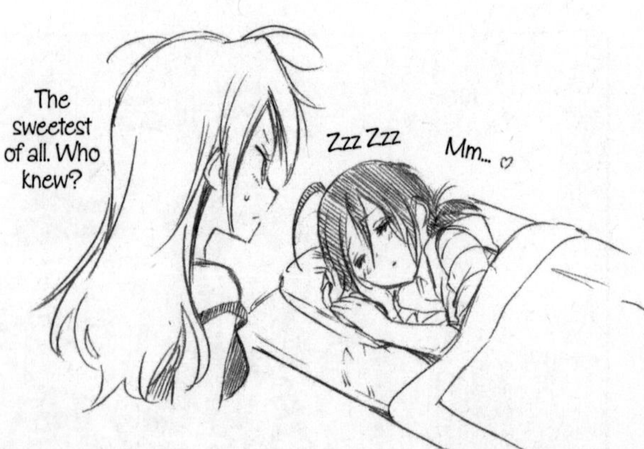
Mm... ♡
Zzz Zzz
The sweetest of all. Who knew?

Question 24: A Dauntless Genius Struggles Against Rumors of [*X*]

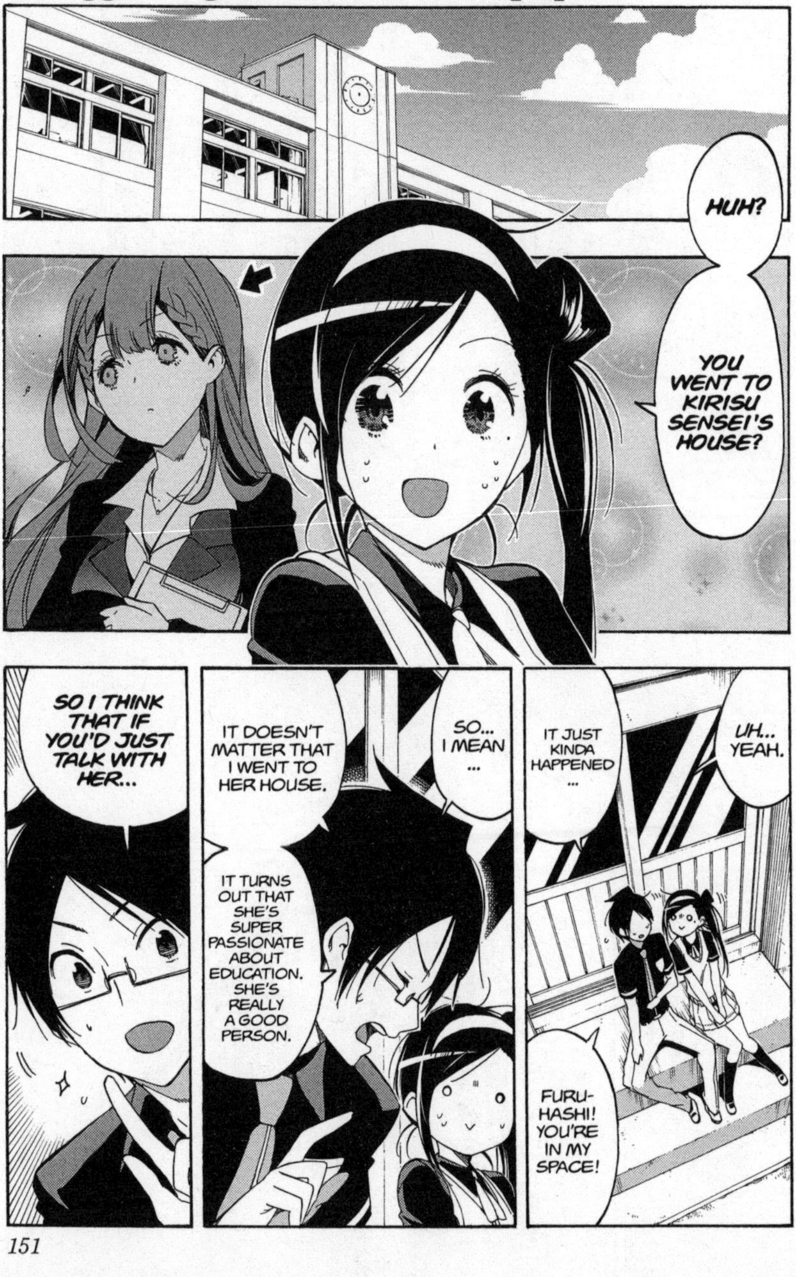
HUH?
YOU WENT TO KIRISU SENSEI'S HOUSE?
UH... YEAH.
IT JUST KINDA HAPPENED ...
FURU-HASHI! YOU'RE IN MY SPACE!
SO... I MEAN ...
IT DOESN'T MATTER THAT I WENT TO HER HOUSE.
IT TURNS OUT THAT SHE'S SUPER PASSIONATE ABOUT EDUCATION. SHE'S REALLY A GOOD PERSON.
SO I THINK THAT IF YOU'D JUST TALK WITH HER...

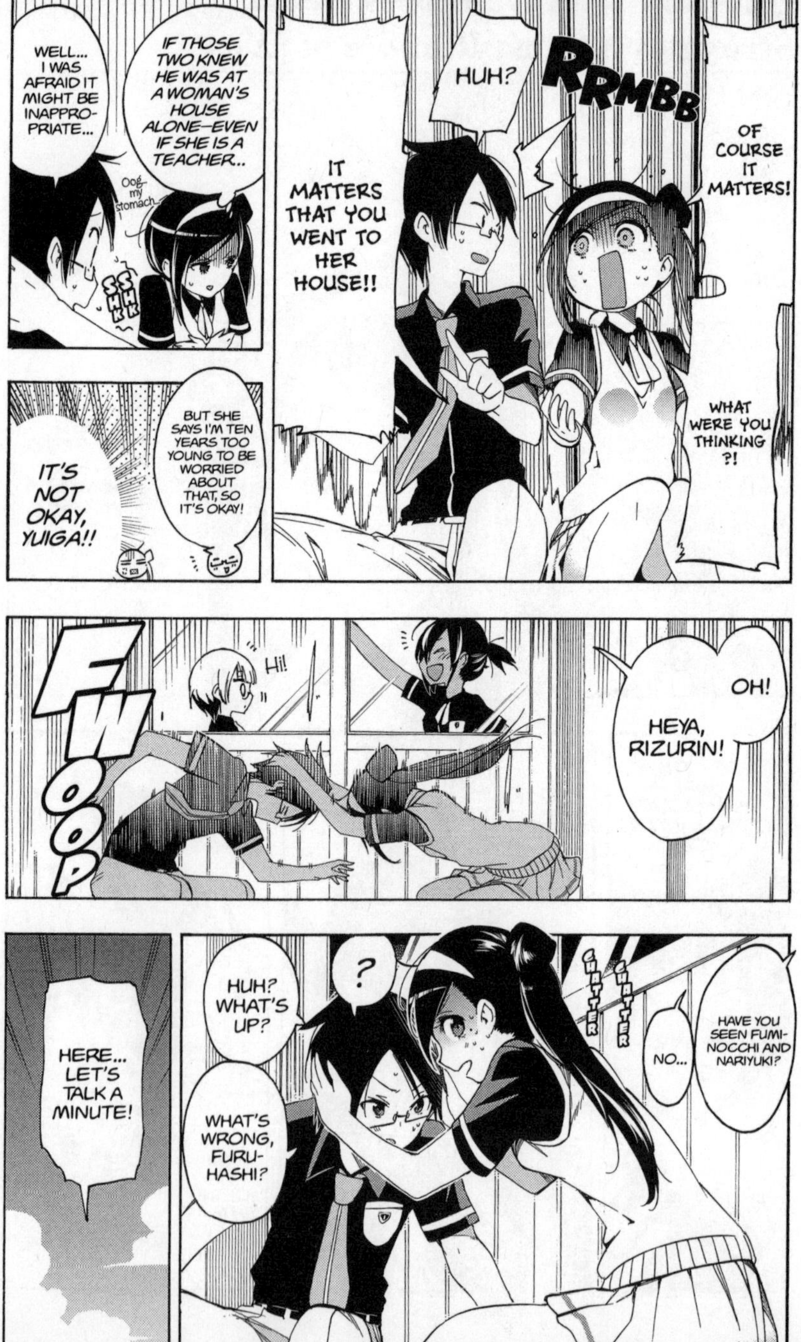
OF COURSE IT MATTERS!
RRMBB
HUH?
IT MATTERS THAT YOU WENT TO HER HOUSE!!
WHAT WERE YOU THINKING?!
IF THOSE TWO KNEW HE WAS AT A WOMAN'S HOUSE ALONE—EVEN IF SHE IS A TEACHER...
WELL... I WAS AFRAID IT MIGHT BE INAPPROPRIATE...
Oog-my stomach...
SHK SHK
BUT SHE SAYS I'M TEN YEARS TOO YOUNG TO BE WORRIED ABOUT THAT, SO IT'S OKAY!
IT'S NOT OKAY, YUIGA!!
OH!
HEYA, RIZURIN!
Hi!
FWOOOP
HAVE YOU SEEN FUMINOCCHI AND NARIYUKI?
NO...
CHATTER CHATTER
?
HUH? WHAT'S UP?
WHAT'S WRONG, FURUHASHI?
HERE... LET'S TALK A MINUTE!

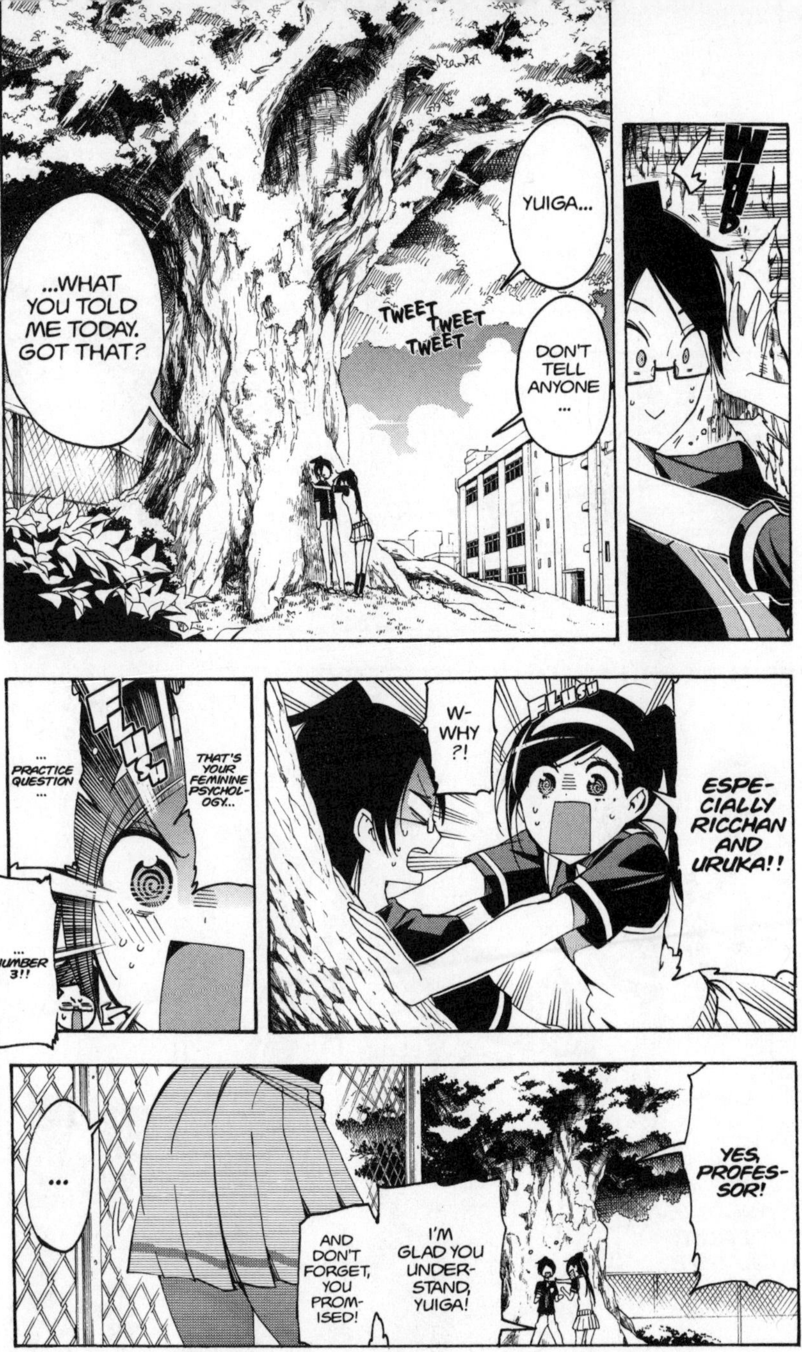
WHUD
YUIGA...
DON'T TELL ANYONE ...
TWEET TWEET TWEET
...WHAT YOU TOLD ME TODAY. GOT THAT?
ESPE-CIALLY RICCHAN AND URUKA!!
FLUSH
W-WHY?!
FLUSH
THAT'S YOUR FEMININE PSYCHOL-OGY...
...PRACTICE QUESTION...
...NUMBER 3!!
YES, PROFES-SOR!
I'M GLAD YOU UNDER-STAND, YUIGA!
AND DON'T FORGET, YOU PROM-ISED!
...

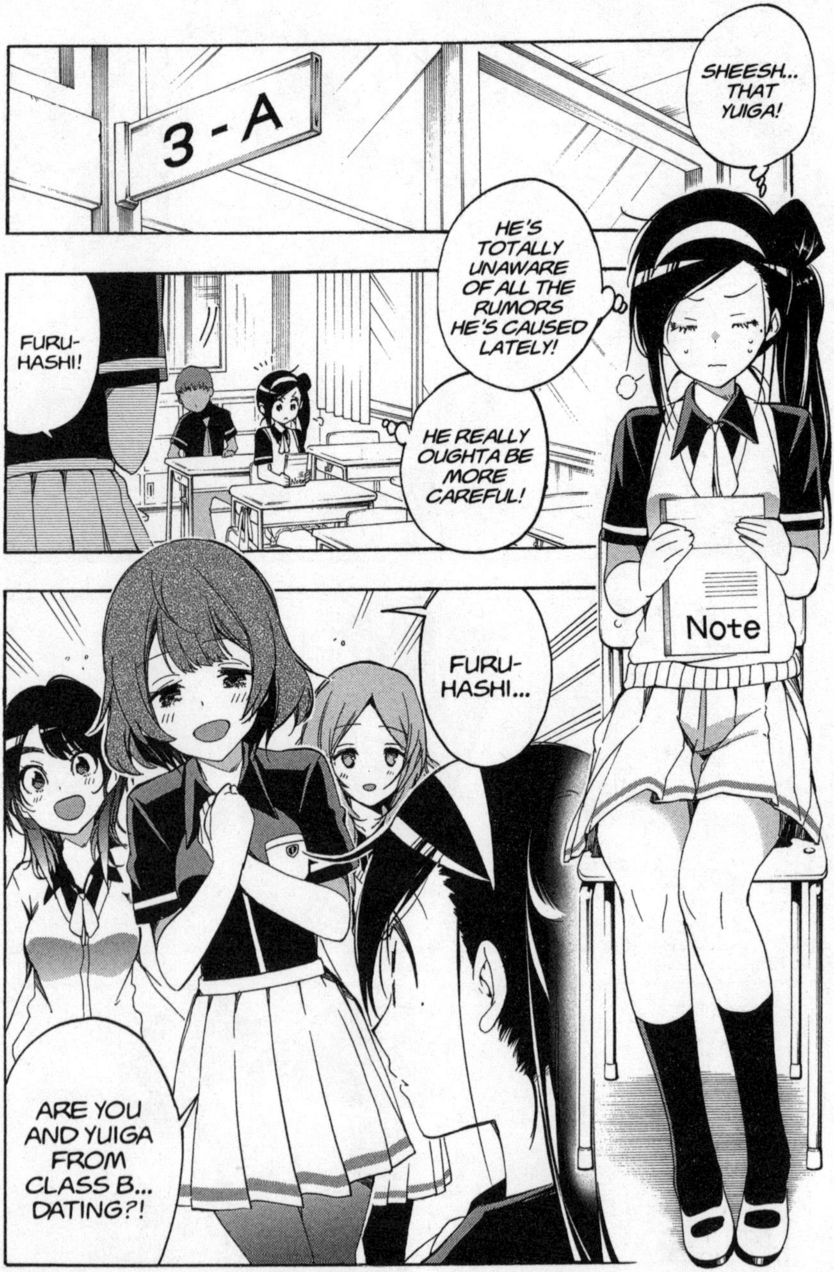
3 - A
SHEESH... THAT YUIGA!
HE'S TOTALLY UNAWARE OF ALL THE RUMORS HE'S CAUSED LATELY!
HE REALLY OUGHTA BE MORE CAREFUL!
Note
FURU-HASHI!
Note
FURU-HASHI...
ARE YOU AND YUIGA FROM CLASS B... DATING?!

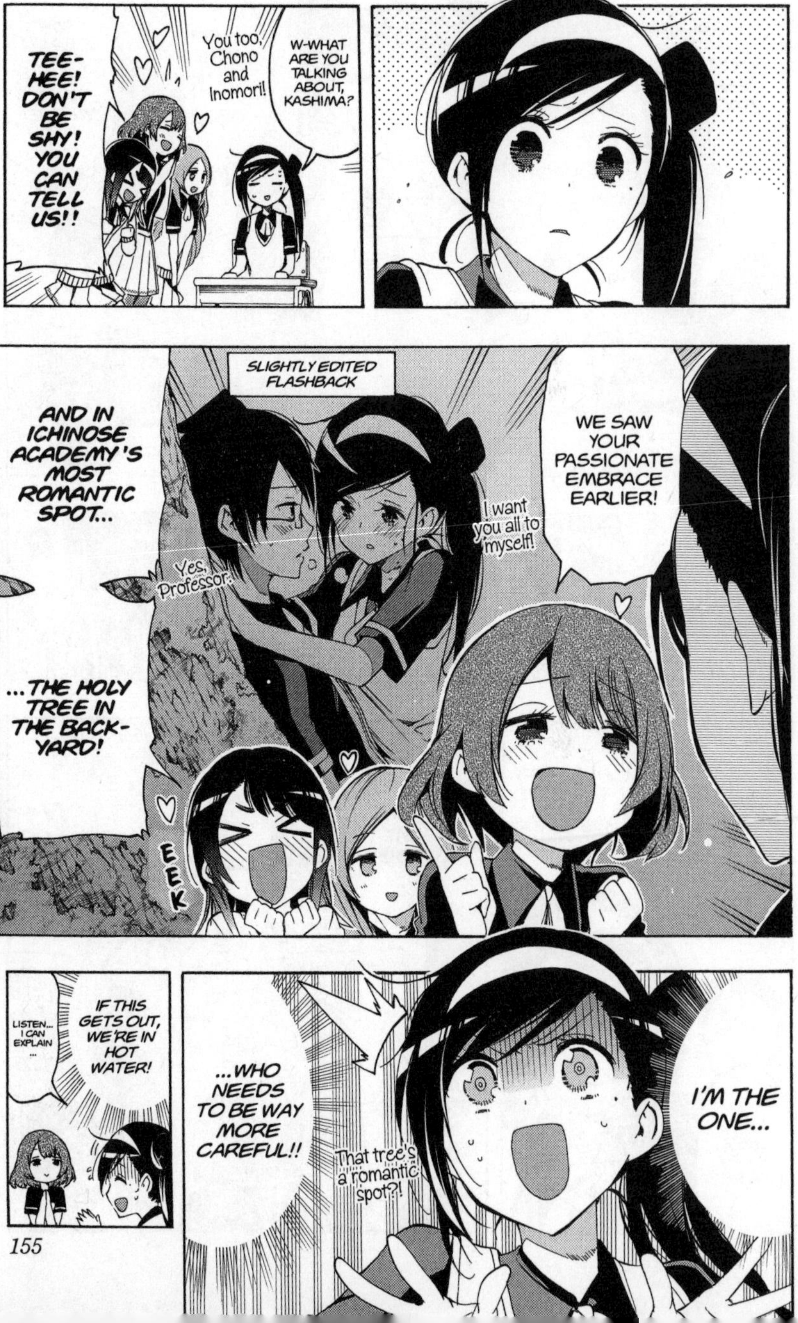
W-WHAT ARE YOU TALKING ABOUT, KASHIMA?
You too, Chono and Inomori!
TEE-HEE! DON'T BE SHY! YOU CAN TELL US!!
WE SAW YOUR PASSIONATE EMBRACE EARLIER!
SLIGHTLY EDITED FLASHBACK
I want you all to myself!
Yes, Professor.
AND IN ICHINOSE ACADEMY'S MOST ROMANTIC SPOT...
...THE HOLY TREE IN THE BACK-YARD!
EEK
I'M THE ONE...
...WHO NEEDS TO BE WAY MORE CAREFUL!!
That tree's a romantic spot?!
IF THIS GETS OUT, WE'RE IN HOT WATER!
LISTEN... I CAN EXPLAIN...

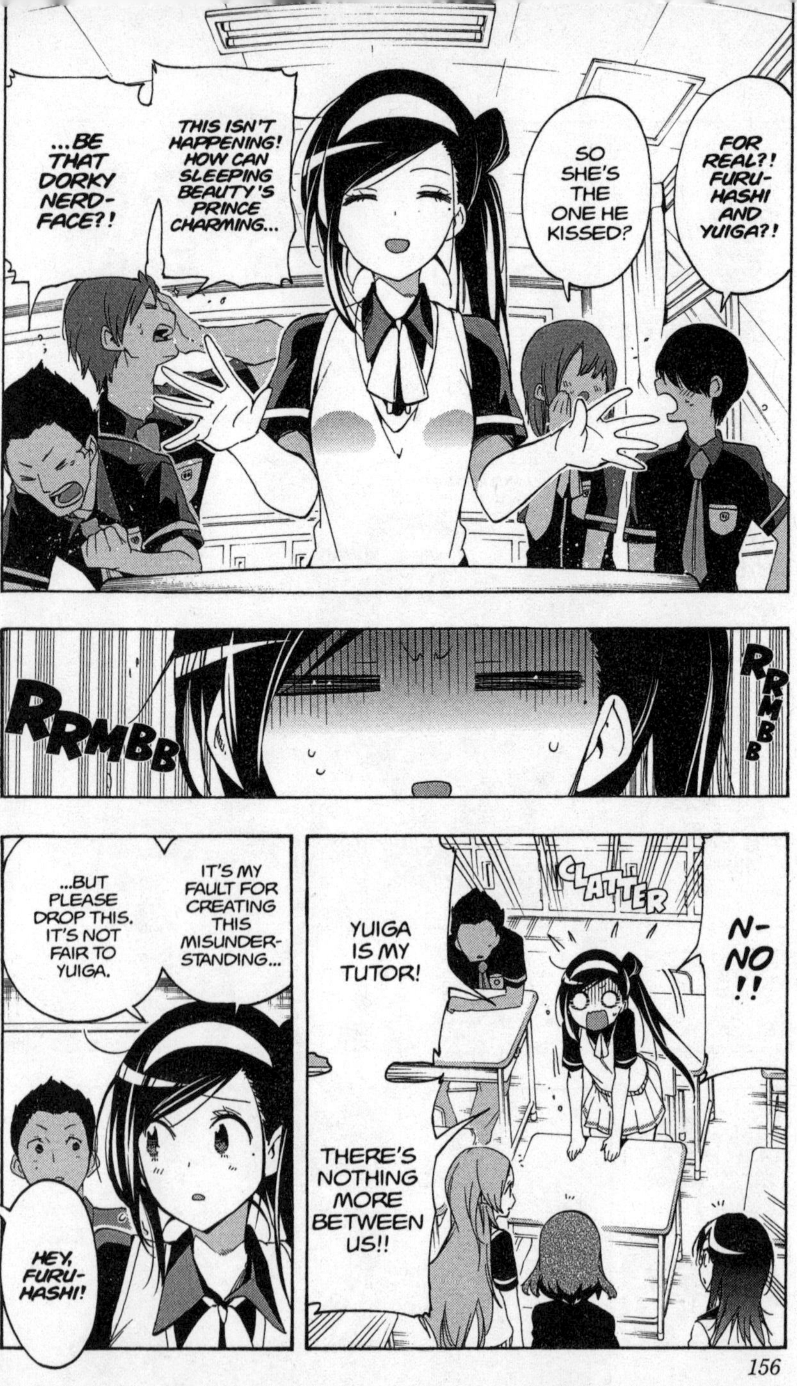
FOR REAL?! FURUHASHI AND YUIGA?!
SO SHE'S THE ONE HE KISSED?
THIS ISN'T HAPPENING! HOW CAN SLEEPING BEAUTY'S PRINCE CHARMING...
...BE THAT DORKY NERD-FACE?!
RRMBB
RRMBB
N-NO!!
CLATTER
YUIGA IS MY TUTOR!
THERE'S NOTHING MORE BETWEEN US!!
IT'S MY FAULT FOR CREATING THIS MISUNDERSTANDING...
...BUT PLEASE DROP THIS. IT'S NOT FAIR TO YUIGA.
HEY, FURUHASHI!

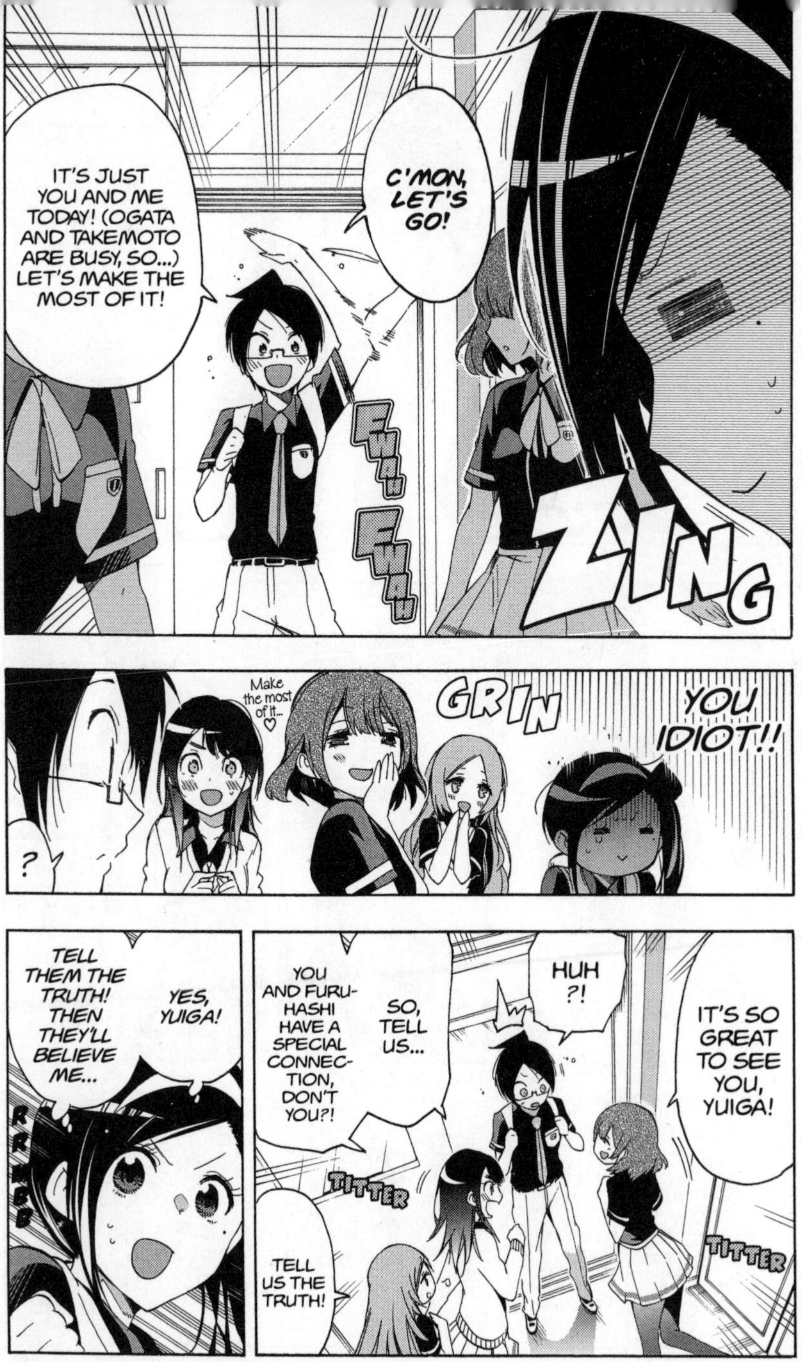
C'MON, LET'S GO!
IT'S JUST YOU AND ME TODAY! (OGATA AND TAKEMOTO ARE BUSY, SO...) LET'S MAKE THE MOST OF IT!
ZING
FWAH FWAH
YOU IDIOT!!
GRIN
Make the most of it... ♡
?
IT'S SO GREAT TO SEE YOU, YUIGA!
HUH ?!
SO, TELL US...
YOU AND FURU-HASHI HAVE A SPECIAL CONNEC-TION, DON'T YOU?!
TITTER
TITTER
TELL US THE TRUTH!
YES, YUIGA!
TELL THEM THE TRUTH! THEN THEY'LL BELIEVE ME...

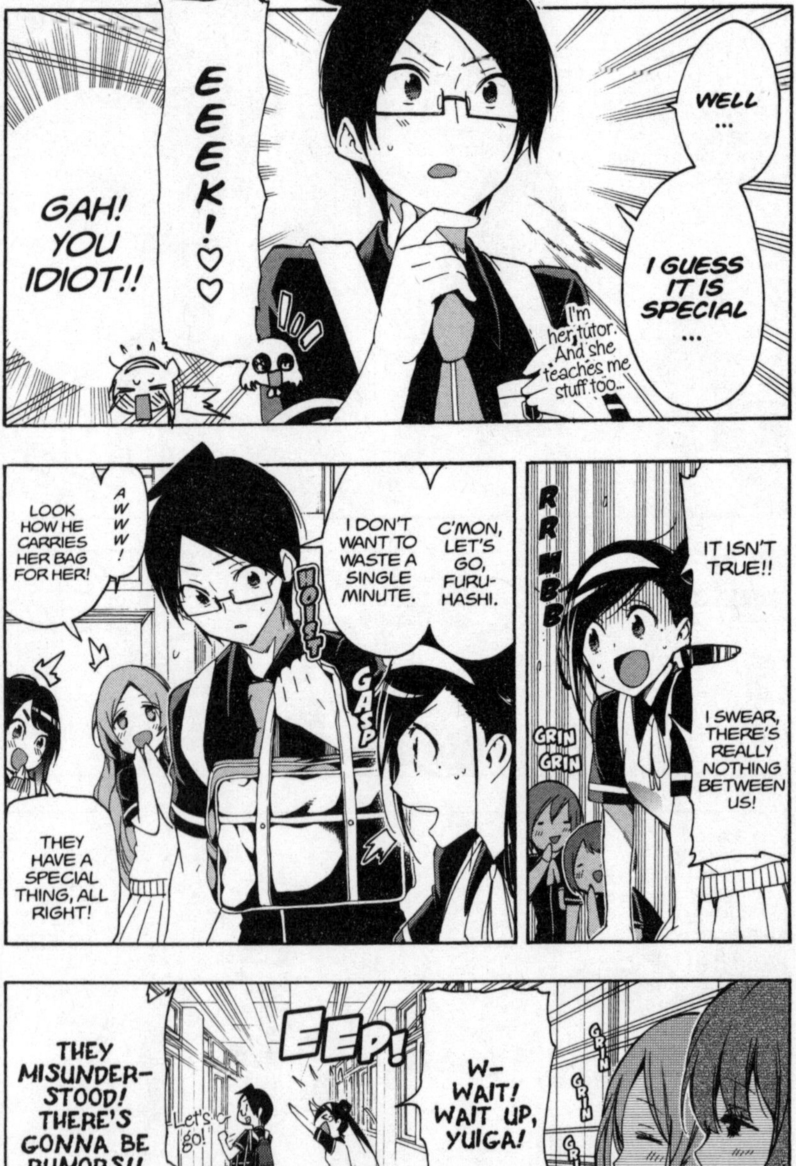
WELL... I GUESS IT IS SPECIAL...
I'm her tutor. And she teaches me stuff too...
EEEK! ♡♡
GAH! YOU IDIOT!!
RRMBB
IT ISN'T TRUE!!
I SWEAR, THERE'S REALLY NOTHING BETWEEN US!
GRIN GRIN
C'MON, LET'S GO, FURU-HASHI.
I DON'T WANT TO WASTE A SINGLE MINUTE.
HOIST
AWWW!
LOOK HOW HE CARRIES HER BAG FOR HER!
GASP
THEY HAVE A SPECIAL THING, ALL RIGHT!
GRIN GRIN GRIN GRIN
W-WAIT! WAIT UP, YUIGA!
EEP!
Let's go!
THEY MISUNDER-STOOD! THERE'S GONNA BE RUMORS!!

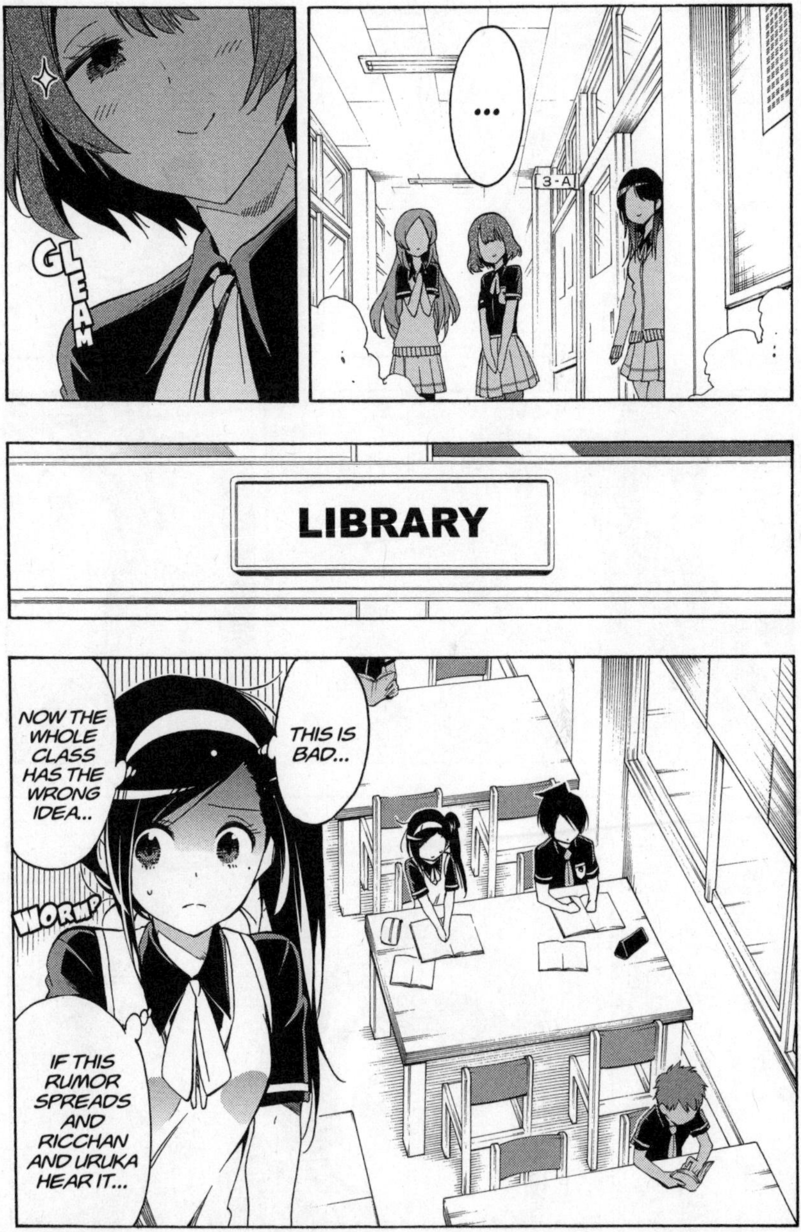
...
GLEAM
LIBRARY
THIS IS BAD...
NOW THE WHOLE CLASS HAS THE WRONG IDEA...
WORMP
IF THIS RUMOR SPREADS AND RICCHAN AND URUKA HEAR IT...

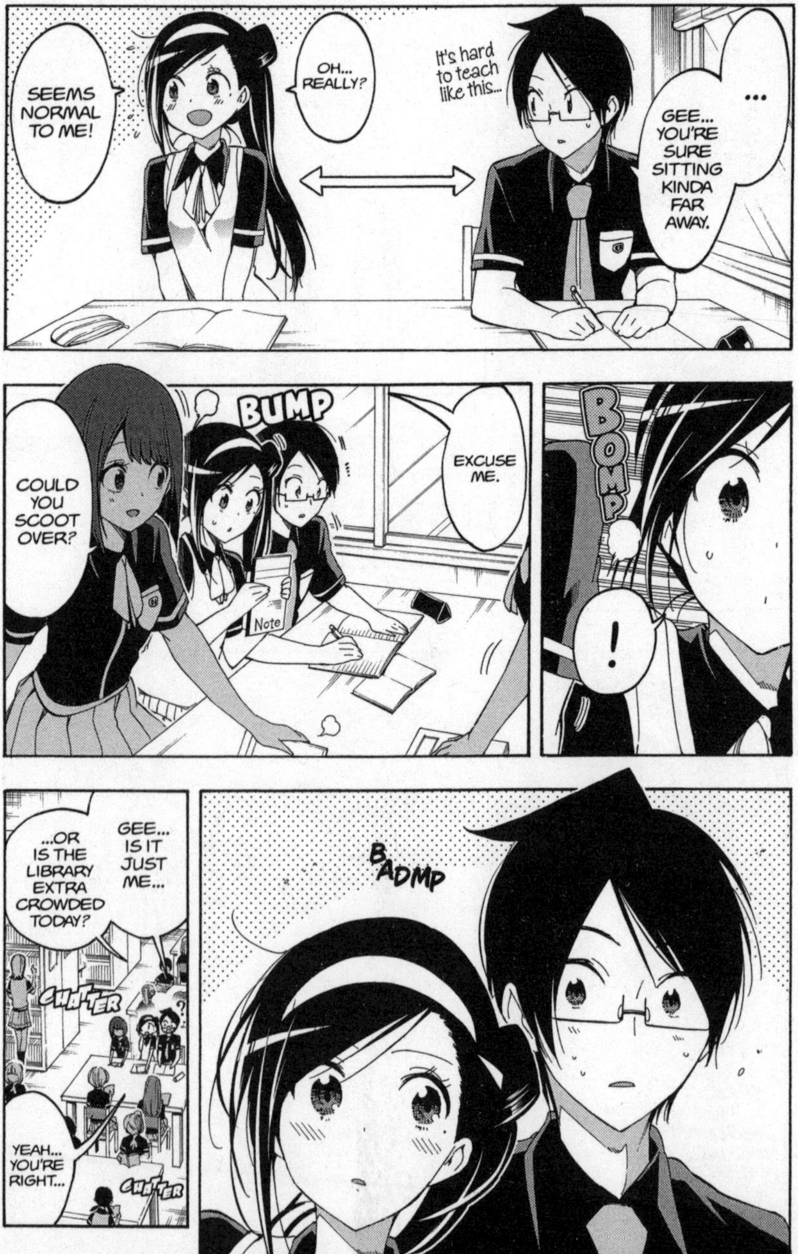
...
GEE... YOU'RE SURE SITTING KINDA FAR AWAY.
It's hard to teach like this...
OH... REALLY?
SEEMS NORMAL TO ME!
BOMP
!
EXCUSE ME.
BUMP
COULD YOU SCOOT OVER?
Note
BADMP
GEE... IS IT JUST ME...
...OR IS THE LIBRARY EXTRA CROWDED TODAY?
CHATTER
YEAH... YOU'RE RIGHT...
CHATTER

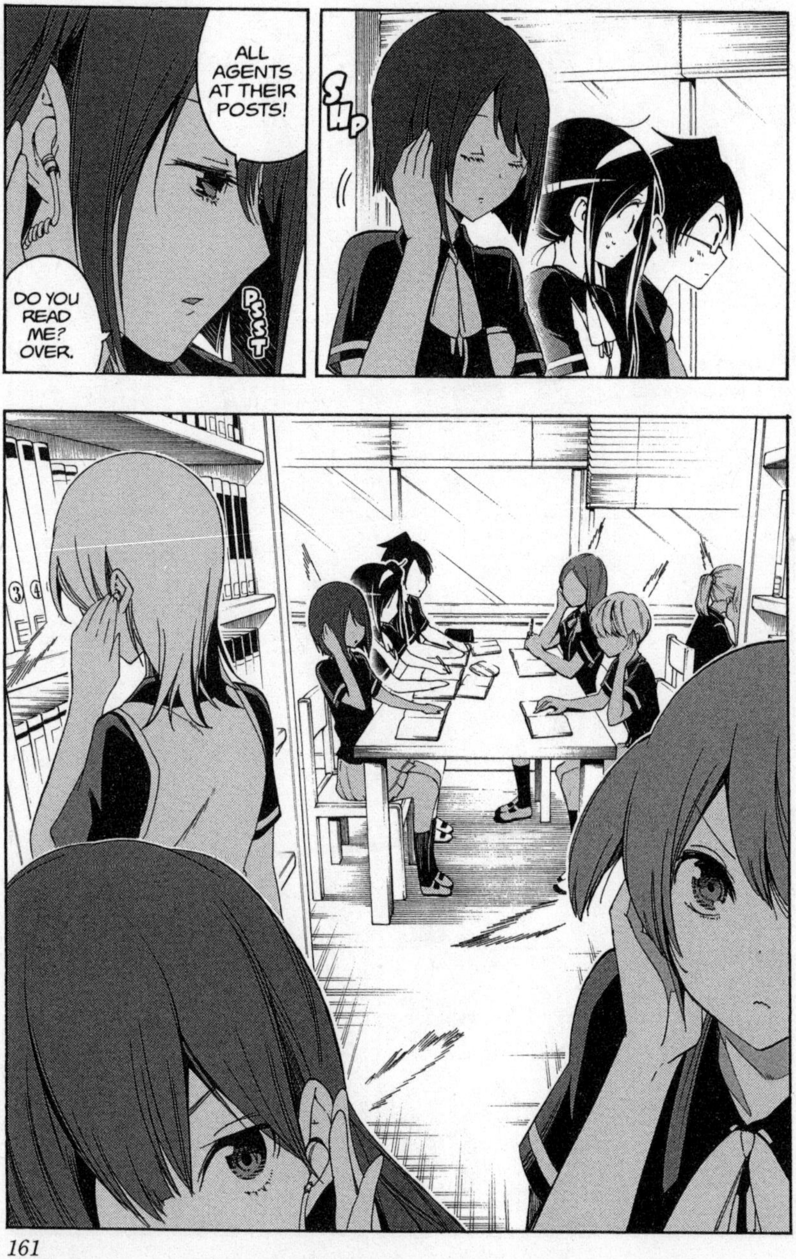
SHP
ALL AGENTS AT THEIR POSTS!
DO YOU READ ME? OVER.
PSSST

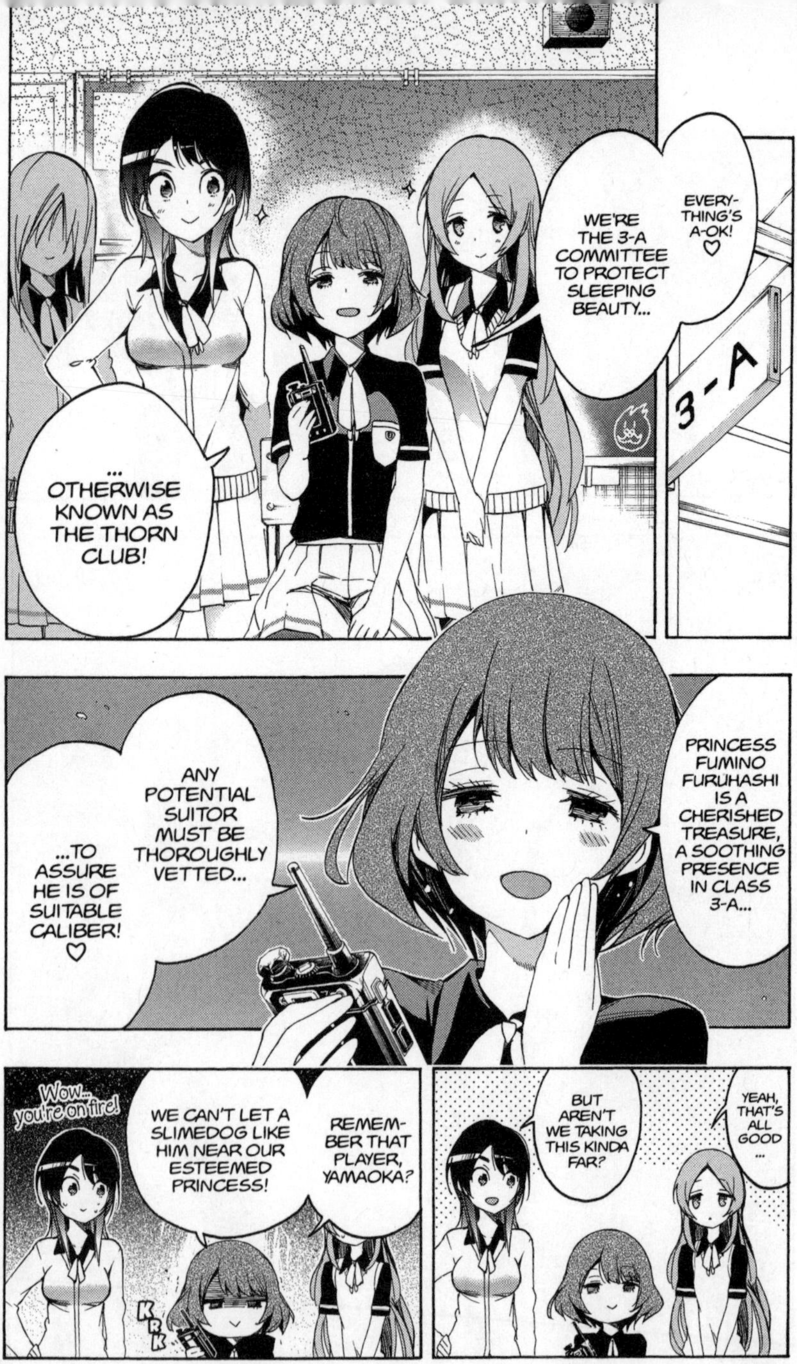
3-A
EVERY-THING'S A-OK! ♡
WE'RE THE 3-A COMMITTEE TO PROTECT SLEEPING BEAUTY...
... OTHERWISE KNOWN AS THE THORN CLUB!
PRINCESS FUMINO FURUHASHI IS A CHERISHED TREASURE, A SOOTHING PRESENCE IN CLASS 3-A...
ANY POTENTIAL SUITOR MUST BE THOROUGHLY VETTED...
...TO ASSURE HE IS OF SUITABLE CALIBER! ♡
YEAH, THAT'S ALL GOOD ...
BUT AREN'T WE TAKING THIS KINDA FAR?
REMEM-BER THAT PLAYER, YAMAOKA?
WE CAN'T LET A SLIMEDOG LIKE HIM NEAR OUR ESTEEMED PRINCESS!
KRK
Wow... you're on fire!

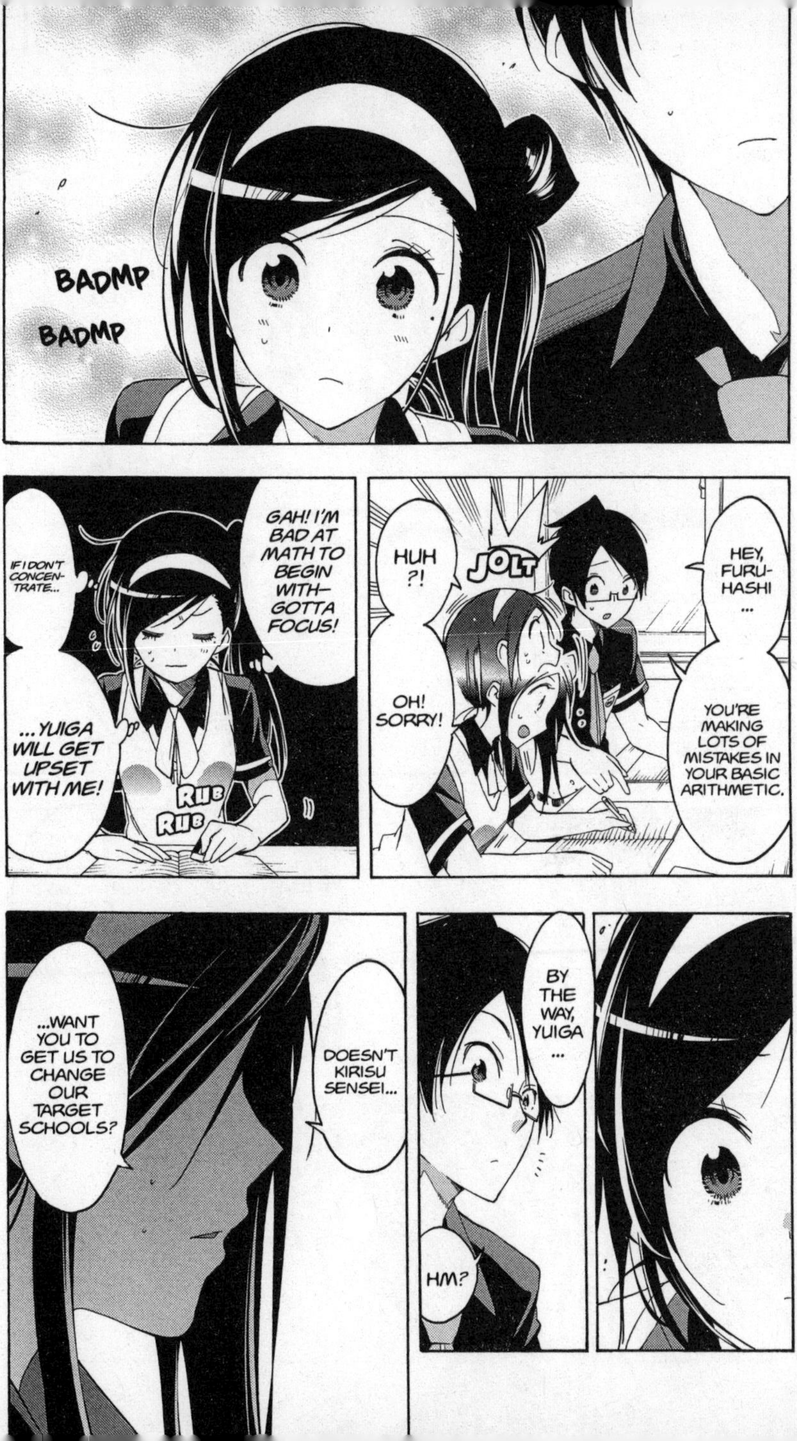
BADMP
BADMP
HEY, FURU-HASHI ...
HUH ?!
JOLT
YOU'RE MAKING LOTS OF MISTAKES IN YOUR BASIC ARITHMETIC.
OH! SORRY!
GAH! I'M BAD AT MATH TO BEGIN WITH—GOTTA FOCUS!
IF I DON'T CONCEN-TRATE...
...YUIGA WILL GET UPSET WITH ME!
RUB
RUB
BY THE WAY, YUIGA ...
HM?
DOESN'T KIRISU SENSEI...
...WANT YOU TO GET US TO CHANGE OUR TARGET SCHOOLS?

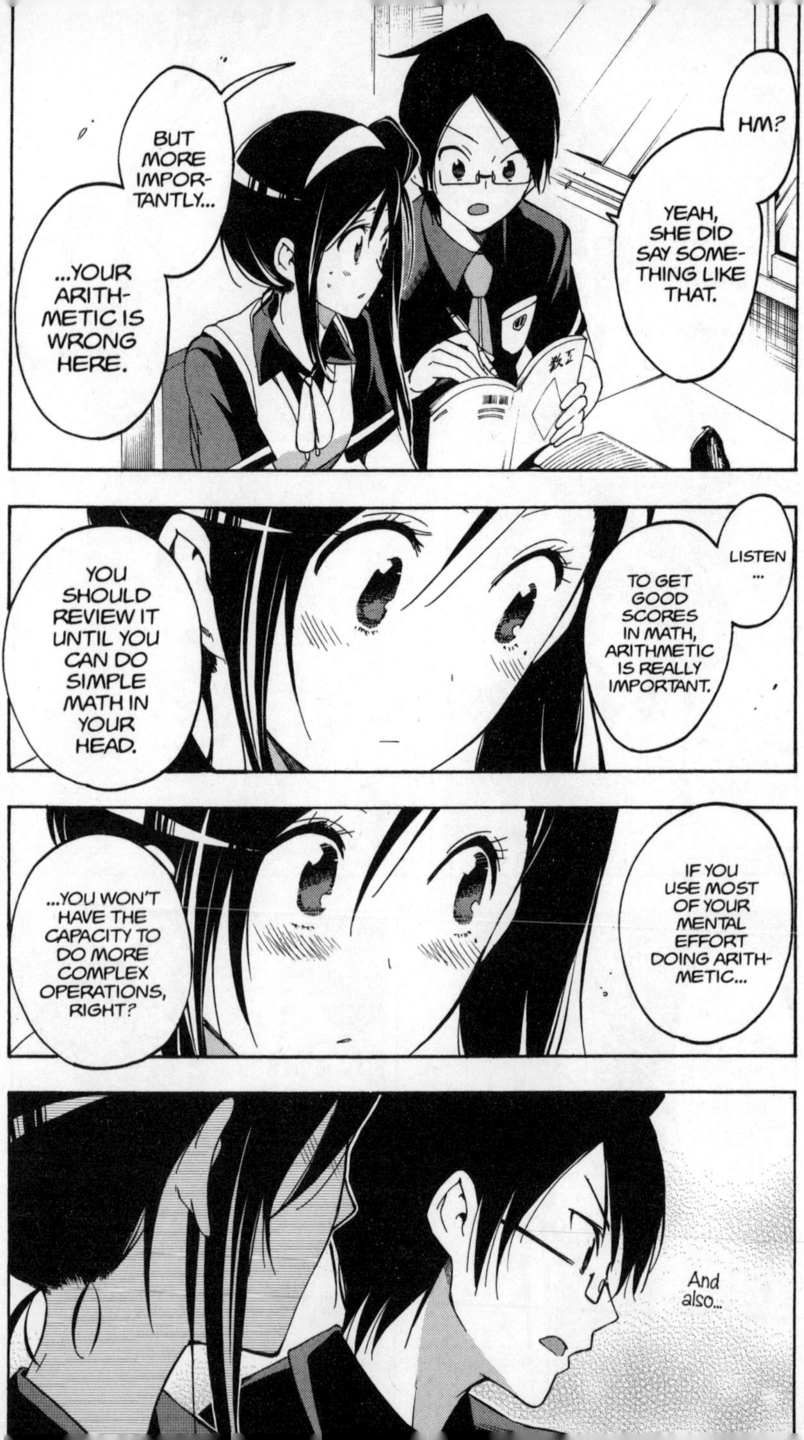
HM?
YEAH, SHE DID SAY SOMETHING LIKE THAT.
BUT MORE IMPORTANTLY...
...YOUR ARITHMETIC IS WRONG HERE.
LISTEN...
TO GET GOOD SCORES IN MATH, ARITHMETIC IS REALLY IMPORTANT.
YOU SHOULD REVIEW IT UNTIL YOU CAN DO SIMPLE MATH IN YOUR HEAD.
IF YOU USE MOST OF YOUR MENTAL EFFORT DOING ARITHMETIC...
...YOU WON'T HAVE THE CAPACITY TO DO MORE COMPLEX OPERATIONS, RIGHT?
And also...

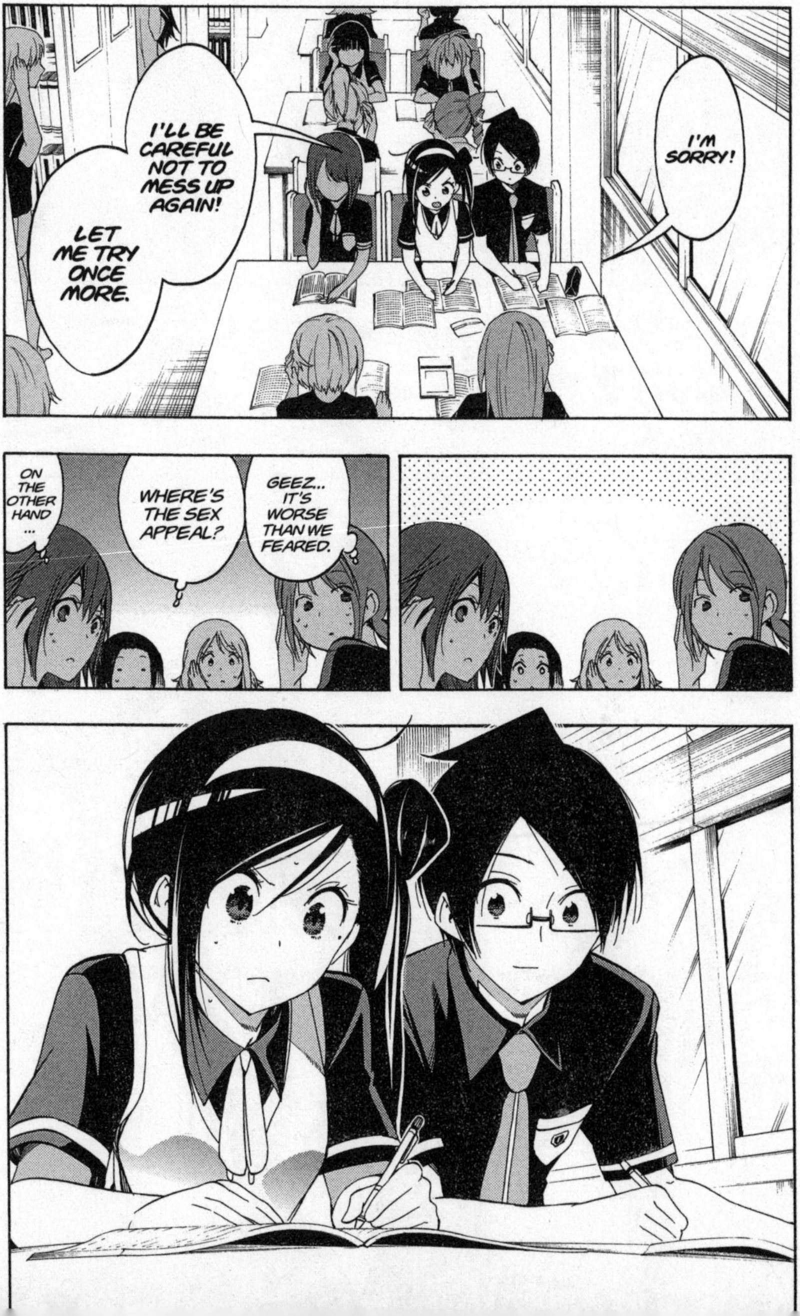
I'M SORRY!
I'LL BE CAREFUL NOT TO MESS UP AGAIN!
LET ME TRY ONCE MORE.
GEEZ... IT'S WORSE THAN WE FEARED.
WHERE'S THE SEX APPEAL?
ON THE OTHER HAND ...

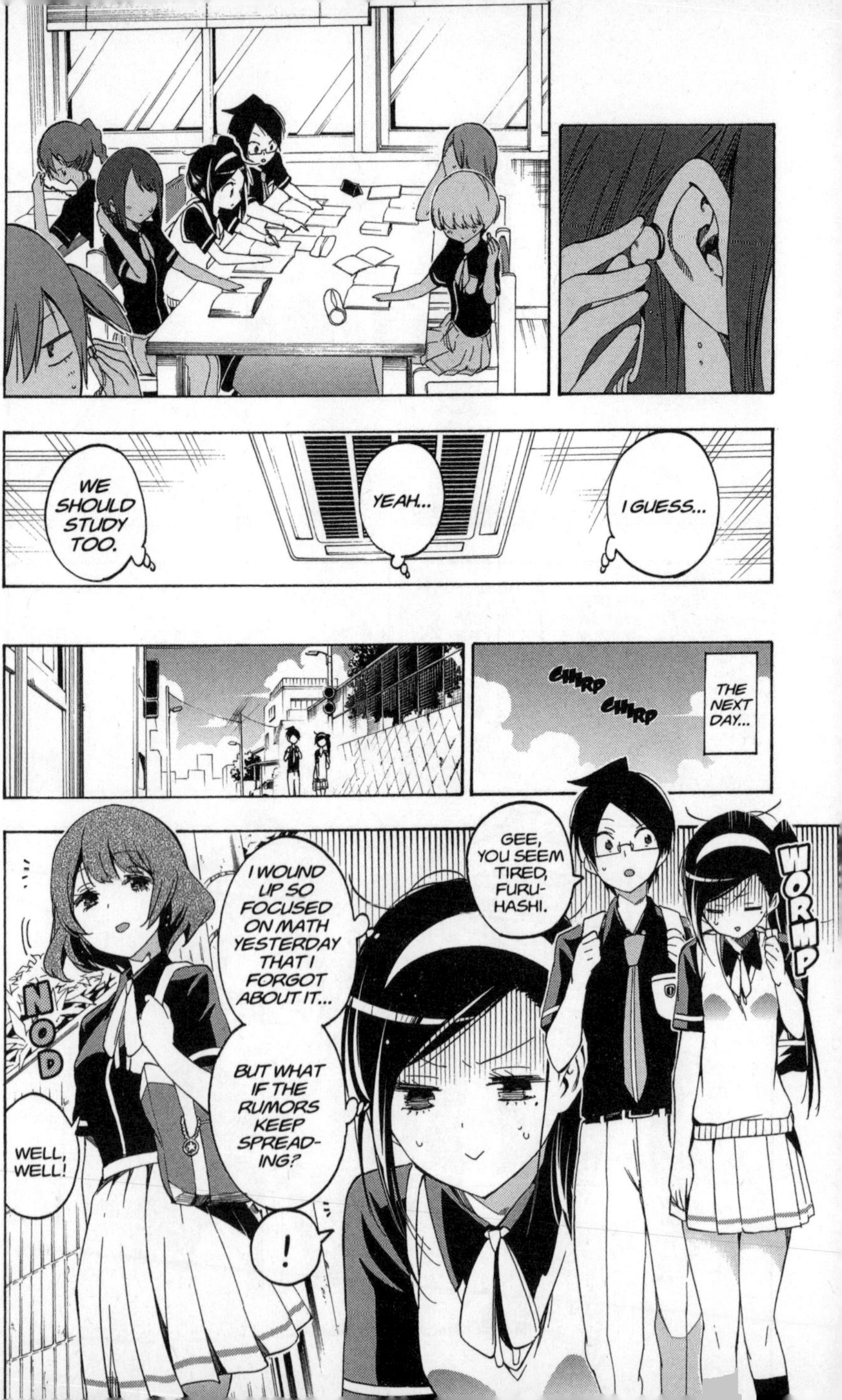
I GUESS...
YEAH...
WE SHOULD STUDY TOO.
THE NEXT DAY...
CHIRP CHIRP
WORMP
GEE, YOU SEEM TIRED, FURU-HASHI.
I WOUND UP SO FOCUSED ON MATH YESTERDAY THAT I FORGOT ABOUT IT...
BUT WHAT IF THE RUMORS KEEP SPREAD-ING?
!
NOD
WELL, WELL!

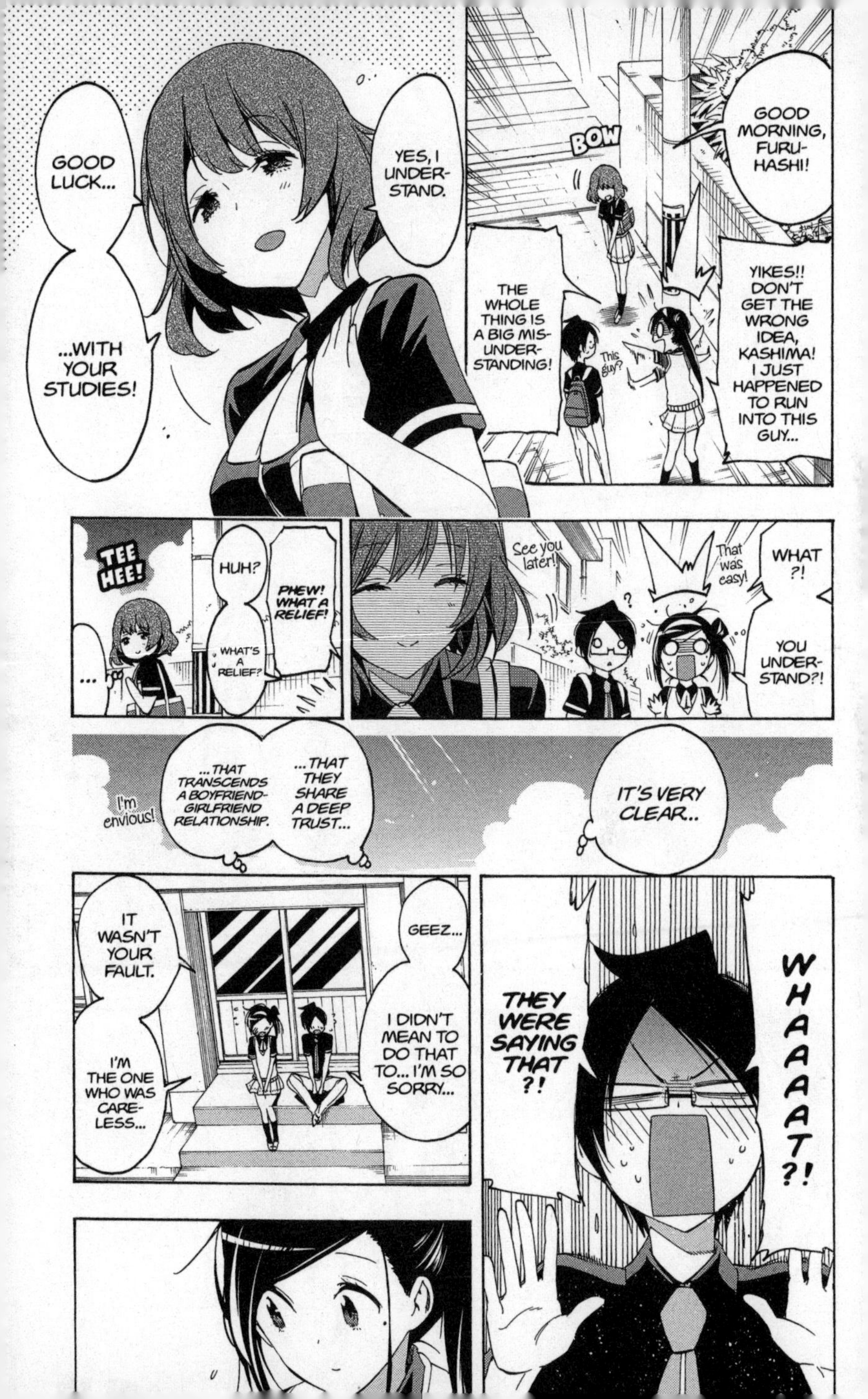
GOOD MORNING, FURU-HASHI!
BOW
YIKES!! DON'T GET THE WRONG IDEA, KASHIMA! I JUST HAPPENED TO RUN INTO THIS GUY...
This guy?
THE WHOLE THING IS A BIG MIS-UNDER-STANDING!
YES, I UNDER-STAND.
GOOD LUCK...
...WITH YOUR STUDIES!
WHAT?!
That was easy!
See you later!
YOU UNDER-STAND?!
PHEW! WHAT A RELIEF!
HUH?
WHAT'S A RELIEF?
...
TEE HEE!
IT'S VERY CLEAR...
...THAT THEY SHARE A DEEP TRUST...
...THAT TRANSCENDS A BOYFRIEND-GIRLFRIEND RELATIONSHIP.
I'm envious!
WHAAAAAT?!
THEY WERE SAYING THAT?!
GEEZ...
I DIDN'T MEAN TO DO THAT TO... I'M SO SORRY...
IT WASN'T YOUR FAULT.
I'M THE ONE WHO WAS CARE-LESS...

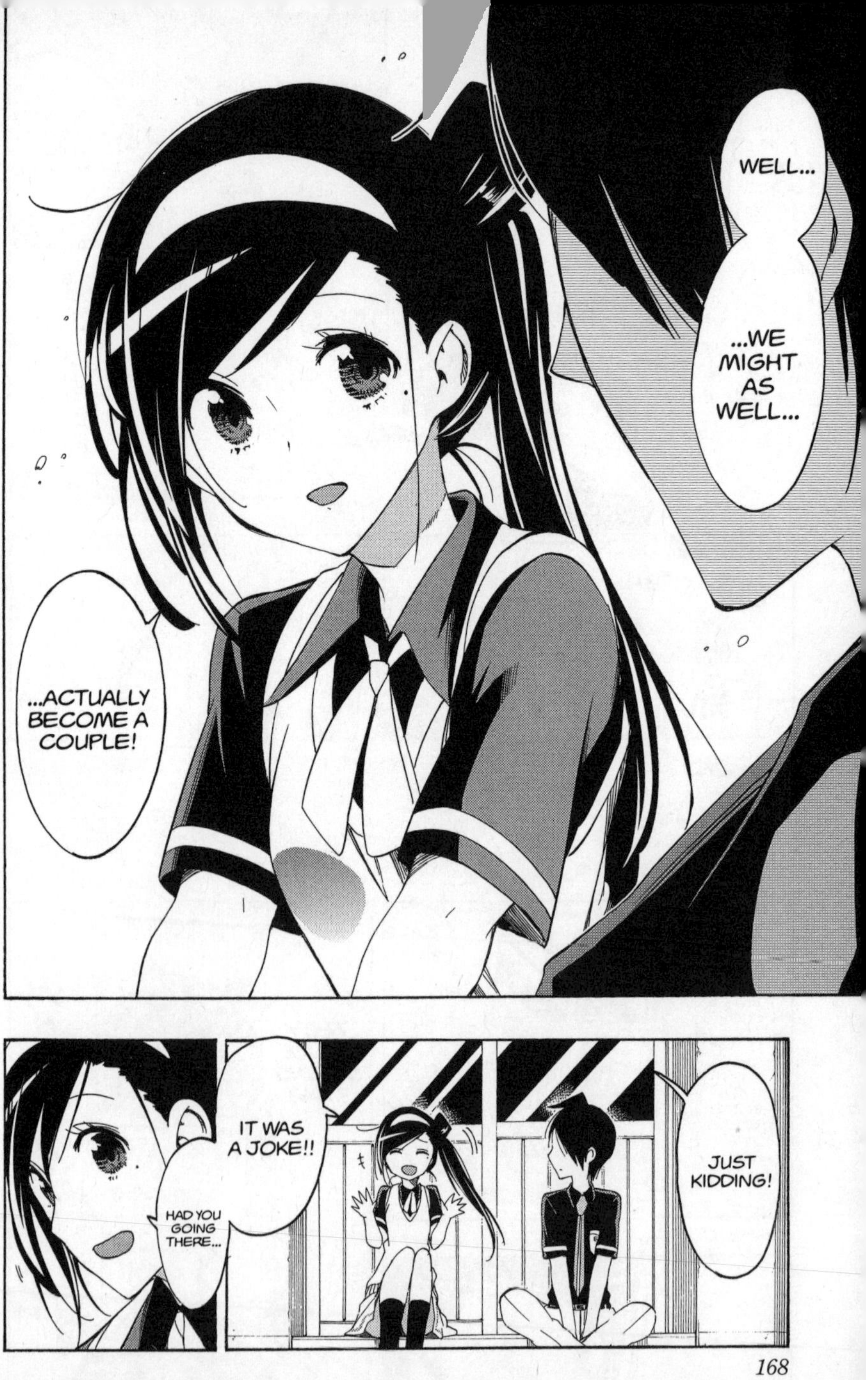
WELL...
...WE MIGHT AS WELL...
...ACTUALLY BECOME A COUPLE!
JUST KIDDING!
IT WAS A JOKE!!
HAD YOU GOING THERE...

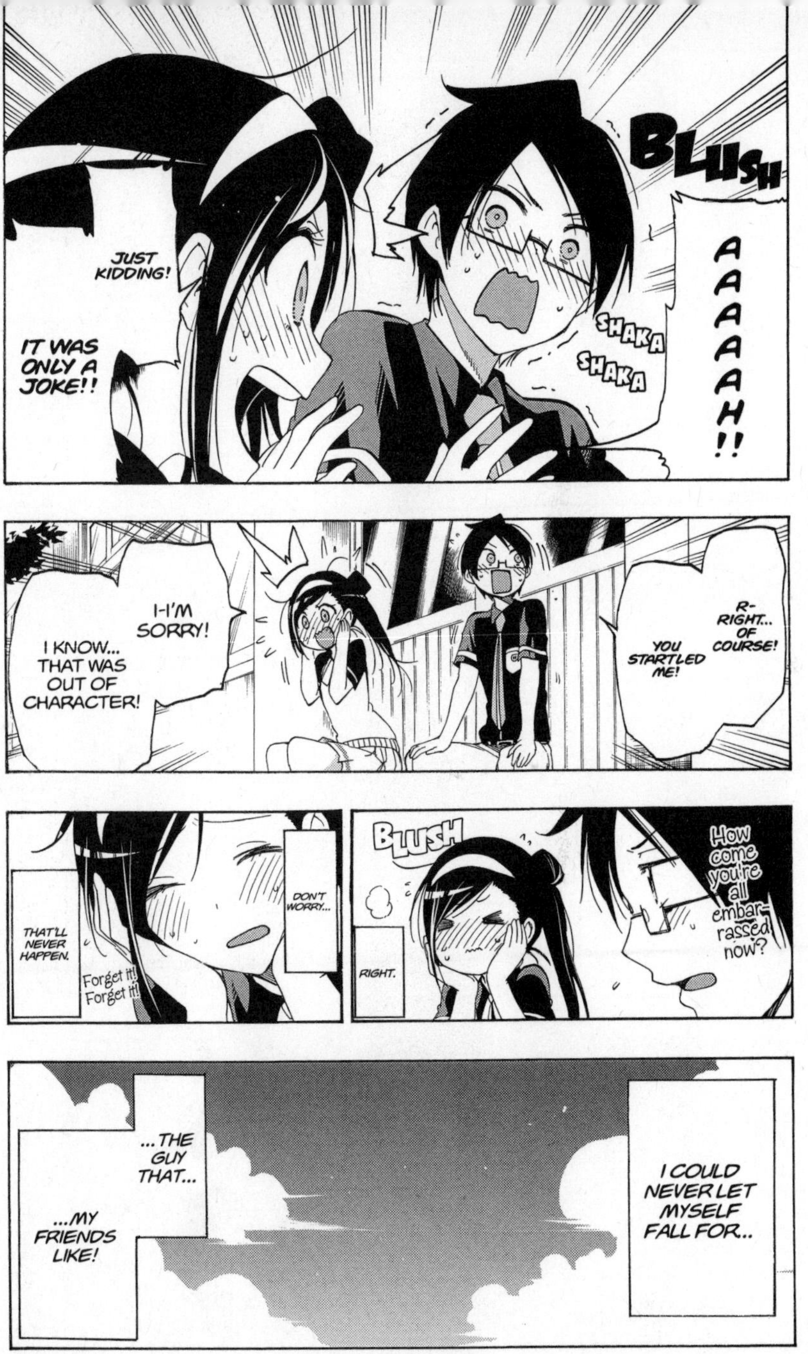
BLUSH
AAAAAAH!!
SHAKA
SHAKA
JUST KIDDING!
IT WAS ONLY A JOKE!!
R-RIGHT... OF COURSE!
YOU STARTLED ME!
I-I'M SORRY!
I KNOW... THAT WAS OUT OF CHARACTER!
How come you're all embar-rassed now?
BLUSH
RIGHT.
DON'T WORRY...
THAT'LL NEVER HAPPEN.
Forget it! Forget it!
I COULD NEVER LET MYSELF FALL FOR..
...THE GUY THAT...
...MY FRIENDS LIKE!

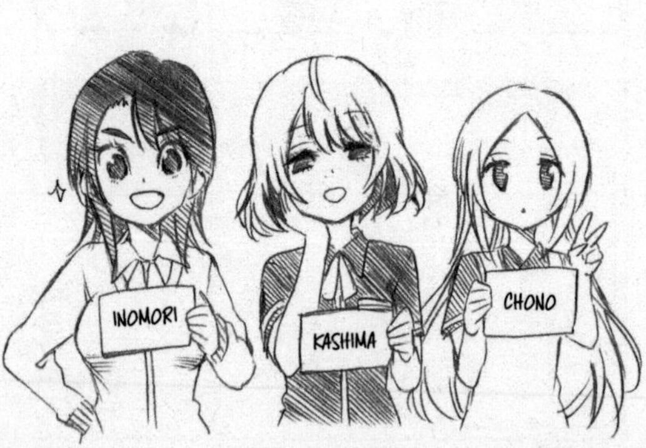
INOMORI
KASHIMA
CHONO

Question 25: It All Begins with a Genius's Struggle with [X]

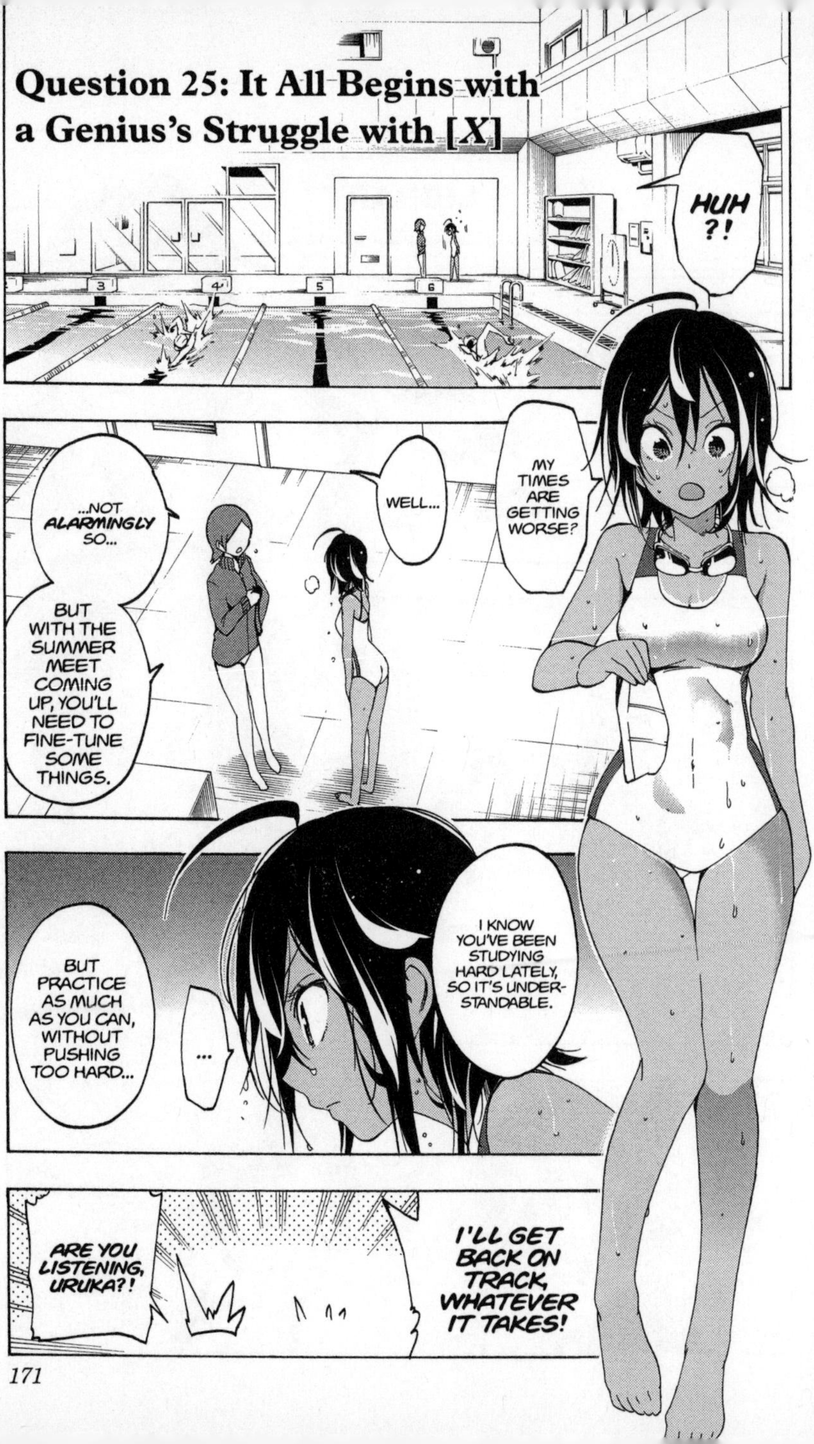
HUH?!
MY TIMES ARE GETTING WORSE?
WELL...
...NOT ALARMINGLY SO...
BUT WITH THE SUMMER MEET COMING UP, YOU'LL NEED TO FINE-TUNE SOME THINGS.
I KNOW YOU'VE BEEN STUDYING HARD LATELY, SO IT'S UNDER-STANDABLE.
...
BUT PRACTICE AS MUCH AS YOU CAN, WITHOUT PUSHING TOO HARD...
I'LL GET BACK ON TRACK, WHATEVER IT TAKES!
ARE YOU LISTENING, URUKA?!

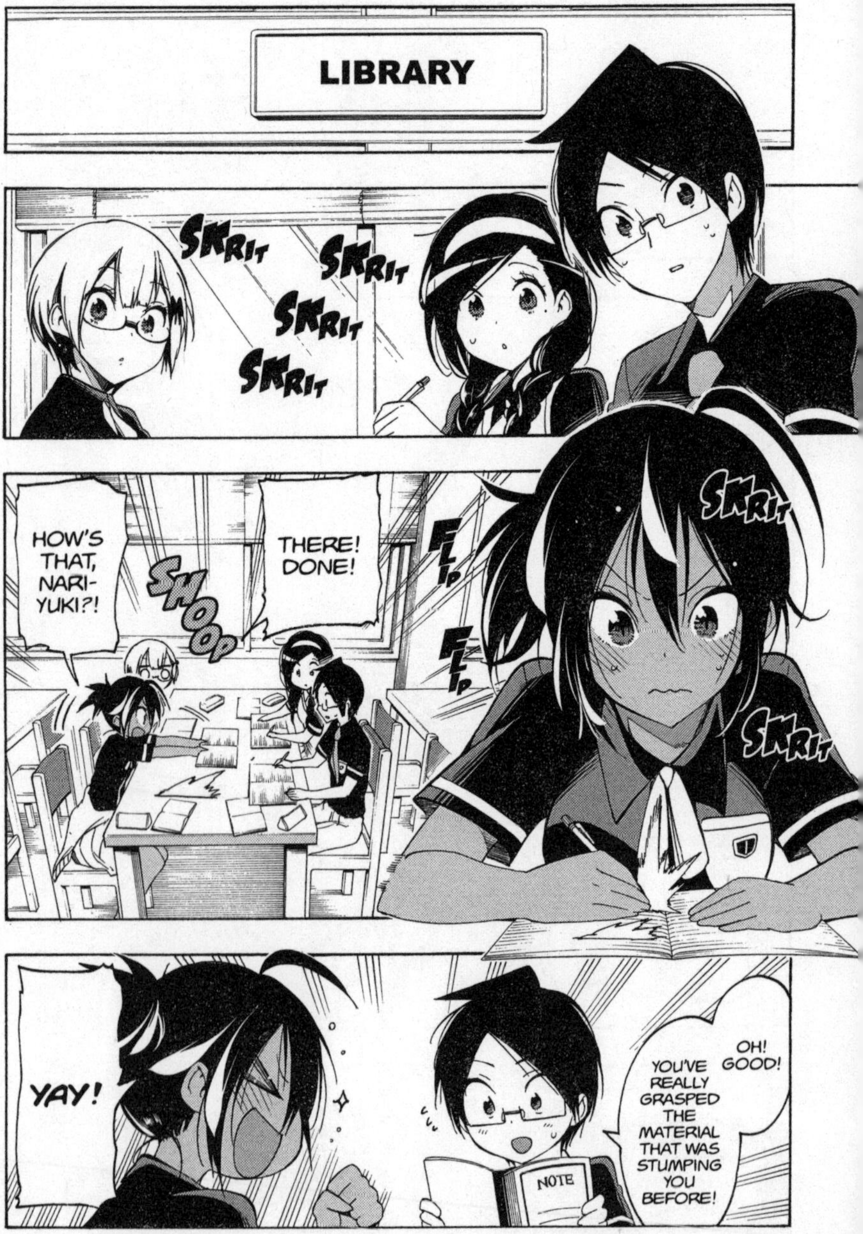
LIBRARY
SKRIT
SKRIT
SKRIT
SKRIT
SKRIT
FLIP
FLIP
SKRIT
THERE! DONE!
SHOOP
HOW'S THAT, NARI-YUKI?!
OH! GOOD!
YOU'VE REALLY GRASPED THE MATERIAL THAT WAS STUMPING YOU BEFORE!
NOTE
YAY!

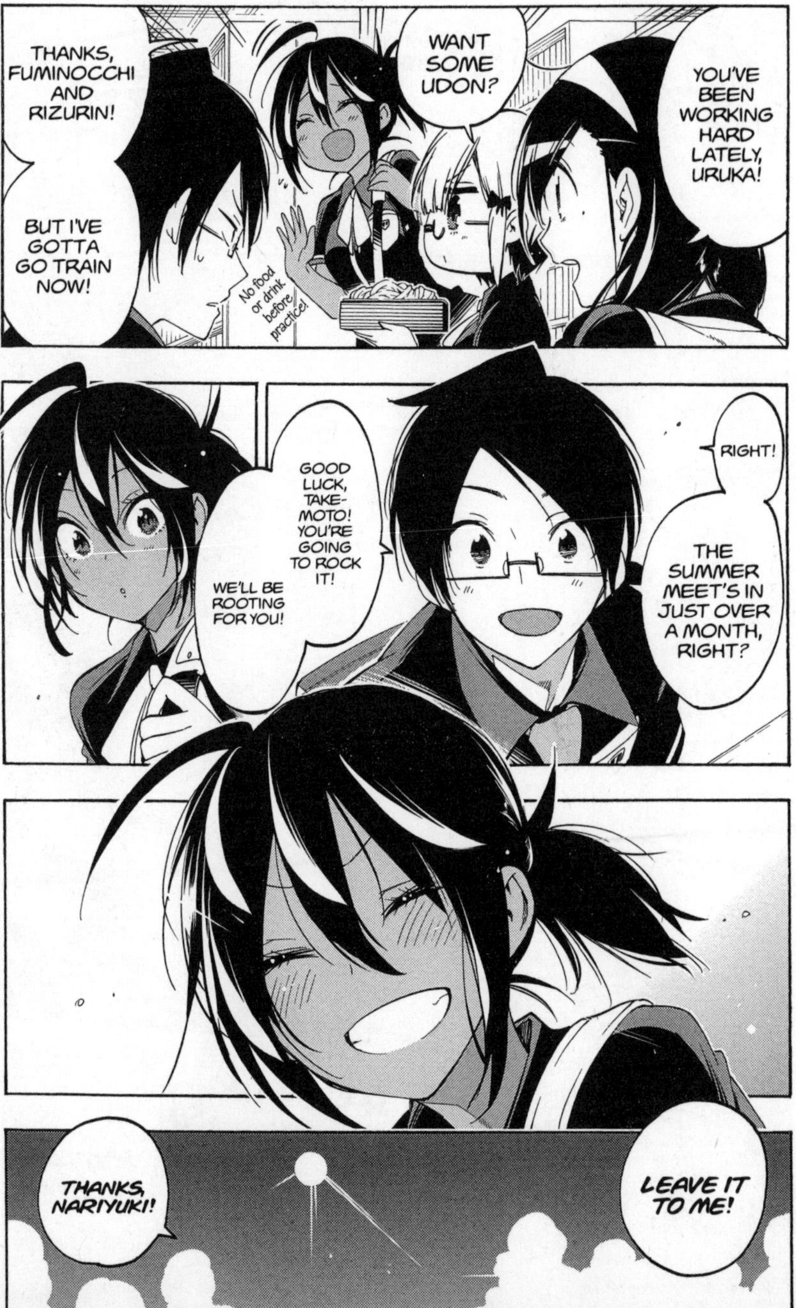
YOU'VE BEEN WORKING HARD LATELY, URUKA!
WANT SOME UDON?
THANKS, FUMINOCCHI AND RIZURIN!
BUT I'VE GOTTA GO TRAIN NOW!
No food or drink before practice!
RIGHT!
THE SUMMER MEET'S IN JUST OVER A MONTH, RIGHT?
GOOD LUCK, TAKE-MOTO! YOU'RE GOING TO ROCK IT!
WE'LL BE ROOTING FOR YOU!
LEAVE IT TO ME!
THANKS, NARIYUKI!

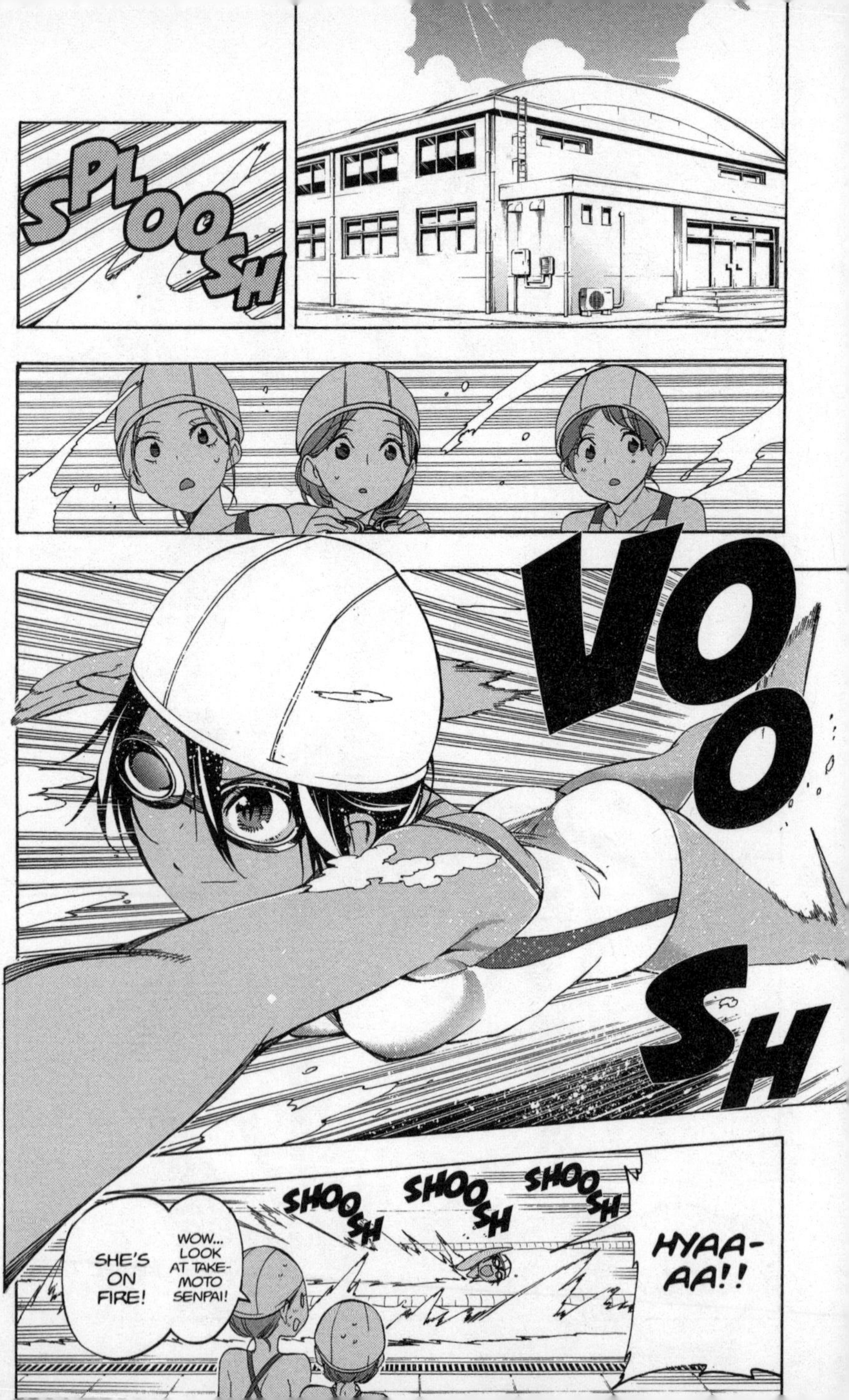
SPLOOSH
VOOSH
HYAAA-AA!!
SHOOSH
SHOOSH
SHOOSH
WOW... LOOK AT TAKE-MOTO SENPAI!
SHE'S ON FIRE!

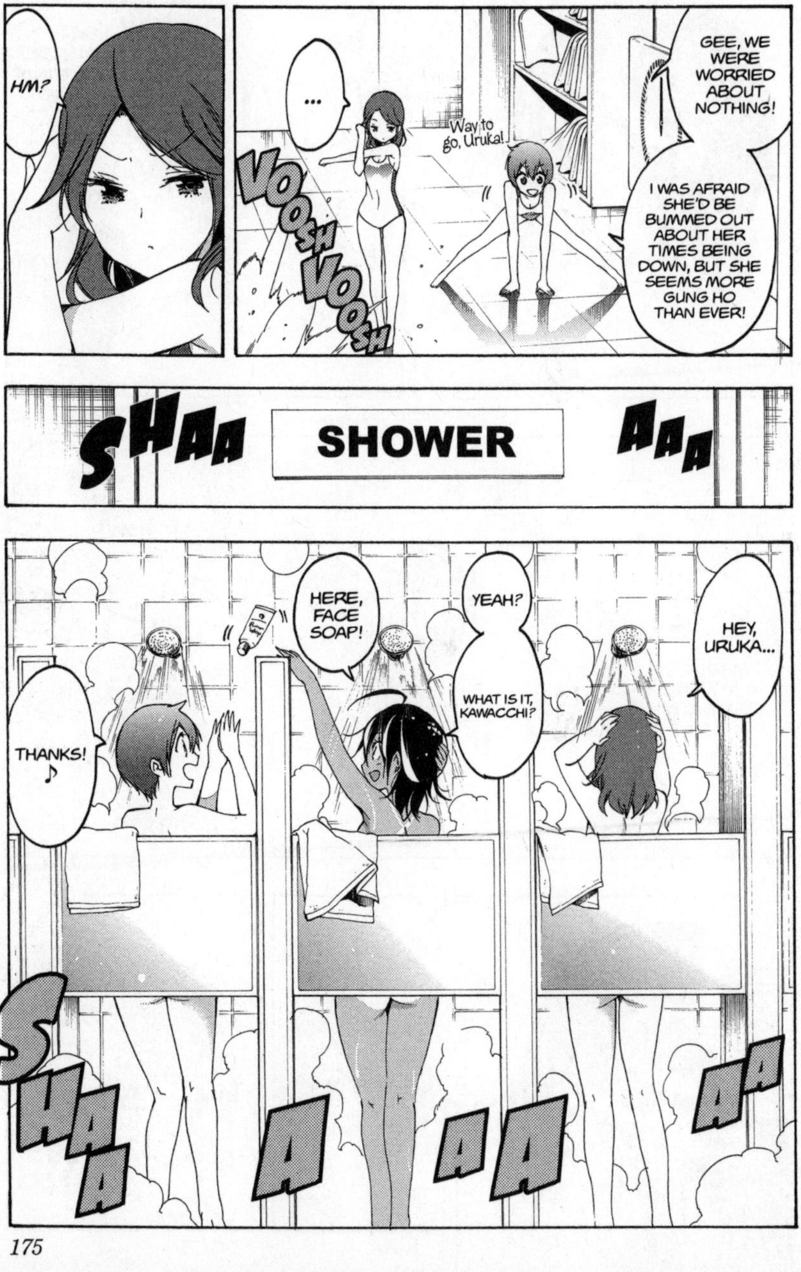
GEE, WE WERE WORRIED ABOUT NOTHING!
I WAS AFRAID SHE'D BE BUMMED OUT ABOUT HER TIMES BEING DOWN, BUT SHE SEEMS MORE GUNG HO THAN EVER!
Way to go, Uruka!
...
VOOSH VOOSH
HM?
SHAA
SHOWER
AAA
HEY, URUKA...
YEAH?
WHAT IS IT, KAWACCHI?
HERE, FACE SOAP!
THANKS! ♪
SHAAAAAAA

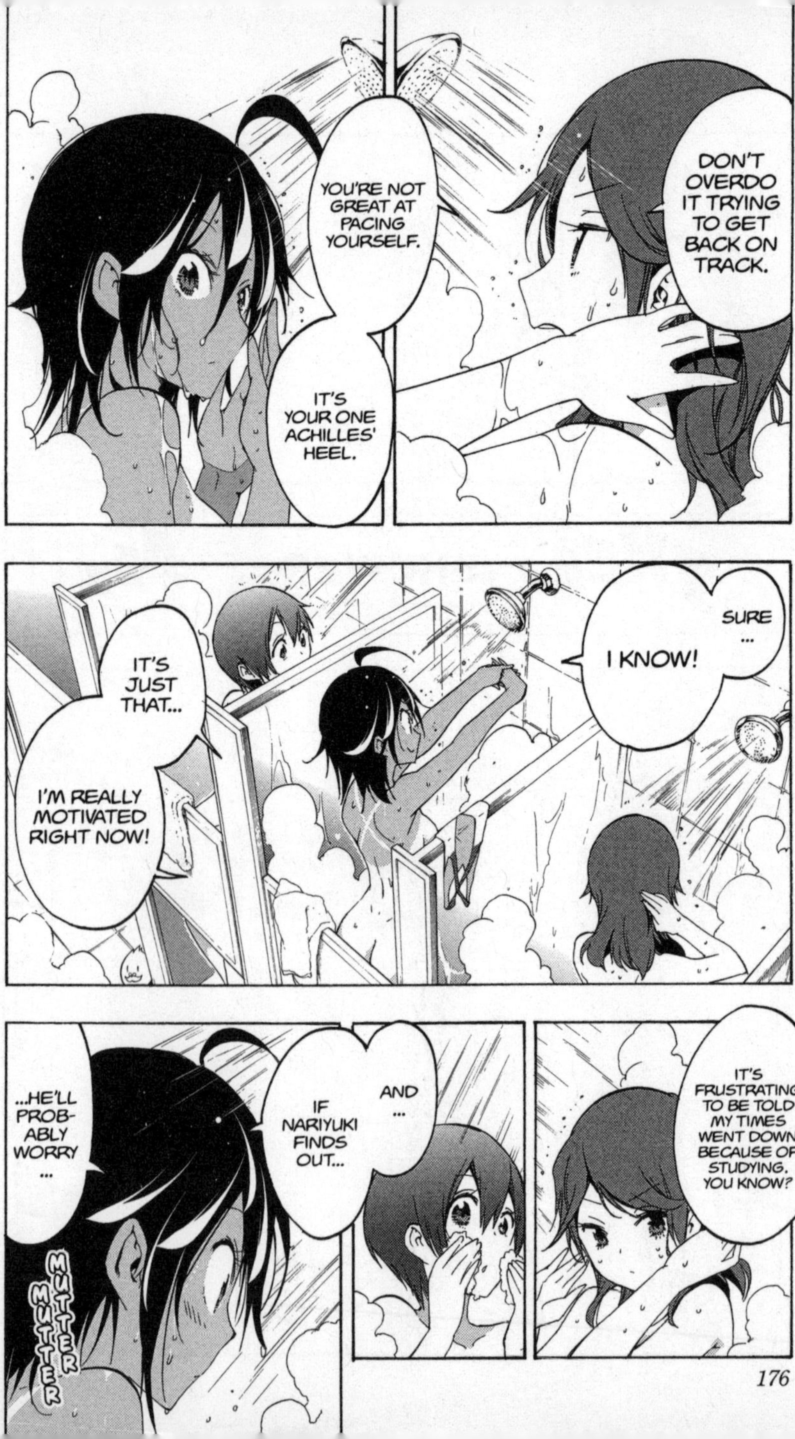
DON'T OVERDO IT TRYING TO GET BACK ON TRACK.
YOU'RE NOT GREAT AT PACING YOURSELF.
IT'S YOUR ONE ACHILLES' HEEL.
SURE ...
I KNOW!
IT'S JUST THAT...
I'M REALLY MOTIVATED RIGHT NOW!
IT'S FRUSTRATING TO BE TOLD MY TIMES WENT DOWN BECAUSE OF STUDYING. YOU KNOW?
AND ...
IF NARIYUKI FINDS OUT...
...HE'LL PROB-ABLY WORRY ...
MUTTER MUTTER

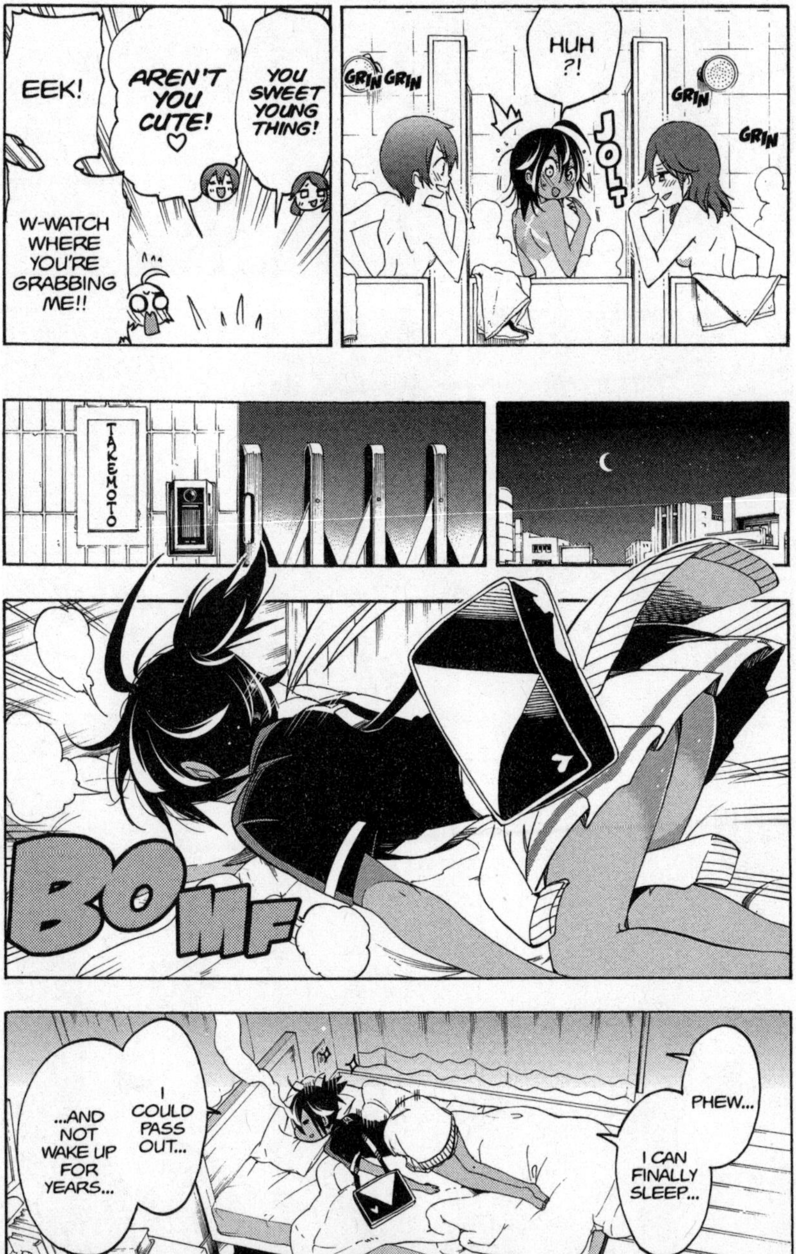
HUH ?!
GRIN GRIN
JOLT
GRIN
GRIN
YOU SWEET YOUNG THING!
AREN'T YOU CUTE! ♡
EEK!
W-WATCH WHERE YOU'RE GRABBING ME!!
TAKEMOTO
BOMF
PHEW... I CAN FINALLY SLEEP...
I COULD PASS OUT...
...AND NOT WAKE UP FOR YEARS...

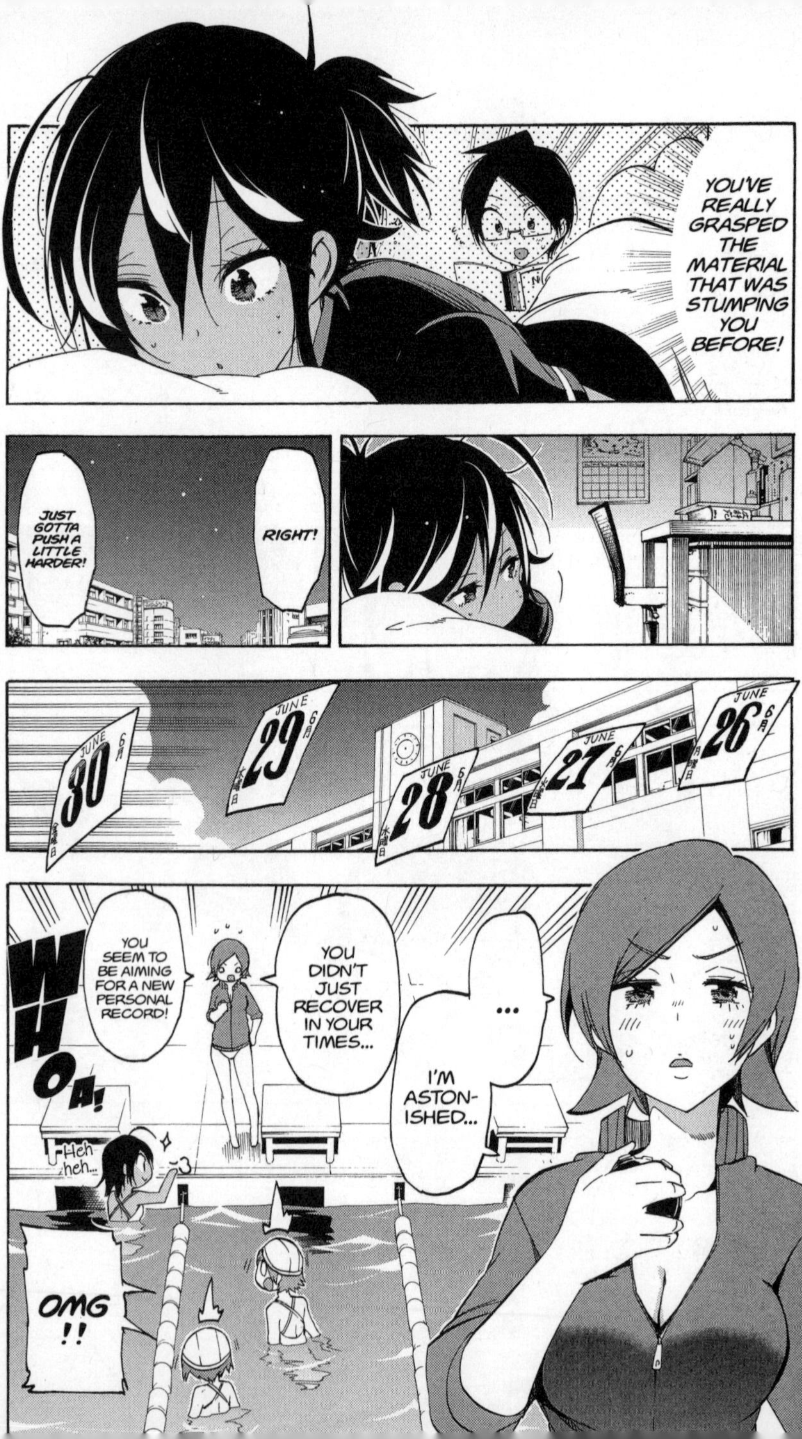
YOU'VE REALLY GRASPED THE MATERIAL THAT WAS STUMPING YOU BEFORE!
RIGHT!
JUST GOTTA PUSH A LITTLE HARDER!
JUNE 26 6月
JUNE 27 6月
JUNE 28 6月
JUNE 29 6月
JUNE 30 6月
...
I'M ASTON-ISHED...
YOU DIDN'T JUST RECOVER IN YOUR TIMES...
YOU SEEM TO BE AIMING FOR A NEW PERSONAL RECORD!
WHOA!
Heh heh...
OMG!!

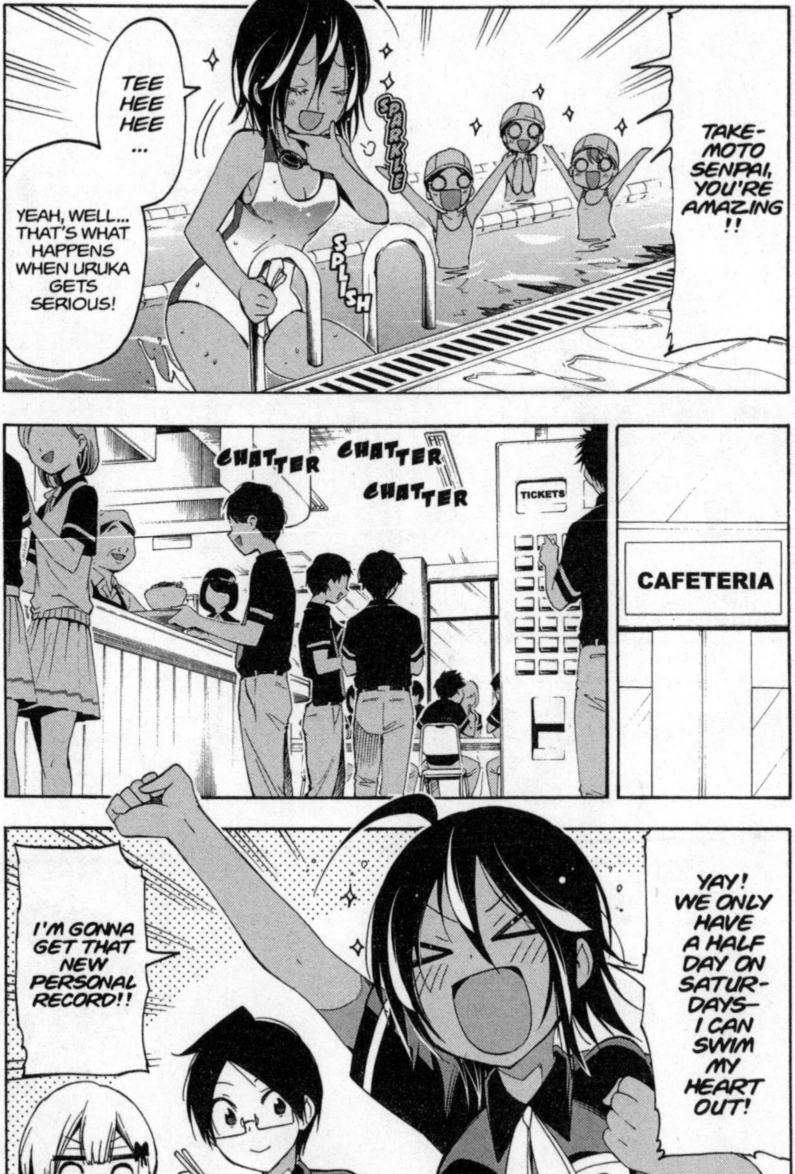
TAKE-MOTO SENPAI, YOU'RE AMAZING!!
TEE HEE HEE...
SPARKLE
SPLISH
YEAH, WELL... THAT'S WHAT HAPPENS WHEN URUKA GETS SERIOUS!
CAFETERIA
TICKETS
CHATTER CHATTER
CHATTER
YAY! WE ONLY HAVE A HALF DAY ON SATUR-DAYS— I CAN SWIM MY HEART OUT!
I'M GONNA GET THAT NEW PERSONAL RECORD!!

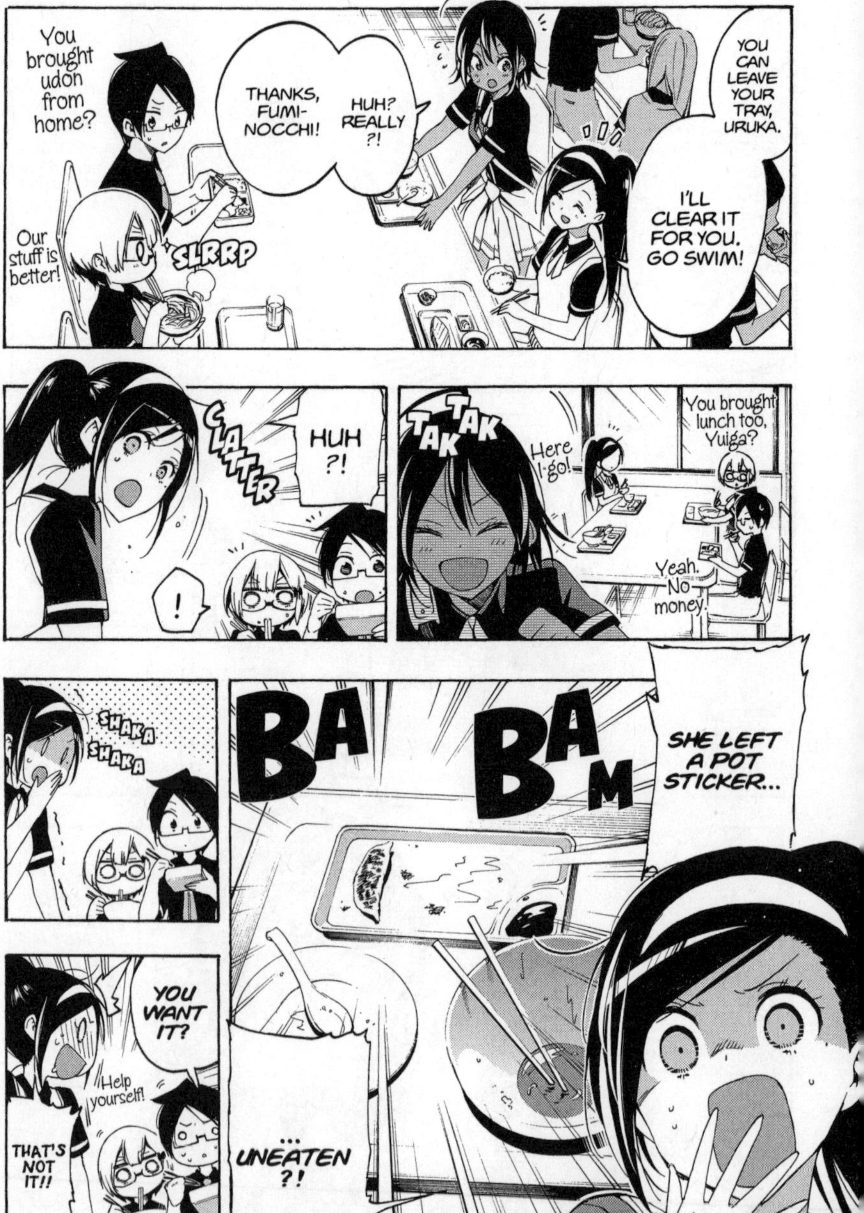
YOU CAN LEAVE YOUR TRAY, URUKA.
I'LL CLEAR IT FOR YOU. GO SWIM!
HUH? REALLY?!
THANKS, FUMI-NOCCHI!
You brought udon from home?
SLRRP
Our stuff is better!
TAK TAK TAK
You brought lunch too, Yuiga?
Here I go!
Yeah. No money.
CLATTER
HUH?!
!
SHE LEFT A POT STICKER...
BAM
BA
...UNEATEN?!
SHAKA SHAKA
YOU WANT IT?
Help yourself!
THAT'S NOT IT!!

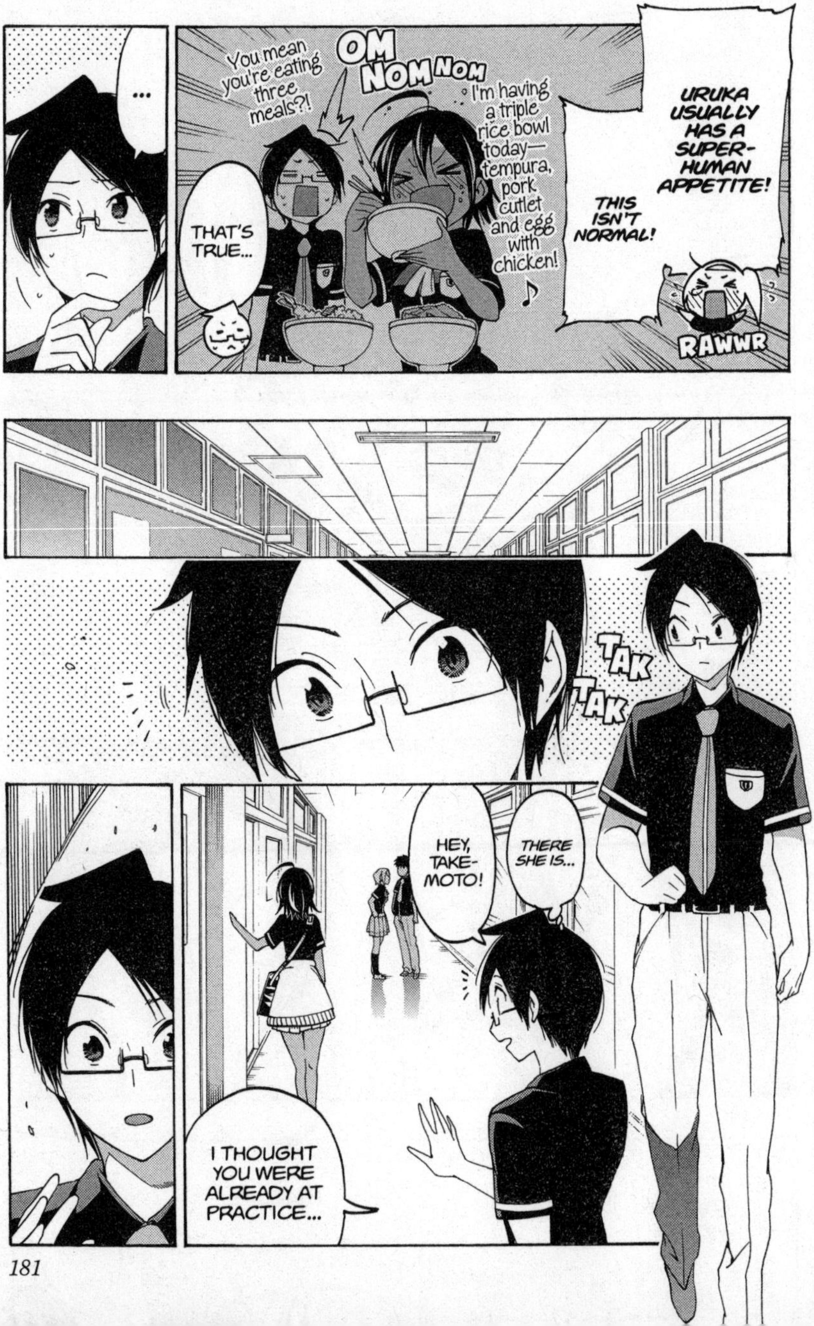
URUKA USUALLY HAS A SUPER-HUMAN APPETITE!
THIS ISN'T NORMAL!
RAWWR
I'm having a triple rice bowl today— tempura, pork cutlet and egg with chicken! ♪
OM NOM NOM
You mean you're eating three meals?!
THAT'S TRUE...
...
TAK TAK
THERE SHE IS...
HEY, TAKE-MOTO!
I THOUGHT YOU WERE ALREADY AT PRACTICE...

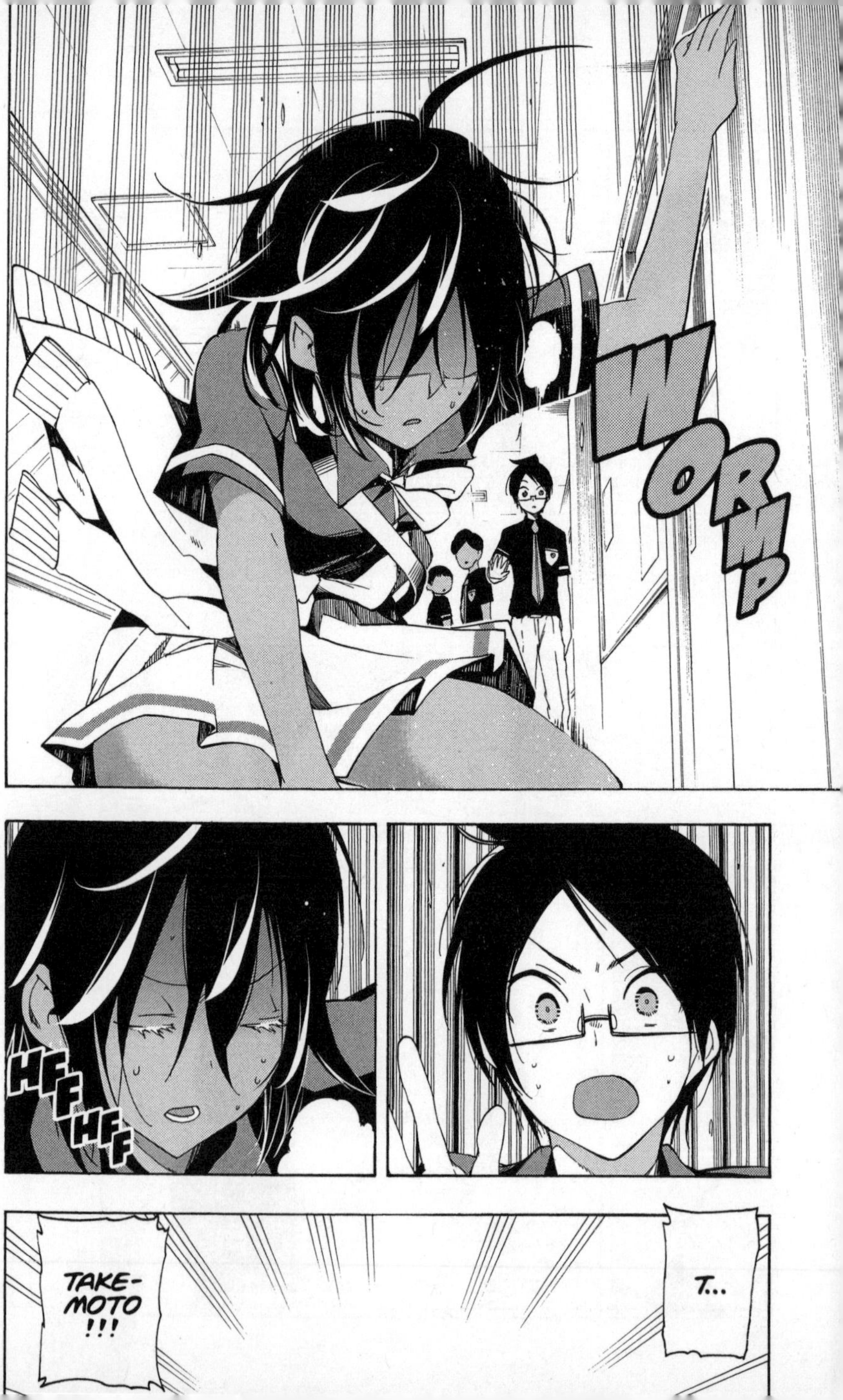
WHOMP
HFF HFF
T...
TAKE-MOTO!!!

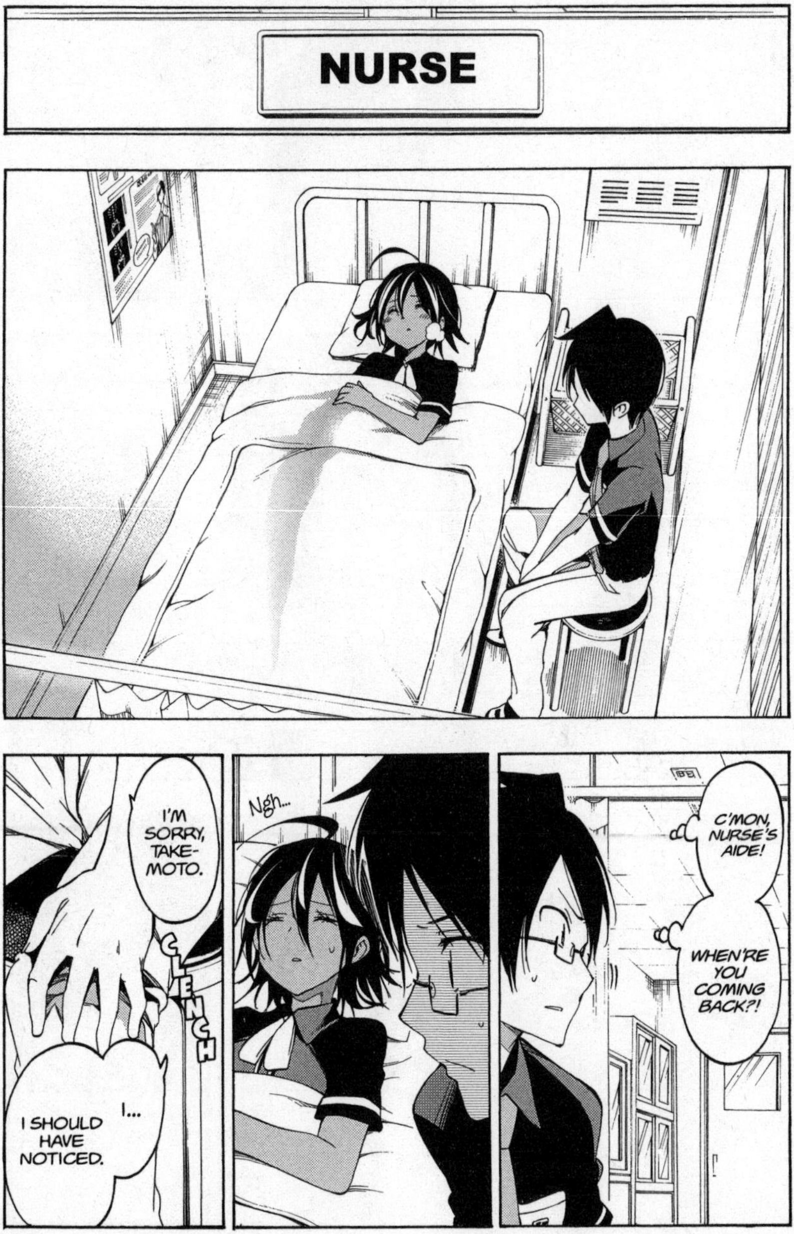
NURSE
C'MON, NURSE'S AIDE!
WHEN'RE YOU COMING BACK?!
Ngh...
I'M SORRY, TAKE-MOTO.
CLENCH
I...
I SHOULD HAVE NOTICED.

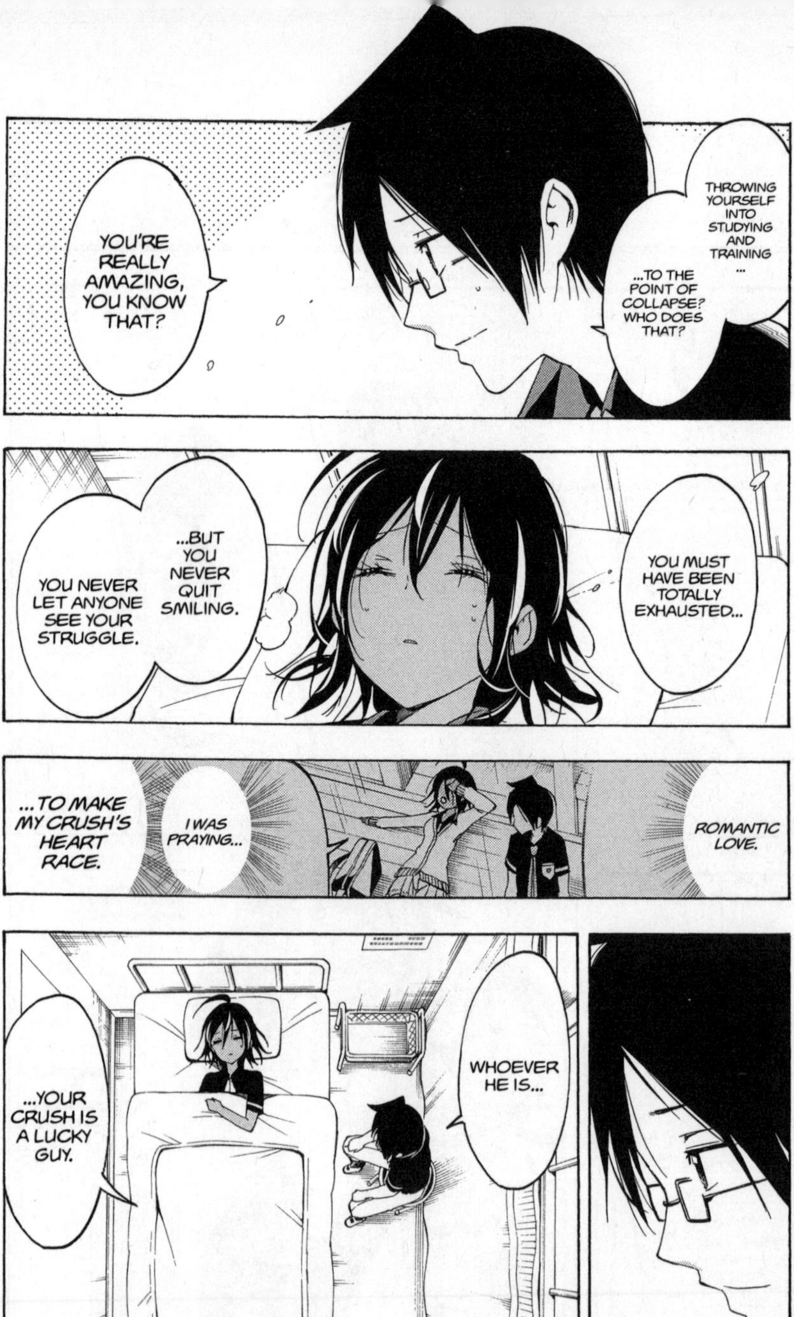
THROWING YOURSELF INTO STUDYING AND TRAINING ...
...TO THE POINT OF COLLAPSE? WHO DOES THAT?
YOU'RE REALLY AMAZING, YOU KNOW THAT?
YOU MUST HAVE BEEN TOTALLY EXHAUSTED...
...BUT YOU NEVER QUIT SMILING.
YOU NEVER LET ANYONE SEE YOUR STRUGGLE.
ROMANTIC LOVE.
I WAS PRAYING...
...TO MAKE MY CRUSH'S HEART RACE.
WHOEVER HE IS...
...YOUR CRUSH IS A LUCKY GUY.

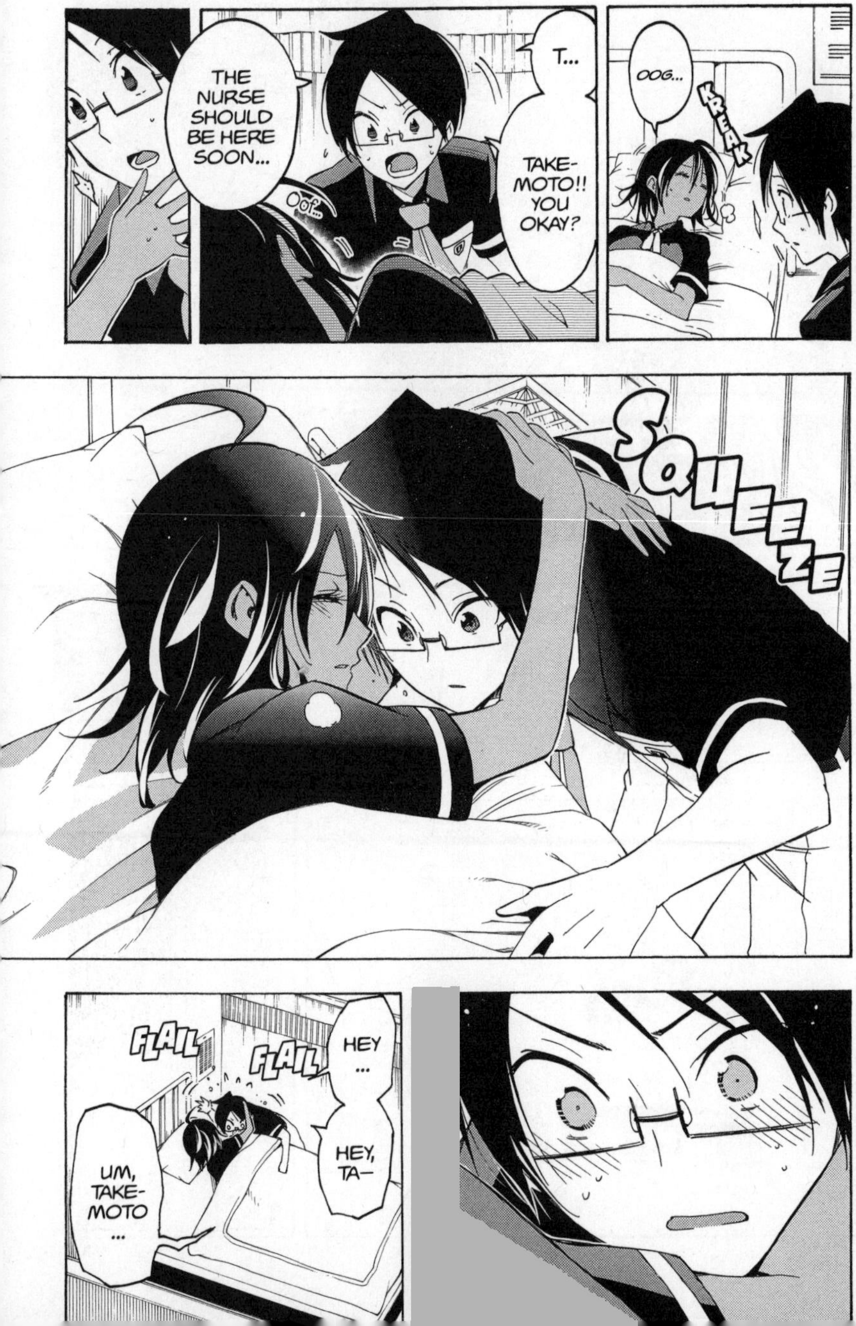
OOG...
KREAK
T...
TAKE-MOTO!! YOU OKAY?
Oof...
THE NURSE SHOULD BE HERE SOON...
SQUEEZE
HEY...
HEY, TA—
FLAIL
FLAIL
UM, TAKE-MOTO...

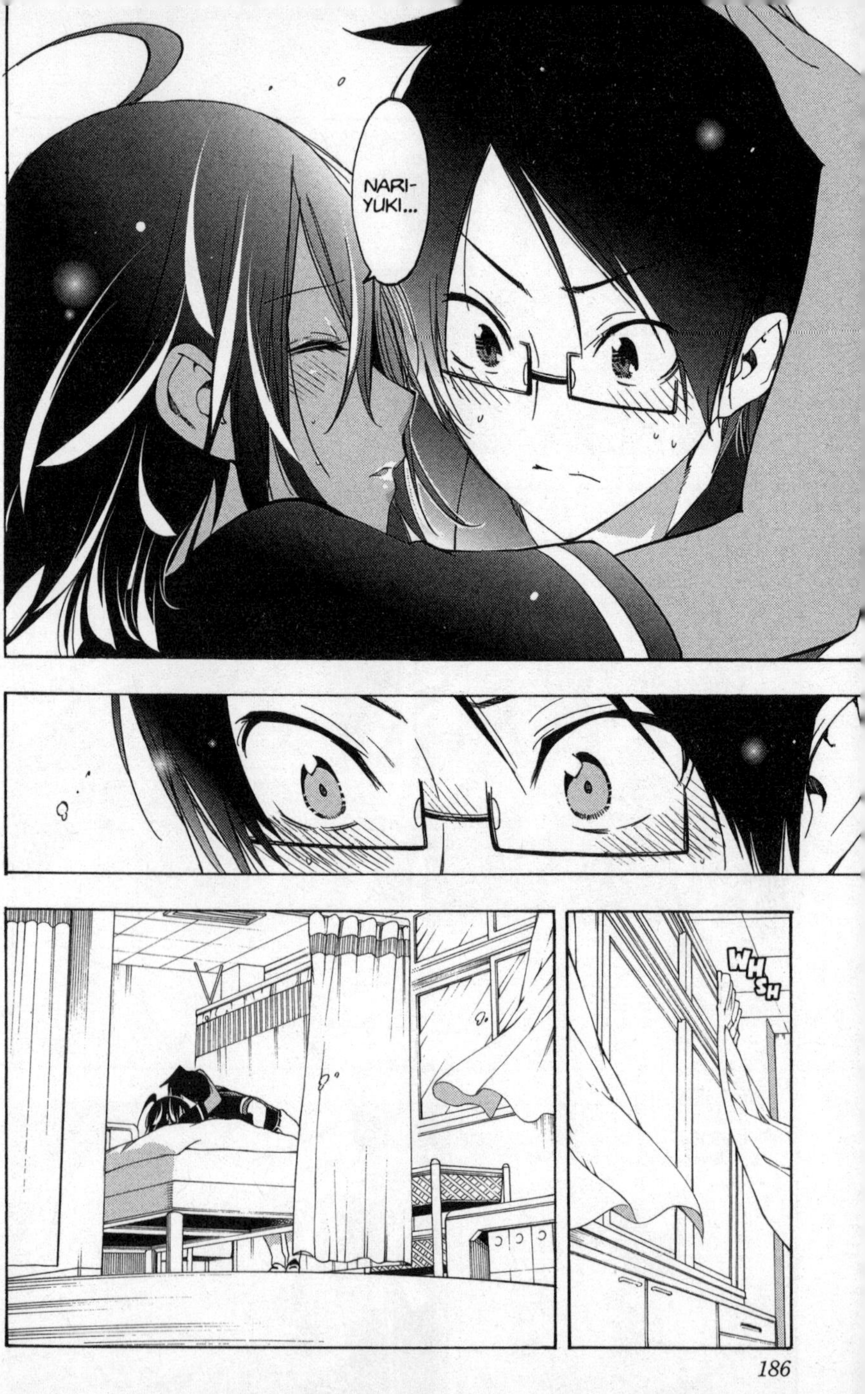
NARI-
YUKI...
WHSH

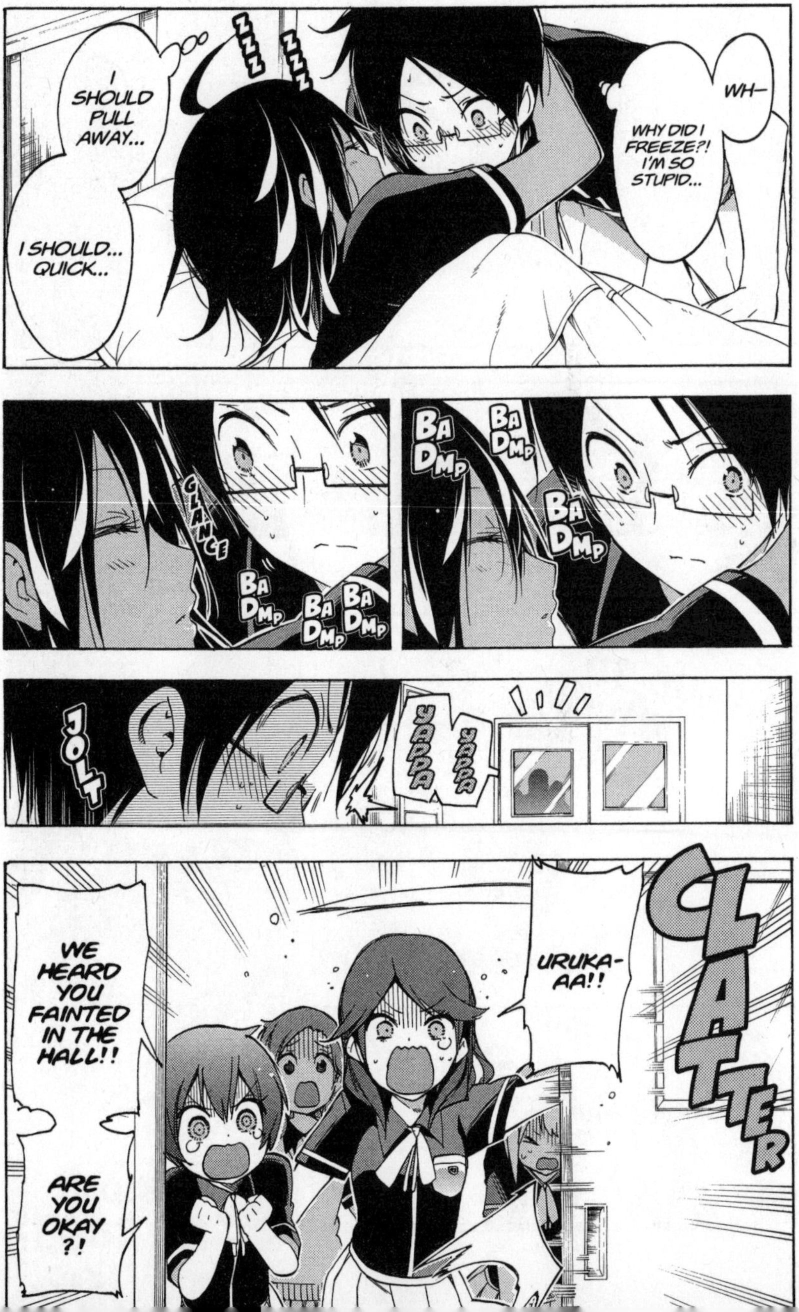
WH—
WHY DID I FREEZE?! I'M SO STUPID...
ZZZ
ZZZ
I SHOULD PULL AWAY...
I SHOULD... QUICK...
BA DMP
BA DMP
BA DMP
GLANCE
BA DMP
BA DMP
BA DMP
YAPPA YAPPA
YAPPA
JOLT
CLATTER
URUKA-AA!!
WE HEARD YOU FAINTED IN THE HALL!!
ARE YOU OKAY?!

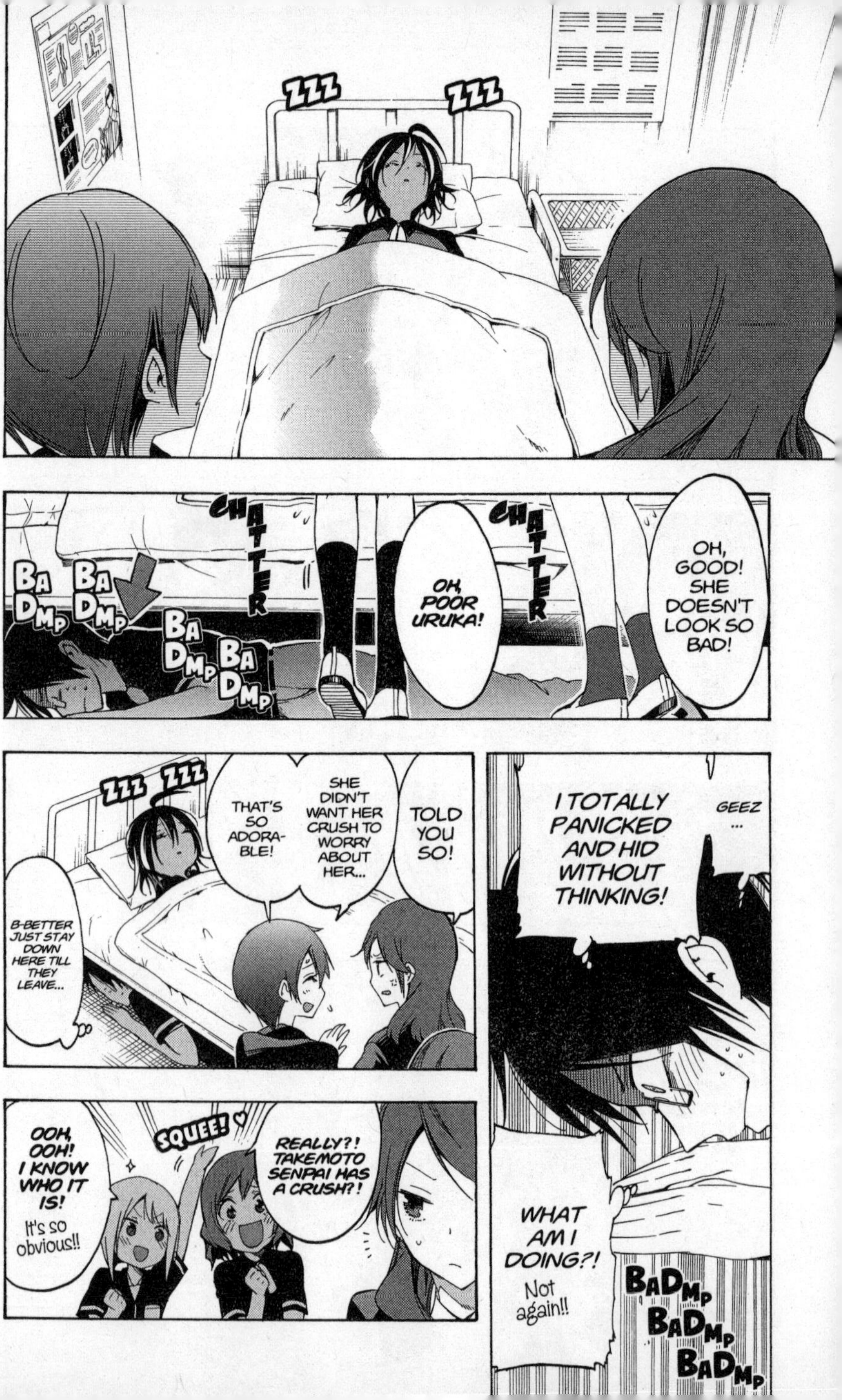
ZZZ
ZZZ
OH, GOOD! SHE DOESN'T LOOK SO BAD!
CHATTER
OH, POOR URUKA!
CHATTER
BADMP
BADMP
BADMP
BADMP
GEEZ ...
I TOTALLY PANICKED AND HID WITHOUT THINKING!
WHAT AM I DOING?!
Not again!!
BADMP
BADMP
BADMP
TOLD YOU SO!
SHE DIDN'T WANT HER CRUSH TO WORRY ABOUT HER...
THAT'S SO ADORABLE!
ZZZ
ZZZ
B-BETTER JUST STAY DOWN HERE TILL THEY LEAVE...
REALLY?! TAKEMOTO SENPAI HAS A CRUSH?!
SQUEE! ♡
OOH, OOH! I KNOW WHO IT IS!
It's so obvious!!

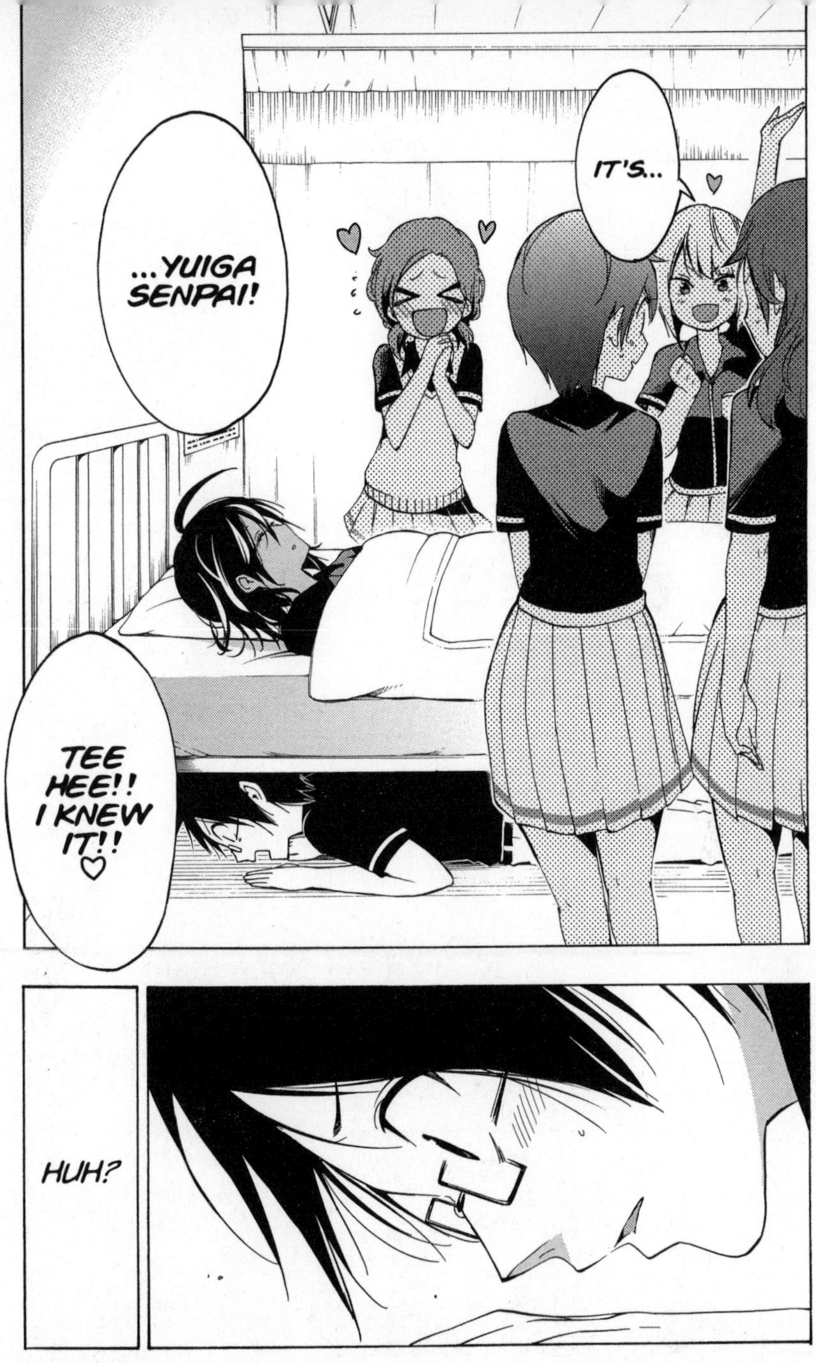
IT'S...
...YUIGA SENPAI!
TEE HEE!! I KNEW IT!! ♡
HUH?

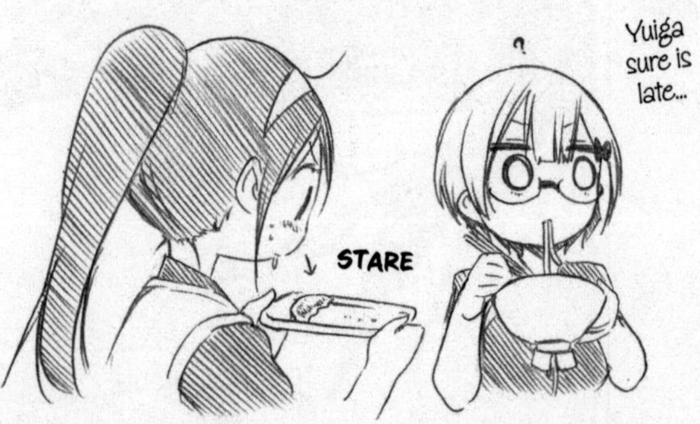
Yuiga sure is late...
STARE

We Never Learn

STAFF

Taishi Tsutsui

Yu Kato

Shinobu Irooki

Yuji Iwasaki

Naoki Ochiai

HELP

Paripoi

Chisato Hatada

Chikomichi

S T A F F   L I S T

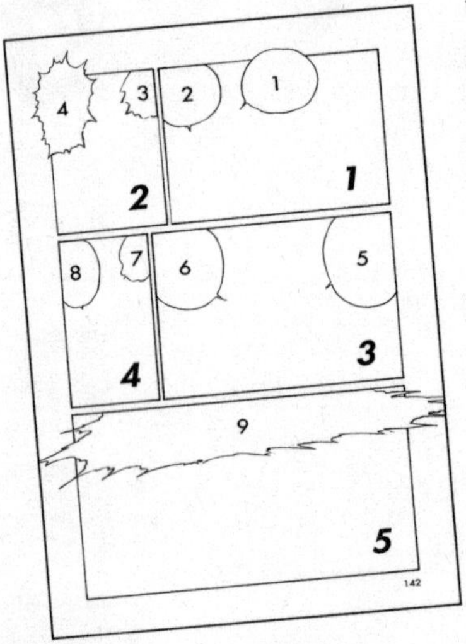
1
2
3
4
1
2
5
6
7
8
3
4
9
5
142

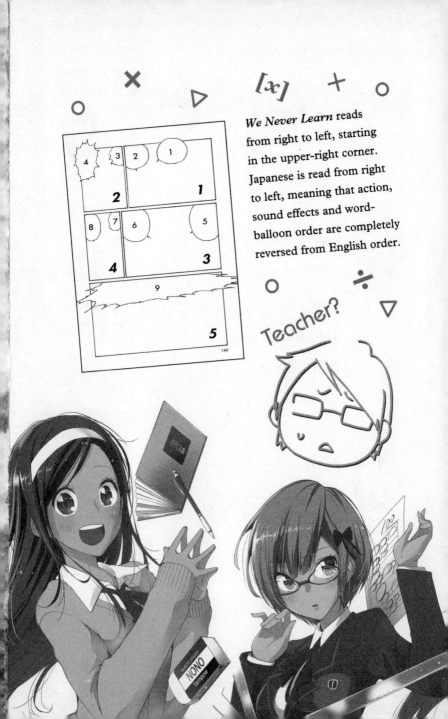

We Never Learn reads from right to left, starting in the upper-right corner. Japanese is read from right to left, meaning that action, word-sound effects and word-balloon order are completely reversed from English order.

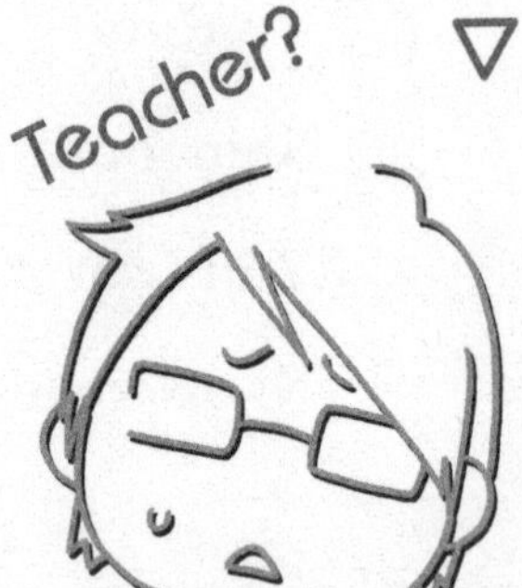
Teacher?

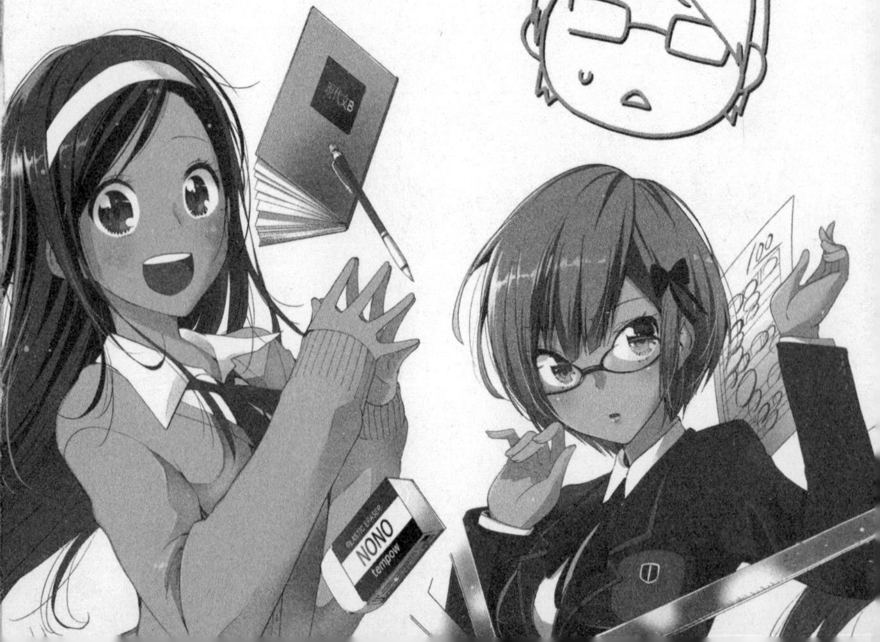
NONO
tempow
100